Birds of Tennessee
A New Annotated Checklist

Scott G. Somershoe
Christopher A. Sloan

Copyright © 2015 Scott G. Somershoe and Christopher A. Sloan
All rights reserved.
Cover photograph Cerulean Warbler Copyright © Ed Schneider
All rights reserved.
ISBN: 1507815751
ISBN-13: 978-1507815755

DEDICATION

I dedicate this project to my wife, Rebecca, and daughter, Jill, who tolerated me working on this project over the last few years; to my parents, Glenn and Linda, who supported me in pursuing a career in birds and conservation; and to Doris and the late Don Cohrs for their knowledge, support and encouragement in my pursuits in ornithology.

Scott G. Somershoe, April 2015

I dedicate this project to the late Barbara Lee, who lit the spark of my passion for birds; to my parents, Mert and Beverly Sloan, who provided all the fuel for that fire that an inquisitive boy could ever want or expect; and to Michael Bierly, who fanned those flames at every opportunity and has been a wonderful birding mentor throughout my life. Last, but not least, I dedicate this project to my wife Shannon, who totally knew what she was signing up for when she married me, but, luckily for me, she decided to do it anyway.

Christopher A. Sloan, April 2015

CONTENTS

Acknowledgments iii

Introduction 1
    Overview 1
    Taxonomy and Use of English Names 1
    Molt and Plumage Terminology 1
    Seasons 2
    Status and Abundance 2
    Geography of Tennessee 4
    Substantiation 6
    Sources 6
    Locations and Abbreviations 6
    Observers 12
    The Mobile App 14
    Feedback and Corrections 14

Species Accounts
    Anatidae: Ducks, Geese, and Swans. 15
    Odontophoridae: New World Quail. 46
    Phasianidae: Grouse and Turkey. 47
    Gaviidae: Loons. 49
    Podicipedidae: Grebes. 52
    Procellariidae: Shearwaters and Petrels. 57
    Hydrobatidae: Storm-Petrels. 58
    Ciconiidae: Storks. 59
    Fregatidae: Frigatebirds. 60
    Sulidae: Boobies and Gannets. 61
    Phalacrocoracidae: Cormorants. 62
    Anhingidae: Darters. 64
    Pelecanidae: Pelicans. 65
    Ardeidae: Bitterns, Herons, and Allies. 67
    Threskiornithidae: Ibises and Spoonbills. 77
    Cathartidae: New World Vultures. 80
    Pandionidae: Ospreys. 82
    Accipitridae: Hawks, Kites, Eagles, and Allies. 83
    Rallidae: Rails, Gallinues, and Coots. 94
    Aramidae: Limpkins. 101
    Gruidae: Cranes. 102
    Recurvirostridae: Stilts and Avocets. 105
    Charadriidae: Lapwings and Plovers. 108

Scolopacidae: Sandpipers, Phalaropes, and Allies. 114
Stercorariidae: Skuas and Jaegers. 142
Alcidae: Auks, Murres, and Puffins. 144
Laridae: Gulls, Terns, and Skimmers. 145
Columbidae: Pigeons and Doves. 163
Cuculidae: Cuckoos, Roadrunners, and Anis. 166
Tytonidae: Barn Owls. 168
Strigidae: Typical Owls. 169
Caprimulgidae: Goatsuckers. 173
Apodidae: Swifts. 176
Trochilidae: Hummingbirds. 178
Alcedinidae: Kingfishers. 182
Picidae: Woodpeckers and Allies. 183
Falconidae: Caracaras and Falcons. 187
Psittacidae: Lories, Parakeets, Macaws, and Parrots. 190
Tyrannidae: Tyrant Flycatchers. 191
Laniidae: Shrikes. 202
Vireonidae: Vireos. 203
Corvidae: Jays and Crows. 209
Alaudidae: Larks. 212
Hirundinidae: Swallows. 213
Paridae: Chickadees and Titmice. 219
Sittidae: Nuthatches. 221
Certhiidae: Creepers. 224
Troglodytidae: Wrens. 225
Polioptilidae: Gnatcatchers and Gnatwrens. 230
Regulidae: Kinglets. 231
Turdidae: Thrushes. 233
Mimidae: Mockingbirds and Thrashers. 240
Sturnidae: Starlings. 243
Motacillidae: Wagtails and Pipits. 244
Bombycillidae: Waxwings. 246
Calcariidae: Longspurs and Snow Buntings. 247
Parulidae: Wood-Warblers. 250
Emberizidae: Sparrows. 286
Cardinalidae: Cardinals, Grosbeaks, and Allies. 303
Icteridae: Blackbirds and Orioles. 310
Fringillidae: Finches and Allies. 318
Passeridae: Old World Sparrows. 325

References 326

Index of English Names 340

ACKNOWLEDGMENTS

The authors would like to thank the following individuals for reviewing and providing comments and suggestions to drafts of this manuscript: Michael Bierly, Kevin Calhoon, Dean Edwards, David Kirschke, Mike Todd, Mark Greene, Brainard Palmer-Ball, and Rick Knight. In particular, the latter three individuals – Mark Greene, Brainard Palmer-Ball, and Rick Knight – devoted a significant amount of time to providing thoughtful, detailed comments, suggestions, edits, and additional records, all of which significantly shaped and improved the project. We also wish to thank Robert Wheat for allowing us to review Tennessee National Wildlife Refuge's database on waterfowl surveys. We are very grateful for their generous support and assistance.

Introduction

Overview

Birds of Tennessee: A New Annotated Checklist provides information on the current status and distribution of all species of birds known to have occurred in Tennessee, excluding species for which only fossil evidence exists (e.g. California Condor). In many respects, this work is a successor to John Robinson's *An Annotated Checklist of the Birds of Tennessee*, which, although published in 1990, has remained an invaluable reference. Since that time, birding has continued to grow in popularity, and online resources (particularly state and local email lists and resources like eBird) have made current information about sightings available to any interested observer on nearly a real-time basis. As a result, much more is known about bird distribution, patterns of occurrence, habitat preferences, and population trends now than was known in 1990. This book (and the accompanying mobile application discussed below) provides a resource for anyone seeking this information.

This book includes all records that have been published through volume 67 of *North American Birds* and volume 83 of *The Migrant*, in addition to select records that are in publication.

Taxonomy and Use of English Names

The accounts are organized taxonomically in accordance with the *Check-list of North American Birds, Seventh Edition* (American Ornithologists' Union 1998), as updated through the *Fifty-Fifth Supplement To The American Ornithologists' Union Check-list of North American Birds* (Chesser et al. 2014). All English names also follow the AOU Checklist, except that, for those field-identifiable subspecies that are discussed in the species accounts, the English names (to the extent one has been adopted) follow eBird, which in most respects follows *The Clements Checklist of Birds of the World, Sixth Edition* (Clements 2007).

Molt and Plumage Terminology

References to molt and plumage follow the Humphrey-Parkes system, in which each plumage correlates to a specific molt, and each species follows complete molt cycles that begin with each pre-basic molt. In some instances, records contain insufficient information to determine a particular age cycle, and in those instances, the less specific term "subadult" or "immature" is used to denote a bird that has not yet achieved its definitive (aka adult) plumage.

Seasons

References to seasons are provided as general guidelines only and are intended more as an indication of the seasonality of movements and less as a reference to a specific period of time. Birds do not have calendars, and rigid categorization of seasons fails to properly take into account the widely varying migration periods for different species. For example, the authors decline to treat an early June White-rumped Sandpiper as a "summer" record or a mid-February Tree Swallow as a "winter" record, when in fact both are almost certainly spring transients. The authors recognize that some records do not lend themselves readily to this approach, and the categorization of those records is simply a matter of opinion with which others may disagree.

Status and Abundance

Status descriptions are based on observations from approximately the last ten years, except where a longer period gives a more accurate picture (such as with certain rarities or vagrants). The following terms are used:

- Resident – Typically present in appropriate habitat during the specified period, although abundance and distribution may vary as transients or seasonal residents come and go.
- Transient – Migrates through the area en route to breeding or wintering areas.
- Visitor – Occurs during the specified period, but not as an established breeder, winter resident, or as a regular transient.
- Extirpated – No longer occurs in the wild in Tennessee.
- Extinct – No longer occurs anywhere.

Abundance descriptions provide an approximation of the likelihood of encountering a species in the right habitat and during the specified period. The following terms are used:

- Common – Easily found, sometimes in large numbers.
- Fairly Common – Expected to be found, but more patchily distributed or in smaller numbers.
- Uncommon – Regularly occurs, but not easily or always detected, or occurs only in very small numbers.
- Irregular – Expected to occur every year but unpredictable and/or difficult to find; applies to species that would be classified as "uncommon" if occurrences were more predictable.

- Rare – Not expected to be found every year, but with an apparently regular pattern of occurrence. "Very rare" applies to circumstances that would be labelled "accidental" but for an apparently regular pattern of occurrence.
- Accidental – Small number of records; not expected to occur; no regular pattern of occurrence.

The following additional descriptive terms are used in some accounts to provide more detail:

- Local – Range is restricted to particular local areas.
- Irruptive – Abundance varies from year to year, often in a loosely cyclical pattern, based on availability of food or habitat in other parts of the country. For irruptive species, the abundance variation from non-irruption years to irruption years is noted in parentheses.
- Introduced – Species for which occurrences in Tennessee are attributable to intentionally or accidentally introduced individuals and that are considered established by the A.O.U.
- Unsubstantiated – Species for which there is no specimen, audio recording, or photographic documentation. May or may not be accepted by the Tennessee Bird Records Committee.

Arrival and departure dates are the expected dates for the earliest and latest transients in that period; any observation that falls outside those expected arrival or departure dates would be unusual and should be documented. For species that are resident in a region of the state during one period but that vacate another region of the state during the same period, early and late dates refer to those regions of the state where the species is not resident during that period (e.g. Blue-winged Warbler, which does not breed in much of west Tennessee).

Although the Tennessee Bird Records Committee (TBRC) of the Tennessee Ornithological Society publishes an *Official List of the Birds of Tennessee*, this book does not strictly follow the decisions of that committee. The authors have, in some instances, treated certain records differently than the TBRC. In particular, the authors treat as Unsubstantiated a few species that are accepted on the official list by the TBRC but for which there is no evidence other than one or more written descriptions. The decision to treat those species as Unsubstantiated is not in any way intended to suggest that those records are invalid, but it simply reflects the opinion of the authors that a specimen, photograph, or sound recording should be required to substantiate all species that are included in the official list.

Geography of Tennessee

In describing the geography of Tennessee with respect to bird distribution, this book adopts the four major Bird Conservation Regions (BCRs) that include portions of Tennessee, as described by the U.S. North American Bird Conservation Initiative. The Appalachian Mountain Bird Conservation Initiative Concept Plan further subdivides the Appalachian Mountain region into subregions, of which three include parts of Tennessee. These six regions provide a more accurate representation of broad habitat areas and general bird distribution than the more traditional division of Tennessee into three major geopolitical "grand divisions" of west, middle, and east Tennessee.

- Mississippi Alluvial Valley
- Southeastern Coastal Plain
- Central Hardwoods
- Appalachian Mountains
    - Cumberland Plateau (subdivision of the Appalachian Mountain BCR)
    - Southern Ridge and Valley (subdivision of the Appalachian Mountain BCR)
    - South Blue Ridge (subdivision of the Appalachian Mountain BCR)

Introduction

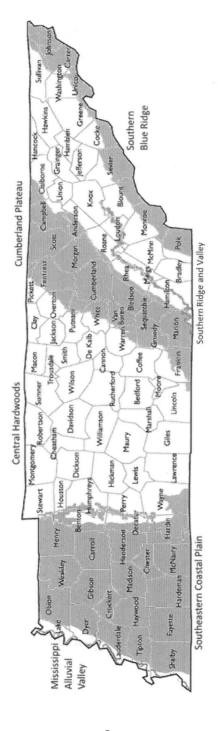

Substantiation

Each species account includes a reference to a specimen, photograph, or sound recording, if one exists, that substantiates the occurrence of the species in Tennessee. In cases where the only substantiation is a photo that has only been published online, the referenced URL also includes that most recent date on which the authors verified the link. The listed reference is not necessarily the first or only substantiated record, but refers to the substantiated record most readily located by the authors. References to "unpublished photographs" mean that photographs exist and have been reviewed by one or both authors, but are not publicly available. Unpublished photographs are only cited as substantiation when no substantiation is publicly available.

Sources

The following sources provide substantially all of the data included in this book and are referenced with the abbreviations set forth below:

- BBS - data published by the U.S. Geological Survey from North American Breeding Bird Surveys conducted in Tennessee
- CBC - data published by the National Audubon Society from Audubon Christmas Bird Counts conducted in Tennessee
- BNash - *Birds of the Nashville Area, 4th Edition*, Parmer, Henry E., 1985. Nashville Chapter, Tennessee Ornithological Society
- eBird - www.eBird.org; Sullivan, B.L., C.L. Wood, M.J. Iliff, R.E. Bonney, D. Fink, and S. Kelling. 2009. eBird: a citizen-based bird observation network in the biological sciences. Biological Conservation 142: 2282-2292.
- MIG - *The Migrant*, a quarterly publication of the Tennessee Ornithological Society
- NAB - *North American Birds*, a quarterly publication of the American Birding Association; previously published at various times as *Bird Lore*, *Audubon Field Notes*, and *American Birds*

Locations and Abbreviations

The following references to locations are used throughout the book:

AEDC – Arnold Engineering Development Center, Coffee Co.
Albany – Greene Co.
Alcoa Marsh – Blount Co.
Amnicola Marsh – Hamilton Co.
Armstrong Bend – Meigs Co.

Introduction

Ashland City – Cheatham Co.
Ashland City Marsh – Cheatham Co.
Austin Springs – Washington Co.
Barkley WMA – Stewart Co.
Bays Mountain Park – Sullivan Co.
Bells Bend – Davidson Co.
Big Bald Mtn. – Unicoi Co.
Big Hill Pond SP – McNairy Co.
Big Sandy Unit – Big Sandy Unit of Tennessee NWR, Henry Co.
Big South Fork NRRA – Fentress, Morgan, and Scott Co.
Big South Fork NRRA, Twin Arches area – Fentress Co.
Bird Island – Cherokee Lake, Hamblen Co.
Black Bayou Refuge – Lake Co.
Black Bayou WMA – Lake Co.
Bluff City – Sullivan Co.
Bogota WMA – Dyer Co.
Booker T. Washington SP – Hamilton Co.
Boone Lake – Sullivan and Washington Co.
Brainerd Levee – Hamilton Co.
Bristol – Sullivan Co.
Britton Ford – Tennessee NWR, Henry Co.
Buena Vista Marsh – Davidson Co.
Burnt Woods Rd – Lake Co.
Bush Lake – Davidson Co. (destroyed by development of Metro Center)
Cades Cove – GSMNP, Blount Co.
Cane Creek Park – Putnam Co.
Carver's Gap – Roan Mountain, Carter Co.
Cates Landing – Lake Co.
Cedar Hill Lake – Davidson Co.
Center Hill Lake – DeKalb Co.
Chattanooga – Hamilton Co.
Chattanooga Point Park – Hamilton Co.
Cherokee Dam – Jefferson-Grainger Co. line
Cherokee Lake – Grainger, Hamblen, and Jefferson Co.
Cherokee NF – Carter, Cocke, Johnson, Monroe, Polk, Unicoi Co.
Chickamauga Lake – Hamilton Co.
Chickamauga Lake dam – Hamilton Co.
Chickasaw NWR – Lauderdale Co.
Chilhowee Lake – Blount, Monroe Co.
Clarksville – Montgomery Co.
Cleveland – Bradley Co.
Clinch River – Anderson, Campbell, Claiborne, Grainger, Co.

Cocklebur Lake – Shelby Co.
Columbia – Maury Co.
Cook Recreation Area – J. Percy Priest Lake, Davidson Co.
Cookeville – Putnam Co.
Cove Lake SP – Campbell Co.
Craven's House – Chickamauga National Battlefield, Hamilton Co.
Cross Creeks NWR – Stewart Co.
Cross Mtn. – Anderson Co.
Dacus Bar – Shelby Co.
Douglas Dam – Sevier Co.
Dresden – Weakley Co.
Duck River Unit – Duck River Unit of Tennessee NWR, Humphreys Co.
Dutch Bottoms – Cocke Co.
Dyersburg – Dyer Co.
Eagle Bend Fish Hatchery – Anderson Co.
Eagle Lake Refuge – Shelby Co.
Eagle Lake WMA – Shelby Co.
Eagleville – Rutherford Co.
Eastern State WMA (now Forks of the River WMA) – Knox Co
Edwin Warner Park – Davidson Co.
Ellington Ag Center – Davidson Co.
Elizabethton – Carter Co.
Ensley – Ensley Bottoms, The Pits, EARTH Works, Shelby Co.
Ensley Bar – Shelby Co.
Erwin – Unicoi Co.
Erwin Fish Hatchery – Unicoi Co.
Everett Lake – Dyer Co.
Fall Creek Falls SP – Van Buren Co.
Foothills Parkway – Blount Co.
Foothills WMA – Blount Co.
Franklin – Williamson Co.
Ft. Campbell – Montgomery and Stewart Co.
Ft. Loudoun Lake – Blount, Knox, Loudon Co.
Frozen Head SP – Morgan Co.
Gallatin – Sumner Co.
Gallatin Steam Plant – Sumner Co.
Gatlinburg – Sevier Co.
Germantown – Shelby Co.
Gooch WMA – Obion Co.
Greeneville – Greene Co.
GSMNP – Great Smoky Mountains National Park, Blount, Sevier Co.
Hampton Creek Cove – Hampton Creek Cove SNA, Carter Co.

Harrison Bay SP – Hamilton Co.
Hatchie NWR – Haywood Co.
Heloise – Dyer Co.
Heritage Marsh – White Co.
Hiwassee Bridge – Meigs Co.
Hiwassee Refuge – Meigs Co.
Hiwassee River Area – includes Rhea , Meigs, Bradley, McMinn Co.
Holston Valley – Sullivan Co.
Hop–in WMA – Obion Co.
Horns Bluff Refuge – Crockett Co.
Horns Bluff WMA – Crockett Co.
Humboldt – Gibson, Madison Co.
Island 13 – Lake Co.
Jackson – Madison Co.
J. Percy Priest Lake – Davidson, Rutherford, Wilson Cos.
Joachim Bible Refuge – Greene Co.
John Sevier Lake – Hawkins Co.
Johnson City – Washington Co.
Kingsport – Hawkins, Sullivan Co.
Kingston Steam Plant – Roane Co.
Knoxville – Knox Co.
Kyker Bottoms Refuge – Blount Co.
Kyker Bottoms WMA – Blount Co.
Lauderdale Refuge – Lauderdale Co.
LBL – Land Between the Lakes NRA, Stewart Co.
Lebanon – Wilson Co.
Lillydale – Clay Co.
Little Elder Island – Woods Reservoir, Franklin Co.
Lower Hatchie NWR – Lauderdale, Tipton Co.
Martin – Weakley Co.
Memphis – Shelby Co.
Millington – Shelby Co.
Monsanto Ponds – Maury Co.
Morristown – Hamblen Co.
Moss Island WMA – Dyer Co.
Mt. Le Conte – GSMNP, Sevier Co.
Mud Island – Shelby Co.
Munford – Tipton Co.
Murfreesboro – Rutherford Co.
Musick's Campground – Sullivan Co.
Narrows of the Harpeth SP – Cheatham Co.
Nashville – Davidson Co.

Natchez Trace SP – Carroll, Henderson Co.
Nickajack Lake – Marion, Hamilton Co.
Norris – Anderson Co.
Norris Dam – Anderson Co.
North Cumberland WMA – Anderson, Campbell, Scott Co.
Oak Ridge – Anderson, Roane Co.
Old Hickory Lake – Davidson, Sumner, Wilson Co.
Orchard Bog – Johnson Co.
Overton Park – Shelby Co.
Pace Point – Big Sandy Unit, Tennessee NWR, Henry Co.
Paris Landing SP – Henry Co.
Patrick Henry Lake – Sullivan Co.
Pennington Bend – Davidson Co.
Percy Warner Park – Davidson Co.
Phillippy – Lake Co.
Phipps Bend – Hawkins Co.
Pickwick Lake – Hardin Co.
Pickwick Dam – Hardin Co.
President's Island – Shelby Co.
Quarry Bog – Johnson Co.
Radnor Lake – Radnor Lake State Natural Area, Davidson Co.
Rankin Bottoms – Cocke Co.
Reelfoot Lake – Lake and Obion Co.
Reelfoot Lake SP – Lake Co.
Ripshin Lake – Carter Co.
Roan Mtn. – Roan Mountain, Carter Co.
Roan Mtn. SP – Roan Mountain State Park, Carter Co.
Roan Creek – Johnson Co.
Robco Lake – Shelby Co.
Round Bald – Roan Mtn., Carter Co.
Samburg – Obion Co.
Savannah – Hardin Co.
Savannah Bay – Hamilton Co.
Savannah Bottoms – Hardin Co.
Sequatchie Valley – Marion, Sequatchie Co.
Seven Islands Wildlife Refuge – Knox Co.
Sevierville – Sevier Co.
Sewanee – Franklin Co.
Shady Valley – Johnson Co.
Shelby Bottoms Park – Davidson Co.
Shelby Farms – Shelby Co.
Shelby Forest SP – Shelby Co.

Introduction

Shelby Forest WMA – Shelby Co.
Shiloh NP – Hardin Co.
Signal Mtn. – Hamilton Co.
Smithville – DeKalb Co.
Snow Bunting Peninsula – Old Hickory Dam, Davidson Co.
S. Holston Lake – Sullivan Co.
S. Holston Dam – South Holston Dam, Sullivan Co.
S. Holston River weir dam – South Holston River weir dam, Sullivan Co.
Soddy Mtn. – Hamilton Co.
Standifer Gap Marsh – Hamilton Co.
Steele Creek Park – Sullivan Co.
Stones River National Battlefield – Rutherford Co.
Sycamore Shoals SP – Washington Co.
Tellico Lake – Blount, Loudon Co.
Tennessee NWR – Decatur, Henry, Humphreys Co.
Tennessee River Gorge – Hamilton, Marion Co.
Tigrett WMA – Dyer Co.
Tiptonville – Lake Co.
Tiptonville Bar – Lake Co.
Tri-Cities Airport – Sullivan Co.
Tullahoma – Coffee Co.
TVA Lake – Shelby Co.
Two Jays – Davidson Co.
Union City – Obion Co.
Upper Douglas Lake – Cocke, Jefferson Co.
Warner Parks – Davidson Co.
Watauga Lake – Carter, Johnson Co.
Watauga River – Carter, Johnson Co.
White Lake Refuge – Dyer Co.
White Lake WMA – Dyer Co.
Wilbur Lake – Carter Co.
Williamsport Lakes WMA – Maury Co.
Wolf River WMA – Fayette Co.
Woodbury – Cannon Co.
Woods Reservoir – Franklin Co.

The following additional abbreviations are used throughout the book:

ad – Adult
APSU – Austin Peay State University Museum of Zoology
BNA – Birds of North America
CBC – Christmas Bird Count

CSM – Cumberland Science Museum, Nashville (now the Adventure Science Center)
Co. – County
f – Female
FBC – Fall Bird Count
imm – Immature
LSUMZ – Louisiana State University Museum of Zoology
m – Male
Mtn. – Mountain
NAMC – North American Migration Count
NP – National Park
NWR – National Wildlife Refuge
Peale Museum – Philadelphia, PA (no longer exists)
SBC – Spring Bird Count
SNA – State Natural Area
SP – State Park
TBRC – Tennessee Bird Records Committee
WMA – Wildlife Management Area
USNM – United States National Museum of Natural History
UTK – University of Tennessee at Knoxville
UTM – University of Tennessee at Martin

Observers

FA – Fred Alsop
HA – Harry Adams
MA – Mark Armstrong
RB – Rob Biller
CB – Carolyn Bullock
CBl – Clyde Blum
KB – Kevin Burke
MLB – Michael Lee Bierly
KAC – Kevin Calhoon
RC – Ron Carrico
GC – Glen Criswell
JPC – J. Paul Crawford
LD – Larry Doyle
DE – Daniel Estabrooks
CF – Clayton Ferrell
FF – Frank Fekel
RF – Robert Ford
MAG – Mark A. Greene

Introduction

BH – Bill Holt
DH – David Hollie
FH – Frank Hixson
JH – James Hurt
JHa – Joyce Haigh
MH – Mark Hopey
SH – Susan Hubley
BL – Bill Lisowsky
DJ – Dan Jacobson
GJ – Greg Jackson
DK – David Kirschke
RLK – Rick L. Knight
EL – Ed LeGrand
RL – Ruth Luckado
TL – Tony Lance
KM – Knox Martin
NM – Nancy Moore
SNM – Susan McWhirter
DM – Daniel Moss
DMi – Don Miller
DaP – David Pitts
DP – Dick Preston
DPa – David Patterson
HP – Henry E. Parmer
JP – James Peters
MP – Michael Plaster
WP – William Pulliam
FR – Fabian F. Romero
JCR – John C. Robinson
TR – Tommie Rogers
CS – Chad Smith
CAS – Chris A. Sloan
DS – Damien Simbeck
ES – Ed Schneider
PS – Paul Super
SGS – Scott G. Somershoe
SJS – Stephen J. Stedman
RS – Ruben Stoll
AT – Allan Trently
MT – Michael Todd
WT – Wallace Todd
DW – Darryl Wilder

GW – Grace Wyatt
JW – Jay Walko
MW – Martha Waldron
MJW – Melinda J. Welton
RW – Robert Wheat
JRW – Jeff R. Wilson
TW – Terry Witt
SZ – Stephen Zipperer

The Mobile App

The authors are also developing a companion mobile application of the same name to enable birders and researchers to more readily access this book's information in the field from any smartphone or other mobile device. The information in the app will be nearly identical to the information in the book, except that subscribers of the app will receive periodic updates in an effort to keep the data current as new records are published. The app will be available sometime in 2015 for both iOS devices (via iTunes) and for Android devices (via the Google Play store).

Feedback and Corrections

Feedback and corrections are welcome. The authors intend to update the mobile app regularly and to publish new editions of the book every few years, so your feedback will help improve each subsequent release. Please email the authors with your suggestions or error corrections at birdsoftennessee@gmail.com.

Anatidae: Ducks, Geese, and Swans.

Thirty-one species have been found in Tennessee, of which 21 occur annually and five are regular breeders. Members of this family are generally found on bodies of water or in other wetland habitats.

Black-bellied Whistling-Duck, *Dendrocygna autumnalis*

Status and Abundance: Fairly common local permanent resident in Shelby Co.; accidental summer and winter visitor elsewhere

Habitat: Ponds, marshes, other wetlands with marshy or vegetated edges

Comments: Nesting has been documented at Ensley since 2008. In prior years, nesting has also been documented at Tully WMA, Tipton Co. and in Lake Co., and has been suspected in Jackson and Madison Cos. (TWRA *fide* SGS). The first state record was of two adults at Reelfoot Lake 1 Aug-8 Oct 1978 (Pitts 1982). This species is found year round at Ensley, but is less abundant and occasionally absent during winter. This species has been observed in the state east to Barkley WMA in Stewart Co., but is highly prone to wander and is possible anywhere.

High Counts – Spring
- 59 on 29 Apr 2012, Ensley (DP, pers. comm.)
- 54 on 12 Apr 2011, Ensley (MIG 82:83)
- 26 on 24 May 2010, Ensley (MIG 81:114)
- 11 on 10 May 2003, Hwy 79, Lake Co. (MIG 74:86)

High Counts – Fall
- 148 on 15 Sep 2012, Shelby Co. FBC (MIG 83:137)
- 106 on 17 Oct 2013, Ensley (SGS, pers. obs.)
- 69 on 6 Sep 2011, Ensley (JRW, unpubl. data)

High Counts – Summer
- 30 on 1 Jul 2012, Ensley (DP, pers. comm.)
- 19 on 29 Jun 2013, Ensley (DW, pers. comm.)

High Counts – Winter
- up to 81 through winter 2011-12, Ensley (JRW, pers. comm.)
- 42 on 10 Dec 2011, Ensley (MIG 83:21)

Substantiation: Photograph: 3 on 28 May 2009, Ensley (NAB 63(3):441)

Fulvous Whistling-Duck, *Dendrocygna bicolor*

Status and Abundance: Very rare visitor to Mississippi Alluvial Valley; accidental visitor elsewhere

Habitat: Wetlands, typically with marshy edges

Comments: Rare visitor at any time of the year and anywhere in the state. Most recent sightings have been in Mississippi Alluvial Valley. One late Apr-May 2006, Robertson Co. (MIG 77:100).

High Counts – Spring
    17 on 18 May 2008, Ensley (MIG 79:61)
    9 on 25-30 May 2003, Lake Co. (MIG 74:86)
    5 on 14 May 2002, Black Bayou WMA (MIG 73:56)
    4 on 14 May 1998, Black Bayou WMA (MIG 69:160)
High Counts – Fall
    9 on 24-26 Nov 1992, Amnicola Marsh (MIG 64:19)
High Counts – Summer
    6 on 17 Jun 2009, TVA Lake (MIG 80:123)
High Counts – Winter
    31 on 29 Jan 1965, Norris Dam (Olson 1965)
Substantiation: Photograph: Sloan, C.A. 2013. "Fulvous Whistling-Duck at Ensley Pits, Memphis, TN (09-02-2013) 008-41". < http://www.chrissloanphotography.com/Birding/Miscellaneous/i-DPjkbdG> Accessed 26 Jun 2015.

Greater White-fronted Goose, *Anser albifrons*
Status and Abundance: Uncommon winter resident and late fall and early spring transient in Mississippi Alluvial Valley and Tennessee NWR; irregular elsewhere; accidental summer visitor
Habitat: Flooded and unflooded crop fields; lakes and ponds
Spring Departure: mid Mar
Fall Arrival: mid Oct
Late Spring
    18 May 2007, John Sevier Lake (MIG 78:103)
    13 May 2007, Rhea Co. (MIG 78:103)
    8 May 2004, Lake Co. NAMC (MIG 75:93)
    15 Apr 1989, Cross Creeks NWR (MIG 60:84)
    8 Apr 2000, Ensley (MIG 71:87)
Early Fall
    5 Oct 1971, Shelby Co. (Waldron 1987)
    7 Oct 2014, Jackson (MAG, pers. comm.)
    9 Oct 1992, Island 13 (MIG 64:15)
High Counts – Spring
    2,500 on 3 Mar 2002, Lake Co. (MIG 73:56)
High Counts – Fall
    600 on 31 Oct 2004, Marshall Co. (MIG 76:29)
    450 on 31 Oct 2004, Ensley (MIG 76:26)
Summer Records
    1 on 13 Jun 1996, Lake Co. (MIG 67:76)
High Counts – Winter
    8,861 on 15 Dec 2007, Reelfoot Lake CBC (MIG 79:35)

4,000 on 4 Feb 2011, Dyer/Lake Co. line (SGS, pers. obs.)
3,589 on 19 Dec 2009, Reelfoot Lake CBC (MIG 81:91)
3,500 on 22 Jan 2005, Reelfoot Lake (MIG 76:78)

Substantiation: Photograph: 1 on 22 Feb 2007, Steele Creek Park (Knight 2008:24)

Snow Goose, *Chen caerulescens*

Status and Abundance: Locally common winter resident and late fall and early spring transient in Mississippi Alluvial Valley and Tennessee NWR; irregular elsewhere; accidental summer visitor

Habitat: Flooded and unflooded crop fields; lakes and ponds

Spring Departure: late Mar

Fall Arrival: early Oct

Comments: Larger numbers are typically found in west and middle Tennessee as far east as Tennessee NWR, with smaller numbers found in rest of the state. Late spring and summer records likely involved injured birds. Snow Goose populations have been rapidly increasing in recent years.

Late Spring
 22 May 2005, Jackson Co. (MIG 76:97)
 15 May 1960, Shelby Co. (MIG 31:30)
 14 May 2005, Anderson Co. NAMC (MIG 76:126)
 5-11 May 1999, Cove Lake SP (MIG 70:101)
 10 May 1997, Cheatham Co. NAMC (MIG 68:98)

Early Fall
 21 Sep 1976, Percy Warner Park (MIG 48:18)
 22 Sep 1965, near Greeneville (MIG 36:97)
 25 Sep 2000, Cates Landing (MIG 72:37)
 25 Sep 2010, Lake Co. (MIG 81:153)
 27 Sep 2002, S. Holston Lake (MIG 74:26)

Summer Records
 1 on 7 Jun 2002, Kingston Steam Plant (MIG 73:113)
 1 on 10 Jun 2011, White Lake Refuge (MIG 82:119)
 1 on 15 May-21 Aug 1960, Shelby Farms (MIG 31:44)
 8 on 6-18 Jul 1951, Tennessee NWR (Cybert 1955)

High Counts – Winter
 700,000 on 5 Feb 2009, Gray's Camp, Reelfoot Lake, Lake Co. (MIG 80:66)
 300,000 on 27 Jan 2014, Dyer Co. (MIG, in press)
 100,000 on 2 Jan 2005, Reelfoot Lake (MIG 76:78)
 80,000 on 14 Dec 2013, Black Bayou Refuge (SGS, pers. obs.)

Substantiation: Specimen: APSU, 1616

Ross's Goose, *Chen rossii*
> Status and Abundance: Uncommon winter resident and late fall and early spring transient in Mississippi Alluvial Valley and Tennessee NWR; irregular elsewhere
> Habitat: Flooded and unflooded crop fields; lakes and ponds
> Spring Departure: early Mar
> Fall Arrival: mid Nov
> Comments: First record was one found 20 Dec 1986, Cross Creeks NWR (Robinson 1988). Likely this species has always been present in small numbers, but is now being detected with greater frequency in part due to heightened observer awareness. Also, Ross's and Snow Goose populations have been rapidly increasing in recent years. Observers should be aware of an increased number of hybrids Ross's x Snow Geese being found annually. Dark morph observed once: 1 on 14-31 Dec 2007, joined by second bird on 30 Dec 2007, Lauderdale Refuge (MIG 79:51).
> Late Spring
>> 22 May 2001, Kingston Steam Plant (MIG 72:96)
>> 10 May 1997, Davidson Co. NAMC (MIG 68:98)
>> 20 Apr 2002, Putnam Co. (MIG 73:58)
>> 1 Apr 1999, Hamilton Co. (MIG 70:101)
>
> Early Fall
>> 29 Oct 2002, Middlebrook Lake, Sullivan Co. (MIG 74:26)
>> 9 Nov 2002, Duck River Unit (MIG 74:18)
>> 12 Nov 2006, Lake Co. (MIG 78:32)
>
> High Counts – Fall
>> 5 on 19 Nov 2010, Duck River Unit (MIG 81:156)
>
> High Counts – Winter
>> 400 on 27 Jan 2014, Dyer Co. (MIG, in press)
>> 387+ on 5 Feb 2009, Gray's Camp, Reelfoot Lake, Lake Co. (MIG 80:66)
>> 112 on 5 Feb 2005, Lake Co. (MIG 76:78)
>> 97 on 18 Dec 2004, Reelfoot Lake CBC (MIG 76:63)
>> 82 on 5 Dec 2009, Lauderdale Refuge (MIG 81:99)
>
> Substantiation: Photograph: 1 ad on 23 Dec 1987, Cross Creeks NWR (TBRC Archives, UTK)

Brant, *Branta bernicla*
> Status and Abundance: Accidental visitor
> Habitat: Flooded and unflooded crop fields; lakes and ponds
> Comments: Pale-bellied Brant (*B. b. hrota*) is most likely, and the published photo from 6 May 1974 is attributable to this subspecies. However, the

Anatidae: Ducks, Geese, and Swans

1965 individual was described as a Black Brant (*B. b. bernicla*).

Records
- (1) 1 on 22-26 Oct 1939, Elkmont, Sevier Co. (Stupka 1963)
- (2) 19 on 29 Dec 1952 and 9 Jan 1953, Duck River Unit (Cybert 1955)
- (3) 2 on 20 Oct 1959, Chattanooga (West 1959a)
- (4) 1 on 31 Oct 1965, one shot at this site in Nov 1965, Hiwassee Island (DeVore and Dubke 1966, DeVore 1969)
- (5) 1 on 2 Mar-28 May 1974, Arlington, Shelby Co. (Coffey 1974)
- (6) 1 on 29 Oct-21 Nov 1974, Hiwassee River Area (MIG 46:21)
- (7) 2 on 17 Dec 1981-28 Feb 1982, Cross Creeks NWR, with one staying until 4 Jan 1983 (Robinson and Blunk 1983)
- (8) 1 on 6 Nov 1986, Harrison Bay SP (DS, pers. comm.)
- (9) 1 imm on 5-7 Nov 1988, Chickamauga Lake (MIG 60:32)
- (10) 1 on 3 Dec 1993, Coffee Co. (MIG 65:42)
- (11) 1 on 7 May 2005, White Co. SBC (MIG 76:138)

Substantiation: Photograph: 1 on 6 May 1974, Arlington, Shelby Co. (MIG 45:93)

Barnacle Goose, *Branta leucopsis*

Status and Abundance: Status uncertain (see comments below); accidental winter and early spring visitor

Habitat: Flooded and unflooded crop fields; lakes and ponds

Comments: All records have been presumed until now to be escapees, and the species is not on the TBRC's Official List. See Howell et al. (2014) for a discussion of natural vagrancy of this species in North America. There will always be some question of provenance for vagrant waterfowl, but the authors believe that it is possible that one or more of Tennessee's records involved wild individuals.

Records
- (1) 2 on 10 Feb-17 Mar 1968, Cove Lake SP (MIG 39:44)
- (2) 1 on 1 Mar-24 Apr 1970, Tennessee NWR (MIG 41:42)
- (3) 1 on 24-27 Jan 1976, Cross Creeks NWR (MIG 47:45)
- (4) 1 on 11 Jan 1983, Tennessee NWR (Nicholson 1983a)

Substantiation: Photograph: 1 on 1 Mar-24 Apr 1970, Tennessee NWR (MIG 41:61)

Cackling Goose, *Branta hutchinsii*

Subspecies: *hutchinsii*

Status and Abundance: Irregular winter resident and late fall and early spring transient in Mississippi Alluvial Valley and Tennessee NWR; rare elsewhere

Habitat: Flooded and unflooded crop fields; lakes and ponds

Spring Departure: mid Feb

Fall Arrival: early Dec

Comments: All well-documented records seem to be referable to Richardson's Goose (*B. h. hutchinsii*), but as identification criteria and observer awareness evolve, other subspecies may be found to occur. Subspecies *B. h. minima* was reported Feb 2003 in Shelby Co. (MIG 74:52), but, given the potential variation within Richardson's Goose and the fact that *B. h. minima* winters almost exclusively in the Central Valley of California, the authors believe that this individual was possibly misidentified.

Late Spring

27 Mar 2007, Steele Creek Park (MIG 78:103)

22 Mar 2009, Ensley (MIG 80:87)

Early Fall

22 Nov 2006, n. Shelby Co. (MIG 78:32)

High Counts – Winter

900 on 17 Feb 2010, Duck River Unit (RW, pers. comm.)

388 on 28 Dec 2011, Duck River Unit (SGS, pers. obs.)

322 on 4 Jan 2014, Duck River Unit (WP, pers. comm.)

300 on 3 Dec 2010, Duck River Unit (RW, pers. comm.)

200 on 4 Dec 2008, Duck River Unit (RW, pers. comm.)

Substantiation: Photograph: 1 on 22 Feb 2007 at Steele Creek Park (Knight 2008:25)

Canada Goose, *Branta canadensis*

Subspecies: *maxima / interior*

Status and Abundance: Common permanent resident

Habitat: Flooded and unflooded crop fields; lakes and ponds

Comments: Most individuals are non-migratory introduced Giant Canada Goose (*B. c. maxima*), initially released by the Tennessee Wildlife Resources Agency in the 1970s. The most common transient subspecies in Tennessee is the St. James Bay subspecies (*B. c. interior*), but they now mostly winter farther north and thus are less common in Tennessee. That subspecies occurs primarily in Mississippi Alluvial Valley, Southeastern Coastal Plain, and western Central Hardwoods, but can occur statewide. Other subspecies are possible, although it may not be possible to identify them in the field.

High Counts – Spring

1,919 on 3 Mar 1994, Duck River Unit (RW, pers. comm.)

High Counts – Fall

1,850 on 15 Nov 1990, Watts Bar Lake, Rhea, Meigs, and Roane Co. (MIG 62:51)

1,745 on 29 Nov 1994, Duck River Unit (RW, pers. comm.)
1,508 on 25 Sep 2010, Elizabethton FBC (MIG 81:142)
1,293 on 29 Nov 1993, Duck River Unit (RW, pers. comm.)
1,010 on 2 Nov 1993, Duck River Unit (RW, pers. comm.)

High Counts – Winter
150,000 on 19 Dec 1989, Reelfoot Lake CBC (MIG 61:3)
112,500 on 20 Dec 1975, Reelfoot Lake CBC (MIG 47:35)
51,000 on 2-3 Jan 1991, Reelfoot Lake (MIG 62:80)
47,000 on 17 Dec 1991, Reelfoot Lake CBC (MIG 63:13)
47,000 on 23 Jan 1991, Reelfoot Lake (MIG 63:60)

Substantiation: Specimen: UTM, 120

Mute Swan, *Cygnus olor*

Status and Abundance: Rare winter visitor; introduced

Habitat: Lakes and ponds

Spring Departure: late Mar

Fall Arrival: late Oct

Comments: Introduced and established in parts of North America; most Tennessee records appear to be natural migrants from those introduced populations, but local escapes are also possible. First state record was 1 on 16 Jan 1970, S. Holston River, Sullivan Co. (Coffey 1970).

High Counts – Winter
8 on 28 Dec 2002-26 Dec 2003, Granville, Jackson Co. (MIG 74:55)
8 on 30-31 Dec 2004, Weakley Co. (MIG 76:78)
6 on 24 Dec 2000, Chickamauga Lake (MIG 72:71)

Substantiation: Specimen: UTM, 407

Trumpeter Swan, *Cygnus buccinator*

Status and Abundance: Rare winter visitor

Habitat: Lakes and ponds

Comments: First recorded by John James Audubon, 26 Nov 1820 in w. Tennessee (Deaderick 1940); no additional records until three were found 28 Dec 2001, Lauderdale Refuge (JRW, pers. comm.). Recent records likely all come from population reintroduced into Great Lakes Region, however one record in northeast Tennessee was from the Ontario introduction program (Knight 2008). Species could occur anywhere in Tennessee; all black-billed swans should be studied carefully.

Substantiation: Photograph: 1 in Jan 2003, Whitetop Creek Park, Bristol (Knight 2008:26)

Tundra Swan, *Cygnus columbianus*
  Status and Abundance: Irregular winter resident and late fall and early spring transient
  Habitat: Lakes and ponds
  Spring Departure: early Mar
  Fall Arrival: late Nov
  Comments: All black-billed swans should be carefully studied to rule out Trumpeter. Minor invasion during winter 1973-74; major invasion during winter 1978-79 (Robinson 1990).
  Late Spring
    11 May 2007, John Sevier Lake (MIG 78:103)
    8 May 2004, Campbell Co. NAMC (MIG 75:92)
    3 Apr 2011, Greene Co. (MIG 82:89)
    3 Apr 2011, John Sevier Lake (MIG 82:89)
  Early Fall
    3 Oct 1993, Wilbur Lake (MIG 65:26)
    18 Oct 1996, Savannah Bay (MIG 68:28)
    25 Oct 1959, Hiwassee Bridge (West 1959)
    7 Nov 1971, Cross Creeks NWR (MIG 43:24)
  High Counts – Fall
    17 on 10 Nov 2011, Watauga Lake (MIG 82:159)
    12 on 23 Nov 1984, S. Holston Lake (MIG 56:27)
  High Counts – Winter
    27 on 27 Nov 1978, Woods Reservoir (MIG 50:42)
    15 on 3-24 Jan 1976, Hatchie NWR (MIG 47:45)
    12 on 14 Jan 1979, near Memphis (MIG 50:41)
  Substantiation: Specimen: LSUMZ, 9152

Wood Duck, *Aix sponsa*
  Status and Abundance: Permanent resident; common spring, summer, and fall. Uncommon during winter in Mississippi Alluvial Valley, Southeastern Coastal Plain, and Central Hardwoods; rare during winter elsewhere
  Habitat: Lakes, ponds, and rivers (typically wooded); swamps
  High Counts – Spring
    500+ on 12 Mar 2000, Dyson's Ditch, Cheatham Co. (MIG 71:89)
    123 on 8 Mar 2004, Duck River Unit (RW, pers. comm.)
  High Counts – Fall
    4,850 on 10 Oct 1967, Reelfoot Lake (MIG:38:94)
    1,191 on 31 Oct 1995, Duck River Unit (RW, pers. comm.)

High Counts – Winter
    1,015 on 28 Dec 1988, Reelfoot Lake CBC (MIG 60:14)
    595 on 12 Nov 1996, Duck River Unit (RW, pers. comm.)
    498 on 30 Jan 1995, Duck River Unit (RW, pers. comm.)
Substantiation: Specimen: LSUMZ, 75673

Gadwall, *Anas strepera*

Status and Abundance: Common (uncommon in Southern Blue Ridge) winter resident and transient; accidental summer visitor

Habitat: Lakes and ponds

Spring Departure: early May

Fall Arrival: mid Sep

Comments: Summer records most likely pertain to sick or injured birds.

Late Spring
    6 Jun 2007, Standifer Gap Marsh (MIG 78:141)
    1 Jun 1963, near Nashville (MIG 34:50)
    29 May 2001, Kingston Steam Plant (MIG 72:96)
    26 May 1980, Kingston Steam Plant (MIG 51:93)
    25 May 2003, Lake Co. (MIG 74:86)

Early Fall
    14 Aug 1977, Nickajack Lake (MIG 49:20)
    29 Aug 1988, Cross Creeks NWR (Robinson 1988a)
    30 Aug 1992, Island 13 (MIG 64:15)
    8 Sep 1968, Reelfoot Lake (MIG 39:89)

High Counts – Spring
    2,411 on 2 Mar 1995, Duck River Unit (RW, pers. comm.)
    1,179 on 8 Mar 2004, Duck River Unit (RW, pers. comm.)

High Counts – Fall
    21,744 on 3 Nov 2008, Duck River Unit (RW, pers. comm.)
    19,360 on 16 Nov 2007, Duck River Unit (RW, pers. comm.)
    16,000 on 22 Oct 2011, Duck River Unit (MIG 82:151)
    10,636 on 21 Nov 2000, Duck River Unit (RW, pers. comm.)
    10,317 on 7 Nov 2005, Duck River Unit (RW, pers. comm.)

Summer Records
    1 m on 8 Jun 2002, Mud Lake, Lake Co. (JRW, unpubl. data)
    2 m on 9 Jun 1996, Mud Lake, Lake Co. (MIG 67:77)
    2 m on 1 Jul 1996, Lake Co. (MIG 67:77)
    1 on 18 Jul 1995, Lake Co. (MIG 66:65)

High Counts – Winter
    22,424 on 3 Dec 2007, Duck River Unit (RW, pers. comm.)
    20,666 on 17 Dec 2007, Duck River Unit (RW, pers. comm.)
    19,445 on 5 Jan 2010, Duck River Unit (RW, pers. comm.)

16,132 on 3 Jan 2009, Cross Creeks CBC (MIG 80:48)
16,100 on 28 Dec 1988, Reelfoot Lake CBC (MIG 60:14)

Substantiation: Specimen: APSU, 1620

Eurasian Wigeon, *Anas penelope*

Status and Abundance: Very rare winter, spring, and fall visitor

Habitat: Lakes and ponds; grain fields near wetlands

Comments: First record was of 2 males and a female and all but one other of the records have been of single males. This is likely due primarily to the difficulty of identifying female wigeon. A male was observed in 5 consecutive years at Cross Creeks NWR and likely represents the same returning individual.

Records
  (1) 3 (2 m, 1 f) on 21 Feb 1944, Chickasaw SP, Chester Co. (Whitt 1944)
  (2) 1 shot between 1950-54, Reelfoot Lake (Pitts 1981)
  (3) 1 m on 20-30 Nov 1982, Savannah Bay (MIG 54:24)
  (4) 1 m on 8-20 Mar 1983, Cross Creeks NWR (MIG 54:61)
  (5) 1 m on 30 Dec 1983-16 Jan 1984, Cross Creeks NWR (MIG 55:45)
  (6) 1 m on 19 Oct-25 Nov 1984, Cross Creeks NWR (MIG 56:19)
  (7) 1 m on 23 Dec 1984, Tennessee NWR, Humphreys Co. (MIG 56:51)
  (8) 1 m on 22-25 Jan 1986, Cross Creeks NWR (MIG 57:56)
  (9) 1 m on 21 Nov-30 Dec 1987, Cross Creeks NWR (Robinson 1990)
  (10) 1 m on 6 Apr 1988, Black Bayou WMA (MIG 69:160)
  (11) 1 m on 15 Dec 1991, Cross Creeks NWR CBC (MIG 62:13)
  (12) 2 (1 m, 1 f) on 21 Oct 1992, Monsanto Ponds (MIG 64:17)
  (13) 1 m on 8 Mar 1995, White Lake WMA (MIG 66:50)
  (14) 1 m on 1 Jan 1997, Lauderdale WMA (MIG 68:62)
  (15) 1 m on 18-22 Feb 2002, Britton Ford (MIG 73:35)
  (16) 1 m on 18 Jan 2009, Robco Lake (MIG 80:66)
  (17) 1 m on 6 Mar 2010, Steele Creek Park (MIG 81:118)
  (18) 1 m on 29 Dec 2010, Savannah CBC, Hardin Co. (MIG 82:58)
  (19) 1 m on 24 Feb 2012, Phillippy (MIG 83:21)
  (20) 1 m on 12-17 Jan 2013, Busseltown Unit, Tennessee NWR (RS, m.ob., pers. comm.)

Substantiation: Photograph: 1 m on 6 Mar 2010, Steele Creek Park (NAB 64(3):51)

American Wigeon, *Anas americana*

Status and Abundance: Fairly common transient and winter resident in Mississippi Alluvial Valley and Southeastern Coastal Plain; irregular elsewhere; accidental summer visitor

Habitat: Lakes and ponds; grain fields near wetlands

Spring Departure: late Apr

Fall Arrival: late Sep

Comments: Becomes less frequently detected by January, especially in the east, but migrants begin to arrive in mid-February. Summer records most likely pertain to sick or injured birds.

Late Spring
- 30 May 1987, Cross Creeks NWR (MIG 58:96)
- 24 May 1972, Radnor Lake (MIG 43:76)
- 23 May 2005, White Lake WMA (MIG 76:95)
- 21 May 1975, Austin Springs (MIG 46:89)

Early Fall
- 24 Aug 1987, Henry Co. (Robinson 1990)
- 1 Sep 2004, Rankin Bottoms (MIG 76:32)
- 3 Sep 1992, Island 13 (MIG 64:15)
- 4 Sep 1988, Cross Creeks NWR (Robinson 1990)
- 5 Sep 1980, Kingston Steam Plant (MIG 52:24)

High Counts – Spring
- 330 on 3 Mar 1994, Duck River Unit (RW, pers. comm.)

High Counts – Fall
- 24,600 on 19 Oct 1967, Reelfoot Lake (USFWS *fide* MAG)
- 4,851 on 16 Nov 2007, Duck River Unit (RW, pers. comm.)
- 4,584 on 3 Nov 2008, Duck River Unit (RW, pers. comm.)
- 4,424 on 21 Nov 2000, Duck River Unit (RW, pers. comm.)
- 4,007 on 12 Nov 1996, Duck River Unit (RW, pers. comm.)

Summer Records
- 1 on 8 Jun 1963, Watauga Lake (MIG 34:53)
- 1 on 24 Jul 1968, Boone Lake (MIG 39:65)
- 1 on 21 Jul 1974, Campbell Co. (MIG 45:102)
- 1 on 6-30 Jun 1977, Sumner Co. (MIG 48:103)
- 1 m on 9-17 Jun 1996, Great River Road, Dyer Co. (MIG 67:77)
- 3 on 8 Jun 2002, Mud Lake, Lake Co. (JRW, unpubl. data)
- 4 (2 m, 2 f) on 5 Jun 2002, Mud Lake, Lake Co. (MIG 73:110)
- 2 on 5 Jun 2005, White Lake WMA (MIG 76:144)

High Counts – Winter
- 15,300 on 27 Dec 1960, Reelfoot Lake CBC (MIG 31:74)
- 9,216 on 29 Nov 1994, Duck River Unit (RW, pers. comm.)
- 8,735 on 2 Jan 2001, Duck River Unit (RW, pers. comm.)
- 8,490 on 8 Jan 2002, Duck River Unit (RW, pers. comm.)
- 7,765 on 30 Jan 1995, Duck River Unit (RW, pers. comm.)
- 7,051 on 13 Feb 1995, Duck River Unit (RW, pers. comm.)
- 6,147 on 16 Dec 1993, Duck River Unit (RW, pers. comm.)

Substantiation: Specimen: USNM, 430872

American Black Duck, *Anas rubripes*

Status and Abundance: Fairly common transient and winter resident; accidental summer visitor

Habitat: Lakes and ponds

Spring Departure: late Mar

Fall Arrival: early Oct

Comments: Regularly hybridizes with Mallards, so individuals showing characteristics of both species are occasionally observed. Breeding was documented in the 1960s at Cross Creeks NWR (Robinson and Blunk 1989), in Blount Co. at Alcoa Marsh in 1972 (MIG 43:52), and at Fort Loudoun Lake in 1974 (MIG 45:77). Nesting has not been documented with more recent summer observations.

Late Spring
- 5 Jun 1999, Lake Co. (JRW, unpubl. data)
- 2 Jun 1997, Island 21, Dyer Co. (MIG 68:134)
- 1 Jun 2003, Hwy 103, Dyer Co. (JRW, unpubl. data)
- 27 May 2003, Dyer Co. (MIG 74:86)
- 25 May 1986, Gallatin Steam Plant (MIG 57:76)
- 19 May 1960, Bush Lake (Parmer 1962)

Early Fall
- 4 Aug 2000, Eagle Bend Fish Hatchery (MIG 72:42)
- 6 Aug 1972, Savannah Bay (MIG 43:101)
- 9 Aug 1987, Cross Creeks NWR (Robinson 1990)
- 20 Aug 1986, Cross Creeks NWR (MIG 58:23)

High Counts – Spring
- 444 on 2 Mar 1995, Duck River Unit (RW, pers. comm.)
- 303 on 18 Feb 1997, Duck River Unit (RW, pers. comm.)

High Counts – Fall
- 3,263 on 29 Nov 1994, Duck River Unit (RW, pers. comm.)
- 2,321 on 27 Nov 1996, Duck River Unit (RW, pers. comm.)
- 1,880 on 21 Nov 2000, Duck River Unit (RW, pers. comm.)
- 1,771 on 18 Nov 1994, Duck River Unit (RW, pers. comm.)
- 1,520 on 12 Nov 1996, Duck River Unit (RW, pers. comm.)

Summer Records
- 1 on 16 Jun 1991, Lake Co. (MIG 63:20)

High Counts – Winter
- 29,000 on 28 Dec 1966, Reelfoot Lake CBC (MIG 37:66)
- 20,676 on 30 Jan 1995, Duck River Unit (RW, pers. comm.)
- 20,000 on 19 Dec 1989, Reelfoot Lake CBC (MIG 61:3)
- 17,939 on 13 Feb 1995, Duck River Unit (RW, pers. comm.)
- 15,928 on 20 Jan 1994, Duck River Unit (RW, pers. comm.)

Substantiation: Specimen: UTM, 99

Anatidae: Ducks, Geese, and Swans

Mallard, *Anas platyrhynchos*
Status and Abundance: Common permanent resident (but summer residents almost entirely comprised of feral populations)
Habitat: Lakes and ponds
Comments: Regularly hybridizes with American Black Ducks, so individuals showing characteristics of both species are occasionally observed.
High Counts – Spring
  2,827 on 2 Mar 1995, Duck River Unit (RW, pers. comm.)
  2,646 on 3 Mar 1994, Duck River Unit (RW, pers. comm.)
  1,685 on 5 Mar 2008, Duck River Unit (RW, pers. comm.)
High Counts – Fall
  29,928 on 28 Nov 1995, Duck River Unit (RW, pers. comm.)
  29,351 on 21 Nov 2000, Duck River Unit (RW, pers. comm.)
  29,138 on 29 Nov 1994, Duck River Unit (RW, pers. comm.)
  25,832 on 24 Nov 1997, Duck River Unit (RW, pers. comm.)
  25,095 on 19 Nov 2008, Duck River Unit (RW, pers. comm.)
High Counts – Winter
  430,000 on 19 Dec 1989, Reelfoot Lake CBC (MIG 61:3)
  314,744 on 16 Dec 1995, Reelfoot Lake CBC (MIG 67:7)
  265,000 on 23 Dec 1979, Reelfoot Lake CBC (MIG 51:31)
  171,898 on 2 Jan 2001, Duck River Unit (RW, pers. comm.)
  155,918 on 20 Jan 1995, Duck River Unit (RW, pers. comm.)
Substantiation: Specimen: UTM, 327

Mottled Duck, *Anas fulvigula*
Status and Abundance: Accidental visitor (mostly fall)
Habitat: Lakes and ponds
Comments: Most likely the sudden regularity of sightings is a function of increased observer awareness and understanding of identification criteria.
Records
  (1) 1 on 4-7 Oct 2003, Ensley (MIG 76:4)
  (2) 1 on 28 Aug-15 Oct 2004, Ensley (MIG 76:4)
  (3) 2 on 27-28 Apr 2005, Ensley (MIG 76:4)
  (4) 2 on 24-30 Sep 2005, Eagle Creek, Henry Co. (MIG 76:3) (documented and accepted by TBRC)
  (5) 1 on 5-9 Sep 2006, Upper Douglas Lake, Jefferson and Cocke Co. (MIG 78:37, Edwards 2012)
  (6) 1 on 7-15 Jun 2008, President's Island (MIG 79:96)
  (7) 1 on 12 Nov 2008, McKellar Lake, Shelby Co. (MIG 80:22)

Substantiation: Photograph: 1 on 28 Aug-15 Oct 2004, Ensley (NAB 59(1):87)

Blue-winged Teal, *Anas discors*
Status and Abundance: Common transient; rare summer resident; very rare winter resident
Habitat: Lakes and ponds
Spring Arrival: late Feb
Spring Departure: late May, overlap with summer residents
Fall Arrival: mid Aug
Fall Departure: late Nov
Comments: Several breeding records have been documented from counties across the state, including Maury (Todd 1944), Shelby (MIG 57:103, MIG 75:158), Hamilton (MIG 75:115), Dyer (MIG 80:124), Anderson, Coffee, Davidson, Grundy, Rutherford, and Lake in 1996 (MIG 67:76), and at Black Bayou Refuge in 2011 (MIG 82:83). Because of the presence of small numbers of regular summering individuals, it is difficult to ascertain whether late spring and early fall individuals are transients or were summer residents.
Early Spring
  25 Feb 1963, near Greeneville (MIG 34:11)
  25 Feb 1986, Cross Creeks NWR (MIG 57:76)
  20 Feb 1982, Ashland City (MIG 53:45)
Late Spring
  31 May into Jun 2001, Brainerd Levee (MIG 72:96)
Early Fall
  2 Aug 1982, Kingston Steam Plant (MIG 54:24)
High Counts – Spring
  1,500 on 5 Apr 2003, Duck River Unit (MIG 74:89)
  500+ on 10 Apr 2000, Rankin Bottoms (MIG 71:91)
High Counts – Fall
  5,350 on 21 Sep 1967, Reelfoot Lake (MIG 38:94)
  1,500 on 17 Sep 1956, Memphis (MIG 27:67)
High Counts – Summer
  6 on 15 Jun 2003, Dyer Co. (MIG 74:129)
  2 m on 6 Jun 2010, Moss Island WMA (MIG 81:125)
Substantiation: Specimen: APSU, 2371

Cinnamon Teal, *Anas cyanoptera*
Status and Abundance: Very rare spring transient; accidental winter visitor
Habitat: Lakes and ponds

Anatidae: Ducks, Geese, and Swans

Records
- (1) 1 on 10-21 Apr 1972, Tennessee NWR, Humphreys Co. (Rauber 1972)
- (2) 1 on 26 Mar 1974, Cross Creeks NWR (Snyder 1974)
- (3) 2 shot on 15 Jan 1987, Tennessee (Shelby Co.)-Arkansas (Crittendon Co.) line (MIG 58:53)
- (4) 1 on 12 Apr 1990, Cross Creeks NWR (MIG 61:73)
- (5) 1 m on 20 Mar-29 Apr 1992, Hwy 79 and Great River Road, Lake Co. (MIG 63:71)
- (6) 1 m on 29-30 Mar 1995, Hwy 152, Middle Fork Forked Deer River, Gibson Co. (MIG 66:50)
- (7) 1 m on 4-14 Mar 1996, Brainerd Levee (MIG 67:62)
- (8) 1 m on 17 Mar-5 Apr 1996, White Lake WMA (MIG 67:59)
- (9) 1 on 29 Mar-12 Apr 1997, Dyer Co. (MIG 68:106)
- (10) 1 m on 18 Mar-2 Apr 1998, Black Bayou WMA (MIG 69:160)
- (11) 1 m on 5 Mar 1999, Duck River Unit (RW, pers. comm.)
- (12) 1 on 9-18 Mar 1999, Reelfoot Lake (MIG 70:97)
- (13) 1 m on 27 Mar 2008, Lincoln Co. (MIG 79:63)
- (14) 1 m on 29 Mar 2013, Humphrey's Co. (MIG, in press)

Substantiation: Photograph: 1 m on 7 Apr 1974, Cross Creeks NWR (TBRC)

Northern Shoveler, *Anas clypeata*

Status and Abundance: Fairly common transient; uncommon winter resident; accidental summer resident

Habitat: Lakes and ponds

Spring Departure: mid May

Fall Arrival: late Aug

Comments: Summer records most likely pertain to injured birds, although a pair was observed copulating at Ensley in Jun 2009 (NAB 63(4):43). One confirmed nesting record of a female with 5 young on 27 June 1998, Lake Co. (JRW, unpubl. data).

Late Spring
- 2 Jun 2008, Washington Co. (MIG 79:98)
- 29 May 2005, White Lake WMA (MIG 76:95)
- 22 May 1967, Amnicola Marsh (MIG 38:50)
- 18 May 2000, Kingston Steam Plant (MIG 71:91)
- 17 May 1967, Nashville (MIG 38:48)

Early Fall
- 8 Aug 1981, Nashville (MIG 53:15)
- 8 Aug 1985, Hiwassee River Area (MIG 57:32)

High Counts – Spring
   869 on 5 Mar 2008, Duck River Unit (RW, pers. comm.)
High Counts – Fall
   3,100 on 23 Nov 1967, Reelfoot Lake (MIG 38:94)
High Counts – Summer
   9 max on 12 Jul-Aug 1996, Shelby Farms (MIG 67:77)
   5 (4 m, 1 f) on 7-8 Jun 1996, Black Bayou WMA (MIG 67:77)
   1-2 on 1 Jun and 24 Jul 1986, Dyer Co. (MIG 57:103)
High Counts – Winter
   3,200 on 23 Dec 1972, Reelfoot Lake CBC (MIG 44:10)
   1,010 on 8 Jan 2009, Duck River Unit (RW, pers. comm.)
Substantiation: Specimen: UTM, 116

Northern Pintail, *Anas acuta*

Status and Abundance: Uncommon winter resident and transient; accidental summer visitor
Habitat: Lakes and ponds
Spring Departure: mid Mar
Fall Arrival: mid Sep
Comments: Summer records most likely pertain to sick or injured birds.
Late Spring
   8 Jun 1997, Mud Lake, Lake Co. (MIG 68:134)
   28 May 2004, Dyer Co. (MIG 75:110)
   26 May 1986, Hiwassee River Area (MIG 57:84)
   23 May 1981, McNairy Co. (Nicholson 1984)
   23 May 2004, Duck River Unit (MIG 75:112)
Early Fall
   15 Aug 1965, Chattanooga (MIG 36:68)
   21 Aug 2004, Lake Co. (MIG 76:26)
   30 Aug 2001, Island 13 (MIG 72:37)
High Counts – Spring
   800 on 8 Mar 2004, Duck River Unit (RW, pers. comm.)
High Counts – Fall
   4,420 on 17 Nov 2005, Duck River Unit (RW, pers. comm.)
   4,370 on 20 Nov 2001, Duck River Unit (RW, pers. comm.)
   3,170 on 24 Nov 2009, Duck River Unit (RW, pers. comm.)
   3,050 on 4 Nov 2002, Duck River Unit (RW, pers. comm.)
   3,030 on 23 Nov 1998, Duck River Unit (RW, pers. comm.)
Summer Records
   1 m on 29 Jun 2002, Great River Road, Dyer Co. (JRW, unpubl. data)
   1 on 29 Jun 1988, Cross Creeks NWR (Robinson 1990)
   2 on 19 Jul 1984, Tennessee NWR (MIG 55:91)

Anatidae: Ducks, Geese, and Swans

High Counts – Winter
  17,000 on 27 Dec 1960, Reelfoot Lake CBC (MIG 31:74)
  16,105 on 2 Jan 2001, Duck River Unit (RW, pers. comm.)
  14,018 on 8 Jan 2009, Duck River Unit (RW, pers. comm.)
  12,860 on 5 Jan 2010, Duck River Unit (RW, pers. comm.)
  10,893 on 21 Jan 1997, Duck River Unit (RW, pers. comm.)
Substantiation: Photograph: Todd, M.C. 2005. "Northern Pintail". <http://www.pbase.com/mctodd/image/39949222> Accessed 15 Dec 2014.

Garganey, *Anas querquedula*
Status and Abundance: Accidental visitor
Habitat: Lakes and ponds
Comments: The TBRC initially rejected the Sep 1994 record on the basis of provenance and the lack of fall records for the interior U.S. To date, this record is one of only four fall records east of the Mississippi River (Howell et al. 2014). However, since the 1990s, fall Garganey have occurred with more regularity in the Pacific states (Howell et al. 2014). The TBRC eventually reconsidered Tennessee's Sep 1994 record and voted to accept it as a wild individual. There will always be some question of provenance for vagrant waterfowl, but given the widespread pattern of vagrancy for this species, the authors believe that both of Tennessee's records are more likely than not to have been wild individuals.
Records
  (1) 1 m on 1-5 Apr 1978, Darwin sewage ponds, Shelby Co. (Nicholson 1983)
  (2) 1 ad m on 3 Sep 1994, Ensley (Greene 1997)
Substantiation: Photograph: 1 m on 3 Apr 1978, Shelby Co. (TBRC Archives, UTK)

Green-winged Teal, *Anas crecca*
Subspecies: *carolinensis*
Status and Abundance: Fairly common transient; uncommon winter resident; accidental summer visitor
Habitat: Lakes and ponds
Spring Departure: late Apr
Fall Arrival: late Aug
Comments: Generally found in small numbers during winter, but can be locally abundant. Summer records most likely pertain to sick or injured birds. Common Teal (*A. c. crecca*) (sometimes called Eurasian Green-winged Teal or Eurasian Teal) is accidental. There are three

unsubstantiated records: 1 ad m on 2 Jun-31 Jul 1988, Cross Creeks NWR (Robinson 1990, MIG 59:125); 1 on 15 Apr 1995, Black Bayou WMA (GC *fide* MAG) and 1 on 2-16 Dec 2001, Lauderdale WMA (MIG 73:35). More records are likely as observer awareness of this possible Eurasian vagrant increases. Some authorities have proposed that this be split into a separate species from Green-winged Teal, as is the case in Europe, although the AOU has not yet accepted this split. The TBRC has not historically evaluated records of subspecies and thus has not considered the validity of any records of this subspecies in Tennessee. As with most vagrant waterfowl records, provenance will likely be a difficult question to resolve.

Late Spring
    11 Jun 1991, Limestone, Washington Co. (MIG 62:112)
    31 May 2004, White Lake WMA (MIG 75:110)
    29 May 2005, White Lake WMA (MIG 76:95)
    14 May 1955, Nashville SBC (MIG 26:27)

Early Fall
    23 Jul 1983, Shelby Co. (MIG 54:86)
    1 Aug 1965, Amnicola Marsh (MIG 36:68)

High Counts – Spring
    10,000 on 31 Mar 2001, Reelfoot Lake (MIG 72:91)
    1,547 on 2 Mar 1995, Duck River Unit (RW, pers. comm.)

High Counts – Fall
    6,730 on 6 Nov 2009, Duck River Unit (RW, pers. comm.)
    5,832 on 24 Nov 2009, Duck River Unit (RW, pers. comm.)
    5,430 on 20 Nov 2006, Duck River Unit (RW, pers. comm.)
    5,374 on 3 Nov 2008, Duck River Unit (RW, pers. comm.)
    4,810 on 25 Oct 2001, Duck River Unit (RW, pers. comm.)

Summer Records
    1 ad m on 2 Jun-31 Jul 1988, Cross Creeks NWR (Robinson 1990, MIG 59:125)
    1 m on 15-22 Jun 1991, Lake Co. (MIG 63:20)
    1 m on 9 Jun 1996, Mud Lake, Lake Co. (MIG 67:76)
    2 (m and f) on 3 Jun 1986, Tatumville Marsh, Dyer Co. (MIG 57:103)

High Counts – Winter
    10,202 on 3 Jan 2006, Duck River Unit (RW, pers. comm.)
    9,200 on 17 Dec 2003, Duck River Unit (RW, pers. comm.)
    7,772 on early Jan 2012, Duck River Unit (RW, pers. comm.)
    6,940 on 22 Nov 1999, Duck River Unit (RW, pers. comm.)
    6,825 on 2 Dec 2002, Duck River Unit (RW, pers. comm.)

Substantiation: Specimen: APSU, 2509

Anatidae: Ducks, Geese, and Swans

Canvasback, *Aythya valisineria*
- Status and Abundance: Uncommon transient and winter resident; accidental summer visitor
- Habitat: Deeper (and usually larger) lakes and ponds
- Spring Departure: late Mar
- Fall Arrival: early Nov
- Comments: Summer records most likely pertain to sick or injured birds.
- Late Spring
    - 19 May 1976, Gallatin (BNA:17)
    - 13 May 1961, Kingsport SBC (MIG 32:30)
    - 13 May 2000, Wilson Co. NAMC (MIG 71:51)
    - 12 May 2007, Anderson Co. NAMC (MIG 78:126)
    - 9 May 1989, Barkley WMA (MIG 60:84)
- Early Fall
    - 29 Sep 1935, Knox Co. (Howell and Monroe 1957)
- High Counts – Fall
    - 900 on 27 Nov 1996, Big Sandy Unit (RW, pers. comm.)
    - 390 on 29 Nov 1993, Big Sandy Unit (RW, pers. comm.)
- Summer Records
    - 1 m on 23-25 Jul 1976, Sumner Co. (MIG 47:99-100)
    - 1 on 30 Jun 1993, Lower Hatchie NWR (MIG 64:84)
    - 1 on 9 Jun 2002, Mud Lake, Lake Co. (MIG 73:110)
- High Counts – Winter
    - 4,965 on 21 Jan 2009, Big Sandy Unit (RW, pers. comm.)
    - 3,098 on 2 Jan 2001, Big Sandy Unit (RW, pers. comm.)
    - 3,000 on 27 Dec 1960, Reelfoot Lake CBC (MIG 31:74)
    - 2,550 on 3 Jan 1995, Big Sandy Unit (RW, pers. comm.)
    - 2,400 on 9 Jan 2008, Big Sandy Unit (RW, pers. comm.)
- Substantiation: Photograph: Todd, M.C. 2013. "Canvasback". <http://www.pbase.com/mctodd/image/148497377> Accessed 25 Sep 2014.

Redhead, *Aythya americana*
- Status and Abundance: Uncommon transient and winter resident; accidental summer visitor
- Habitat: Deeper (and usually larger) lakes and ponds
- Spring Departure: mid Apr
- Fall Arrival: late Oct
- Comments: Summer records most likely pertain to sick or injured birds.
- Late Spring
    - 24 May 1980, Cedar Hill Lake (BNA:17)

13 May 2000, Lake Co. NAMC (MIG 71:50)
5 May 1963, Reelfoot Lake SBC (MIG 34:30)
4 May 1986, Chattanooga SBC (MIG 57:66)
Early Fall
12 Oct 1985, Cross Creeks NWR (MIG 57:25)
13 Oct 1977, Savannah Bay (MIG 49:20)
High Counts – Spring
160 on 6 Mar 2007, Ft. Loudoun Lake (MIG 78:103)
123 on 9 Mar 1996, Ft. Loudoun Lake (MIG 67:63)
70 on 13 Mar 1989, Boone Lake (MIG 60:89)
High Counts – Fall
30 on 10 Nov 1996, Boone Lake (MIG 68:28)
24 on 29 Nov 2004, Chickamauga Lake (MIG 76:32)
Summer Records
1 on 3 Jul 1983, Greene Co. (MIG 54:90)
1 Aug 1965, Chattanooga (MIG 36:68)
31 Aug 1985, Lake Co. (MIG 57:22, summered in area)
High Counts – Winter
1,500 on 12 Nov 1979, Woods Reservoir (MIG 51:39)
600 on 20 Dec 1975, Reelfoot Lake CBC (MIG 47:35)
500 on 28 Dec 1967, Lebanon CBC (MIG 38:87)
Substantiation: Photograph: 1 in Sep 2002, Bays Mountain Park (Knight 2008:29)

Ring-necked Duck, *Aythya collaris*

Status and Abundance: Fairly common transient and winter resident; accidental summer visitor
Habitat: Lakes and ponds
Spring Departure: early May
Fall Arrival: early Oct
Late Spring
25 May 2005, Chickasaw NWR (MIG 76:95)
10 May 1997, Wilson Co. NAMC (MIG 68:98)
Early Fall
10 Sep 1978, Kingston Steam Plant (MIG 50:22)
17 Sep 2005, Roane Co. FBC (MIG 76:16)
20 Sep 1987, Henry Co. (Robinson 1990)
High Counts – Spring
610 on 8 Mar 2004, Big Sandy Unit (RW, pers. comm.)
281 on 12 Mar 1989, Stewart Co. (MIG 60:84)
High Counts – Fall
4,860 on 16 Nov 2007, Duck River Unit (RW, pers. comm.)

4,430 on 24 Nov 2009, Duck River Unit (RW, pers. comm.)
3,150 on 19 Nov 2008, Big Sandy Unit (RW, pers. comm.)
1,942 on 19 Nov 2002, Duck River Unit (RW, pers. comm.)
1,562 on 17 Nov 2005, Duck River Unit (RW, pers. comm.)

Summer Records
1 f on 7 Jun 1994, Monsanto Ponds (MIG 64:86)
1 on 7 Jul 1997, Washington Co. (MIG 68:136)
1 f on 2 Jun 2002, Mud Lake, Lake Co. (MIG 73:110)
1 on 20 Jul 2002, Eagle Lake WMA (MIG 73:110)
1 on 31 Jul 2002, Phillippy (MIG 73:110)
1 m on 14 Jun and 19 Jul 2003, Livingston, Overton Co. (MIG 74:131)
3 on 5 Jun 2005, White Lake WMA (MIG 76:144)

High Counts – Winter
25,000 on 30 Dec 1958, Reelfoot Lake CBC (MIG 30:16)
10,870 on 21 Jan 2009, Big Sandy Unit (RW, pers. comm.)
10,520 on 9 Jan 2008, Big Sandy Unit (RW, pers. comm.)
9,352 on 18 Dec 2006, Cross Creeks CBC (MIG 78:62)
9,270 on 18 Jan 2006, Big Sandy Unit (RW, pers. comm.)

Substantiation: Specimen: LSUMZ, 75674

Greater Scaup, *Aythya marila*

Status and Abundance: Irregular transient and winter resident (uncommon in Mississippi Alluvial Valley and Southeastern Coastal Plain); accidental summer visitor

Habitat: Deeper (and usually larger) lakes and ponds

Spring Departure: late Mar

Fall Arrival: early Nov

Comments: Summer records most likely pertain to sick or injured birds.

Late Spring
31 May 2004, Dyer Co. (MIG 75:110)
27 May 2003, Dyer Co. (MIG 74:86)
14 May 2008, Mud Lake, Lake Co. (MIG 80:124)
4 May 2009, Austin Springs (MIG 80:91)
3 May 1970, Chattanooga SBC (MIG 41:36)

Early Fall
17 Oct 1987, Hiwassee River Area (Robinson 1990)
20 Oct 2010, Mississippi River, Shelby Co. (MIG 81:153)
30 Oct 1983, Old Hickory Lake (MIG 55:19)

High Counts – Spring
450 on 4 Mar 1974, Chickamauga Lake (MIG 45:23)
350 on 2 Mar 1991, Chickamauga Lake (MIG 62:112)

High Counts – Fall
    88 on 30 Nov 2010, TVA Lake (MIG 81:153)
Summer Records
    1 on 16 May-8 Jul 1976, Fort Loudoun Lake (MIG 47:101)
    1 on 7 Jun 1983, Kingston Steam Plant (MIG 54:90)
High Counts – Winter
    500+ on 4 Dec 2007, Pace Point (MIG 79:51)
    500 on 26 Jan 1971, Chickamauga Lake (MIG 42:20)
    214 on 21 Dec 2009, TVA Lake (MIG 81:99)
Substantiation: Photograph: Somershoe, S.G. 2014. "Greater Scaup". <http://www.pbase.com/shoeman/image/154159939> Accessed 25 Sep 2014.

Lesser Scaup, *Aythya affinis*
Status and Abundance: Fairly common transient and winter resident; rare summer visitor
Habitat: Deeper (and usually larger) lakes and ponds
Spring Departure: mid May
Fall Arrival: mid Oct
Comments: There are over 20 summer records, which most likely pertain to sick or injured birds.
Late Spring
    29 May 2004, McKellar Lake, Shelby Co. (MIG 75:110)
    29 May 2007, Upper Douglas Lake (MIG 78:103)
    24 May 2001, Reelfoot Lake (MIG 72:91)
Early Fall
    15 Sep 2001, Bristol NAMC (MIG 73:30)
    6 Oct 1938, North Lake, Shelby Co. (MIG 9:95)
    6 Oct 1984, Radnor Lake (MIG 56:19)
    9 Oct 1976, Wilbur Lake (MIG 48:23)
High Counts – Spring
    5,000 on 15 Mar 2009, TVA Lake (MIG 80:87)
    4,000 on 5 Mar 2006, Ensley (MIG 77:98)
    3,000 on 3 Mar 2001, Ensley (MIG 72:91)
High Counts – Fall
    3,000 on 30 Nov 2003, Robco Lake (MIG 75:23)
    3,000 on 17 Nov 2011, Boone Lake (MIG 82:154)
    2,000 on 16 Nov 1970, Woods Reservoir (MIG 42:19)
High Counts – Winter
    8,000 on 1 Dec 2007, Robco Lake (MIG 79:51)
    6,800 on 23 Dec 1972, Reelfoot Lake CBC (MIG 44:10)
    5,494 on 17 Dec 1994, Reelfoot Lake CBC (MIG 66:12)

5,283 on 20 Dec 2003, Reelfoot Lake CBC (MIG 75:57)

Substantiation: Photograph: Todd, M.C. 2005. "Lesser Scaup". <http://www.pbase.com/mctodd/image/40255861> Accessed 25 Sep 2014.

King Eider, *Somateria spectabilis*

Status and Abundance: Accidental winter visitor

Habitat: Lakes and other large bodies of water

Records

(1) 1 f shot in the Opossum Branch area of Woods Reservoir between 1964 and 1967 (Bierly 1976)

Substantiation: Specimen: CSM, AV-267

Harlequin Duck, *Histrionicus histrionicus*

Status and Abundance: Accidental winter visitor

Habitat: Lakes, ponds, and fast-flowing rivers

Records

(1) 2 shot on Norris Lake on 8 Jan 1984 (MIG 55:49)

(2) 1 m shot on 5 Jan 1985, Cheatham Lake (MIG 56:51)

(3) 1 imm m photographed at South Holston Dam, 1 Jan through early Feb 2000 (MIG 71:46, Knight 2008)

(4) 1 f on 10-11 Feb 2000, Chilhowee Lake, Blount Co. (MIG 71:46, Calhoon 2000)

(5) 1 f on 31 Jan-11 May 2013, Kingsport (RLK, m. ob., photos)

Substantiation: Photograph: 1 imm m in Jan 2000, South Holston Dam (Knight 2008:30)

Surf Scoter, *Melanitta perspicillata*

Status and Abundance: Irregular transient and winter resident

Habitat: Deeper (and usually larger) lakes and ponds

Spring Departure: late Mar

Fall Arrival: mid Oct

Comments: Small numbers of individuals may be found throughout winter with unknown migratory status, although February birds are thought to be early spring transients.

Late Spring

23 May 2006, Cane Creek Park (MIG 77:100)

17 May 1995, Reelfoot Lake (MIG 66:50)

14 Apr 1996, Hatchie NWR (MIG 67:59)

6 Apr 1998, Radnor Lake (MIG 69:164)

Early Fall

1 Oct 1984, Austin Springs (MIG 56:24)

8 Oct 1980, Radnor Lake (BNA:18)
High Counts – Spring
8 on 22 Apr 1989, Chickamauga Lake, Hamilton Co. (MIG 60:89)
7 on 14 Apr 1996, Hatchie NWR (MIG 67:59)
6 on 19 Mar 2007, Chickamauga Lake, Hamilton Co. (MIG 78:103)
High Counts – Fall
9 on 20 Oct 2011, Austin Springs (MIG 82:158)
9 on 9 Nov 1991, Wilbur Lake (MIG 63:57)
8 on 17 Nov 2011, Ft. Patrick Henry Lake, Sullivan Co. (MIG 82:154)
7 on 16 Nov 1970, Woods Reservoir (MIG 42:19)
7 on 27 Nov 1998, Midway, Dyer Co. (MIG 70:46)
7 on 29 Oct 1987, Paris Landing SP (Robinson 1990)
High Counts – Winter
14 on 29 Jan 2014, S. Holston Lake (RLK, pers. comm.)
9 on 27 Jan 2014, Woods Reservoir (SGS, pers. obs.)
8 on 12 Dec 2004, S. Holston Lake (MIG 76:82)
Substantiation: Photograph: 1 on 5 Apr 2005, Austin Springs (Knight 2008:30)

White-winged Scoter, *Melanitta fusca*
Status and Abundance: Irregular transient and winter resident
Habitat: Deeper (and usually larger) lakes and ponds
Spring Departure: late Mar
Fall Arrival: early Nov
Comments: Although rare, it is the most commonly detected scoter in Tennessee and may be found throughout the winter months. A major influx occurred statewide Jan-Feb 2014 with counts up to 100 individuals.
Late Spring
11 May 1989, Boone Lake (MIG 60:89)
29 Apr 1988, Dickson Co. (Robinson 1990)
27 Apr 1968, Fort Loudoun Lake (MIG 39:45)
Early Fall
16-17 Oct 1993, Wilbur Lake (MIG 65:26)
20 Oct 2002, Henry Co. (MIG 74:16)
21 Oct 1949, Tennessee NWR (Cybert 1955)
25 Oct 1986, Old Hickory Lake, Sumner Co. (MIG 58:23)
High Counts – Spring
6 on 27 Mar 2014, Nickajack Lake, Marion Co. (TR, pers. comm.)
3 on 31 Mar 2009, Pickwick Lake (MIG 80:87)
High Counts – Fall
8 on 1 Nov 2009, S. Holston Lake (MIG 81:58)

High Counts – Winter
> up to 100 on 27 Jan 2014, Tennessee River, Hamilton Co. (DH, pers. comm.)
> 62 on 14 Feb 2014, Sale Creek, Hamilton Co. (MP *fide* SGS)
> 28 on 30 Dec 1981, Chickamauga Lake (MIG 53:47)
> 26 on 27 Jan 2014, Woods Reservoir (SGS, pers. obs.)
> 26 on 8 Feb 2014, Seven Points Rec. Area (MIG, in press)

Substantiation: Specimen: UTM, 300

Black Scoter, *Melanitta americana*

Status and Abundance: Rare transient and winter resident
Habitat: Deeper (and usually larger) lakes and ponds
Spring Departure: early Feb
Fall Arrival: late Oct
Late Spring
> 19 May 2008, Bunge Road, Dyer Co. (MIG 80:124)
> 14 May-14 Jun 1967, Cardwell's Lake, Knox Co. (Alsop and Wallace 1970)
> 29 Apr 1988, Dickson Co. (Robinson 1990)
> 5 Apr 2008, TVA Lakes (MIG 79:61)

Early Fall
> 14 Oct 2002, Britton Ford (MIG 74:16)
> 14 Oct 2006, Mud Island (MIG 78:33)
> 16 Oct 2005, Mississippi River, Shelby Co. (MIG 76:23)

High Counts – Spring
> 20 on 19 Apr 1985, Stewart Co. (Robinson and Blunk 1989)

High Counts – Fall
> 10 on 2 Nov 2010, Upper Douglas Lake (MIG 81:158)
> 7 on 16 Nov 2010, S. Holston Lake (MIG 81:162)

Summer Records
> 1 on 14 May-14 Jun 1967, Cardwell's Lake, Knox Co. (Alsop and Wallace 1970)

High Counts – Winter
> 5 m on 30 Jan 2014, Tennessee River, Hamilton Co. (CBl, pers. comm.)
> 5 on 11 Dec 2001, Cherokee Lake (MIG 73:38)
> 4 (3 m, 1 f) on 10 Dec 1989, Woods Reservoir (MIG 61:59)
> 4 on 20 Dec 1997, Chickamauga Lake, Chattanooga CBC (MIG 69:111)

Substantiation: Photograph: Somershoe, S.G. 2014. "Black Scoter". <http://www.pbase.com/shoeman/image/154154937> Accessed 25 Sep 2014.

Long-tailed Duck, *Clangula hyemalis*
    Status and Abundance: Rare transient and winter resident
    Habitat: Deeper (and usually larger) lakes and ponds
    Spring Departure: late Mar
    Fall Arrival: mid Nov
    Late Spring
        8-11 May 2002, Cane Creek Park (MIG 73:58)
        3 May 1930, Radnor Lake (Monk 1932)
        25 Apr 1987, Austin Springs (MIG 58:102)
        23 Apr 1992, Tellico Lake (MIG 63:76)
        20 Apr 2004, Dutch Bottoms (MIG 75:116)
    Early Fall
        26 Oct 1985, Pace Point (MIG 57:22)
        29 Oct 1988, Britton Ford (MIG 60:25)
        30 Oct 1980, Boone Lake (MIG 52:24)
        31 Oct 1975, Radnor Lake (MIG 47:18)
    High Counts – Fall
        4 on 19 Nov 1996, Reelfoot NWR (MAG, pers. comm.)
        4 on 21 Nov 2000, Boone Lake (MIG 72:42)
        3 on 23 Nov 2006, S. Holston Lake (MIG 78:41)
    High Counts – Winter
        31 on 3 Feb 1929, Radnor Lake (Monk 1932)
        13 on 7 Jan 1968, S. Holston Lake (MIG 39:23)
        12 on 17 Jan 1976, Watauga Lake (MIG 47:49)
        11 on 17-22 Jan 2011, S. Holston Lake (MIG 82:62)
    Substantiation: Specimen: LSUMZ, 75675

Bufflehead, *Bucephala albeola*
    Status and Abundance: Fairly common transient and winter resident; accidental summer visitor
    Habitat: Lakes and ponds
    Spring Departure: early May
    Fall Arrival: late Oct
    Comments: At least 5 summer records from Wilbur Lake between 1966 and 1982, including 2 birds present throughout summer of 1969 (MIG 40:93) and 2 birds from May-July 1970 (MIG 41:72).
    Late Spring
        27 May 2003, Dyer Co. (MIG 74:86)
        26 May 2010, Old Hickory Lake (JH *fide* SGS)
        24 May 1975, Wilbur Lake (MIG 46:91)
        19 May 2002, Reelfoot Lake (MIG 73:56)

Anatidae: Ducks, Geese, and Swans

Early Fall
    9 Oct 1983, Wilbur Lake (MIG 55:27)
    20 Oct 1981, Radnor Lake (MIG 53:15)
    21 Oct 1987, Paris Landing SP (Robinson 1990)

High Counts – Fall
    1,083 on 20 Nov 2003, Duck River Unit (RW, pers. comm.)
    671 on 21 Nov 2000, Duck River Unit (RW, pers. comm.)
    632 on 20 Nov 2001, Duck River Unit (RW, pers. comm.)

Summer Records
    10 Aug 2010, S. Holston River weir dam (MIG 81:162)
    11 Jun 1992, Old Hickory Lake (MIG 63:97)

High Counts – Winter
    1,000 on 14 Jan 1940, Norris Lake (MIG 11:27)
    980 on 22 Dec 1999, Duck River Unit (RW, pers. comm.)
    952 on 5 Jan 2000, Duck River Unit (RW, pers. comm.)
    948 on 18 Dec 2006, Duck River Unit (RW, pers. comm.)
    916 on 28 Feb 2000, Duck River Unit (RW, pers. comm.)

Substantiation: Specimen: UTM, 309

Common Goldeneye, *Bucephala clangula*

Status and Abundance: Uncommon transient and winter resident; accidental summer visitor

Habitat: Deeper (and usually larger) lakes and ponds

Spring Departure: early Apr

Fall Arrival: mid Nov

Comments: Among the latest waterfowl species to arrive during fall (along with Common Merganser).

Late Spring
    18 May 1996, Chickamauga Lake, Hamilton Co. (MIG 67:63)
    11 May 1975, Reelfoot Lake SBC (MIG 46:56)
    7 May 1978, Knoxville SBC (MIG 49:56)
    29 Apr 1972, Nashville SBC (MIG 43:45)

Early Fall
    16 Oct 1953, Kingsport (Switzer 1957)
    3 Nov 1984, Woods Reservoir (MIG 56:19)
    8 Nov 1986, Paris Landing SP (MIG 58:19)

High Counts – Spring
    120 on 29 Nov 1994, Big Sandy Unit (RW, pers. comm.)

Summer Records
    1 on 12 Jun 1963-summer 1964, Wilbur Lake (Dubke 1963)
    1 injured bird on 5 Aug-11 Oct 1966, Wilbur Lake (MIG 37:85)
    1 m on 23 Jul 2002, Chickmauga Lake (MIG 73:113)

High Counts – Winter
>3,000 on 28 Dec 1964, Dyersburg CBC (MIG 35:111)
>1,996 on 16 Jan 2001, Big Sandy Unit (RW, pers. comm.)
>1,874 on 20 Dec 2000, Big Sandy Unit (RW, pers. comm.)
>1,531 on 21 Jan 1997, Big Sandy Unit (RW, pers. comm.)
Substantiation: Specimen: APSU, 1636

Barrow's Goldeneye, *Bucephala islandica*
Status and Abundance: Accidental winter visitor
Habitat: Deeper (and usually larger) lakes and ponds
Comments: One record of one f on 26-28 Dec 2009, Antioch Harbor, Henry Co., poor photo, seen by JRW and MT. Photo of female accepted by authors but record has not been submitted to TBRC. One male was described on the Cumberland River in Montgomery Co. on 21 Jan 1940 (Clebsch 1940), but record not officially accepted (Alsop 1972). A goldeneye photographed and observed 18 Nov-30 Dec 1978, Radnor Lake (MIG 50:42) was thought possibly to be this species, but the authors have reviewed the photos and are of the opinion that the individual is either an aberrant Common or possibly a hybrid.
Records
>(1) 1 f on 26-28 Dec 2009, Antioch Harbor, Henry Co., poor photo, seen by JRW and MT (not submitted to TBRC)
Substantiation: Photograph: Wilson, J.R. 2009. "Barrow's Goldeneye". <http://www.pbase.com/ol_coot/image/147619771> Accessed 25 Sep 2014.

Hooded Merganser, *Lophodytes cucullatus*
Status and Abundance: Fairly common transient and winter resident; uncommon summer resident in Mississippi Alluvial Valley, Southeastern Coastal Plain, Central Hardwoods; rare summer resident in Cumberland Plateau, Ridge and Valley, Southern Blue Ridge
Habitat: Lakes and ponds
Spring Departure: late Apr
Fall Arrival: mid Oct
Early Fall
>5 Sep 1936, Rutherford Co. (DeVore 1975)
>17 Sep 2005, Putman Co. FBC (MIG 76:16)
>5 Oct 2002, Old Hickory Lake (CAS, pers. obs.)
High Counts – Spring
>123 on 5 Mar 2008, Duck River Unit (RW, pers. comm.)
High Counts – Fall
>569 on 21 Nov 2000, Big Sandy Unit (RW, pers. comm.)

Anatidae: Ducks, Geese, and Swans

>484 on 19 Nov 2002, Big Sandy Unit (RW, pers. comm.)
>460 on 19 Nov 2008, Duck River Unit (RW, pers. comm.)
>423 on 17 Nov 2005, Big Sandy Unit (RW, pers. comm.)

High Counts – Winter
>3,000 on 2 Jan 1955, Tennessee NWR (MIG 25:77)
>2,002 on 26 Dec 1955, Reefoot Lake CBC (MIG 26:61)
>1,636 on 8 Dec 2996, Big Sandy Unit (RW, pers. comm.)
>1,189 on 6 Jan 2005, Big Sandy Unit (RW, pers. comm.)
>1,067 on 1 Dec 2000, Duck River Unit (RW, pers. comm.)

Substantiation: Specimen: UTM, 100

Common Merganser, *Mergus merganser*

Status and Abundance: Irregular winter resident and late fall and early spring transient (most regularly at Big Sandy Unit, Tennessee NWR)

Habitat: Deeper (and usually larger) lakes and ponds

Spring Departure: late Mar

Fall Arrival: late Nov

Comments: One historic documented breeding record from Smith Co. 1896-1899 (Kiff 1989, Knight 1989, MIG 60:93-94). More numerous in cold winters.

Late Spring
>25 May 2014, Beaver Creek, Sullivan Co. (MIG, in press)
>24 May 1971, Lillydale (MIG 42:69)
>23 May 1973, Austin Springs (MIG 44:86)
>7 May 1967, Paris Landing SP (MIG 38:31)

Early Fall
>16 Oct 1953, near Kingsport (Switzer 1957)
>26 Oct 1974, Old Hickory Lake (MIG 46:19)
>9 Nov 1967, Reelfoot Lake (MIG 38:94)

High Counts – Spring
>14 on 27 Apr 1997, Cheatham Co. (MIG 68:109)

High Counts – Winter
>648 on 1 Feb 1994, Normandy Reservoir (MIG 65:42)
>200 on 29 Feb 1964, Old Hickory Lake (MIG 35:14)
>180 on 1 Feb 1994, Tims Ford Lake (MIG 65:42)
>125 on 24 Feb 1979, Norris Lake (MIG 50:44)
>100 on 2 Jan 1955, Tennessee NWR (MIG 25:77)

Substantiation: Specimen: UTK

Red-breasted Merganser, *Mergus serrator*

Status and Abundance: Uncommon transient and winter resident; accidental summer visitor

Habitat: Deeper (and usually larger) lakes and ponds
Spring Departure: early May
Fall Arrival: mid Nov
Late Spring
    31 May 1967, Reelfoot Lake (MIG 38:46)
    31 May 1997, Old Hickory Lake (MIG 68:109)
    30 May 1983, Watauga Lake (MIG 53:70)
Early Fall
    19 Sep 2009, Blount Co. FBC (MIG 81:41)
    29 Sep 1974, J. Percy Priest Lake (MIG 46:19)
High Counts – Spring
    100 on 5 Mar 2001, Reelfoot Lake (MIG 72:91)
    96 on 31 Mar 2001, Watauga Lake (MIG 72:99)
High Counts – Fall
    600 on 21-27 Nov 1972, Woods Reservoir (MIG 44:22)
    200 on 24 Nov 1997, Big Sandy Unit (RW, pers. comm.)
    120 on 22 Nov 2003, Chilhowee Lake (MIG 75:34)
High Counts – Winter
    1000+ on 15 Feb 2007, Pace Point (MIG 78:78)
    600 on 5 Jan 2010, Big Sandy Unit (RW, pers. comm.)
    400+ on 12 Jan 2009, Pace Point (MIG 80:66)
    295 on 6 Jan 2005, Big Sandy Unit (RW, pers. comm.)
    269 on 5 Dec 2005, Boone Lake (MIG 77:60)
Substantiation: Specimen: UTM, 354

Ruddy Duck, *Oxyura jamaicensis*
    Status and Abundance: Common transient and winter resident; accidental summer visitor (although has been resident in some recent summers at Robco Lake, Shelby Co.)
    Habitat: Lakes and ponds
    Spring Departure: late Apr
    Fall Arrival: mid Oct
    Comments: Most summers records are from Shelby Co., particularly at Robco Lake.
    Late Spring
        27 May 1976, Maury Co. (MIG 47:100)
        22 May 1981, Kingston Steam Plant (MIG 52:97)
        12 May 2001, Cane Creek Park (MIG 72:94)
        11 May 1958, Reelfoot Lake (MIG 29:30)
        11 May 1989, Austin Springs (MIG 60:89)
    Early Fall
        5 Sep 1964, near Greeneville (MIG 35:103-104)

16 Sep 1979, Maury Co. (MIG 51:16)

High Counts – Spring
  3,000+ on 19 Mar 1991, Reelfoot Lake, Lake Co. (MIG 62:109)
  2,050 on 5 Mar 2008, Big Sandy Unit (RW, pers. comm.)

High Counts – Fall
  5,000 on 17 Nov 2000, Reelfoot Lake (MIG 73:10)
  1,768 on 12 Nov 1998, Big Sandy Unit (RW, pers. comm.)
  1,585 on 19 Nov 2008, Big Sandy Unit (RW, pers. comm.)
  1,530 on 20 Nov 2003, Big Sandy Unit (RW, pers. comm.)
  1,486 on 1 Dec 2000, Big Sandy Unit (RW, pers. comm.)

High Counts – Summer
  70 (62 m in alternate plumage, 8 f) on 8 Jun 2002, Mud Lake, Lake Co. (JRW, unpubl. data)
  7 on 2 Jun 2002, Mud Lake, Lake Co. (JRW, unpubl. data)
  3-5 on 2 Jun-7 Jul 2002, Reelfoot Lake (JRW, unpubl. data)

High Counts – Winter
  8,515 on 14 Dec 2013, Reelfoot Lake CBC (MIG, in press)
  6,610 on 18 Dec 1990, Reelfoot Lake CBC (MIG 62:80)
  5,050 on 14 Dec 2002, Reelfoot Lake CBC (MIG 74:39)
  5,000+ on 26 Feb 1989, Reelfoot Lake (MIG 60:60)
  4,718 on 16 Dec 1995, Reelfoot Lake CBC (MIG 67:8)

Substantiation: Specimen: UTM, 302

Odontophoridae: New World Quail. Only one species occurs in Tennessee, and, despite being a popular gamebird, it is declining statewide in large part due to the loss of grassland-shrubland habitats.

Northern Bobwhite, *Colinus virginianus*
>Status and Abundance: Uncommon (locally common) permanent resident
>Habitat: Unmowed or ungrazed pasture or native warm season grasses with shrubs and/or adjacent hedgerows and second growth to mature forest. Also found in mature forest adjacent to open fields. Found on high elevation grassy balds spring through fall.
>Comments: The species has declined dramatically over the last 25 years; the decline is thought to be largely due to loss of habitat resulting from changes in farming practices and growth of old fields and grasslands into less suitable habitats due to lack of management (i.e. fire). The future viability of this species in Tennessee should be a high conservation priority.
>High Counts – Spring
>>209 on 28 Apr 1968, Knoxville (MIG 39:31)
>>124 on 7-8 May 1988, Murfreesboro SBC (MIG 60:48
>>91 on 11 May 2002, Montgomery Co. NAMC (MIG 73:95)
>>43 on 12 May 2001, Montgomery Co. NAMC (MIG 72:14)
>
>High Counts – Fall
>>21 on 15 Sep 2012, Montgomery Co. FBC (MIG 83:137)
>>13 on 18 Oct 2010, White Co. FBC (MIG 81:142)
>>8 on 29 Sep 2001, Davidson Co. NAMC (MIG 73:30)
>
>High Counts – Winter
>>183 on 21 Dec 1958, Memphis CBC (MIG 29:70)
>
>Substantiation: Specimen: LSUMZ, 6118

Phasianidae: Grouse and Turkey. Two species are permanent residents in Tennessee. Several attempts to establish a huntable population of one additional species – Ring-necked Pheasant – have been unsuccessful thus far.

Ruffed Grouse, *Bonasa umbellus*
- Status and Abundance: Uncommon permanent resident in Ridge and Valley, Southern Blue Ridge; rare in Cumberland Plateau
- Habitat: Forest with dense undergrowth and/or extensive woody debris
- Comments: Formerly common on the Cumberland Plateau, but is extirpated from most areas with small numbers still found in the Cumberland Mountains, i.e. Frozen Head SP and North Cumberland WMA. Historical survey data indicates that its former range may have included Central Hardwoods (Robinson 1990); there have been several unsuccessful attempts to "reintroduce" the species into several Central Hardwoods counties since 1980.
- High Counts – Spring
    - 15 on 26 Apr 1997, Elizabethton SBC (MIG 68:57)
- High Counts – Winter
    - 25 on 19 Dec 1937, GSMNP (MIG 9:7)
    - 12 on 30 Dec 1989, GSMNP CBC (MIG 61:4)
- Substantiation: Specimen: LSUMZ, 75717

Wild Turkey, *Meleagris gallopavo*
- Status and Abundance: Fairly common permanent resident
- Habitat: Open forest and adjacent clearings
- Comments: The species has increased dramatically in the last 25 years as a result of a very successful TWRA reintroduction program, and there is now a huntable population in every county.
- High Counts – Spring
    - 38 on 8 May 2004, Nashville SBC (MIG 75:104)
    - 21 on 12 May 2001, Montgomery Co. NAMC (MIG 72:14)
- High Counts – Fall
    - 1,556 on 29 Sep 2012, Elizabethton FBC (MIG 83:137)
    - 122 on 4 Oct 2008, Nashville FBC (MIG 80:14)
    - 106 on 2 Oct 2004, Nashville FBC (MIG 76:20)
    - 98 on 3 Oct 2009, Nashville FBC (MIG 81:41)
- High Counts – Winter
    - 563 on 19 Dec 2009, Clarksville CBC (MIG 81:90)
    - 381 on 3 Jan 2004, Clarksville CBC (MIG 75:56)
    - 351 on 16 Dec 2006, Clarksville CBC (MIG 78:62)

315 on 18 Dec 2004, Clarksville CBC (MIG 76:62)
294 on 19 Dec 2003, Cross Creeks CBC (MIG 74:40)
Substantiation: Specimen: UTM, 408

Gaviidae: Loons.

Four species have been found in Tennessee, principally during the late fall and winter. Three of those occur annually. Loons are widely and regularly found throughout Tennessee, particularly at deep water reservoirs.

Red-throated Loon, *Gavia stellata*

Status and Abundance: Rare winter visitor and late fall and early spring transient

Habitat: Deeper (and usually larger) lakes and ponds

Spring Departure: mid Mar

Fall Arrival: early Nov

Comments: Occurs annually on Kentucky Lake and nearby areas, but can be found on larger lakes and rivers statewide.

Late Spring
- 8 May 1976, Maury Co. (MIG 47:90)
- 7 May 1950, Watauga Lake (Herndon 1950)
- 4-5 May 1974, Pickwick Landing SP (MIG 45:45)
- 2 May 2000, Pennington Bend (MIG 71:89)
- 1 May 2004, Nickajack Lake (MIG 75:116)

Early Fall
- 8 Oct 2006, S. Holston Lake (MIG 78:41)
- 21 Oct 1971, Woods Reservoir (MIG 42:92)
- 21 Oct 2000, Pace Point (MIG 73:10)
- 22 Oct 1979, Cherokee Lake (MIG 51:17)
- 23 Oct 1971, Knoxville (MIG 42:92)

High Counts – Fall
- 2 on 13 Nov 1997, Boone Lake (MIG 69:45)
- 2 on 26-27 Nov 2009, Pace Point (MIG 81:49)

High Counts – Winter
- 8 on 22 Apr 1950, Watauga Lake (Herndon 1950)
- 5-6 on 6 Nov 1949, Watauga Lake (Herndon 1950)
- 5 on 9 Feb 2014, Pickwick Lake (RH, pers. comm.)
- up to 5 on 12 Jan-28 Feb 2004, Pace Point (MIG 75:73)
- up to 5 on 15 Jan-17 Feb 2014, Chickamauga Lake (MIG, in press)

Substantiation: Photograph: 1 on 24 Nov 2006, S. Holston Lake (Knight 2008:33)

Pacific Loon, *Gavia pacifica*

Status and Abundance: Rare winter resident and late fall and early spring transient; accidental summer visitor

Habitat: Deeper (and usually larger) lakes and ponds

Spring Departure: mid Mar

Fall Arrival: early Nov

Comments: The first state record was of 1 on 6-20 Mar 1988, J. Percy Priest Lake, Davidson Co. (Knight 2007). In the last 20 years, likely as a result of increased observer awareness, this species has been found to occur annually, most often in areas with concentrations of Common Loons. Most records are from Kentucky Lake in the northern part of the state. Observers should be aware of the possibility that an Arctic Loon could occur here.

Late Spring

    30 Mar 2011, Pickwick Dam (MIG 82:83)

    20 Mar 1988, J. Percy Priest Lake, Davidson Co. (Knight 2007)

    19 Mar 2004, Port Road overlook, Henry Co. (JRW, unpubl. data)

Early Fall

    6 Nov 2006, Henry Co. (MIG 78:33)

    29 Nov 2005, Pace Point (MIG 76:23)

High Counts – Fall

    3 on 16 Nov 2002, Henry Co. (MIG 74:15)

    3 on 29 Nov 1996, Pace Point (JRW, unpubl. data)

    2 on 5 Nov 2000, Big Sandy (MIG 72:37)

Summer Records

    1 dead on 29 Jun 2003, Lauderdale Co. (MIG 74:129)

    1 on 22 Jun 1996, Lake Co. (MIG 67:76)

    1 on 4-11 Jun 1996, Lake Co. (MIG 67:76)

High Counts – Winter

    5 on 8 Dec 2014, Cook Recreation Area (SGS, pers. obs.)

    up to 3 on 13 Dec 2003-28 Feb 2004, Pace Point (MIG 75:73)

    2 on 11-13 Feb 2000, Paris Landing SP (MIG 71:42)

Substantiation: Photograph: Somershoe, S.G. 2014. "Pacific Loon". < http://www.pbase.com/shoeman/image/154446713> Accessed 25 Sep 2014.

Common Loon, *Gavia immer*

Status and Abundance: Fairly common transient and winter resident; rare summer visitor

Habitat: Deeper (and usually larger) lakes and ponds

Spring Departure: mid May

Fall Arrival: mid Oct

Comments: Individuals observed during spring are almost always in basic plumage aspect are presumed second-year birds. Notable concentrations occur on Kentucky Lake in the northern part of the state in Nov and Dec.

Late Spring
- 27 May 2001, Armstrong Bend (MIG 72:96)
- 27 May 2010, Old Hickory Lake, Sumner Co. (MIG 81:115)

Early Fall
- 31 Aug 2005, Chickamauga Lake (MIG 76:28)

High Counts – Spring
- 88 on 11 Apr 2004, J. Percy Priest Lake (MIG 75:113)
- 85 on 29 Mar 2013, J. Percy Priest Lake, Rutherford Co. (DE, pers. comm.)
- 84 on 3 Apr 2004, Watauga Lake (MIG 75:119)

High Counts – Fall
- 900+ on 7 Nov 2010, Pace Point, Paris Landing SP area (MIG 81:153)
- 800 on 6 Nov 2006, Henry Co. (MIG 78:33)
- 719 on 16 Nov 2002, Pace Point (JRW, unpubl. data)
- 580 on 13 Nov 1996, S. Holston Lake (MIG 68:30)
- 505 on 14 Nov 1996, Boone Lake (MIG 68:27)

High Counts – Summer
- 2 on 23 Jul 2005, Tennessee River, Hamilton Co. (MIG: 76:146)

High Counts – Winter
- 350 on 5 Dec 2004, Henry Co. (MIG 76:78)
- 316 on 22 Jan 2011, J. Percy Priest Lake, Davidson Co. (SGS, pers. obs.)

Substantiation: Specimen: USNM, 195681

Yellow-billed Loon, *Gavia adamsii*

Status and Abundance: Accidental late fall and winter visitor

Habitat: Deeper (and usually larger) lakes and ponds

Records
- (1) 1 on 18-19 Feb 1995, Dale Hollow Lake, Clay Co. (Stedman 1995)
- (2) 1 on 30 Nov 1999, Watauga Lake (Calhoon 2000, Knight 2008, MIG 71:38)
- (3) 1 on 6 Nov 2000, Chickamauga Lake (MIG 72:42)
- (4) 1-2 on 21 Feb-8 Mar 2004, Pace Point (NAB 58(3), MIG 75:73)
- (5) 1 on 26 Nov-4 Dec 2005, Pace Point (NAB 60(1), MIG 76:23)
- (6) 1 imm on 26 Dec 2009, Pace Point (MIG 81:99)
- (7) 1 imm on 7-27 Nov 2010, Pace Point-Paris Landing SP area (MIG 81:153)

Substantiation: Photograph: 1 on 18-19 Feb 1995, Dale Hollow Lake, Clay Co. (Stedman 1995)

Podicipedidae: Grebes. Six species are found in Tennessee, with two occurring regularly and the others infrequently to rarely. Grebes are widespread and occur primarily on larger rivers and lakes.

Pied-billed Grebe, *Podilymbus podiceps*
> Status and Abundance: Fairly common transient and winter resident; rare summer resident
>
> Habitat: Lakes and ponds
>
> Comments: Rare breeding bird, but breeding has been documented in Hardeman, Lake, and Shelby Cos. (MIG 75:158) and in Blount, Carter, Davidson, Dyer, Franklin, Hamilton, Knox, Lauderdale, Maury, Meigs, Rutherford, and Warren (Robinson 1990). Nesting building seen at Lower Hatchie NWR in late May 2003 (MIG 74:86). At least 10 nests with eggs found in May 2011 at Black Bayou Refuge (SGS, pers. obs.). Birds may linger into summer and can be found in any month of the year.
>
> High Counts – Spring
>> 20 on 13 May 2006, Lake Co. NAMC (MIG 77:130)
>> 11 on 8 May 2004, Shelby Co. NAMC (MIG 75:93)
>
> High Counts – Fall
>> 142 on 28 Sep 2009, Natchez Trace SP (MIG 81:49)
>> 100 on 25 Sep 1997, Old Hickory Lake (MIG 69:42)
>
> High Counts – Winter
>> 357 on 30 Dec 2006, Nickajack CBC (MIG 78:63)
>> 350 on 3 Jan 1987, Nickajack CBC (MIG 58:2)
>> 311 on 18 Dec 1972, Woods Reservoir (MIG 44:22)
>> 305 on 29 Dec 2007, Nickajack CBC (MIG 79:35)
>> 286 on 27 Dec 2003, Nickajack CBC (MIG 75:57)
>
> Substantiation: Specimen: LSUMZ, 75661

Horned Grebe, *Podiceps auritus*
> Status and Abundance: Fairly common transient and winter resident, accidental summer visitor.
>
> Habitat: Deeper (and usually larger) lakes and ponds
>
> Spring Departure: late Apr
>
> Fall Arrival: mid Oct
>
> Late Spring
>> 23 May 1974, Tennessee NWR (MIG 45:100)
>> 4 May 1985, Gallatin Steam Plant (MIG 56:75)
>> 4 May 2014, Milan Tennessee Army National Guard facility, Carroll Co. (MJW, pers. comm.)

Early Fall
    7 Aug 1921, Radnor Lake (BNA:14)
    31 Aug 1977, Kingsport (MIG 49:20)
    31 Aug 1998, S. Holston Lake (MIG 70:54)
    5 Sep 1994, Coffee Co. (MIG 66:22)
    18 Sep 2004, Greene Co. FBC (MIG 76:14)
High Counts – Spring
    430 on 26 Mar 2005, Center Hill Lake (MIG 76:97)
    405 on 15 Mar 2006, Center Hill Lake (MIG 77:100)
High Counts – Fall
    1,100 on 26 Nov 2009, Pace Point (MIG 81:49)
    1,000 on 24 Nov 2006, Henry Co. (MIG 78:33)
    550 on 9 Nov 1991, Boone Lake (MIG 63:54)
    405 on 23 Nov 1971, Booker T. Washington SP (MIG 43:26)
Summer Records
    1 on 30 May-19 Jun 1954, Lake Phillip Nelson near Elizabethton (Behrend 1954)
    1 to 2 on 8 May-1 Jun 1967, Bush Lake (MIG 38:47)
High Counts – Winter
    852 on 22 Dec 2002, Pace Point (JRW, unpubl. data)
    766 on 21 Dec 2009, Franklin/Coffee Co. CBC (MIG 81:91)
    744 on 19 Dec 2009, Chattanooga CBC (MIG 81:90)
    740 on 5 Dec 2005, Boone Lake (MIG 77:60)
    575 on 23 Feb 1997, Center Hill Lake (MIG 68:63)
Substantiation: Specimen: UTM, 200

Red-necked Grebe, *Podiceps grisegena*

Status and Abundance: Rare transient and winter resident
Habitat: Deeper (and usually larger) lakes and ponds
Spring Departure: mid Mar
Fall Arrival: mid Nov
Comments: Major influx into eastern half of state Mar-Apr 2014, concentrated in northeast Tennessee with significant high counts on Boone Lake.
Late Spring
    6-16 May 2003, Austin Springs (MIG 74:91)
    14 Apr-2 May 2013, Watauga Lake (FA, pers. comm.)
    1 May 1920, Radnor Lake (Dubke and Dubke 1975)
    1 May 2014, Boone Lake (RLK, pers. comm.)
    30 Apr-1 May 1977, Lebanon SBC (MIG 48:90)
Early Fall
    7 Sep 1975, Nashville (MIG 47:18)

2-4 Oct 1997, S. Holston Lake (MIG 69:48)
31 Oct-2 Nov 1976, Old Hickory Lake (MIG 48:18)

High Counts – Spring
180 on 19 Mar 2014, Boone Lake (RLK, SGS, pers. obs.)
15 on 10 Mar 2004, S. Holston Lake, Sullivan Co. (MIG 75:119)

High Counts – Winter
6 on 12-27 Feb 1988, Chickamauga Lake (Robinson 1990)

Substantiation: Photograph: Somershoe, S.G. 2014. "Red-necked Grebe". <http://www.pbase.com/shoeman/image/154753885> Accessed 15 Dec 2014.

Eared Grebe, *Podiceps nigricollis*

Status and Abundance: Very rare transient and winter resident

Habitat: Deeper (and usually larger) lakes and ponds

Spring Departure: late Mar

Fall Arrival: early Nov

Comments: Since 1995, a small number have wintered regularly off Musick's Campground, S. Holston Lake, Sullivan Co. The highest count was 21 on 6 Oct 1996 (Knight 2008). These birds can arrive much earlier (as early as late Aug) and depart later (as late as late Apr) than is the norm for records elsewhere in the state.

Late Spring
30 Apr 2006, S. Holston Lake (MIG 77:106)
18 Apr 2000, S. Holston Lake (MIG 71:94)
16 Apr 2002, S. Holston Lake (MIG 73:63)
14 Apr 2003, S. Holston Lake (MIG 74:94)
12 Apr 2003, Center Hill Lake (MIG 74:89)

Early Fall
10 Aug 1998, Shelby Farms (MIG 70:46)
19-21 Aug 1996, Shelby Farms (MIG 68:24)
25 Aug 1997, S. Holston Lake (MIG 69:48)
26 Aug-2 Oct 1983, Kingston Steam Plant (MIG 55:23)
4-9 Sep 1987, Radnor Lake (MIG 59:34)

High Counts – Spring
8 on 25 Mar 2005, S. Holston Lake (MIG 76:103)
7 on 16 Apr 2002, S. Holston Lake (MIG 73:63)

High Counts – Fall
21 on 6 Oct 1996, S. Holston Lake (MIG 68:30)
14 on 26 Oct 2005, S. Holston Lake (MIG 77:32)

High Counts – Winter
16 on 19 Jan 1997, S. Holston Lake (MIG 62:66)
11 in Jan 2001, S. Holston Lake (MIG 72:73)

10 on 1 Jan 2006, S. Holston Lake (MIG 77:40)

8 on 26 Dec 2004, S. Holston Lake (MIG 76:62)

Substantiation: Photograph: Todd, M.C. 2002. "Eared Grebe". <http://www.pbase.com/mctodd/image/26541780> Accessed 15 Dec 2014.

Western Grebe, *Aechmophorus occidentalis*

Status and Abundance: Very rare winter visitor

Habitat: Deeper (and usually larger) lakes and ponds

Comments: Robinson (1990) cites five records of *Aechmorphus* grebes that pre-dated the species split in 1985 and notes that none are documented well-enough to identify to species.

Records

(1) 1 on 23 Nov 1996, Britton Ford, likely same bird on 7 Dec 1996, Pace Point (JRW, unpubl. data)

(2) up to 3 on 22 Dec 1998-4 Feb 1999, Old Hickory Lake (MIG 70:70)

(3) 1 on 2 May 1999, TVA Lake (MIG 70:96)

(4) 1 on 11-12 Nov 2000, Reelfoot Lake (MIG 73:10)

(5) 1 on 22 Aug-15 Sep 2002, Norris Lake, Grainger Co. (MIG 74:21, Edwards 2012)

(6) 1 on 21 Dec 2002-19 Jan 2003, Nickajack Lake (MIG 74:56)

(7) 1 on 16-18 Nov 2003, Britton Ford (MIG 75:23)

(8) 2 on 23 Dec 2005-26 Feb 2006, Britton Ford (MIG 77:57) and likely same 2 on 26 Feb-9 Mar 2006, Pace Point (MIG 77:57, MIG 77:98)

(9) 1-2 on 6-29 Nov 2006, Pace Point (MIG 78:33) and likely same 2 on 7 Mar 2007, Pace Point (MIG 78:99)

(10) 1 on 28 Dec 2008-4 Jan 2009, Cherokee Lake (MIG 80:70)

(11) 2 on 12-23 Dec 2009, Lake Tansi (MIG 81:103)

(12) 1 on 27 Jan 2010, Center Hill Lake, DeKalb Co. (MIG 81:101)

(13) 1 on 31 Dec 2011, Reelfoot Lake (MIG 83:21)

(14) 1 on 7-13 Nov 2012, S. Holston Lake (MIG 83:157)

(15) 1 on 1-5 Dec 2012, J. Percy Priest Lake, Davidson Co. (MIG, in press)

(16) 1 on 28 Jan-24 Feb 2013, Chickamauga Lake (MIG, in press)

Substantiation: Photograph: 2 on 12-23 Dec 2009, Lake Tansi (NAB 64(2):46)

Clark's Grebe, *Aechmophorus clarkii*

Status and Abundance: **Unsubstantiated**; accidental late fall and winter visitor

Habitat: Deeper (and usually larger) lakes and ponds

Comments: Although there are no known photographs from Tennessee, the 1993 individual was well-documented at close range by numerous observers. Robinson (1990) cites five records of *Aechmorphus* grebes that pre-date the species split in 1985, and notes that none are documented well-enough to determine which species was involved. An *Aechmorphus* grebe 21 Nov 2009, Reelfoot Lake (MIG 81:49) was identified as a possible Clark's Grebe.

Records
(1) 1 on 18-21 Mar 1993, Nickajack Lake (MIG 64:68, Knight 1996)
(2) 5 Nov 2004, Mud Island (MIG 76:27)

Procellariidae: Shearwaters and Petrels. Only one species of this pelagic family has occurred in Tennessee, and that was in association with the passing of a hurricane. Any future occurrences of the same or other species in this family will surely also be storm waifs; for example, Kentucky has a 2005 record of Audubon's Shearwater and older records of Black-capped Petrel.

Great Shearwater, *Puffinus gravis*
    Status and Abundance: Accidental visitor
    Records
        (1) 1 injured bird found 1 Sep 2005 following Hurricane Katrina,
            Murfreesboro, later died during rehab (Sloan 2011)
    Substantiation: Specimen (UTC, B147)

Hydrobatidae: Storm-Petrels. One species is known from two records, one with multiple individuals, and both are associated with the passing of tropical storms or hurricanes. As with the shearwaters and petrels, future occurrences of this pelagic family in Tennessee will also certainly be in connection with tropical storms or hurricanes.

Band-rumped Storm-Petrel, *Oceanodroma castro*
  Status and Abundance: Accidental fall visitor
  Habitat: Large open bodies of water (following a hurricane)
  Comments: Two other unidentified storm-petrels have been reported. One was in Collegedale, Hamilton Co. following the same tropical storm that produced the first record of Band-rumped (Jacobson 1976), and another from Watauga Lake following Hurricane Hugo (Langridge and Cross 1991).
  Records
    (1) 3 found dead or dying at GSMNP on 24-26 Sep 1975 following Hurricane Eloise (MIG 47:23)
    (2) 1-2 on 30 Aug 2005, Bruton Branch Area of Pickwick Lake following Hurricane Katrina (MIG 76:23, Edwards 2012)
  Substantiation: Specimen: USNM, 526349

Ciconiidae: Storks. One species occurs in shallow water wetlands primarily in the Mississippi Alluvial Valley during late summer and early fall.

Wood Stork, *Mycteria americana*
    Status and Abundance: Very rare spring visitor in Mississippi Alluvial Valley; rare to irregular late summer and fall visitor in Mississippi Alluvial Valley, rare elsewhere during fall
    Habitat: Shallow wetlands
    Fall Arrival: mid Jul
    Fall Departure: mid Sep
    Comments: Most individuals occur during post-breeding dispersal in late summer and early fall primarily in Shelby Co., but also they occur elsewhere in Mississippi Alluvial Valley and rarely elsewhere in the state. Numbers increasing in recent years.
    Early Fall
        12-19 Jul 1999, Duck River Unit (MIG 70:130)
    Late Fall
        17 Nov 2014, Duck River Unit (CF, pers. comm.)
        18 Sep 2009, Dacus Bar (MIG 81:49)
        11 Sep-7 Oct 1983, Knox Co. (Nicholson 1990)
    Spring Records
        16 Apr 1937, Knox Co. (Howell and Monroe 1958)
        17 Apr 1945, Reelfoot Lake (Spofford 1945)
        24 Apr 2001, Hamilton Co. (MIG 72:96)
        17 May 1944, Lauderdale Co. (Monroe 1944)
        25 May 1975, Stewart Co. (Dinsmore 1975)
    Summer Records
        13 Jun 1932, Claiborne Co. (Ogden 1933)
        14 Jun 1984, Reelfoot Lake (MIG 55:87)
    High Counts – Fall
        720 on 8 Sep 2001, Great River Road, Dyer Co. (JRW, unpubl. data)
        500 on 27 Sep 1953, Lauderdale Co. (MIG 25:15)
        362 on 26 Aug 2001, Mud Lake, Shelby Co. (JRW, unpubl. data)
        206 on 13 Sep 1988, Ensley Bar (MIG 60:25)
        up to 128 on 22 Aug-2 Sep 2012, Riverport Road, Shelby Co. (MIG 83:147)
        116 on 17 Sep 1996, President's Island (JRW, unpubl. data)
    Substantiation: Photograph: Todd, M.C. 2006. "Wood Stork". <http://www.pbase.com/mctodd/image/65558850> Accessed 15 Dec 2014.

Fregatidae: Frigatebirds. One species is known from four records and all are associated with the passing of tropical storms or hurricanes. However, observers who are fortunate enough to find a frigatebird in Tennessee should not assume that it is a Magnificent; both Lesser and Great Frigatebird have occurred as vagrants in the interior of the continental U.S.

Magnificent Frigatebird, *Fregata magnificens*
    Status and Abundance: Accidental fall visitor
    Habitat: Large bodies of water (after a tropical storm)
    Records
        (1) 1 ad f on 24 Sep 1988, Cherokee Lake, Hamblen Co. (MIG 60:31, Knight 1993) (following Hurricane Gilbert)
        (2) 1 imm on 27 Sep 1988, Columbia, Maury Co. (MIG 60:28, Knight 1993) (following Hurricane Gilbert)
        (3) 1 on 30 Aug 2005, Pickwick Lake, Hardin Co. (MIG 76:23, Edwards 2012) (following Hurricane Katrina)
        (4) 1 f on 5 Sep 2011, Old Hickory Lake, Davidson Co. (NAB 66(1), MIG 82:151) (following Tropical Storm Lee)
    Substantiation: Photograph: 1 f on 24 Sep 1988, Cherokee Lake, Hamblen Co. (TBRC Archives, UTK)

Sulidae: Boobies and Gannets. One species is known from one record. Brown Booby could potentially also occur as a vagrant; at least four have been recorded in recent years in Arkansas.

Northern Gannet, *Morus bassanus*
> Status and Abundance: ***Unsubstantiated***; accidental visitor
> Comments: Accepted by the TBRC on the basis of written documentation.
> Records
>> (1) One well described imm was observed 29 Nov 1987 in Robertson Co. on I-65 flying from Kentucky into Tennessee (Braun 1988)

Phalacrocoracidae: Cormorants. Two species are found in Tennessee. One is a widespread breeding bird on nearly all large rivers in the state, while the other species is accidental in west Tennessee.

Neotropic Cormorant, *Phalacrocorax brasilianus*
Status and Abundance: Very rare spring, summer, and fall visitor in Mississippi Alluvial Valley, accidental elsewhere

Habitat: Medium to large bodies of water, especially with dead trees and snags

Records
- (1) 1 on 19-20 Jun 1993, Mud Lake, Lake Co. (Greene 1997)
- (2) 1 on 30 Jun 1996, Mud Lake, Lake Co. (Greene 1997)
- (3) 1 on 11 August 1996, Ensley (Greene 1997)
- (4) 1 on 22 Mar 1997, Robco Lake (JRW, unpubl. data)
- (5) 1 on 5-7 Jul 1997, Mud Lake, Lake Co. (MIG 68:134)
- (6) 1 on 7 Jun 1998, Lake Co. (JRW, unpubl. data)
- (7) 1 imm on 5 Sep 1998, Phillippy (MIG 70:46)
- (8) 1 on 7 Jun 2004, White Lake WMA (MIG 76:91)
- (9) 1 on 12 Sep 2004, Ensley (MIG 76:27)
- (10) 1 on 13 Sep 2007, Ensley (MIG 79:20)
- (11) 1 on 25 Apr 2010, Hatchie NWR (MIG 81:114)
- (12) 1 on 25 Jul 2010, TVA Lakes (MIG 81:125)
- (13) 2 on 12 Jun 2011, White's Lake Refuge (MIG 82:119)
- (14) 1 on 19 Jun 2011, Phillippy (MIG 82:119)
- (15) 1-2 on 10-16 Jul 2011, Great River Road, Dyer Co. (MIG 82:119)
- (16) 1 on 12 Jul 2011, Mud Lake, Lake Co. (MIG 82:119)
- (17) 1 on 16 Jul 2011, Moss Island WMA (MIG 82:119)
- (18) 1 on 12/15 Aug 2012, Duck River Unit (MIG 83:149)
- (19) 1 on 19 Aug-2 Sep 2012, TVA Lakes (MIG 83:147)

Substantiation: Photograph: 1 on 25 Apr 2010, Hatchie NWR (NAB 64(3):52)

Double-crested Cormorant, *Phalacrocorax auritus*
Status and Abundance: Fairly common transient, uncommon (locally common) summer resident, locally common winter resident

Habitat: Large lakes and rivers

Comments: Increasingly common breeding bird across Tennessee, with significant colonies on Old Hickory Lake, Kentucky Lake, Cherokee Lake, and the Tennessee River in east Tennessee (2012 statewide survey by SGS). First Nashville summer record in Jul 1993 (MIG 64:86).

High Counts – Spring
    1,500 on 4 Mar 1999, Reelfoot Lake (MIG 70:97
    1,000 on 10 Mar 1997, Reelfoot Lake (MIG 68:106)
    1,000 on 25 Apr 1997, Old Hickory Lake (MIG 68:108)

High Counts – Fall
    5,000+ on 10 Oct 2000, Reelfoot Lake (MIG 72:37)
    3,250 on 19 Oct 1991, Reelfoot Lake, Lake Co. (MIG 63:52)
    3,145 on 26 Nov 2002, Mud Island (MIG 74:15)

High Counts – Summer
    450 on 2 Jun 2008, Bird Island (MIG 79:98)
    190 on 3 Jun 2006, Bird Island (MIG 77:144)

High Counts – Winter
    4,500 on 20 Dec 1952, Reelfoot Lake CBC (MIG 23:69)
    3,000 on 3 Jan 1954, Tennessee NWR (MIG 24:81)

Substantiation: Specimen: LSUMZ, 80269

Anhingidae: Darters. One species occurs as a rare breeding bird in the Mississippi Alluvial Valley.

Anhinga, *Anhinga anhinga*
- Status and Abundance: Locally uncommon transient and summer resident, and accidental winter visitor, in Mississippi Alluvial Valley and Southeastern Coastal Plain; accidental elsewhere
- Habitat: Lakes, rivers, and cypress swamps
- Spring Arrival: mid Apr
- Fall Departure: late Sep
- Comments: Very small numbers breed in the Mississippi and likely Hatchie River valleys. Has nested at Big Hill Pond SP in 1980 (Waldron 1980) and Tennessee NWR, Humphrey's Co. in 1953 (Cypert 1955). Nest found 2 June 2011 on J. Percy Priest Lake, Rutherford Co. (SGS, pers. obs.). Formerly nested in moderate to large numbers at Reelfoot Lake.
- Early Spring
    - 27 Mar 2012, Fayette Co. (MIG 83:64)
    - 30 Mar 2006, Loosehatchie Bottoms, Fayette Co. (MIG 77:98)
    - 8 Apr 2008, near Brownsville, Haywood Co. (MIG 79:61)
- Late Fall
    - 6 Nov-8 Dec 1994, Samburg, Reelfoot Lake (MIG 66:19)
    - 8 Nov 1996, Shelby Co. (MIG 68:24)
    - 29 Oct 1950, President's Island (MIG 22:12)
    - 16 Oct 2003, Brewer's Bar, Reelfoot Lake, Obion Co. (USFWS *fide* NM)
    - 11 Oct 1987, Amnicola Marsh (Robinson 1990)
- High Counts – Spring
    - 50 on 29 May 1933, Reelfoot Lake (MIG 4:15)
    - 24 on 9 May 2009, Chickasaw NWR (MIG 80:87)
    - 6 (3 pairs with nests) on 22 Apr 2009, Eagle Lake, Shelby Forest WMA (MIG 80:87)
- High Counts – Fall
    - 13 on 29 Oct 1950, President's Island (MIG 22:12)
- High Counts – Summer
    - 16 on 15 Jul 2014, Macedonia Bottoms, Gibson Co. (MAG, pers. comm.)
- Winter Records
    - 1 on 2-8 Dec 1994, Samburg (MIG 66:40)
- Substantiation: Egg set: AFG-LSUMZ

Pelecanidae: Pelicans. Two species occur in Tennessee. One species is widespread and occurs regularly, while the other species is accidental.

American White Pelican, *Pelecanus erythrorhynchos*
Status and Abundance: Fairly common fall transient and uncommon spring transient in Mississippi Alluvial Valley and Southeastern Coastal Plain; irregular transient elsewhere. Uncommon summer visitor in Mississippi Alluvial Valley, Southeastern Coastal Plain, and Central Hardwoods. Rare winter visitor in Cumberland Plateau, Ridge and Valley, Southern Blue Ridge; uncommon to locally common winter resident in Mississippi Alluvial Valley, Southeastern Coastal Plain, and Central Hardwoods.

Habitat: Large lakes and rivers, rests on shorelines, sandbars, and mudflats

Comments: Numbers reported in Tennessee have increased significantly since Robinson (1990) was published. Small numbers of non-breeding birds can be found during summer along the Mississippi River and along the Tennessee River in w. Tennessee. Locally common during winter on Reelfoot Lake, Cross Creeks NWR, and along upper Kentucky Lake.

High Counts – Spring
  2,000 on 31 Mar 2001, Reelfoot Lake (MIG 72:91)
  500+ on 7 Mar 1999, Shelby Co. (MIG 70:97)
  300 on 3 Apr 2005, Dyer Co. (MIG 76:95)

High Counts – Fall
  5,000 on 13 Nov 2013, Duck River Unit (MIG, in press)
  4,892 on 7 Oct 2005, Mississippi River, Shelby Co. (MIG 77:23)
  3,263 on 23 Oct 2005, Mississippi River, Shelby Co. (MIG 77:23)
  2,620 on 1 Nov 2000, Shelby Co. (MIG 73:10)
  2,470 on 19 Nov 2008, Duck River Unit (RW, pers. comm.)

High Counts – Summer
  460 on 6 Jul 2002, Tiptonville Bar (JRW, unpubl. data)
  75 on 5 Jul 2010, Moss Island WMA (MIG 81:125)
  75 on 8 Jul 2010, Bogota WMA (MIG 81:125)

High Counts – Winter
  1,150 on 25 Feb 2011, Reelfoot Lake, Lake Co. (SGS, pers. obs.)
  550 on 14 Jan 2006, Henry Co. (MIG 77:57)

Substantiation: Photograph: Todd, M.C. 2003. "American White Pelican". <http://www.pbase.com/mctodd/image/26808881> Accessed 15 Dec 2014.

Brown Pelican, *Pelecanus occidentalis*
    Status and Abundance: Very rare spring, summer, and fall visitor
    Habitat: Large lakes and rivers
    Comments: Several records during spring since 2012 from east Tennessee.
    Records
        (1) 1 on 17 May 1936, Tennessee/Mississippi state line in Shelby Co. (M'Camey 1936)
        (2) 1 on 6 Jun 1937, Norris Lake (Foster 1937)
        (3) 1 on 12 Apr 1983, Memphis (MIG 54:59)
        (4) 1 on 27 Aug-1 Sep 1996, Reelfoot Lake SP (MIG 68:24)
        (5) 1 imm on 5-11 Jul 2002, Chickamauga Lake (MIG 73:113)
        (6) 1 imm on 20-25 May 2003, Chickamauga Lake, Hamilton Co. (MIG 74:91)
        (7) 1 on 11 Jul-10 Oct 2005, Chickamauga Dam (MIG 76:28, MIG 76:146)
        (8) 1 on 2 Nov 2008, McKellar Lake, Shelby Co. (MIG 80:22)
        (9) 1 on 9-13 Apr 2009, J. Percy Priest Lake, Davidson Co., likely same bird later seen on 10 May 2009, Old Hickory Lake (MIG 80:89)
        (10) 1 on 27-30 Jul 2009, Duck River Unit (MIG 80:125)
        (11) 1 imm on 2-3 Aug 2009, Boone Lake (MIG 81:54)
        (12) 1 on mid-May 2012, Cordell Hull Lake, Smith Co. (MIG 83:66)
        (13) 1 on 19 May 2012, Chickamauga Lake (MIG 83:69)
        (14) 1 on 12 Apr 2013, Cherokee Lake (MIG, in press)
        (15) 1 imm on 25-27 May 2013, Ft. Loudoun/Tellico Dams, Loudon Co. (MIG, in press)
        (16) 1 ad on 5 Jun 2013, Watts Bar Lake, Roane Co. (MIG, in press)
        (17) 1 on 6 May 2014, Nickajack Dam, Marion Co. (KAC, pers. comm.)
    Substantiation: Photograph: 1 on 2 Nov 2008, McKellar Lake, Shelby Co. (NAB 63(1):56)

Ardeidae: Bitterns, Herons, and Allies.

Twelve species occur in a variety of wetlands, flooded forests, riverine and other open water habitats. Ten species breed in Tennessee, while one species formerly bred and one species occurs accidentally.

American Bittern, *Botaurus lentiginosus*

Status and Abundance: Irregular transient, rare summer and winter resident

Habitat: Marshes

Spring Arrival: mid Mar

Spring Departure: early May

Fall Arrival: mid Sep

Fall Departure: mid Nov

Comments: There are 4 nesting records with the most recent in 1976. There are several June and July records without documented nesting.

Early Spring

    3 Mar 1974, Amnicola Marsh (FH, pers. comm.)

Late Spring

    7 Jun 2003, Standifer Gap Marsh (MIG 74:132)

    22 May 1994, Dyer Co. (JRW, unpubl. data)

    20 May 1990, Ensley (MIG 61:70)

Early Fall

    7 Aug 2004, Tennessee NWR (MIG 76:29)

    18 Aug 1990, Limestone, Washington Co. (MIG 62:51)

Late Fall

    29 Nov 1938, GSMNP (Stupka 1963)

    28 Nov 1996, Black Bayou WMA (MIG 68:24)

    26 Nov 1998, Hiwassee River Area (MIG 60:31)

    22 Nov 2006, Brainerd Levee (MIG 78:37)

    19 Nov 1972, Cross Creeks NWR (MIG 44:22)

High Counts – Spring

    7 on 17 Apr 1972, Goose Pond, Grundy Co. (MIG 43:50)

Winter Records

    1 on 2 Jan 1961, Lebanon CBC (MIG 31:74)

    1 on 14 Feb 1976, Hamilton Co. (MIG 47:47)

    1 on 14 Feb 1976, Kingsport (Knight 2008)

    1 on 9 Dec 1978, Nashville (BNA:15)

    1 on 12 Dec 1986, Kingsport (Knight 2008)

    1 on 17 Dec 2005, Standifer Gap Marsh (DPa, pers. comm.)

Substantiation: Specimen: LSUMZ, 75672

Least Bittern, *Ixobrychus exilis*
> Status and Abundance: Irregular (locally uncommon) transient and summer resident
> Habitat: Marshes
> Spring Arrival: late Apr
> Fall Departure: late Sep
> Comments: Found as a migrant across the state. Recently only known to breed at Standifer Gap Marsh (although not since 2012, Patterson 2006) and Reelfoot Lake, Lake/Obion Co. Five nests with eggs found at Black Bayou Refuge, 25-26 May 2011 (SGS, pers. obs.). Sixteen nests found 28 June 1971 on Reelfoot Lake (MIG 42:67). Nested in Meigs Co. in 1997 (MIG 68:136) and at Brainard Levee in 1998 (MIG 69:188).
> Early Spring
>> 4 Apr 1968, Knoxville (MIG 39:44)
>> 17 Apr 1972, Goose Pond, Grundy Co. (MIG 43:50)
> Late Fall
>> 23 Oct 1979, Austin Springs (MIG 51:17)
>> 19 Oct 2009, Putnam Co. FBC (MIG 81:41)
>> 10 Oct 1937, Knox Co. (Howell and Monroe 1957)
> High Counts – Spring
>> 5 on 25 May 2011, Black Bayou Refuge (MIG 82:83)
>> 4 on 21 May 1994, Ensley (JRW, unpubl. data)
>> 3 on 14 May 2005, Hamilton Co. NAMC (MIG 76:126)
> High Counts – Fall
>> 3 on 17 Sep 2004, TVA Lake, Ensley (JRW, unpubl. data)
> High Counts – Summer
>> 18 on 28 Jun 1971, near Samburg, Reelfoot Lake (MIG 42:67)
>> 12 on 26 Jun 2006, Standifer Gap Marsh (DPa, pers. comm.)
> Substantiation: Specimen: LSUMZ, 75671

Great Blue Heron, *Ardea herodias*
> Status and Abundance: Fairly common permanent resident
> Habitat: Wetlands; also plowed or harvested fields (feeding on rodents)
> Comments: Rookeries, many under 20 nesting pairs, are found on nearly all navigable waterways in the state. Development of dams by TVA has likely increased nesting opportunities in east Tennessee. Many small rookeries are found on smaller creeks and in dry woodlots away from bodies of water (SGS, pers. obs.). Before 1950, there were no nesting records east of the Southeastern Coastal Plain (Robinson 1990). Few rookeries have as many as 300 nesting pairs now (SGS, pers. obs.), whereas Robinson (1990) reported several sites with 500 or more

nests through the late 1980s. Great White Heron (*A. h. occidentalis*) is a very rare spring, summer, and fall visitor to Cumberland Plateau, Ridge and Valley, and Southern Blue Ridge, with 11 records (including several documented with photographs):
(1) 1 on 15-19 Oct 1990, S. Holston Lake (MIG 62:53, Knight et al. 1992)
(2) 1 on 29 Aug 1991, S. Holston Lake (MIG 63:57)
(3) 1 on 7-29 Aug 2002, S. Holston Lake (MIG 74:26)
(4) 1 on 21 Sep-11 Nov 2002, DeKalb and Putnam Co. (MIG 76:91)
(5) 1 on 19 Oct 2003, Center Hill Lake (MIG 75:26)
(6) 1 on 20 Aug 2004, S. Holston Lake (MIG 76:37)
(7) 1 on 5 Dec 2006-11 Jan 2007, 10-27 Mar 2007, Little River, Townsend, Blount Co. (MIG 78:84, MIG 78:106, Edwards 2012)
(8) 1 on 7 Jun-early Jul 2008, Watauga River (MIG 79:100)
(9) 1 on 9 Jun-3 Jul 2009, Chickamauga Dam (MIG 80:126)
(10) 1 on 8 and 12 Jul 2011, Hamilton Co. (NAB 65(4), MIG 82:121)
(11) 1 on 16 Jul-24 Sep 2011, Nolichucky River, Unicoi/Washington Co. (NAB 65(4), MIG 82:123)

High Counts – Spring
1,000+ on 2 Apr 1991, Little Ronaldson Slough, Reelfoot Lake, Lake Co. (MIG 62:109)
500 on 24 Apr 1954, Tennessee NWR (MIG 25:28)
450 on 22 Apr 2009, Shelby Forest WMA (SGS, pers. obs.)

High Counts – Fall
500 on 10 Sep 1988, Hatchie NWR (MIG 60:25)
98 on 30 Oct 1988, Mississippi River, Shelby Co. (MIG 60:25)
76 on 27 Sep 2003, Nashville FBC (MIG 75:15)

High Counts – Winter
419 on 22 Dec 2001, Chattanooga CBC (MIG 72:114)
275 on 1 Jan 2006, Hiwassee CBC (MIG 77:41)
254 on 1 Jan 2003, Hiwassee CBC (MIG 74:39)
199 on 1 Jan 1996, Hiwassee CBC (MIG 67:7)

Substantiation: Specimen: LSUMZ, 75663

Great Egret, *Ardea alba*

Status and Abundance: Fairly common spring and fall visitor and summer resident; rare winter resident (perhaps uncommon in Mississippi Alluvial Valley, Southeastern Coastal Plain, Central Hardwoods)

Habitat: Wetlands

Comments: Small breeding colonies (typically less than ten pairs) occur across the state, with a few sizeable ones (up to 300 pairs) along the Mississippi River. Seems to be increasing as a winter resident from Cumberland Plateau east.

High Counts – Spring
- 260 on 12 May 2001, Lake Co. NAMC (MIG 72:14)
- 72 on 8 May 2004, Lake Co. NAMC (MIG 75:93)
- 15 on 8 May 2005, Rankin Bottoms (MIG 76:100)

High Counts – Fall
- 3,500 on 27 Aug 1994, Cates Landing (MIG 66:19)
- 1,500 on 13 Sep 1988, Ensley Bar (MIG 60:25)
- 1,219 on 6 Aug 1988, Mud Lake, Shelby Co. (Robinson 1988a)
- 1,200 on 18 Aug 1996, Phillippy (MIG 68:25)
- 850+ on 23 Aug 2012, Riverport Road, Shelby Co. (MIG 83:147)

High Counts – Winter
- 23 on 6 Jan 2007, Robco Lake (MIG 78:78)
- 9 on 28 Jan 2007, Robco Lake (MIG 78:78)
- 6 on 1 Jan 2000, Hiwassee CBC (MIG 71:15)
- 6 on 2 Dec 1989, Rankin Bottoms (MIG 61:60)

Substantiation: Egg set: AFG-LSUMZ

Snowy Egret, *Egretta thula*

Status and Abundance: Uncommon spring and fall visitor (fairly common fall visitor in Mississippi Alluvial Valley); rare summer resident; accidental winter visitor

Habitat: Wetlands

Spring Arrival: early Apr

Fall Departure: early Oct

Comments: Probably nests more commonly in Mississippi Alluvial Valley than is known. One nesting location active in 2009, 2011, 2012, 2013 at Little Elder Island and one on Old Hickory Lake, Sumner Co. in 2008. Fall dispersal of birds from southern locations can result in large numbers seen in Mississippi Alluvial Valley.

Early Spring
- 19 Mar 2008, Cane Creek Park (SJS, pers. comm.)
- 23 Mar 2003, Hatchie NWR (MIG 74:86)
- 27 Mar 2005, J. Percy Priest Lake (MIG 76:97)
- 27 Mar 1994, Everett Lake (MIG 65:50)
- 29 Mar 1988, Putnam Co. (MIG 59:96)

Late Fall
- 6 Oct 1986, Austin Springs (MIG 58:27)
- 14 Oct 1993, Lake Co. (MIG 65:20)
- 25 Oct 2009, Joachim Bible Refuge (MIG 81:54)
- 28 Oct 2002, Everett Lake (MT, pers. comm.)

High Counts – Spring
- 172 on 22 Apr 2007, Heloise, Dyer Co. (MIG 68:106)

61 on 8 May 2004, Lake Co. NAMC (MIG 75:93)
26 on 13 May 2000, Lake Co. NAMC (MIG 71:50)
High Counts – Fall
600 on 21 Aug 2005, Everett Lake (MIG 77:24)
156 on 11 Aug 1988, Ensley Bar, Shelby Co. (Robinson 1988a)
High Counts – Summer
145 on 26 Jun 2010, White Lake Refuge (MIG 81:125)
Winter Records
1 (injured) on 12 Dec 2004, Ensley (MIG 76:78)
1 on 24 Dec 1955, Reelfoot Lake CBC (MIG 26:59)
Substantiation: Photograph: Somershoe, S.G. 2012. "Snowy Egret". <http://www.pbase.com/shoeman/image/143594660> Accessed 25 Sep 2014.

Little Blue Heron, *Egretta caerulea*
Status and Abundance: Uncommon spring and fall visitor (but fairly common fall visitor in Mississippi Alluvial Valley); rare summer resident; accidental winter visitor
Habitat: Wetlands
Spring Arrival: late Mar
Fall Departure: early Oct
Comments: Rare breeder. In 2009, 6 pairs nested on Little Elder Island (SGS, pers. obs.); 12 pairs were found nesting there on 25 May 2012 (SGS, pers. obs.). Historically nested in large numbers, e.g. 500 pairs in Dyersburg in 1960 (Ganier 1960).
Early Spring
12 Mar 1989, Cross Creeks NWR (MIG 60:84)
17 Mar 1996, Reelfoot Lake, Lake Co. (MIG 67:59)
22 Mar 2011, Fayette Co. (MIG 82:83)
23 Mar 1991, Hiwassee River Area (MIG 62:112)
Late Fall
23 Nov 1977, Nashville (MIG 49:42)
7 Nov 1992, Dyer Co. (MIG 64:15)
23 Oct 1979, Nashville (MIG 51:16)
23 Oct 2005, Benton Co. (MIG 76:24)
High Counts – Spring
113 on 8 May 2004, Lake Co. NAMC (MIG 75:93)
52 on 13 May 2000, Lake Co. NAMC (MIG 71:50)
26 on 12 May 2001, Lake Co. NAMC (MIG 72:14)
High Counts – Fall
2,882 on 6 Aug 1988, Mud Lake, Shelby Co. (Robinson 1988a)
2,000+ on 14 Aug 1994, Cates Landing (MIG 66:19)

High Counts – Summer
> 3,000 on 30 Jun 1962, Dyersburg (MIG 33:47)
> 320 on 30 Jun 2002, White Lake WMA (MIG 73:110)

Winter Records
> 1 on 26 Dec 1936, Memphis CBC (MIG 8:7)
> 1 on 28 Dec 1970, Lebanon CBC (MIG 42:8)
> 1 on 19 Dec 1971, Knoxville CBC (MIG 43:11)

Substantiation: Specimen: APSU, 2312

Tricolored Heron, *Egretta tricolor*

Status and Abundance: Rare spring, late summer, and fall visitor
Habitat: Wetlands
Spring Arrival: late Apr
Spring Departure: late May
Fall Arrival: late Jul
Fall Departure: mid Sep
Comments: Most likely in late July to late Aug. Can occur through summer. Occurrence during summer poorly known. One nesting record with one fledgling from 15 Jun-13 Jul 1997, Island 18, Dyer Co. (JRW, unpubl. data).

Early Spring
> 1-2 Apr 1988, Great Lakes Pond, Carter Co. (MIG 59:103)
> 2 Apr 2000, Watauga River (MIG 71:94)
> 13 Apr 2002, Kyker Bottoms Refuge (MIG 73:61)
> 18 Apr 1991, Austin Springs (MIG 62:112)
> 20 Apr 2002, Lillydale Campground, Clay Co. (MIG 73:58)

Late Spring
> 31 May-5 Jun 1999, Lake Co. (JRW, unpubl. data)
> 30 May 2003, Dyer Co. (MIG 74:86)
> 26 May 2011, Black Bayou Refuge (MIG 82:83)

Late Fall
> 21 Sep 2011, Upper Douglas Lake (MIG, in press)
> 19 Sep 2004, Brainerd Levee (MIG 76:33)
> 28 Aug-17 Sep 1998, White's Lake Refuge (MIG 70:46)
> 16 Sep 1978, Hiwassee River Area (MIG 50:22)

High Counts – Fall
> Up to 26 on 31 Jul-14 Aug 1988, Ensley Bar (Robinson 1988a)

High Counts – Summer
> 3 on 23 Jul 2006, White Lake Refuge (MIG 77:143)
> 2 imm on 31 Jul-8 Aug 2012, Duck River Unit (MIG 83:103)

Substantiation: Photograph: 2 imm on 5 Aug 2012, Duck River Unit (NAB 67(1):86)

Reddish Egret, *Egretta rufescens*
Status and Abundance: Accidental late summer and fall visitor
Habitat: Wetlands
Records
(1) 1 imm on 23 Aug 1997, Gallatin Steam Plant (MIG 68:40)
(2) 1 imm on 12-20 Jul 2008, Rankin Bottoms (MIG 79:98)
Substantiation: Photograph: 1 imm on 23 Aug 1997, Gallatin Steam Plant (MIG 68:40)

Cattle Egret, *Bubulcus ibis*
Status and Abundance: Irregular (uncommon Mississippi Alluvial Valley) transient and locally uncommon summer resident (rare Southern Blue Ridge); accidental winter visitor
Habitat: Wetlands; pastures
Spring Arrival: late Mar
Fall Departure: early Nov
Comments: First state record on 5-6 May 1961 in Anderson Co. (Olson 1961). May be found breeding into Sep. Only 5-6 nesting locations known in 2012 (SGS, pers. obs.)
Early Spring
7 Mar 1976, Memphis (MIG 47:45)
8 Mar 1974, Cove Lake SP (MIG 45:23)
11 Mar 2006, Hamilton Co. (MIG 77:102)
Late Fall
28 Nov 1972, Cannon Co. (MIG 44:22)
26 Nov 1993, Lauderdale WMA (MIG 65:20)
25 Nov 1965, Chickamauga Lake (MIG 36:95)
24 Nov 2009, Robco Lake (MIG 81:49)
High Counts – Spring
1,884 on 6 Aug 1988, Ensley Bar (Robinson 1988b)
1,500 on 14 May 2004, Dyer Co. (MIG 75:110)
641 on 8 May 2004, Lake Co. NAMC (MIG 75:93)
High Counts – Fall
2,600+ on 14 and 26 Aug 1994, Cates Landing (MIG 66:19)
2,381 on 22 Aug 2009, Little Elder Island (MIG 81:51)
2,000+ on 6 Sep 2008, Little Elder Island (MIG 80:25)
1,884 on 6 Aug 1988, Mud Lake, Shelby Co. (Robinson 1988a)
801 on 9 Sep 2006, Little Elder Island (MIG 78:35)
High Counts – Summer
1000 on 20 Jul 2009, Little Elder Island (MIG 80:125)

High Counts – Winter
    1 on 22 Dec 1973, Reelfoot Lake CBC (MIG 45:11)
    1 on 22 Dec 1984, Reelfoot Lake CBC (MIG 56:6)
    1 on 16 Dec 1990, Elizabethton CBC (MIG 62:15, 87)
    1 on 12 Feb 1999, Lake Co. (MIG 70:68)
    1 on 3 Jan 2004, Knox CBC (MIG 75:67, 77)
Substantiation: Specimen: UTM, 411

Green Heron, *Butorides virescens*

Status and Abundance: Fairly common transient and summer resident; accidental winter visitor
Habitat: Streams, ponds, and small lakes (generally wooded)
Spring Arrival: late Mar
Fall Departure: late Oct
Comments: Many winter records, most in Dec. Some birds may linger throughout winter where suitable habitat and open water remain.
Early Spring
    11 Mar 1979, Radnor Lake (BNA:15)
    12 Mar 1983, Red Bank, Hamilton Co. (MIG 54:64)
Late Fall
    29 Nov 2004, City Lake, Putnam Co. (MIG 76:30)
    28 Nov 1963, Knoxville (MIG 34:74)
High Counts – Spring
    30 on 26 Apr 1980, Elizabethton SBC (MIG 51:55)
    19 on 9 May 1992, Chattanooga SBC (MIG 63:47)
    15 on 12 May 2001, Hamilton Co. NAMC (MIG 72:14)
    15 on 12 May 2001, Maury Co. NAMC (MIG 72:14)
    13 on 14 May 2005, Montgomery Co. NAMC (MIG 76:127)
High Counts – Fall
    55 on 4 Aug 1985, Hiwassee River Area (MIG 57:31)
High Counts – Summer
    31 on 31 Jul 1988, Stewart Co. (MIG 59:125)
High Counts – Winter
    1 on 14 Feb 1968, Ft. Loudoun dam (MIG 39:44)
    1 on 21 Feb 1983, Chickamauga Lake (MIG 54:45)
    1 on 1 Jan 1992, Hamilton Co. (MIG 63:62)
    1 on 30 Dec 1992, Chickamauga Lake (MIG 64:49)
Substantiation: Specimen: APSU, 2311

Black-crowned Night-Heron, *Nycticorax nycticorax*

Status and Abundance: Fairly common transient and summer resident; locally uncommon winter resident

Habitat: Lakes and ponds

High Counts – Spring
- 366 on 11 May 2002, Nashville SBC (MIG 73:104)
- 326 on 4 May 2008, Nashville NAMC (MIG 79:89)
- 203 on 11 May 2002, Davidson Co. NAMC (MIG 73:94)
- 150 on 11 May 2002, Sumner Co. NAMC (MIG 73:94)
- 114 on 12 May 2007, Davidson Co. NAMC (MIG 78:126)

High Counts – Fall
- 200+ on 5 Sep 1983, Cherokee Lake, Hawkins Co. (*fide* RLK)
- 100 on 13 Sep 2000, Rankin Bottoms (MIG 72:42)
- 99 on 5 Oct 2002, Nashville FBC (MIG 73:50)
- 31 on 2 Nov 2001, Douglas Dam (MIG 73:15)
- 30 on 22 Aug 1989, Boone Dam (MIG 61:17)

High Counts – Summer
- 700 during summer 1984, Bordeaux heronry, Nashville (BNA:15)
- 150 on 3 Jun 2013, Pear Island, J. Percy Priest Lake, Davidson Co. (SGS, pers. obs.)
- 124 on 3 Jun 2006, Bird Island (MIG 77:146)

High Counts – Winter
- 52 on 1 Jan 2002, Hickory-Priest CBC (MIG 72:115)
- 34 on 1 Jan 1998, Hickory-Priest CBC (MIG 69:20)
- 31 on 26 Jan 2006, Douglas Dam (MIG 77:60)
- 27 on 14 Dec 2002, Douglas Dam (MIG 74:56)
- 22 on 30 Dec 1989, Kingsport CBC (MIG 61:3)

Substantiation: Specimen: LSUMZ, 75669

Yellow-crowned Night-Heron, *Nyctanassa violacea*

Status and Abundance: Uncommon transient and summer resident; accidental winter resident

Habitat: Small wooded creeks and ponds

Spring Arrival: late Mar

Fall Departure: late Sep

Comments: Arrival and departure dates difficult to establish due to reclusive nature. Typically nests in small colonies, usually 5 pairs or fewer, but has nested in large groups with 67 nests counted in Memphis in 1977 (MIG 48:75). Small colonies can be found in urban neighborhoods where nests are in large trees over yards and roads.

Early Spring
- 7 Mar 1988, Memphis (MIG 59:94)
- 16 Mar 2010, Elizabethton (MIG 81:121)
- 16 Mar 2013, Kingsport (RLK, pers. comm., MIG in press)
- 25 Mar 2010, Sylvan Park, Davidson Co. (MIG 81:116)

25 Mar 1996, Gooch WMA (MIG 67:59)
Late Fall
21 Nov 1970, Cross Creeks NWR (MIG 42:19)
19 Nov 1972, Cross Creeks NWR (MIG 44:22)
High Counts – Spring
14 on 26 May 2011, Black Bayou Refuge (MIG 82:83)
9 on 9 May 1992, Chattanooga SBC (MIG 63:47)
High Counts – Summer
29 on 15 Jun 1985, Hatchie NWR (MIG 56:107)
12 (11 ad, 1 imm) on 18 Jun 2010, Sycamore Shoals SP (SGS, pers. obs.)
High Counts – Winter
1 on 27 Feb 1976, Gallatin (MIG 47:45)
1 on 30 Dec 1978, Highland Rim CBC (MIG 50:10)
1 on 16 Dec 1979, Memphis CBC (MIG 51:31)
1 on 24 Feb 1980, Nashville (MIG 51:39)
Substantiation: Specimen: LSUMZ, 75670

Threskiornithidae: Ibises and Spoonbills.

All four species found in Tennessee are rare to accidental and could occur anywhere that suitable shallow water wetlands occur.

White Ibis, *Eudocimus albus*

Status and Abundance: Very rare spring visitor; rare late summer and fall visitor

Habitat: Shallow wetlands

Fall Arrival: early Jul

Fall Departure: late Aug

Comments: Most records are of immature birds.

Early Fall
- 21 Jun 2000, Carter Co. (MIG 71:122)
- 22 Jun-7 Jul 2005, Hatchie NWR (MIG 76:144)
- 27 Jun 1973, Sequatchie Valley (MIG 44:86)

Late Fall
- 13 Oct 1977, Dyersburg (Criswell 1979)
- 24-26 Oct 2005, Savannah Bay (MIG 76:28)

High Counts – Spring
- 51 (all ad) on 14 May 2011, Hatchie NWR (MIG 82:83)
- 7 ad on 22 May 2011, Lauderdale Co. (MIG 82:83)

High Counts – Fall
- 103 on 7 Aug 1980, Dyersburg (MIG 51:91)

High Counts – Summer
- 35 on 29 Jun 2005, near Loretto, Lawrence Co. (MIG 76:145)
- 23 (possible nesting) on 18 Jun 1996, Dyer Co. (JRW, unpubl. data)
- 16 (9 ad, 7 imm) on 26 Jul 2003, Mud Lake, Shelby Co. (JRW, unpubl. data)
- 15 imm on 25 Jul 2010, White Lake Refuge (MIG 81:125)
- 14 imm on 4 Jul 2010, Mud Lake, Shelby Co. (MIG 81:125)

Substantiation: Photograph: 1 imm on 2 Jul 2008, Watauga River, Carter Co. (Knight 2008:39)

Glossy Ibis, *Plegadis falcinellus*

Status and Abundance: Rare spring, late summer, and fall visitor; accidental winter visitor

Habitat: Shallow wetlands

Spring Arrival: late Apr

Fall Departure: late Sep

Comments: Older records of *Plegadis* sp. were often attributed to this species but in many cases lack sufficient documentation to determine the species. Dark ibis should be studied closely, since White-faced is now known to occur regularly. Key identification criteria are eye color, leg color, and color of the edge of the bare loral skin. Knight (2011b) provides an excellent summary of the status of dark ibises in Tennessee.

Early Spring
> 19 Apr 1990, Ensley (JRW, unpubl. data)

Late Spring
> 28-31 May 2003, Dyer Co. (MIG 74:86)
> 28 May 1998, Hwy 79, Lake Co. (MIG 69:160)

Late Fall
> 2/18 Oct 2012, Rankin Bottoms (MIG, in press)
> 27 Sep 1999, Cross Creeks NWR (MIG 71:33)
> 16-17 Sep 2009, Paddle Creek, Sullivan Co. (MIG 81:54)
> 6 Sep 1996, White Lake WMA (MIG 68:25)

High Counts – Spring
> 14 on 8 May 1971, Kingsport (Robinson 1990)
> 10 on 15 Apr 1943, Reelfoot NWR (HA *fide* MAG)

High Counts – Fall
> 2 on 2 Sep 1988, Gallatin Steam Plant (MIG 60:28)
> 2 on 22 Sep 1990, Duck River Unit (JRW, unpubl. data)

Summer Records
> 1 on 30 Jun 1976, Haywood Co. (MIG 47:99)
> 2 ad on 24 Jun 1993, Lake Co. (MIG 64:84)
> 1 on 16 Jun 2007, Little Elder Island (MIG 78:140)

Winter Records
> 1 on 11 Dec 2007, Standifer Gap Marsh (MIG 79:54)
> 1 on 9-15 Jan 2004, Duck River Unit (NAB 58(2))

Substantiation: Photograph: 1 imm on 14 Sep 2009, Anderson Co. (NAB 64(1):51)

White-faced Ibis, *Plegadis chihi*

Status and Abundance: Very rare visitor (most records from Mississippi Alluvial Valley)

Habitat: Shallow wetlands

Comments: Approximately 15 records. See notes under Glossy Ibis. A well-described "White-faced Glossy Ibis" from Mud Lake, Shelby Co. on 23 Sep 1945 (MIG 16:44) likely constitutes the first record of this species in Tennessee. Knight (2011b) provides an excellent summary of the status of dark ibises in Tennessee.

High Counts – Spring
> 26 on 19 Apr 1990, Ensley (Waldron 1990, Knight 1993)

High Counts – Summer
> 14 on 5 Jun 2003, Great River Road, Dyer Co. (MIG 74:129)
> 8 ad on 3-4 Jun 1996, Dyer Co. (MIG 67:76)

Winter Records
> 1 on 1-9 Dec 2006 (and during fall), Lake Co. (MIG 78:78)
> 1 on 30 Nov into Dec 2006, Lake Co. (MIG 78:33)

Substantiation: Photograph: 1 on 12 May 2010, John Sevier Lake (NAB 64(3):52)

Roseate Spoonbill, *Platalea ajaja*

Status and Abundance: Accidental spring visitor, very rare late summer and fall visitor (most likely in Mississippi Alluvial Valley)

Habitat: Shallow wetlands

Fall Arrival: late Jul

Fall Departure: mid Sep

Comments: Likely an annual post-breeding visitor to Mississippi Alluvial Valley, especially sw. Shelby Co., but occurs statewide.

Early Fall
> 3 Jul 2013, Rhea Co. (MIG, in press)
> 5 Jul 2009, Chickamauga Dam (MIG 80:127)

Late Fall
> 7-16 Oct 2002, Kinser Park, Greene Co. (MIG 74:21) and 22 Oct 2002, Dutch Bottoms (MIG 74:22)
> 28 Sep 2008, Mud Lake, Shelby Co. (MIG 80:22)
> 14 Sep 1994, Phillippy (JRW, unpubl. data)

High Counts – Fall
> 7 on 28 Sep 2008, Mud Lake, Shelby Co. (MIG 80:22)
> 3 on 27 Aug 2002, Cocklebur Lake (MIG 74:15)
> 2 on 2 Aug 2005, Buckelew Slough, Obion Co. (JRW, unpubl. data)
> 2 on 23 Aug-1 Sep 2009, Moss Island WMA (MIG 81:49)

Substantiation: Photograph: 1 imm on 19 Aug 2010, Phipps Bend (NAB 65(1):57)

Cathartidae: New World Vultures. Two species occur statewide year round.

Black Vulture, *Coragyps atratus*
Status and Abundance: Common permanent resident

Habitat: Open areas, wooded edges, urban and suburban areas; often roosts on large dead trees, dams, high voltage transmission towers, cell towers

Comments: Increasing greatly in abundance statewide in last 20 years for unknown reasons.

High Counts – Spring
- 250 on 15 Apr 2009, Jefferson Springs, Smyrna, Rutherford Co. (SGS, pers. obs.)
- 161 on 8 May 1999, Hamilton Co. SBC (MIG 70:37)
- 136 on 8 May 2004, Nashville SBC (MIG 75:104)
- 109 on 13 May 2006, Nashville SBC (MIG 77:122)

High Counts – Fall
- 570 on 8 Oct 2005, Nashville FBC (MIG 77:9)
- 511 on 4 Oct 2008, Nashville FBC (MIG 80:14)
- 450 on 1 Nov 1986, Gallatin Steam Plant (MIG 58:23)

High Counts – Winter
- 689 on 3 Jan 2009, Clarksville CBC (MIG 80:48)
- 463 on 17 Dec 1988, Duck River Reservoir CBC (MIG 60:14)
- 450 on 1 Feb 2014, Long Hunter SP (SGS, pers. obs.)
- 450 on 12 Dec 1951, near Nashville (Ganier 1952)
- 450 on 18 Jan 2008, Long Hunter SP, Davidson Co. (MIG 79:52)

Substantiation: Specimen: APSU, 2302

Turkey Vulture, *Cathartes aura*
Status and Abundance: Common permanent resident

Habitat: Open areas, wooded edges, urban and suburban areas; often roosts on large dead trees, dams, high voltage transmission towers, cell towers

Comments: Increasing greatly in abundance statewide in last 20 years for unknown reasons. Range retracts from some breeding areas in coldest part of winter. Large movement of northern populations through the state, more noticeable during fall.

High Counts – Spring
- 355 on 3 Mar 1997, S. Holston Lake (MIG 68:113)
- 145 on 24 Apr 2004, Elizabethton SBC (MIG 75:104)
- 137 on 14 May 2005, Montgomery Co. NAMC (MIG 76:127)

123 on 26 Apr 1997, Elizabethton SBC (MIG 68:57)
High Counts – Fall
1,845 on 21 Oct 1982, Blount Co. (MIG 54:36)
1,000+ on 10 Oct 1988, Townsend (MIG 60:35)
763 on 9 Nov 1997, Soddy Mtn. (MIG 69:45)
High Counts – Winter
500+ on 28 Jan 1996, Chickamauga Lake (MIG 67:32)
475 on 28 Dec 2004, DeKalb Co. CBC (MIG 76:62)
Substantiation: Specimen: APSU, 1258

Pandionidae: Ospreys. The only member of this family is a widespread transient and summer resident around larger bodies of water.

Osprey, *Pandion haliaetus*
> Status and Abundance: Fairly common transient and summer resident, very rare winter visitor
> Habitat: Large lakes and rivers
> Spring Arrival: early Mar
> Fall Departure: early Nov
> Comments: Fairly common nesting bird on nearly all large lakes and rivers in Tennessee. They nest on bridges, river markers, communication towers, artificial nesting structures and other suitable elevated structures over or near water. Hacking of immature Osprey began in 1980 with a collaboration of numerous partners including Tennessee Wildlife Resources Agency and Tennessee Valley Authority. Between 1980 and 1988, 165 immature Osprey were hacked in Tennessee.
> Early Spring
>> 5 Mar 2010, Rankin Bottoms (MIG 81:118)
>> 6 Mar 2005, Lake Co. (MIG 76:95)
>
> Late Fall
>> 20 Nov 1998, Chickamauga Lake (MIG 70:52)
>> 14 Nov 2005, Eagle Bend Fish Hatchery (MIG 76:28)
>> 14 Nov 2009, Greene Co. (MIG 81:54)
>
> High Counts – Spring
>> 15 on 25 Apr 1987, Elizabethton SBC (MIG 58:81)
>> 15 on 26 Apr 1987, Knoxville SBC (MIG 58:81)
>
> High Counts – Fall
>> 9 on 19 Sep 2009, Elizabethton FBC (MIG 81:42)
>> 4 on 30 Sep 2006, Nashville FBC (MIG 78:26)
>
> Substantiation: Specimen: LSUMZ, 75704

Acciptridae: Hawks, Kites, Eagles, and Allies. Fifteen species occur in Tennessee. 10 occur annually statewide and 5 are accidental.

Swallow-tailed Kite, *Elanoides forficatus*
    Status and Abundance: Accidental spring visitor; rare fall visitor
    Habitat: Farmland and river bottoms
    Fall Arrival: late Jul
    Fall Departure: late Aug
    Comments: Mostly occurs during this species' northward dispersal this in late summer and early fall. Most recent records in mid-August. There are a small number of spring records, but few in recent years. First state record was 5 May 1810 in Maury Co. by Alexander Wilson (Yeatman 1965).
    Early Fall
        17 Jul 2008, Knoxville (MIG 79:99)
        20 Jul 2011, Bledsoe Co. (MIG 82:121)
        26 Jul 2002, Hiwassee River, Polk Co. (MIG 73:114)
    Late Fall
        25 Sep 1933, S. Harpeth River near Nashville (Ganier 1933)
        25 Sep 1993, Forked Deer River Bottoms, Weakley Co. (MAG, pers. comm.)
        19 Sep 1983, Memphis (MIG 55:17)
        19 Sep 2012, Montgomery Co. (MIG 83:149)
        13 Sep 1983, Millington (JRW, unpubl. data)
    Spring Records
        1 on 10 Apr 1977, Shelby Co. (MIG 48:75)
        1 on 7 May 2008, Hatchie NWR (MIG 79:61)
        1 on 27 Apr 2010, Cades Cove (MIG 81:121)
    High Counts – Fall
        10 max on 2-19 Aug 2012, south of Pikeville, Bledsoe Co. (MIG 83:153)
        8 or 10 on 9 Aug 1886, near Woodland Mills, Obion Co. (Yeatman 1965)
        2 on 15 Aug 1929, S. Harpeth River near Nashville (Ganier 1933)
    Substantiation: Specimen: LSUMZ, 75676

White-tailed Kite, *Elanus leucurus*
    Status and Abundance: Accidental spring, summer, and fall visitor
    Records
        (1) 1 on 20 May 1991, Millsfield, Dyer Co. (Criswell 1991a, Knight 1993)
        (2) 1 on 22 Jun 1991, Little Turkey Creek, Humphrey's Co. (Knight

1993)
- (3) 1 on 1 Jun 1994, Rutherford Co. (MIG 64:86)
- (4) wing found 9 Apr 1995, Volunteer Army Ammunitions Plant, Hamilton Co. (MIG 67:63)
- (5) 1 on 14 Apr 1996, Volunteer Army Ammunitions Plant, Hamilton Co. (MIG 67:63)
- (6) 1 on 20-21 Apr 2001, Black Bayou WMA (MIG 72:91)
- (7) 1 on 23 Mar 2002, Black Bayou WMA (JRW, unpubl. data)
- (9) 1 on 7-8, 11 May 2003, Ft. Campbell (MIG 74:89, MIG 76:4)

Substantiation: Unpublished photograph: 1 on 7-8, 11 May 2003, Ft. Campbell (DM)

Mississippi Kite, *Ictinia mississippiensis*

Status and Abundance: Fairly common spring transient and summer resident, and uncommon fall transient in Mississippi Alluvial Valley and Southeastern Coastal Plain; rare spring and fall visitor elsewhere

Habitat: Found along wooded rivers and swamps; farmland; also nests in residential areas

Spring Arrival: mid Apr

Fall Departure: mid Sep

Comments: Over 400 Mississippi Kites have been released in west Tennessee from 1983-2010 through a hacking program (Martin 2012). Three records for upper east Tennessee:
- (1) 1 on 19 May 1995, western Washington Co. (Knight 2008)
- (2) 1 on 22 Apr 1997, Austin Springs (Knight 2008)
- (3) 2 on 14 May 2008, western Washington Co. (SGS, pers. obs., Knight 2008)

Early Spring
- 22 Mar 2011, Shelby Co. (JRW, pers. comm.)
- 30 Mar 1985, Memphis (MIG 56:74)

Late Fall
- 1 Nov 2000, Memphis (MIG 73:10)
- 23 Oct 1996, Millington, Shelby Co. (MIG 68:25)
- 13 Oct 1983, Cross Creeks NWR (MIG 55:19)
- 11 Oct 1997, Shelby Co. (MIG 69:40)

High Counts – Spring
- 130 on 24 May 2003, Black Bayou WMA (MIG 74:86)
- 102 on 5 May 1990, Shelby Forest SP (MIG 61:70)
- 100 on 16 May 1998, President's Island (JRW, unpubl. data)
- 72 on 12 May 2007, Shelby Co. NAMC (MIG 78:126)
- 63 on 12 May 2001, Shelby Co. NAMC (MIG 72:15)

Acciptridae: Hawks, Kites, Eagles, and Allies

High Counts – Fall
   208 on 22 Aug 1987, Island 13 (Hoff 1988)
   197 on 22 Aug 1987, Mud Island (MIG 59:32)
High Counts – Summer
   133 on 14 Jun 1992, Lauderdale Co. (JRW, unpubl. data)
   130 on 24 May 2003, Black Bayou WMA (MIG 74:86)
   127 on 2 Jun 1996, Tipton Co. (JRW, unpubl. data)
   88 on 13 Jun 1988, Lauderdale Co. (MIG 59:123)
   86 on 2 Jun 1991, Hwy 79W, Dyer Co. (MIG 63:20)
Substantiation: Specimen: LSUMZ, 9535

Bald Eagle, *Haliaeetus leucocephalus*
Status and Abundance: Uncommon (locally fairly common) year round
Habitat: Larger lakes and rivers
Comments: Populations have increased dramatically since the mid-1980s. In 2013, there were approximately 175 known nesting pairs across the state (SGS, pers. comm.). Hacking of immature Bald Eagles began in 1980 with a collaboration of numerous partners including Tennessee Wildlife Resources Agency and the American Eagle Foundation. Through 2013, 353 immature Bald Eagles were hacked in Tennessee.
High Counts – Winter
   297 (175 ad, 122 imm) on 5 Feb 1987, Reelfoot Lake (MIG 58:53)
   242 (132 ad, 110 imm) on 17 Dec 1994, Reelfoot Lake CBC (MIG 66:13)
Substantiation: Specimen: TWRA office, Nashville

Northern Harrier, *Circus cyaneus*
Status and Abundance: Uncommon transient and winter resident, very rare summer resident
Habitat: Large weedy fields, often associated with wetlands, open marshes, also harvested agriculture fields
Spring Departure: early May
Fall Arrival: late Aug
Comments: There is one confirmed (but unsuccessful) nesting attempt from Ft. Campbell 15 May 2002 (MIG 73(1):187). An adult male and female there 27-29 Jun 1998 (MIG 69(4):187) and another adult male and female seen at Bark Camp Barrens WMA, Coffee Co. in May and June 2006 (SGS, pers. obs.) are suspected nesting birds, but nests were not located. There are several records from June and July of possibly late transients or nonbreeding birds.
Late Spring
   31 May 2006, Bark Camp Barrens WMA (MIG 77:100)
   30 May 1999, Hardeman Co. (MIG 70:97)

29 May 1975, Hatchie NWR (MIG 46:87)
21 May 1986, Putnam Co. (MIG 57:78)

Early Fall
3 Aug 1969, Ashland City Marsh (MIG 40:89)
13 Aug 1985, Elizabethton (MIG 57:35)
13 Aug 2002, Shelby Farms (MIG 74:16)
17 Aug 1997, Shady Valley (MIG 69:49)
17 Aug 2008, Putnam Co. (MIG 80:25)

High Counts – Spring
24 on 9 Mar 1986, Humphreys Co. (MIG 57:78)

High Counts – Fall
6 on 30 Sep 2006, Elizabethton FBC (MIG 78:26)

Summer Records
2 (1 ad f, 1 ad m) on 6 Jul 2008, Dyer/Lake Co. line (MIG 80:124)
2 (1 ad f, 1 ad m) on 27-29 Jun 1998, Ft. Campbell (MIG 69(4):187)
1 on 28 Jul 1996, Carroll Co. (MIG 67:77)

High Counts – Winter
34 on 24 Feb 2004, Ft. Campbell, Montgomery Co. (DM, pers. comm.)
32 on 4 Jan 2003, Savannah CBC (MIG 74:41)
30 on 14 Dec 2002, Reelfoot Lake CBC (MIG 74:41)
29 on 21 Dec 1996, Memphis CBC (MIG 68:20)
26 on 30 Dec 2009, Savannah CBC (MIG 81:93)

Substantiation: Specimen: LSUMZ, 75703

Sharp-shinned Hawk, *Accipiter striatus*

Status and Abundance: Uncommon transient and winter resident; uncommon summer resident in Cumberland Plateau, Ridge and Valley, Southern Blue Ridge; rare summer resident Mississippi Alluvial Valley, Southeastern Coastal Plain, Central Hardwoods

Habitat: Forest and forest edge, including suburban areas

Spring Departure: mid May

Fall Arrival: early Sep

Comments: Summer records are primarily in upper east Tennessee where they are rare breeding birds. Occasionally found across middle and west Tennessee during summer.

Late Spring
29 May 1989, Rutherford Co. (MIG 60:85)
28 May 2001, Dyersburg (MIG 72:92)
28 May 2005, Ensley (MIG 76:95)

Early Fall
9 Aug 2003, Dyer Co. (MIG 75:23)
25 Aug 2000, Shelby Co. (MIG 73:10)

High Counts – Spring
> 5 on 9 May 1992, Chattanooga SBC (MIG 63:47)
> 4 on 21 Apr 1990, Greeneville SBC (MIG 61:50)

High Counts – Fall
> 77 on 12 Oct 1997, Soddy Mtn. (MIG 69:45)
> 67 on 15 Oct 1977, Kyle's Ford Fire Tower, Hawkins Co. (MIG 49:50)
> 46 on 20 Oct 1996, Soddy Mtn. (MIG 68:28)

High Counts – Winter
> 14 on 20 Dec 1997, Chattanooga CBC (MIG 69:21)
> 9 on 1 Jan 1998, Hickory-Priest CBC (MIG 69:20)
> 8 on 2 Jan 2005, Knoxville CBC (MIG 76:65)
> 7 on 18 Dec 1988, Memphis CBC (MIG 60:60)
> 7 on 3 Jan 2004, Fayette Co. CBC (MIG 75:58)

Substantiation: Specimen: LSUMZ, 75683

Cooper's Hawk, *Accipiter cooperii*

Status and Abundance: Fairly common transient and winter resident, uncommon summer resident

Habitat: Forest and forest edge, including suburban areas

Comments: Breeds locally across the state. This species has increased both as a winter and summer resident during the last 20+ years. An apparent hybrid Northern Goshawk x Cooper's Hawk was banded on 5 Nov 2008 on Little Bald Mtn., Unicoi Co. (NAB 64(3):524).

High Counts – Spring
> 13 on 26 Apr 1981, Knoxville SBC (MIG 52:64)

High Counts – Fall
> 12 on 3 Oct 2009, Nashville FBC (MIG 81:42)
> 11 on 25 Sep 1977, Kyle's Ford Fire Tower, Hawkins Co. (MIG 49:50)

High Counts – Winter
> 15 on 2 Jan 2005, Knoxville CBC (MIG 76:65)
> 14 on 16 Dec 2006, Nashville CBC (MIG 78:65)
> 12 on 4 Jan 2003, Knoxville CBC (MIG 74:41)

Substantiation: Specimen: LSUMZ, 75689

Northern Goshawk, *Accipiter gentilis*

Status and Abundance: Rare winter visitor and transient and very rare summer visitor in Southern Blue Ridge; very rare elsewhere

Habitat: Forest and forest edge

Spring Departure: late Mar

Fall Arrival: mid Oct

Comments: Almost all records are of single birds, rarely are individuals relocated. One bird overwintered from 4 Oct 1975 to 24 Apr 1976,

Roan Creek (MIG 47:79). Observers should take care to document all sightings; few reports have been adequately documented, and separation from Cooper's Hawk and imm Red-shouldered Hawk can be tricky. An apparent hybrid Northern Goshawk x Cooper's Hawk was banded on 5 Nov 2008 on Little Bald Mtn., Unicoi Co. (NAB 64(3):524).

Late Spring
    1 May 1994, Roan Mtn. (MIG 65:32)
    1 Apr 2006, Kyker Bottoms Refuge (MIG 77:103)

Early Fall
    13 Aug 1981, Roan Mtn. (MIG 53:22)
    15 Aug 1988, Roan Mtn. (MIG 60:35)
    27 Aug 1991, S. Holston Lake (MIG 63:57)
    2 Sep 1988, Bristol (MIG 60:35)
    7 Sep 2002, Roan Mtn. (MIG 74:26)

High Counts – Fall
    2 on 26 Sep 2009, Ripshin Lake (MIG 81:58)

Summer Records
    1 on 1 Jun 1991, Roan Mtn. (MIG 81:4, Knight 2008)
    1 on 18 Jun 1971, Indian Gap, GSMNP (MIG 42:72)

Substantiation: Specimen: LSUMZ, 75681

Red-shouldered Hawk, *Buteo lineatus*

Status and Abundance: Uncommon permanent resident
Habitat: Forests and forest edge, primarily lowland deciduous forests near wetlands

High Counts – Spring
    25 on 9 May 1992, Chattanooga SBC (MIG 63:47)
    21 on 8 May 1999, Hamilton Co. SBC (MIG 70:37)
    18 on 10 May 1997, Chattanooga SBC (MIG 68:57)
    16 on 12 May 2007, Putnam Co. NAMC (MIG 78:127)
    16 on 12 May 2007, Shelby Co. NAMC (MIG 78:127)

High Counts – Fall
    27 on 18 Oct 2010, White Co. FBC (MIG 81:143)
    19 on 16 Sep 2006, Putnam Co. FBC (MIG 78:19)
    14 on 17 Sep 2005, Shelby Co. FBC (MIG 77:16)

High Counts – Winter
    27 on 1 Jan 1999, Hiwassee CBC (MIG 70:13)
    27 on 18 Dec 2010, Cookeville CBC (MIG 82:49)
    27 on 4 Jan 2003, Savannah CBC (MIG 74:41)
    24 on 1 Jan 2000, Hiwassee CBC (MIG 71:17)
    23 on 20 Dec 1997, Chattanooga CBC (MIG 69:21)

Substantiation: Specimen: LSUMZ, 75693

Broad-winged Hawk, *Buteo platypterus*
Status and Abundance: Fairly common transient, uncommon summer resident, accidental winter visitor
Habitat: Forest and forest edge
Spring Arrival: late Mar
Fall Departure: mid Oct
Comments: Six winter records, but only two records (Nashville CBC in 1984 and Johnson Co. in 1935-36) have adequate documentation.
Early Spring
    1 Mar 1967, Waconda Bay, Hamilton Co. (MIG 38:50)
    3 Mar 1969, Savannah (MIG 40:44)
    12 Mar 1961, Nashville (MIG 32:5)
    12 Mar 1973, Hiwassee River Area (MIG 44:25)
Late Fall
    24 Nov 1987, Union Co. (MIG 59:40)
    10 Nov 1986, Shelby Co. (MIG 58:19)
    7 Nov 2004, Britton Ford (JRW, unpubl. data)
High Counts – Spring
    340 on 14 Apr 2002, Soddy Mtn. (MIG 73:61)
    245 on 16 Apr 2004, Soddy Mtn. (MIG 75:116)
    115 on 14 Apr 2003, Soddy Mtn. (MIG 74:92)
High Counts – Fall
    7,630 on 25 Sep 2011, Big Bald Mtn. (MH, pers. comm.)
    4,985 on 25 Sep 1960, Elder Mtn., Hamilton Co. (MIG 32:27)
    4,246 on 25 Sep 1970, near Fall Creek Falls SP (MIG 42:3)
    3,992 on 27 Sep 2009, Soddy Mtn. (MIG 81:55)
High Counts – Winter
    1 on 1 Dec 1935-mid-Jan 1936, Cox's Lake, Johnson Co. (Tyler and Lyle 1936)
    1 on 30 Dec 1958, Reelfoot Lake CBC (MIG 31:16)
    1 on 22 Dec 1984, Nashville CBC (MIG 56:51)
    1 on 20 Dec 1991, Millington, Shelby Co. (MIG 63:60)
    1 on 20 Dec 1997, Chattanooga CBC (MIG 69:21)
    1 on 1 Jan 2001, Hiwassee CBC (MIG 72:72)
Substantiation: Specimen: LSUMZ, 75698

Swainson's Hawk, *Buteo swainsoni*
Status and Abundance: Very rare transient
Habitat: Open areas

Records
- (1) 1 on 27 Sep 1980, Chilhowee Mtn. (Stedman and Stedman 1981)
- (2) 1 on 4 Nov 1990, Pace Point (JRW, unpubl. data)
- (3) 1 on 27 Apr 1996, Ensley (JRW, unpubl. data)
- (4) 1 on 3 May 1997, Ensley (JRW, unpubl. data)
- (5) 1 light morph on 11 Apr 1998, Soddy Mtn. (MIG 69:166)
- (6) 1 on 25 Apr 1998, Airpark Inn, Reelfoot Lake, Lake Co. (MIG 69:161)
- (7) 1 on 6 Oct 2000, Dyer Co. (MIG 73:7)
- (8) 1 ad on 22 Sep 2001, White Lake Refuge (JRW, unpubl. data)
- (9) 1 imm on 25 Apr 2009, Ensley (MIG 80:87)
- (10) 1 ad on 24 Apr 2010, Eagle Lake Refuge (MIG 81:114)
- (11) 1 on 27 Sep 2010, Trezevant, Hwy 79, Carroll Co. (MIG 81:154)

Substantiation: Photograph: 1 imm on 25 Apr 2009, Ensley (NAB 63(3):442)

Red-tailed Hawk, *Buteo jamaicensis*

Subspecies: *borealis*

Status and Abundance: Fairly common permanent resident

Habitat: Open fields and forest edges, including urban and suburban areas

Comments: Western Red-tailed Hawk (*B. j. calurus*) is a rare winter resident in the Mississippi Alluvial Valley and an accidental rare winter visitor elsewhere (see, e.g., Somershoe, S.G. 2013. "Western Red-tailed Hawk". <http://www.pbase.com/shoeman/image/149126629> Accessed 25 Sep 2014).

Krider's Hawk (*B. j. krideri*) is a rare winter resident in the Mississippi Alluvial Valley and an accidental winter visitor elsewhere (see, e.g., Somershoe, S.G. 2011. "Krider's Red-tailed Hawk" <http://www.pbase.com/shoeman/image/157564030> Accessed 25 Sep 2014.).

Harlan's Hawk (*B. j. harlani*) is a rare winter resident in the Mississippi Alluvial Valley and an accidental winter visitor elsewhere (see, e.g., Somershoe, S.G. 2014. "Harlan's Red-tailed Hawk". <http://www.pbase.com/shoeman/image/153797107> Accessed 25 Sep 2014.).

High Counts – Spring
- 40 on 8 May 1999, Hamilton Co. SBC (MIG 70:37)
- 39 on 12 May 2007, Montgomery Co. NAMC (MIG 78:127)
- 29 on 10 May 1997, Chattanooga SBC. (MIG 68:57)

High Counts – Fall
  69 on 15 Nov 1994, Soddy Mtn. (MIG 66:24)
  63 on 22 Nov 1996, Soddy Mtn. (MIG 68:28)
  45 on 14 Nov 1979, Chickamauga Lake dam (MIG 51:82)
High Counts – Winter
  86 on 18 Dec 1999, Reelfoot Lake CBC (MIG 71:16)
  85 on 20 Dec 1998, Memphis CBC (MIG 70: 13)
  84 on 21 Dec 1996, Memphis CBC (MIG 68:20)
  81 on 20 Dec 1997, Chattanooga CBC (MIG 69:21)
  79 on 19 Dec 1999, Memphis CBC (MIG 71:16)
Substantiation: Specimen: LSUMZ, 75691

Rough-legged Hawk, *Buteo lagopus*

Status and Abundance: Rare winter resident and late fall and early spring transient
Habitat: Large open fields
Spring Departure: late Mar
Fall Arrival: mid Nov
Comments: More common during winters with more severe weather. Light morph is more commonly detected. The authors are not aware of any documentation of the three early fall records; all are extraordinarily early.
Late Spring
  7 May 1994, Montgomery Co. SBC (MIG 65:32)
  29 Apr 1956, Greeneville SBC (MIG 27:32)
  25 Apr 1998, Greeneville NAMC (MIG 69:149)
  21 Apr 2001, Lake Co. (MIG 72:92)
Early Fall
  24 Sep 1957, Joelton, Davidson Co. (BNA:20)
  26 Sep 1975, Rockwood, Roane Co. (MIG 47:26)
  6 Oct 1985, Shelby Co. (MIG 57:22)
High Counts – Spring
  4 (1 dark, 3 light) on 9 Apr 1989, Ft. Campbell, Montgomery Co. (MIG 60:85)
High Counts – Winter
  5 on 15 Jan 1983, Ft. Campbell, Montgomery Co. (MIG 54:44)
Substantiation: Photograph: 1 on 17 Feb 1979, Piney Flats, Sullivan Co. (Knight 2008:43)

Ferruginous Hawk, *Buteo regalis*

Status and Abundance: Accidental winter visitor
Comments: All birds have been light morph.

Records
(1) 1 on 22 Nov 2010, Jolly's Landing, Lake Co. (MAG, pers. comm.)
(2) 1 on 9-10 Nov 2012, Bogota WMA (MIG 83:147)
(3) 1 on 27 Jan 2014, Pea Ridge Road, Lake Co. (MAG, pers. comm.)
Substantiation: Photograph: Wilson, J.R. 2012. "Ferruginous Hawk". <http://www.pbase.com/ol_coot/image/147619737> Accessed 25 Sep 2014.

Golden Eagle, *Aquila chrysaetos*

Status and Abundance: Irregular transient; irregular (locally uncommon) winter resident

Habitat: Large tracts of mature forest; forest interspersed with patches of open fields or near wetlands

Spring Departure: early Mar

Fall Arrival: mid Nov

Comments: Although there is anecdotal evidence of nesting in the state in late 1800s and in the 1930s and 1940s, the authors are skeptical that this species historically bred in Tennessee. Notwithstanding the scant historical breeding evidence, Tennessee Wildlife Resources Agency and American Eagle Foundation hacked 47 immature Golden Eagles from 1995-2006. One pair that nested near Cordell Hull Lake (1993, 94, 96, 2000, 2001, 2007, 2012) was likely the progeny of a pair of hacked birds; one of the adults was confirmed as a hacked bird from Georgia. Evidence of apparent nesting along Caney Fork River in Smith Co. in 2007 with two adults and one immature bird photographed and recorded on video in late Sep 2007. There are occasional, undocumented summer reports. Robinson (1990) summarizes at least nine summer records from 1924 through 1986. Recent research has documented wintering Golden Eagles from the escarpment of the Cumberland Plateau to the highest elevations of the Southern Blue Ridge, with multiple individuals appearing on study sites simultaneously. At least 15 different individuals were present on Bear Hollow Mountain WMA, Franklin Co. in Jan-Mar 2014 (SGS, pers. comm.).

Late Spring
20 May 2010, Shelby Co. (MIG 81:114)
29 Apr 1971, Rutherford Co. (DeVore 1975)
24 Apr 2004, Greeneville SBC (MIG 75:104)
17 Apr 1955, Bristol SBC (MIG 26:28)

Early Fall
28 Aug 1996, Hawkins Co. (MIG 68:28)
6 Sep 1964, Greene Co. (MIG 35:104)

13 Sep 1996, Soddy Mtn. (MIG 68:28)
24 Sep 2009, Steele Creek Park (MIG 81:55)
2 Oct 1969, Rutherford Co. (DeVore 1975)
High Counts – Winter
7 on 3 Jan 1954, Tennessee NWR (MIG 24:77)
4 on 27 Dec 1968, Reelfoot Lake CBC (*fide* MAG)
Substantiation: Specimen: LSUMZ, 75702

Rallidae: Rails, Gallinues, and Coots.
Nine species have been found in Tennessee. Three species formerly bred in the state and are currently rare to accidental, while three other species are accidental. All species except American Coot are dependent on marshes, a habitat which is now severely limited in Tennessee.

Yellow Rail, *Coturnicops noveboracensis*
Status and Abundance: Accidental spring transient and summer visitor; very rare fall transient

Habitat: Wet or dry grassy fields, especially rice fields

Fall Arrival: late Sep

Fall Departure: mid Oct

Comments: This species likely occurs annually but is difficult to detect due to its secretive nature. If you have the good fortune to find a rice field harvest in progress in late Sep or early Oct, watch closely for this species and other rails and marsh birds flushed in front of the harvester. The majority of records are in late Sep through mid Oct. Half of records are window kills (Robinson 1990). One winter record. One record in upper east Tennessee at Round Bald on Roan Mtn. on 4 Oct 2002 (Knight 2008).

Late Fall
  19 Oct 2011, Duck River Unit (MIG 82:152)

Spring Records
  1 on 13 Apr 2002, Standifer Gap Marsh (MIG 73:61)

High Counts – Fall
  2 on 25 Sep 1999, Hwy 78, Lake Co. (JRW, unpubl. data)

Summer Records
  1 on 8 Jun 1996, Black Bayou WMA (JRW, unpubl. data)

Winter Records
  1 on 8 Dec 1953, Pickett Co. (Hassler 1984)

Substantiation: Specimen: LSUMZ, 75734

Black Rail, *Laterallus jamaicensis*
Status and Abundance: **Unsubstantiated**; very rare transient

Habitat: Found in wet, grassy fields, including rice fields

Comments: The 1915 individual was purportedly collected and mounted (Walker 1935) but the current location of the specimen is unknown. Most records are from east Tennessee. A pair was documented nesting at Roaring Fork in western Greene Co. in 1964 (Nevius 1964).

Records
  (1) 1 between 10 and 20 Jun 1915, near Del Rio, Cocke Co. (Walker

1935)
(2) 7 (2 ad, 5 young) during spring 1964, Bluff Mtn., Greene Co. (Nevius 1964)
(3) 1 on 27 Apr 1980, Knoxville SBC (MIG 51:55)
(4) 1 on 5 May 1980, Jefferson Co. (MIG 51:62)
(5) 1 on 1 May 1983, Knoxville SBC (MIG 54:51)
(6) 1 on 11 May 2002, Standifer Gap Marsh (MIG 73:61)
(7) 1 on 21 Sep 2002, Standifer Gap Marsh (MIG 74:22)
(8) 1 on 14 Oct 2002, Lake Co. (MIG 74:16)

Clapper Rail, *Rallus longirostris*
Status and Abundance: Accidental visitor
Records
(1) 1 on 9 Apr 1986 of an injured bird that was captured, banded, and released on 17 Apr 1986 in Elizabethton (MIG 57:87)
(2) 1 on 23 Sep 2005, Chattanooga, found injured and died (MIG 76:29, Edwards 2012)
Substantiation: Specimen: UTK 148

King Rail, *Rallus elegans*
Status and Abundance: Rare transient and summer resident; very rare winter visitor
Habitat: Marshes with dense vegetation and some shallow open water
Spring Arrival: early Apr
Fall Departure: early Oct
Comments: Few records in last 10-15 yrs. Most recent records are from the Duck River Unit of Tennessee NWR where nesting was documented in 2008 and 2009 with several pairs present.
Early Spring
   1 Mar 1961, Bristol (MIG 32:10)
   29 Mar 1956, Buena Vista Marsh (BNA:21)
Late Fall
   26 Nov 1992, Amnicola Marsh (MIG 64:20)
   17 Nov 1976, Alcoa Marsh (MIG 48:49)
   3 Nov 1942, Nashville (MIG 13:71)
   30 Oct 1975, Alcoa Marsh (MIG 47:21)
High Counts – Spring
   12 on 20 May 2000, Black Bayou WMA (MIG 71:87)
   4 on 13 May 2000, Lake Co. NAMC (MIG 71:50)
High Counts – Summer
   19 (2 ad, 17 downy young) on 14 Jul 1996, Dyer Co. (JRW, unpubl. data)

15 (11 ad, 4 young) on 2 Jul 1995, Reelfoot NWR, Obion Co. (JRW, unpubl. data)
12 on 5 Jun 1999, Lake Co. (JRW, unpubl. data)

Winter Records
1 on 24 Dec 1940, Knox. Co. (MIG 12:18)
1 on 2 Jan 1943, near Nashville (MIG 13:71)
1 on 4 Dec 1952, Nashville (BNA:21)
1 on 24 Dec 1971, Dresden (MAG *fide* DaP)
1 on Nov 1974-Mar 1975, Alcoa Marsh (MIG 46:46)
3/1 on 16/17 Jan 1999, Black Bayou WMA (MIG 70:68, JRW, unpubl. data)

Substantiation: Specimen: LSUMZ, 75721

Virginia Rail, *Rallus limicola*

Status and Abundance: Uncommon transient; locally uncommon summer resident; rare (locally uncommon) winter resident

Habitat: Marshes and vegetated edges of lakes and ponds

Spring Arrival: late Apr

Fall Departure: mid Oct

Comments: Some Virginia Rails overwinter in various places in the state, sometimes in moderate numbers (up to 13 birds, see below). Sightings occur year round at a few locations and the winter records make identification of arrival and departure dates difficult. Virginia Rails have been known to nest in recent years at Standifer Gap Marsh (Hamilton Co.), Shady Valley (Johnson Co.), and Heritage Marsh (White Co.) (MIG 75:160). Also recently found year round at Meadowview Marsh, Kingsport (Sullivan Co.). Early spring records could be overwintering birds.

Early Spring
13 Mar 1987, Sullivan Co. (MIG 58:102)
18 Mar 1978, Buena Vista Marsh (MIG 49:67)

Late Fall
21 Nov 2009, Fentress Co. (MIG 81:51)
16 Nov 1986, Monroe Co. (MIG 58:13)
26 Oct 1966, Nashville (Laskey 1966)

High Counts – Spring
11 on 10 May 2003, Hamilton Co. NAMC (MIG 74:114)
8 on 14 May 2005, Hamilton Co. NAMC (MIG 76:126)

High Counts – Fall
5 on 11 Sep 1993, Gallatin Steam Plant (MIG 65:23)

High Counts – Winter
13 on 16 Dec 2006, Standifer Gap Marsh (MIG 78:82))

13 on 17 Dec 2005, Chattanooga CBC (MIG 77:42)
8 on 18 Dec 2004, Chattanooga CBC (MIG 76:64)
8 on 23 Dec 1974, Alcoa Marsh (MIG 46:46)
Substantiation: Specimen: LSUMZ, 75723

Sora, *Porzana carolina*

Status and Abundance: Uncommon transient; rare summer and winter resident

Habitat: Marshes and vegetated edges of lakes and ponds

Spring Arrival: late Mar

Spring Departure: mid May

Fall Arrival: early Sep

Fall Departure: mid Nov

Comments: There are a few summer records, including individuals heard at dawn 21 Jun 2006 in McNairy Co. (Applegate 2006). One was documented nesting in 1990 at Ensley (MIG 61:70). Birds are very difficult to detect during summer. There are over 20 winter records, which may be lingering migrants; however some may overwinter if habitat remains suitable.

Early Spring
   6 Mar 1951, near Bristol (MIG 22:19)
   12 Mar 2000, Shelby Farms (MIG 71:87)
   13 Mar 1987, Hardin Co. (MIG 58:92)
   18 Mar 1990, Macedonia Bottoms, Gibson Co. (MAG, pers. comm.)
   23 Mar 1985, Maury Co. (MIG 56:76)

Late Spring
   30 May 1986, Shelby Co. (MIG 57:74)
   27 May 1985, Lawrence Co. (MIG 56:76)

Early Fall
   2 Aug 1961, Goose Pond, Grundy Co. (MIG 32:43)
   20 Aug 1964, Knoxville (MIG 35:63)
   21 Aug 1978, Shelby Co. (MIG 50:19)

Late Fall
   16 Nov 1986, J. Percy Priest Lake (MIG 58:23)
   15 Nov 1999, Kingston Steam Plant (MIG 71:36)
   11 Nov 1971, Buena Vista Marsh (MIG 43:25)

High Counts – Spring
   37 on 6 May 1988, Stewart Co. (Robinson 1990)
   20+ on 15 May 2011, Ensley (MIG 82:84)
   10 on 21 Apr 1996, Brainerd Levee (MIG 67:63)
   9 on 10 May 1997, Chattanooga SBC (MIG 68:57)
   9 on 27-28 Apr 1990, Columbia SBC (MIG 61:50)

High Counts – Fall
 55 on 25 Sep 1999, Lake Co. (JRW, unpubl. data)
 50+ on 13 Sep 2011, Duck River Unit (MIG 82:152)
 50+ on 18 Sep 2000, Hwy 78 rice fields, Lake Co. (MIG 72:38)
 43 on 18 Oct 2002, Lake Co. (MIG 74:16)
 30 on 14 Oct 2002, Hwy 78 rice fields, Lake Co. (JRW, unpubl. data)
Summer Records
 1 on 21 Jun 1956, Greene Co. (MIG 27:52)
 1 on 22 Jul 1972, Tennessee NWR (MIG 43:75)
 1 on 23 Jul 1972, Buena Vista Marsh (MIG 43:76)
 3-4 in late May-8 Jun 2006, Shady Valley (MIG 77:148)
Substantiation: Specimen: LSUMZ, 75731

Purple Gallinule, *Porphyrio martinicus*
Status and Abundance: Rare spring and very rare fall transient, very rare summer resident
Habitat: Marshes and other wetlands with thick floating aquatic vegetation
Spring Arrival: early May
Spring Departure: early Jun
Comments: Most sightings from late Apr through mid-Jun. Scattered records after July. Nested at Reelfoot Lake as recently as 1984 (Pitts 1985).
Early Spring
 16 Mar 1936, Coffee Co. (MIG 7:47)
 7 Apr 1983, Memphis (MIG 54:59)
 10 Apr 2005, Standifer Gap Marsh (MIG 76:101)
 29 Apr 1991, Dyer Co. (GC *fide* MAG)
Fall Records
 10 Nov 1923, Radnor Lake (BNA:21)
 12 Oct 1958, Knox Co. (MIG 30:9)
 5 Oct 1975, Nashville (MIG 47:18)
 10 Sep 1981, Hiwassee River Area (MIG 53:19)
Substantiation: Specimen: LSUMZ, 75736

Common Gallinule, *Gallinula galeata*
Status and Abundance: Irregular transient, rare summer resident, accidental winter visitor
Habitat: Marshes and other wetlands with dense growth of emergent vegetation
Spring Arrival: late Apr
Fall Departure: late Sep

Comments: Although rare during summer, there are several nesting records, including in Cheatham Co. in 1993 (MIG 64:86). Formerly common during summer at Reelfoot Lake as late as the 1990s.

Early Spring
    19 Mar 1956, Memphis (MIG 27:17)
    7 Apr 1988, Nashville (Robinson 1990)
    8 Apr 1969, Reelfoot NWR (USFWS unpubl. data)
    14 Apr 1973, Erwin Fish Hatchery (MIG 44:52)

Late Fall
    21 Oct 1937, Reelfoot Lake (Wetmore 1939)
    27 Oct 1984, Maury Co. (MIG 56:20)
    2 Nov 1982, Hiwassee River Area (MIG 54:24)
    20 Nov 2009, John Sevier Lake (MIG 81:55)

High Counts – Spring
    30 on 30 May 1932, Reelfoot Lake (Ganier 1933b)
    8 on 13 May 2000, Sumner Co. NAMC (MIG 71:53)

High Counts – Fall
    11 on 26 Aug 1994, Reelfoot NWR, Obion Co. (JRW, unpubl. data)

High Counts – Summer
    22 on 22 Jul 1995, Reelfoot NWR, Obion Co. (JRW, unpubl. data)

Winter Records
    1 on 26 Dec 1949, Reelfoot Lake CBC (MIG 20:61)

Substantiation: Specimen: LSUMZ, 75738

American Coot, *Fulica americana*

Status and Abundance: Fairly common transient; common winter resident, rare (locally uncommon) summer resident

Habitat: Marshes, lakes, ponds

Comments: There are records for every month of the year, including several documented nesting records. Nesting was documented at Old Hickory Lake in 1984 (MIG 55:91), in Hamilton Co. in 1971 (MIG 42:46), at Camden in Benton Co. in 1971 (Robinson 1990), and in Sullivan Co. in 2012 (RLK, pers. comm.). There are historical records of nesting at Reelfoot Lake before 1930 (Rhoads 1895, Ganier 1933b).

High Counts – Spring
    5,000 on 8 May 1996, Black Bayou WMA (MIG 67:59)
    3,806 on 5 Mar 2008, Big Sandy Unit (RW, pers. comm.)
    2,775 on 5 Mar 2008, Duck River Unit (RW, pers. comm.)

High Counts – Fall
    42,428 on 6 Nov 2009, Duck River Unit (RW, pers. comm.)
    37,400 on 10 Nov 1999, Duck River Unit (RW, pers. comm.)
    36,520 on 16 Nov 2007, Duck River Unit (RW, pers. comm.)

21,450 on 25 Oct 2001, Duck River Unit (RW, pers. comm.)
20,350 on 3 Nov 2008, Duck River Unit (RW, pers. comm.)

High Counts – Winter
36,000 on 29 Dec 1965, Reelfoot Lake CBC (MIG 36:88)
18,760 on 29 Dec 2001, Nickajack CBC (MIG 72:115)
18,660 on 27 Dec 2003, Nickajack CBC (MIG 75:59)
16,001 on 28 Dec 2002, Nickajack CBC (MIG 74:41)

Substantiation: Specimen: LSUMZ, 75739

Aramidae: Limpkins. One species is known from two records.

Limpkin, *Aramus guarauna*
> Status and Abundance: Accidental visitor
> Records
>> (1) 1 well described bird from Radnor Lake on 10-11 Jun 1961 (Morlan 1961)
>> (2) 1 on 27 Jul-18 Sep 1999, Hatchie NWR (MIG 71:31)
>
> Substantiation: Photograph: Wilson, J.R. 1999. "Limpkin". <http://www.pbase.com/ol_coot/image/28382772> Accessed 25 Sep 2014.

Gruidae: Cranes. Three species have been documented in Tennessee; one is uncommon to locally common statewide and two species are rare to accidental. All favor farmland for feeding and loafing and roost in shallow water wetlands.

Sandhill Crane, *Grus canadensis*
    Status and Abundance: Irregular (locally common) late fall transient and winter resident, irregular early spring transient, very rare summer resident
    Habitat: Rivers, lakes, mudflats; grain and wheat fields
    Spring Departure: mid Mar
    Fall Arrival: late Oct
    Comments: Population has increased greatly in the last 20 years. Abundant in the Hiwassee River area from Nov through Feb. A significant number of birds are now wintering on Hop-In Refuge (Obion Co.). Few summer records, but the first state record was of a bird shot near Chattanooga on 1 Jun 1935 (Butts 1936).
    Late Spring
        18 May 1986, Fort Pillow SP (MIG 57:74)
        16 May 1986, Hiwassee River Area (MIG 57:84)
        13 May 2006, Hamilton Co. (MIG 77:103)
        4 May 2002, Lauderdale Co. (MIG 73:56)
    Early Fall
        1 Aug 1965, near Chattanooga (DeVore 1966)
        20 Sep 2008, John Sevier Lake (MIG 80:28)
        21 Sep 1987, Memphis (MIG 59:23)
        21 Sep 1997, Anderson Co. (MIG 69:46)
        25 Sep 2006, Shady Valley (MIG 78:42)
    High Counts – Spring
        1,007 on 1 Mar 2000, Hop-in WMA (MIG 71:87)
    High Counts – Summer
        3 on 7 Jun-13 Jul 2011, Duck River Unit (MIG 82:120)
    High Counts – Winter
        15,761 on 1 Jan 2006, Hiwassee CBC (MIG 77:43)
        14,600 on 1 Jan 2005, Hiwassee CBC (MIG 76:65)
        13,951 on 1 Jan 2004, Hiwassee CBC (MIG 75:59)
    Substantiation: Specimen: CSM, F82-11

Hooded Crane, *Grus monacha*
    Status and Abundance: Accidental winter visitor
    Comments: This crane was surely one of the most visited birding rarities

in recent memory; records kept by several dedicated observers estimated that over 7,000 people visited from 47 states and 15 countries! A couple of weeks after it was last seen in Tennessee, what most likely was the same individual appeared in Indiana. While its provenance may never truly be known, the Nebraska Bird Records Committee, while in the process of voting on a Hooded Crane record from spring 2011 (possibly the same individual?), uncovered evidence indicating that it is unlikely to have been an escapee. Kevin Calhoon, a member of the TBRC, worked with NBRC chair Mark Brogie to research information on captive Hooded Cranes in North America. All known captive individuals have been accounted for, save for four individuals that escaped from a private facility in Idaho; all are believed to have been pinioned, and therefore flightless. Experts at the International Crane Foundation, and the studbook keeper for the species, have expressed strong opinions that these Hooded Crane records are of wild birds (KAC, pers. comm.), and the TBRC agreed. In late 2014, the American Birding Association Checklist Committee voted against adding the species to the official list of birds of North America due to concerns about provenance (Pranty et al. 2014). The authors disagree with that decision and believe that the preponderance of the evidence indicates that this record most likely involves a wild individual.

Records

(1) 1 on 13 Dec 2011-30 Jan 2012, Hiwassee Refuge, Meigs Co. (Murray 2012)

Substantiation: Photograph: Kuehnel, J.W. 2012. "Hooded Crane" <http://www.tnbirds.org/TBRC/TBRC_actions.html> Accessed 26 Jun 2015.

Whooping Crane, *Grus americana*

Status and Abundance: Very rare to locally uncommon (Hiwassee Refuge and vicinity) winter resident; accidental elsewhere

Habitat: Rivers, lakes, mudflats; grain fields

Spring Departure: late Feb

Fall Arrival: mid Nov

Comments: All birds seen in Tennessee during the last decade or so are part of an experimental population and not yet countable on ABA bird lists. Often associates with Sandhill Cranes. The primary winter location is Hiwassee River area, but the migration route is now taking immatures through Carroll Co., and individuals from this population have wandered widely, including individuals that wintered in Lawrence and Davidson counties.

Substantiation: Photograph: Somershoe, S.G. 2007. "Whooping Crane" <http://www.pbase.com/shoeman/image/157564338> Accessed 25 Sep 2014.

Recurvirostridae: Stilts and Avocets. Two species occur regularly and can be found nearly anywhere in the state where suitable shallow water habitat is present, although the stilt is rare outside of its breeding range in the Mississippi Alluvial Valley.

Black-necked Stilt, *Himantopus mexicanus*

Status and Abundance: Uncommon (common at Ensley) transient and summer resident in Mississippi Alluvial Valley; very rare elsewhere; accidental during winter

Habitat: Sandbars, mudflats, and muddy edges of lakes and ponds

Spring Arrival: mid Mar

Fall Departure: late Sep

Comments: Nesting occurs in several locations along the Mississippi River with a large colony at Ensley. Breeding numbers and range have increased steadily over past 25 years. First state record on 21 Mar 1981 in Shelby Co. (MIG 52:71).

Early Spring
- 16 Mar 2003, Ensley (MIG 74:87)
- 18 Mar 2001, Eagle Lake WMA (MIG 72:92)
- 19 Mar 1989, Ensley (MIG 60:83)
- 20 Mar 2010, TVA Lakes (MIG 81:114)

Late Fall
- 6 Nov 1994, Ensley (JRW, unpubl. data)
- 24 Oct 2004, Blount Co. (MIG 76:34)
- 13 Oct 2004, Austin Springs (MIG 76:34)
- 8 Oct 2005, Gallatin Steam Plant (MIG 76:26)

High Counts – Spring
- 128 on 8 May 2011, Ensley (MIG 82:84)
- 90 on 10 May 2003, Shelby Co. NAMC (MIG 74:114)
- 86 on 8 May 2004, Shelby Co. NAMC (MIG 75:95)
- 60 on 12 May 2001, Lake Co. NAMC (MIG 72:16)

High Counts – Fall
- 134 on 8 Aug 1996 (JRW, unpubl. data)
- 52 on 15 Aug 1999, Eagle Lake WMA (MIG 71:31)
- 28 on 1 Sep 2002, Shelby Co. FBC (MIG 73:51)

High Counts – Summer
- 307 on 13 Jul 2002, Ensley (MIG 73:111)
- 233 on 4 Jul 2002, Ensley (JRW, unpubl. data)
- 192 on 2 Jun 2003, Lake and Dyer Co. (JRW, unpubl. data)
- 174 on 29 Jun 2002, Ensley (JRW, unpubl. data)
- 161 ad max in Jun 2011, Ensley (MIG 82:119)

High Counts – Winter
    1 on 24 Nov 2013-2 Jan 2014, Robertson Co. (TL, pers. comm.)
Substantiation: Photograph: 1 on 1 Aug 1985, Eagle Bend Fish Hatchery (MIG 57:19)

American Avocet, *Recurvirostra americana*

Status and Abundance: Irregular (uncommon Mississippi Alluvial Valley) spring transient, uncommon fall transient

Habitat: Sandbars, mudflats, and edges of lakes and ponds

Spring Arrival: mid Apr

Spring Departure: mid May

Fall Arrival: mid Aug

Fall Departure: late Oct

Comments: More frequently found during fall than spring. Late June records are likely early fall migrants.

Late Spring
    16 Jun 2008, Mud Lake, Lake Co. (MIG 80:124)
    14 Jun 2002, Greene Co. (MIG 73:113)
    3 Jun 2008, Dyer Co. (MIG 80:124)
    1 Jun 2011, Dyer Co. (MIG 82:119)
    29 May 2004, Ensley (MIG 75:111)

Early Fall
    6 Jul 1999, Mississippi River mile 771 (MIG 70:130)
    9 Jul 1987, Cross Creeks NWR (MIG 59:35)
    20 Jul 1981, Kingston Steam Plant (MIG 52:98)
    23 Jul 2002, Chickamauga Lake (MIG 73:113)

Late Fall
    22 Nov 1975, Johnson City (MIG 47:48)
    18 Nov 2009, Eagle Bend Fish Hatchery (MIG 81:55)
    14 Nov 2006, Pace Point (MIG 78:33)
    8 Nov 1996, Ensley (JRW, unpubl. data)
    7 Nov 1974, Tennessee NWR (MIG 46:44)

High Counts – Spring
    36 on 16 Apr 1982, Chickamauga Lake (MIG 53:68)
    36 on 27 Apr 2013, Steele Creek Park (RB, pers. comm.)
    29 on 28 Apr 2000, Old Hickory Lake (MIG 71:89)
    27 on 9 May 1984, Dyer Co. (MIG 55:67)

High Counts – Fall
    71 on 21 Oct 1994, Lake Co. (MIG 66:22)
    14 on 21 Oct 2001, Middlebrook Lake, Sullivan Co. (MIG 73:18)
    13 on 22 Aug-1 Sep 2007, Upper Douglas Lake (MIG 79:25)
    12 on 1-2 Sep 1985, Island 13 (JRW, unpubl. data)

10 on 15 Sep 2005, Celina, Clay Co. (MIG 77:26)
10 on 18 Sep 1997, Kingsport (MIG 69:46)
Summer Records
2 on 19 Jun 1977, Washington Co. (MIG 48:105)
1 on 28 Jun 1987, Polk Co. (MIG 58:147)
Winter Records
1 on 1-4 Dec 1998, White Lake WMA (MIG 70:68)
Substantiation: Photograph: Somershoe, S.G. 2011. "American Avocet". <http://www.pbase.com/shoeman/image/138053154> Accessed 15 Dec 2014.

Charadriidae: Lapwings and Plovers. Seven species of plover have occurred in Tennessee. One is a widespread resident breeding species, four are regular transients, and two are accidental. All species could occur nearly anywhere in the state where suitable shallow water habitat is present.

Black-bellied Plover, *Pluvialis squatarola*
    Status and Abundance: Uncommon transient
    Habitat: Sandbars, mudflats, and muddy edges of lakes and ponds
    Spring Arrival: late Apr
    Spring Departure: late May
    Fall Arrival: early Aug
    Fall Departure: mid Oct
    Comments: Late northbound migrants may linger into early June, while early southbound birds may occur in late June and early July.
    Early Spring
        15 Mar 1986, Lawrence Co. (MIG 57:78)
        2 Apr 1972, Jefferson Co. (MIG 43:53)
    Late Spring
        3 Jun 2007, Rankin Bottoms (MIG 78:142)
        1 Jun 2002, Dyer Co. (MIG 73:111)
        31 May 1980, Anderson Co. (MIG 51:94)
        31 May 2004, White Lake WMA (MIG 75:111)
        29 May 2007, Wal-Mart Distribution Center, Greene Co. (MIG 78:104)
    Early Fall
        18 Jul 1987, Kingston Steam Plant (MIG 58:145)
        26 Jul 2003, Ensley (JRW, unpubl. data)
    Late Fall
        15 Nov 1970, Kingston Steam Plant (MIG 42:21)
        18 Nov 2000, Pace Point (MIG 73:10)
        24 Nov 1984, Tennessee NWR (MIG 56:20)
        29 Nov 1992, Ensley (MIG 64:15)
        30 Nov 1987, Henry Co. (MIG 59:23)
    High Counts – Spring
        19 on 17 May 1980, Kingston Steam Plant (MIG 51:94)
        18 on 12 May 2001, Lake Co. NAMC (MIG 72:14)
        13 on 18 May 1997, Lake Co. (JRW, unpubl. data)
        13 on 8 May 2010, Lake Co. (MIG 81:114)
    High Counts – Fall
        17 on 8 Sep 2004, S. Holston Lake (MIG 76:38)
        up to 17 on 18 Sep-23 Oct 1982, Rankin Bottoms (MIG 54:25)

15 on 25 Sep 1990, Island 13 (MAG, pers. comm.)
11 on 17 Oct 1993, Ensley (JRW, unpubl. data)
6 on 12 Oct 2010, Big Sandy Unit (MIG 81:154)
Summer Records
1 on 10/15 Jun 1993, Dyer Co. (MIG 64:84)
1 on 22 Jun 1991, Great River Road, Lake Co. (MIG 63:20)
Winter Records
1-9 Dec 2000, Dyer Co. (MIG 72:68)
Substantiation: Photograph: Todd, M.C. 2010. "Black-bellied Plover". <http://www.pbase.com/mctodd/image/124481855> Accessed 25 Sep 2014.

American Golden-Plover, *Pluvialis dominica*

Status and Abundance: Uncommon spring and irregular fall transient
Habitat: Sandbars, mudflats, and muddy edges of lakes and ponds; during spring, often in plowed fields, sod farms, and similar open field habitats
Spring Arrival: mid Mar
Spring Departure: early May
Fall Arrival: early Aug
Fall Departure: early Nov
Comments: Mid-June records are possibly lingering northbound migrants that may not have completed migration. Similarly, early December records could possibly be late southband migrants. A vagrant Pacific Golden-Plover or even a European Golden-Plover is possible (and a possible Pacific has been reported at Ensley), so observers should familiarize themselves with the identification criteria.
Early Spring
27 Feb 1997, Shelby Farms (MIG 68:62)
28 Feb 1971, Tennessee NWR (MIG 42:43)
1 Mar 2001, Gibson Co. (MIG 72:92)
4 Mar 1955, Shelby Farms (MIG 26:46)
Late Spring
6 Jun 1991, Dyer Co. (MIG 63:20)
31 May 1988, Sumner Co. (Robinson 1990)
31 May 2003, Lake Co. (MIG 74:87)
Early Fall
29 Jun 2002, Ensley (JRW, unpubl. data)
30 Jun 1996, Island 13 (JRW, unpubl. data)
1 Jul 1996, Island 13 Road (MIG 67:77)
4 Jul 2002, Ensley (JRW, unpubl. data)
5 Jul 1975, Lake Co. (MIG 46:87)

Late Fall
: 28 Nov 1978, Shelby Co. (MIG 50:41)

High Counts – Spring
: 2,500 on 17 Mar 1996, Ensley (JRW, unpubl. data)
: 2,500 on 23 Apr 1989, Tennemo Levee, Dyer Co. (JRW, unpubl. data)
: 2,500 on 28 Mar 2011, Obion Co. (MIG 82:84)
: 1,750 on 5 Apr 2003, Hall's Airport, Lauderdale Co. (JRW, unpubl. data)
: 1,500 on 31 Mar 2011, Tipton Co. (MIG 82:84)
: 1,500 on 5 Apr 2003, Lauderdale Co. (MIG 74:87)
: 1,500 on 6 Apr 1996, Ensley (JRW, unpubl. data)

High Counts – Fall
: 22 on 10 Oct 2004, Ensley (MIG 76:27)
: 19 on 17 Sep 1994, Ensley (JRW, unpubl. data)
: 19 on 4 Oct 1990, Ensley (JRW, unpubl. data)
: 17 on 14 Sep 1996, Ensley (JRW, unpubl. data)
: 15 on 3 Oct 1991, Ensley (MIG 63:52)

Summer Records
: 2 on 16 Jun 2002, Mud Lake, Lake Co. (MIG 73:111)
: 2 on 19 Jun 2003, Black Bayou WMA (MIG 74:130)
: 1 on 21-22 Jun 1991, Great River Road, Lake Co. (MIG 63:20)
: 4/2 on 6-7 Jul 1991, Hwy 103 and Great River Rd, Dyer Co. (MIG 63:20)

Winter Records
: 2 Dec 1979, Savannah Bay (MIG 51:42)
: 4 Dec 1988, Tellico Lake, Monroe Co. (MIG 60:64)
: 9 Dec 1990, Ensley (MIG 62:80)
: 4 Dec 1995, Ensley (MIG 66:41)

Substantiation: Photograph: Somershoe, S.G. 2011. "American Golden Plover". <http://www.pbase.com/shoeman/image/137672737> Accessed 25 Sep 2014.

Snowy Plover, *Charadrius nivosus*

Status and Abundance: Accidental visitor

Records
: (1) 1 on 19-25 May 1977, Gallatin Steam Plant, Sumner Co. (Crawford and Crawford 1977)
: (2) 1 on 9-18 Sep 1985, Island 13 (MIG 57:22, Knight 1993)
: (3) 1 on 27 Mar 1992, near Lenox, Dyer Co. (Knight 1993)
: (4) 1 on 20-21 Aug 1994, Island 13 (MIG 66:20)

Substantiation: 1 on 19-25 May 1977, Gallatin Steam Plant (Crawford and Crawford 1977)

Charadriidae: Lapwings and Plovers

Wilson's Plover, *Charadrius wilsonia*
>Status and Abundance: **Unsubstantiated**
>Comments: Accepted by the TBRC on the basis of written documentation. The authors have not reviewed the documentation that was submitted to the TBRC but note that there are very few inland records of this species anywhere in the U.S. The published description (Waldron 1989a) lacks sufficient detail to evaluate the record. Two earlier sightings from the Chattanooga area lacked sufficient documentation.
>Records
>>(1) 1 on 17 Apr 1988, Ensley (Waldron 1989a, Knight 1993)

Semipalmated Plover, *Charadrius semipalmatus*
>Status and Abundance: Fairly common transient; accidental winter visitor
>Habitat: Sandbars, mudflats, and muddy edges of lakes and ponds
>Spring Arrival: mid Apr
>Spring Departure: late May
>Fall Arrival: late Jul
>Fall Departure: late Oct
>Early Spring
>>6 Mar 1978, Shelby Co. (MIG 49:65)
>>15 Mar 2003, Eagle Lake WMA (MIG 74:87)
>>1 Apr 1991, Shelby Farms (MIG 62:110)
>
>Late Spring
>>7 Jun 2004, White Lake WMA (MIG 75:158)
>>6 Jun 2010, Ensley (MIG 81:114)
>>5 Jun 2002, Lake Co. (MIG 73:111)
>>4 Jun 1996, Lake Co. (JRW, unpubl. data)
>>3 Jun 2000, Black Bayou Refuge (MAG, pers. comm.)
>
>Early Fall
>>4 Jul 2000, Greene Co. (MIG 71:121)
>>13 Jul 1997, Ensley (JRW, unpubl. data)
>>14 Jul 2002, Ensley (MIG 73:111)
>
>Late Fall
>>22 Nov 1987, Henry Co. (MIG 59:32)
>>6 Nov 2014, Gibson Co. Lake (MAG, pers. comm.)
>>5 Nov 1991, Ensley (JRW, unpubl. data)
>>1 Nov 1982, Gallatin Steam Plant (MIG 54:22)
>
>High Counts – Spring
>>217 on 9 May 2014, near Black Bayou Refuge (MAG, pers. comm.)
>>159 on 12 May 2001, Lake Co. NAMC (MIG 72:14)
>>114 on 15 May 1979, Gallatin Steam Plant (MIG 50:87)

Winter Records
    6 on 23 Dec 1971-1 Jan 1972, Cherokee Lake (MIG 43:27)
    2 on 21 Dec 1969, Knoxville CBC (MIG 41:8)
    1 on 1-11 Dec 2000, Everett Lake (MIG 72:68)
Substantiation: Specimen: LSUMZ, 8991

Piping Plover, *Charadrius melodus*
Status and Abundance: Very rare spring transient; uncommon summer and fall transient
Habitat: Sandbars, mudflats, and muddy edges of lakes and ponds
Fall Arrival: mid Jul
Fall Departure: mid Sep
Comments: Likely annual from mid-July through August on sandbars in the Mississippi River, but access and birder effort is very limited. All spring records are listed below.
Early Fall
    5 Jul 2000, Shelby Farms (MIG 71:118)
    12 Jul 1992, Island 13 (JRW, unpubl. data)
Late Fall
    15 Oct 1983, Gallatin Steam Plant (MIG 55:20)
    3 Oct 1977, Hiwassee Island, Meigs Co. (MIG 49:21)
    24 Sep 1991, Ensley (JRW, unpubl. data)
    17 Sep 1992, Island 13 (MIG 64:15)
Spring Records
    1 on 5 May 1935, Shelby Co. (Coffey 1935)
    1 on 9 Apr 1955, Nashville (Weise 1958)
    1 on 3 May 1973, Columbia SBC (MIG 44:45)
    1 on 28 Apr-6 May 1984, Columbia SBC (MIG 55:69)
    1 on 7 May 1984, Lake Co. (Robinson 1990)
    1 on 20 Apr 1993, Lake Co. (MIG 64:63)
    2 on 20 Apr 2011, Old Hickory Lake, Davidson Co. (MIG 82:86)
High Counts – Fall
    6 on 17 Aug 2002, Island 13 (MIG 74:16)
    4 on 23 Jul 1998, Ensley (MIG 69:186)
    2 on 12 Jul 1992, Island 13 (JRW, unpubl. data)
    2 on 7/13 Aug 1989, Island 13 (JRW, unpubl. data)
Substantiation: Photograph: 2 on 20 Apr 2011, Old Hickory Lake, Davidson Co. (NAB 65(3):48)

Killdeer, *Charadrius vociferus*
Status and Abundance: Common permanent resident
Habitat: Sandbars, mudflats, and muddy edges of lakes and ponds; lawns

and other short, grassy fields

Comments: Interesting late nesting of an adult seen incubating 3 eggs on 16 Nov 2008, Ensley (MIG 80:22).

High Counts – Spring
    300 on 13 Mar 2013, Eagleville (SGS, pers. obs.)
    105 on 26 Apr 1992, Knoxville SBC (MIG 63:47)

High Counts – Fall
    2,258 on 24 Aug 1997, Ensley (MIG 69:40)
    1,250 on 24 Sep 1995, Ensley (JRW, unpubl. data)
    1,200 on 1 Oct 1995, Ensley (JRW, unpubl. data)
    600 on 26 Aug 2002, Gibson Co. (MIG 74:16)
    480 on 30 Aug 2006, Rankin Bottoms (MIG 78:38)

High Counts – Summer
    250 on 26 Jul 2006, Upper Douglas Lake (MIG 78:142)

High Counts – Winter
    1,094 on 27 Dec 2003, Jackson CBC (MIG 75:59)
    995 on 20 Dec 2003, Reelfoot Lake CBC (MIG 75:59)
    823 on 18 Dec 2004, Reelfoot Lake CBC (MIG 76:65)
    811 on 30 Dec 1996, Savannah CBC (MIG 68:20)

Substantiation: Specimen: LSUMZ, 75744

Scolopacidae: Sandpipers, Phalaropes, and Allies.

Thirty-four species have been documented in Tennessee. Only one species is a resident breeder, while 24 species occur regularly as transients, and nine species are rare to accidental. All species could occur nearly anywhere in the state where suitable shallow water habitat is present. Several other species could potentially occur as vagrants.

Spotted Sandpiper, *Actitis macularius*

Status and Abundance: Fairly common transient, very rare summer and winter resident

Habitat: Sandbars, mudflats, and muddy edges of lakes and ponds; rocky shorelines

Spring Arrival: late Mar

Spring Departure: early Jun

Fall Arrival: mid Jul

Fall Departure: early Nov

Comments: Accidental breeder. One wintered for 7 consecutive years (2006-2012) on the S. Holston River in Kingsport.

Early Spring
- 9 Feb 1989, President's Island (JRW, unpubl. data)
- 15 Mar 1976, Carter Co. (MIG 47:50)

Late Spring
- 4 Jun 1989, Ensley (JRW, unpubl. data)
- 2 Jun 2002, Great River Road, Dyer Co. (JRW, unpubl. data)
- 28 May 2007, Ensley (MIG 78:99)

Early Fall
- 1 Jul 1989, Cross Creeks NWR (MIG 60:106)
- 1 Jul 1995, Island 13 (JRW, unpubl. data)
- 3 Jul 2000, Pennington Bend (MIG 71:120)
- 3 Jul 2011, Lake Co. (MIG 82:119)
- 3-4 Jul 1994, Ensley (JRW, unpubl. data)

High Counts – Spring
- 109 on 8 May 1976, Kingsport SBC (MIG 47:90)
- 46 on 1 May 1994, Elizabethton SBC (MIG 65:32)
- 34 on 12 May 1990, Elizabethton SBC (MIG 61:50)

High Counts – Fall
- 24 on 6 Aug 1999, Rankin Bottoms (MIG 71:36)
- 20 on 18 Jul 1998, Ensley (JRW, unpubl. data)
- 12 on 17 Aug 1991, Ensley (JRW, unpubl. data)
- 8 on 25 Sep 2012, Elizabethton FBC (MIG 83:142)
- 6 on 26 Sep 2009, Elizabethton FBC (MIG 80:42)

High Counts – Summer
- 3 (1 ad, 2 young) on 24 Jul 2009, Ensley (MIG 80:124)
- 2 (1 ad, 1 young) on 4 Jun 1989, Metro Center, Davidson Co. (MIG 60:106)
- 2 ad with young on 12 Jul 2008, Ensley (MIG 79:96)
- 2 on 5 Jun 2003, Dyer Co. (MIG 74:130)

Winter Records
- 2 through winter 2006-2007, Kingsport, Sullivan Co. (NAB 61(2):78)
- 1 on 9-11 Feb 1989, Ensley (MIG 60:60)
- 1 on 21 Dec 1997, Memphis CBC (MIG 69:22)

Substantiation: Specimen: LSUMZ, 75763

Solitary Sandpiper, *Tringa solitaria*

Status and Abundance: Fairly common transient

Habitat: Mudflats, creeks, edges of lakes and ponds, particularly with emergent vegetation

Spring Arrival: mid Mar

Spring Departure: late May

Fall Arrival: mid Jul

Fall Departure: mid Oct

Comments: Late spring transients may linger into early and mid-June, while early southbound transients may appear in late June. June birds may also represent birds not completing a migration to the breeding grounds and overlapping with southbound birds.

Early Spring
- 1 Mar 1973, Woodbury (MIG 44:23)
- 16 Mar 1996, Eagle Lake WMA (MIG 67:60)
- 16 Mar 1996, Gibson Co. (MIG 67:60)
- 18 Mar 1934, Mud Lake, Shelby Co. (MIG 5:26)

Late Spring
- 10 Jun 1995, President's Island (MIG 66:66)
- 4 Jun 1994, Lake Co. (MIG 65:62)
- 2 Jun 2000, Greene Co. (MIG 71:121)

Early Fall
- 30 Jun 2000, Bledsoe Co. (MIG 71:121)
- 1 Jul 1972, Reelfoot Lake (MIG 43:75)
- 1-2 Jul 1995, Ensley (JRW, unpubl. data)
- 2 Jul 1994, Burnt Woods Road (MIG 65:62)
- 3 Jul 1987, Carter Co. (MIG 58:147)
- 3 Jul 2011, Lake Co. (MIG 82:119)

Late Fall
- 27 Nov 1975, Buena Vista Marsh (MIG 47:46)

22 Nov 1986, Shelby Co. (MIG 58:20)

High Counts – Spring
900 on 23 Apr 1989, Tennemo Levee, Dyer Co. (JRW, unpubl. data)
345 on 25 Apr 1992, Ensley (JRW, unpubl. data)
300+ on 3 May 2008, Ensley (MIG 79:61)
298 on 25 Apr 1991, Ensley (MIG 62:110)
212 on 16 Apr 2011, Ensley (MIG 82:84)

Winter Records
1 on 15 Dec 1956, Bush Lake, Davidson Co. (BNA:23)
1 on 3 Nov 1973-8 Jan 1974, Buena Vista Marsh (MIG 45:21)

Substantiation: Specimen: LSUMZ, 75758

Greater Yellowlegs, *Tringa melanoleuca*

Status and Abundance: Uncommon (fairly common Mississippi Alluvial Valley) transient, rare winter visitor

Habitat: Sandbars, mudflats, and edges of lakes and ponds, particularly with emergent vegetation

Spring Arrival: late Feb

Spring Departure: late May

Fall Arrival: early Jul

Fall Departure: mid Nov

Comments: Late spring transients can linger into early or mid-June while the first likely southbound migrants appear in late June to the beginning of July. A few birds linger into winter with some likely overwintering in some years. High counts in late February are likely early northbound migrants.

Early Spring
7 Feb 1999, Ed Davis Fish Farm, Gibson Co. (MAG, pers. comm.)
20 Feb 1994, Ensley (JRW, pers. comm.)
21 Feb 1983, Hiwassee River Area (MIG 54:46)
23 Feb 1955, Buena Vista Marsh (BNA:22)

Late Spring
13 Jun 2004, White Lake WMA (MIG 75:158)
6 Jun 1997, Eagle Lake WMA (JRW, unpubl. data)
4 Jun 2004, White Lake WMA (MIG 75:158)

Early Fall
24 Jun 2004, White Lake WMA (MIG 75:158)
28 Jun 1999, Kingston Steam Plant (MIG 70:132)
29 Jun 1992, Lake Co. (MIG 63:95)
30 Jun 1997, White Lake Refuge (GC *fide* MAG)

Late Fall
25 Nov-1 Dec 1977, Hiwassee River Area (MIG 49:46)

30 Nov 1975, Buena Vista Marsh (MIG 47:46)
29 Nov 1994, Ensley (JRW, unpubl. data)
27 Nov 1998, Everett Lake (JRW, unpubl. data)
26 Nov 1989, Hiwassee River Area (MIG 61:18)

High Counts – Spring
2,410 on 22-23 Apr 2011, Lauderdale, Dyer, Lake Co. (MIG 82:84)
1,700+ on 8 Apr 2010, Lake Co. (MIG 81:114)
800 on 23 Apr 1989, Tennemo Levee, Dyer Co. (JRW, unpubl. data)
300 on 20 Apr 1986, Lake Co. (Robinson 1990)
200 on 25 Apr 1955, Nashville (Weise 1958)

High Counts – Winter
8 on 24 Dec 2001, Great River Road, Dyer Co. (JRW, unpubl. data)
2 on 17 Dec 1994, Reelfoot Lake CBC (JRW, unpubl. data)

Substantiation: Specimen: LSUMZ, 75754

Willet, *Tringa semipalmata*
Subspecies: *inornata*
Status and Abundance: Uncommon transient
Habitat: Sandbars, mudflats, and edges of lakes and ponds
Spring Arrival: late Apr
Spring Departure: mid May
Fall Arrival: mid Jul
Fall Departure: mid Sep
Comments: Most sightings are concentrated during the last few days of April and the first few days of May. All individuals that have been identified to subspecies appear to refer to the expected Western Willet (*T. s. inornata*), but observers should be aware of the possibility that an Eastern Willet (*T. s. semipalmata*) could occur, perhaps in connection with a tropical storm.

Early Spring
2 Apr 1972, Jefferson Co. (MIG 43:53)
7 Apr 2012, Ensley (MIG, in press)
10 Apr 1993, Ensley (JRW, unpubl. data)
16 Apr 2008, N. Memphis (MIG 79:61)

Late Spring
27 May 2001, Brainerd Levee (MIG 72:97)
24-25 May 2003, Hwy 79W, Lake Co. (MIG 74:87)
23 May 1999, Island 13 (GC *fide* MAG)

Early Fall
22 Jun 2004, Tennemo Levee, Lake Co. (MIG 75:158)
27 Jun 1989, Ensley (JRW, unpubl. data)
29 Jun 1995, Island 13 (MIG 66:66)

3 Jul 1965, Amnicola Marsh (MIG 36:68)
4 Jul 2004, Ensley (MIG 75:158)
Late Fall
8 Nov 1986, Roan Creek (MIG 58:31)
High Counts – Spring
175 on 3 May 1979, Center Hill Lake (MIG 50:69)
120 on 27 Apr 1999, Cheatham Co. (MIG 70:99)
77 on 6 May 1984, Ashland City Marsh (BNA:23)
75 on 30 Apr 2006, Knoxville SBC (MIG 77:123)
High Counts – Fall
13 on 2 Aug 1994, Ensley (JRW, unpubl. data)
9 on 21-31 Aug 1998, Shelby Farms (MIG 70:47)
8 on 20 Aug 2005, Rhea Co. (MIG 77:30)
Winter Records
1 on 6 Dec 1995, Ripley, Lauderdale Co. (MIG 67:31)
Substantiation: Specimen: LSUMZ, 3394

Lesser Yellowlegs, *Tringa flavipes*

Status and Abundance: Fairly common transient, rare winter visitor
Habitat: Sandbars, mudflats, and edges of lakes and ponds, particularly with emergent vegetation
Spring Arrival: early Mar
Spring Departure: late May
Fall Arrival: early Jul
Fall Departure: late Nov
Comments: Late spring transients can linger into early or mid-June while the first likely southbound migrants appear in late June to the beginning of July. A few birds linger into winter.
Early Spring
14 Feb 1987, Lake Co. (MIG 58:53)
16 Feb 1992, Ensley (MIG 63:60)
16 Feb 2003, Black Bayou WMA (JRW, unpubl. data)
19 Feb 1997, Black Bayou WMA (MIG 68:62)
26 Feb 1995, Britton Ford (JRW, unpubl. data)
26 Feb 1996, Ensley (JRW, unpubl. data)
Late Spring
2 Jun 2004, White Lake WMA (MIG 75:158)
31 May 1979, Savannah Bay (MIG 50:89)
30 May 1988, Cross Creeks NWR (Robinson 1990)
30 May 2004, Ensley (MIG 75:111)
Early Fall
23 Jun 1993, Lake Co. (GC *fide* MAG)

Scolopacidae: Sandpipers, Phalaropes, and Allies

   28 Jun 1993, Dyer Co. (GC *fide* MAG)
   29 Jun 2002, Ensley (MIG 73:111)
   1 Jul 1973, Sequatchie Valley (MIG 44:86)
   1 Jul 1996, White Lake WMA (MIG 67:77)
   1 Jul 2001, Ensley (JRW, unpubl. data)
Late Fall
   30 Nov 1989, Ensley (MIG 61:13)
   29 Nov 1972, Buena Vista Marsh (MIG 44:23)
   29 Nov 1994, Ensley (JRW, unpubl. data)
   24 Nov 1994, Ensley (JRW, unpubl. data)
   26 Nov 1994, Ensley (JRW, unpubl. data)
High Counts – Spring
   7,630 on 22-23 Apr 2001, Lauderdale, Dyer, and Lake Co. (MIG 82:84)
   1,500 on 23 Apr 1989, Tennemo Levee, Dyer Co. (JRW, unpubl. data)
   1,368 on 26 Apr 2011, Ensley (MIG 82:84)
   1,420 on 2 May 2004, Ensley (MIG 75:111)
   1,100 on 25 Apr 1992, Ensley (JRW, unpubl. data)
High Counts – Fall
   328 on 12 Oct 1989, Ensley (MIG 61:13)
   310+ on 23 Sep 1989, Ensley (MIG 61:13)
   254 on 23 Sep 1992, Ensley (JRW, unpubl. data)
   233 on 3 Oct 1993, Ensley (MIG 65:21)
   220 on 30 Sep 1989, Island 13 (JRW, unpubl. data)
High Counts – Winter
   22 on 6 Dec 1994, Ensley (JRW, unpubl. data)
   6 on 16 Dec 2001, Lake Co. (MIG 73:36)
   6 on 9/17 Dec 1989, Ensley (MIG 61:57)
   5 on 14 Dec 2003, Memphis CBC (MIG 75:59)
   5 on 17 Dec 1994, Black Bayou WMA (JRW, unpubl. data)
Substantiation: Specimen: LSUMZ, 75755

Upland Sandpiper, *Bartramia longicauda*
   Status and Abundance: Irregular (uncommon Mississippi Alluvial Valley) transient
   Habitat: Grassy pastures and fields, including airports and sod farms
   Spring Arrival: early Apr
   Spring Departure: late Apr
   Fall Arrival: mid Jul
   Fall Departure: mid Sep
   Comments: Late spring transients can linger into early or mid-June while the first likely southbound migrants appear in late June to the beginning of July.

Early Spring
: 10 Mar 1937, Murfreesboro (Todd 1937)
: 12 Mar 1950, Memphis (MIG 21:13)

Late Spring
: 18 May 1960, Rutherford Co. (DeVore 1975)
: 12 May 2001, Hwy 79W, Lake Co. (MIG 72:92)
: 12 May 2007, Anderson Co. NAMC (MIG 78:128)
: 11 May 1991, Ensley (MIG 62:110)

Early Fall
: 18 Jun 1972, Nashville (MIG 43:76)
: 21 Jun 1953, Shelby Farms (MIG 24:55)
: 23 Jun 1991, Ensley (MIG 63:21)
: 5 Jul 1997, Dyer Co. (MIG 68:134)

Late Fall
: 13 Nov 1943, Memphis (MIG 15:76)
: 27 Oct 2003, Standifer Gap Marsh (MIG 75:31)
: 22 Oct 1964, Buena Vista Marsh (MIG 35:102)

High Counts – Spring
: 20 on 22 Apr 1993, Ensley (JRW, unpubl. data)
: 17 on 7 Apr 1991, Ensley (JRW, unpubl. data)
: 14 on 7 Apr 1990, Ensley (JRW, unpubl. data)
: 12 on 8 Apr 2007, Ensley (MIG 78:99)
: 10 on 17 Apr 1993, Ensley (MIG 64:64)

High Counts – Fall
: 100 on 28 Jun 1946, Rutherford Co. (Layne 1946)

Substantiation: Photograph: Somershoe, S.G. 2012. "Upland Sandpiper". <http://www.pbase.com/shoeman/image/145552438> Accessed 25 Sep 2014.

Whimbrel, *Numenius phaeopus*

Subspecies: *hudsonicus*

Status and Abundance: Very rare transient

Habitat: Sandbars, mudflats, and edges of lakes and ponds; also occasionally high elevation grassy balds

Spring Arrival: mid May

Spring Departure: early Jun

Fall Arrival: mid Jul

Fall Departure: late Sep

Late Spring
: 4 Jun 1977, Austin Springs (MIG 48:105)

Early Fall
: 6-7 Jul 2002, Island 13 (MIG 73:111)

21 Jul 1990, Ensley (MIG 62:22)
21-22 Jul 1990, Ensley (JRW, unpubl. data)
24 Jul 1971, Ashland City Marsh (Riggins and Riggins 1972)
Late Fall
26 Sep 1975, Gallatin Steam Plant (MIG 47:18)
16-21 Sep 2010, Big Bald Mtn. (MIG 81:163)
20 Sep 1971, Buena Vista Marsh (Bierly 1972)
High Counts – Spring
18 on 27 May 1979, Kingston Steam Plant (Stedman 1980)
15 on 23 May 1989, Island 13 (MIG 65:52)
10 on 25 May 2000, S. Holston Lake (MIG 71:95)
5 on 26 May 1994, Lake Co. (MIG 65:51)
High Counts – Fall
2 on 30-31 Aug 1980, Big Bald Mtn. (Mayfield 1981)
Substantiation: Photograph: 1 on 29 May 2012, Dyer Co. (NAB 66(3):496)

Long-billed Curlew, *Numenius americanus*
Status and Abundance: ***Unsubstantiated***; accidental transient
Records
(1) 1 on 1 Sep 1985, Island 13 (MIG 57:22)
(2) 1 on 31 Oct 1987, Dacus Bar (JRW, unpubl. data)
(3) 1 on 11 Sep 1991, Tiptonville (Knight 1993)
(4) 1 on 27 Sep 1993, Ensley (Knight 1996)

Hudsonian Godwit, *Limosa haemastica*
Status and Abundance: Rare transient
Habitat: Sandbars, mudflats, and edges of lakes and ponds
Spring Arrival: mid Apr
Spring Departure: mid May
Fall Arrival: late Aug
Fall Departure: mid Oct
Comments: Nearly annual. Most records are of single birds and they rarely linger for more than one day.
Early Spring
30 Mar-1 Apr 2007, Ensley (MIG 78:99)
17 Apr 1982, Shelby Farms (MIG 53:66)
Late Spring
6 Jun 2004, Ensley (MIG 75:158)
4 Jun 2004, White Lake WMA (MIG 75:158)
28 May 2004, White Lake WMA (MIG 75:111)
Late Fall
12 Nov 1983, Hiwassee River Area (MIG 55:24)

2-4 Nov 1995, Savannah Bay (MIG 67:22)
High Counts – Spring
 11 on 21 May 2011, Dyer Co. (MIG 82:84)
 9 on 23 Apr 2011, Lake Co. (MIG 82:84)
 3 on 13-14 May 2002, Lake Co. (MIG 73:56)
 3 on 14 May 2002, Little Levee Road, Dyer Co. (MIG 73:56)
 2 on 13 May 1978, Gallatin Steam Plant (MIG 49:67)
 2 on 28 May 2004, White Lake WMA (MIG 75:111)
 2 on 8 May 1983, Reelfoot Lake SBC (Brown 1985)
High Counts – Fall
 3 ad on 12 Sep 2008, Big Sandy River flats, Henry Co. (MIG 80:23)
Substantiation: Photograph: 1 on 17 May 2009, Ensley (NAB 63(3):443)

Marbled Godwit, *Limosa fedoa*

Status and Abundance: Rare transient
Habitat: Sandbars, mudflats, and edges of lakes and ponds
Spring Arrival: mid Apr
Spring Departure: mid May
Fall Arrival: mid Aug
Fall Departure: mid Sep
Comments: Most fall records in August.
Late Spring
 26 May 1998, Shelby Farms (MIG 69:161)
Early Fall
 24 Jun 1995, Island 13 (MIG 66:66)
 4 Aug 1993, Levee Road, Lake Co. (MIG 65:21)
 7 Aug 1993, Shelby Farms (MIG 65:21)
 13 Aug 1990, Ensley (MIG 62:47)
Late Fall
 6 Oct 1976, Douglas Lake (MIG 48:21)
High Counts – Spring
 16 on 20 Apr 2002, Austin Springs (MIG 73:61)
 9 on 13 Apr 2001, S. Holston Lake (MIG 72:99)
 8 on 30 Apr 1997, Ensley (MIG 68:107)
 3 on 13 Apr 2001, Kingston Steam Plant (MIG 72:97)
High Counts – Fall
 4 on 14 Aug 1999, Lake Co. (JRW, unpubl. data)
Substantiation: Photograph: 1 on 8 Sep 2011, Rankin Bottoms (NAB 66(1):95)

Ruddy Turnstone, *Arenaria interpres*

Status and Abundance: Uncommon transient

Habitat: Sandbars, mudflats, and edges of lakes and ponds
Spring Arrival: late Apr
Spring Departure: late May
Fall Arrival: late Jul
Fall Departure: mid Sep
Early Spring
    18 Apr 1987, Old Hickory Lake (MIG 58:97)
Late Spring
    3 Jun 1990, Phillippy (MIG 62:22)
    2 Jun 1998, Dyer Co. (GC *fide* MAG)
    1 Jun 1997, Cross Creeks NWR (MIG 68:135)
Early Fall
    26 Jul 1990, Ensley (JRW, unpubl. data)
    26 Jul 1991, Ensley (JRW, unpubl. data)
Late Fall
    4 Nov 2004, Rankin Bottoms (MIG 76:34)
    31 Oct 1996, Island 13 (GC *fide* MAG)
    25 Oct 2007, Austin Springs (MIG 79:25)
    13 Oct 1985, Shelby Co. (MIG 57:22)
High Counts – Spring
    28 on 18 May 1998, Hwy 79 and Great River Road (MIG 69:161)
    15 on 26 May 1989, Phillippy (MIG 60:83)
    7 on 20 May 1997, Black Bayou WMA (GC *fide* MAG)
High Counts – Fall
    21 on 21 Sep 1985, Island 13 (MIG 57:22)
    13 on 5 Aug 1995, Phillippy (JRW, unpubl. data)
High Counts – Summer
    7 on 29 Jul 2006, Dacus Bar (MIG 77:143)
Substantiation: Specimen: APSU, 2458

Red Knot, *Calidris canutus*
    Status and Abundance: Accidental spring and rare fall transient
    Habitat: Sandbars, mudflats, and edges of lakes and ponds
    Fall Arrival: mid Aug
    Fall Departure: mid Sep
    Comments: Few records in the last 20 years as the population of the eastern subspecies (*C. c. rufa*) has crashed.
    Early Fall
        6 Aug 1955, Memphis (MIG 26:47)
        10 Aug 1993, Phillippy (MIG 65:21)
    Late Fall
        10 Oct 1979, Gallatin Steam Plant (BNA:23)

Spring Records
   7 on 28 May 1979, Gallatin Steam Plant (MIG 50:87)
High Counts – Fall
   14 on 8 Sep 2004, S. Holston Lake (MIG 76:38)
   13 on 27 Aug 2000, Tiptonville Bar (JRW, unpubl. data)
   10 on 20 Aug 1989, Island 13 (JRW, unpubl. data)
   10 on 5 Sep 2011, Old Hickory Lake, Davidson Co. (JH, pers. comm., photos)
   5 on 28 Aug 2000, Mud Island (MIG 73:10)
Substantiation: Specimen: LSUMZ, 75770

Ruff, *Calidris pugnax*
Status and Abundance: Very rare transient
Habitat: Sandbars, mudflats, and edges of lakes and ponds
Records
   (1) 1 on 6-9 Apr 1972, Sequatchie Valley (Shafer 1972)
   (2) 1 on 7 Sep 1987, Ensley (Robinson 1990)
   (3) 1on 24 Apr 1988, Ensley (Robinson 1990)
   (4) 1 on 21 Aug 1988, Ensley (MIG 60:26, Waldron 1989, Knight 1993)
   (5) 1 on 10-13 May 1989, Austin Springs (Knight 1990, Knight 1993)
   (6) 1 on 27 Sep-12 Oct 1989, Ensley (MIG 61:14)
   (7) 1 f on 4 May 1992, Ensley (MIG 63:72)
   (8) 1 on 9 May 1993, Ensley (JRW, unpubl. data)
   (9) 1 f on 2 May 1994, Ensley (JRW, unpubl. data)
   (10) 1 f on 11 May 1994, Dyer Co. (MIG 65:51)
   (11) 1 Oct-29 Nov 1994, Ensley (MIG 66:20; JRW, unpubl. data)
   (12) 1 on 4-7 Aug 2001, Ensley (MIG 73:11)
   (13) 2 imm on 23 Sep 2001, Rankin Bottoms (MIG 73:16)
   (14) 1 f on 20-28 Jul 2002, Ensley (MIG 73:111)
   (15) 1 imm on 18 Aug 2002, Rankin Bottoms (MIG 74:23)
   (16) 1 on 31 Aug 2002, Ensley (MIG 74:16)
   (17) 1 ad m on 17 Mar 2003, Hardin Co. (MIG 74:87)
   (18) 1 f on 23 Apr 2003, Eagle Lake WMA (MIG 74:87)
   (19) 1 ad m on 27 Apr-1 May 2007, Phillippy (MIG 78:99)
   (20) 1 on 8 Aug 2008, Phillippy (MIG 80:23)
   (21) 1 on 28 Apr 2011, Ensley (MIG, in press)
   (22) 1 f on 27 Aug-1 Sep 2011, Rankin Bottoms (RLK, pers. comm.)
Substantiation: Photograph: 1 on 27 Apr 2007, Lake Co. (NAB 61(3):454)

Sharp-tailed Sandpiper, *Calidris acuminata*
Status and Abundance: Accidental transient

Records
(1) 1 on 12-19 Sep 1992, Ensley (MIG 64:16, Knight 1993)
Substantiation: Photograph: 1 on 12-19 Sep 1992, Ensley (NAB 47(1))

Stilt Sandpiper, *Calidris himantopus*
Status and Abundance: Uncommon transient
Habitat: Sandbars, mudflats, and edges of lakes and ponds
Spring Arrival: mid Apr
Spring Departure: mid May
Fall Arrival: mid Jul
Fall Departure: late Oct
Comments: Much less common during spring than during fall migration.
Early Spring
   10 Mar 1985, Shelby Co. (MIG 56:74)
   20 Mar 2005, Brainerd Levee (MIG 76:101)
   23 Mar 2003, Hatchie NWR (MIG 74:87)
   23 Mar 2000, Austin Springs (MIG 71:92)
   24 Mar 1991, Ensley (MIG 62:110)
Late Spring
   15 Jun 2003, Dyer Co. (MIG 74:130)
   2 Jun 1982, Kingston Steam Plant (MIG 53:89)
Early Fall
   1 Jul 1980, Gallatin Steam Plant (BNA:24)
   3 Jul 1987, Kingston Steam Plant (MIG 58:145)
   4 Jul 1987, Shelby Co. (MIG 58:137)
   7 Jul 2007, Ensley (MIG 78:140)
Late Fall
   15 Nov 1986, Shelby Co. (MIG 58:20)
   8 Nov 2003, Ensley (MIG 75:24)
   5 Nov 1991, Ensley (JRW, unpubl. data)
   4 Nov 2011, Ensley (MIG 82:150)
   2 Nov 1981, Gallatin Steam Plant (MIG 58:25)
High Counts – Spring
   54 on 18 May 1997, White Lake WMA (JRW, unpubl. data)
   45 on 14 May 2005, Shelby Co. NAMC (MIG 76:129)
High Counts – Fall
   235 on 26 Sep 2004, Ensley (MIG 76:28)
   184 on 28 Sep 1996, Ensley (JRW, unpubl. data)
   174 on 21 Sep 1998, Heloise (MIG 70:47)
   121 on 21 Aug 1994, Ensley (JRW, unpubl. data)
   117 on 27 Sep 1995, Ensley (MIG 67:19)
Substantiation: Specimen: LSUMZ, 75794

Curlew Sandpiper, *Calidris ferruginea*
    Status and Abundance: Accidental transient
    Habitat: Sandbars, mudflats, and edges of lakes and ponds
    Records
        (1) 1 on 3-4 Jun 1996, Hwy 79, Lake Co. (Criswell 1997)
        (2) 1 on 8 Oct 2004, Britton Ford (MIG 76:28)
    Substantiation: Photograph: 1 on 3-4 Jun 1996, Hwy 79, Lake Co. (NAB 50(5))

Red-necked Stint, *Calidris ruficollis*
    Status and Abundance: ***Unsubstantiated***; accidental fall transient
    Habitat: Sandbars, mudflats, and edges of lakes and ponds
    Comments: Accepted by the TBRC on the basis of written documentation.
    Records
        (1) 1 on 7 Aug 1993, Ensley (Greene 1997)
        (2) 1 on 8-21 Oct 1994, Ensley (Greene 1997)

Sanderling, *Calidris alba*
    Status and Abundance: Rare spring transient, uncommon fall transient, very rare winter visitor
    Habitat: Sandbars, mudflats, and edges of lakes and ponds
    Spring Arrival: late Apr
    Spring Departure: late May
    Fall Arrival: late Jul
    Fall Departure: mid Oct
    Comments: Most common along the Mississippi River during fall migration.
    Early Spring
        24 Apr 1971, Woodbury (MIG 42:44)
        29 Apr 1961, Bristol (MIG 32:30)
    Late Spring
        29 May 2001, Kingston Steam Plant (MIG 72:97)
        28 May 1979, Gallatin Steam Plant (MIG 50:87)
        28 May 1979, Kingston Steam Plant (MIG 50:89)
        28 May 1987, Island 13 (MIG 58:92)
        28 May 2001, Ensley (MIG 72:92)
    Early Fall
        9 Jul 1985, Sumner Co. (MIG 57:27)
        9 Jul 1988, Island 13 (MIG 59:123)
        13 Jul 2003, Ensley (MIG 74:130)

Late Fall
- 19 Nov-1 Dec 2004, Ensley (JRW, unpubl. data)
- 21 Nov 1992, Island 13 (MIG 64:16)
- 11 Nov 1984, Island 13 (MIG 56:17)
- 6 Nov 1961, Bush Lake, Davidson Co. (MIG 33:13)
- 4 Nov 2011, Austin Springs (MIG 81:155)

High Counts – Spring
- 23 on 6-7 May 1994, Columbia SBC (MIG 65:32)
- 8 on 13 May 2000, Tiptonville Bar (JRW, unpubl. data)
- 8 on 15 May 2001, Kingston Steam Plant (MIG 72:97)

High Counts – Fall
- 42 on 22 Sep 1984, Island 13 (MIG 56:17)
- 35 on 8 Sep 1990, Island 13 (JRW, unpubl. data)
- 20-25 on 13-21 Sep 1980, Rankin Bottoms (MIG 52:25)

Winter Records
- 15 on 1 Dec 2004, Ensley (MIG 76:78)
- 12 on 11 Dec 2004, Ensley (MT, pers. comm.)
- 3 on 19 Dec 2004, Ensley (MT, pers. comm.)
- 1 on 1 Jan 1987, Hiwassee CBC (MIG 58:3)
- 1 on 9 Dec 1984, Shelby Co. (MIG 56:48)

Substantiation: Photograph: 1 on 29 Aug 2006, Musick's Campground (Knight 2008:51)

Dunlin, *Calidris alpina*

Status and Abundance: Uncommon transient, irregular winter resident Ridge and Valley (accidental winter visitor elsewhere)

Habitat: Sandbars, mudflats, and edges of lakes and ponds

Spring Arrival: late Apr

Spring Departure: late May

Fall Arrival: late Aug

Fall Departure: late Nov

Comments: Some fall birds may linger into winter, which blurs fall departure dates.

Early Spring
- 1 Apr 2008, Gibson Co. (MIG 79:62)
- 1 Apr 1990, Ensley (JRW, unpubl. data)
- 2 Apr 1995, Ensley (JRW, unpubl. data)
- 7 Apr 1973, Reelfoot Lake (MIG 44:50)
- 8 Apr 2005, Rankin Bottoms (MIG 76:101)

Late Spring
- 12 Jun 1971, Gallatin Steam Plant (MIG 42:69)
- 4 Jun 1992, Limestone, Washington Co. (MIG 63:76)

3-4 Jun 1996, Lake Co. (MIG 67:77)
2 Jun 2002, Great River Road, Dyer Co. (JRW, unpubl. data)
1 Jun 1986, Kingston Steam Plant (MIG 57:113)

Early Fall
11 Jul 2004, Mud Lake, Lake Co. (MIG 75:159)
1 Aug 1976, Sumner Co. (MIG 55:22)
10 Aug 1978, Kingston Steam Plant (MIG 50:22)
14 Aug 1993, Ensley (JRW, unpubl. data)
17 Aug 2002, Island 13 (MIG 74:16)

High Counts – Spring
500 on 24 May 2003, Dyer and Lake Co. (MIG 74:87)
110 on 24 May 2005, Chickasaw NWR (MIG 76:95)
103 on 11 May 2011, Lake Co. (MIG 82:84)
76 on 20 May 2001, Black Bayou WMA (MIG 72:92)

High Counts – Fall
800 on 1 Nov 2002, Dutch Bottoms (MIG 74:22)
390 on 27 Nov 1982, Douglas Lake (MIG 54:25)
355 on 4 Nov 2007, Upper Douglas Lake (MIG 79:25)
330+ on 7 Nov 2003, Upper Douglas Lake (MIG 75:31)
260 on 30 Nov 1980, Douglas Lake (MIG 52:49)

High Counts – Winter
230 on 4 Jan 1981, Upper Douglas Lake (MIG 52:49)
150 on 19 Jan 1980, Upper Douglas Lake (MIG 51:42)
141 on 1 Jan 1989, Hiwassee CBC (MIG 60:17)
100 on 11 Dec 1988, Hiwassee River Area (MIG 60:64)
94 on 11 Dec 2001, Douglas Lake (MIG 73:38)

Substantiation: Specimen: Milligan College, 65

Purple Sandpiper, *Calidris maritima*

Status and Abundance: **Unsubstantiated**; accidental visitor

Comments: Accepted by the TBRC on the basis of written documentation.

Records
(1) 1 on 25 Nov 1962, Hiwassee Island, Meigs Co. (Alsop 1972)
(2) 1 on 8 Jun 1967, Bays Mtn. Lake, Sullivan Co. (Alsop 1972, Knight 2008)
(3) 1 on 6 Jun 1975, Gallatin Steam Plant (Crawford and Crawford 1975)
(4) 1 on 29-30 Nov 1976, Shelby Co. (Holt 1979)

Baird's Sandpiper, *Calidris bairdii*

Status and Abundance: Rare spring transient; irregular (uncommon Mississippi Alluvial Valley) fall transient

Scolopacidae: Sandpipers, Phalaropes, and Allies

Habitat: Sandbars, mudflats, and edges of lakes and ponds
Spring Arrival: late Mar
Spring Departure: mid May
Fall Arrival: late Jul
Fall Departure: early Nov
Early Spring
- 12 Mar 2004, Shelby Farms (MIG 75:111)
- 14 Mar 1995, White Lake WMA (MIG 66:51)
- 22 Mar 1977, Ensley (JRW, unpubl. data)

Late Spring
- 11 Jun 1980, Sumner Co. (BNA:24)
- 8 Jun 1971, Amnicola Marsh (MIG 42:71)
- 6 Jun 1971, Tennessee NWR (MIG 42:68)
- 5 Jun 1993, Ensley (JRW, unpubl. data)
- 25-27 May 2007, Brainerd Levee (MIG 78:104)

Early Fall
- 13 Jul 1981, Kingston Steam Plant (MIG 52:98)
- 15 Jul 1985, Lawrence Co. (MIG 57:27)
- 20-27 Jul 2002, Ensley (MIG 73:111)
- 22 Jul 2007, Ensley (MIG 78:140)

Late Fall
- 29 Nov 1972, Austin Springs (MIG 44:26)
- 25 Nov 2004, Ensley (MIG 76:27)
- 22 Nov 1992, Island 13 (GC *fide* MAG)
- 21 Nov 1992, Dyer Co. (GC *fide* MAG)
- 20 Nov 1989, Island 13 (GC *fide* MAG)

High Counts – Spring
- 21 on 2 May 2010, Ensley (MIG 81:114)
- 4 on 24 May 2003, Greene Co. (MIG 74:92)

High Counts – Fall
- 23 on 26 Aug 1989, Paris Landing SP (JRW, unpubl. data)
- 21 on 3 Sep 1989, Paris Landing SP (JRW, unpubl. data)
- 19 on 8 Sep 2002, Ensley (MIG 74:16)
- 18 on 9 Sep 2010, Island 13 (MIG 81:154)
- 16 on 3 Sep 1989, Island 13 (MIG 61:13)
- 16 on 3 Sep 1995, Dyer Co. (MIG 67:18)

Substantiation: Photograph: Somershoe, S.G. 2011. "Baird's Sandpiper". <http://www.pbase.com/shoeman/image/137672763> Accessed 25 Sep 2014.

Least Sandpiper, *Calidris minutilla*

Status and Abundance: Common transient, irregular winter visitor

Habitat: Sandbars, mudflats, and edges of lakes and ponds; more tolerant of emergent vegetation than other peeps except Pectoral

Spring Arrival: mid Mar

Spring Departure: early Jun

Fall Arrival: early Jul

Fall Departure: mid Nov

Comments: Fall birds linger into winter period and small numbers may be found throughout winter where suitable habitat remains.

Early Spring
- 26 Feb 1995, Reelfoot NWR (JRW, unpubl. data)
- 2 Mar 1957, Nashville (MIG 28:2)
- 11 Mar 1950, Shelby Farms (MIG 21:13)
- 13 Mar 1987, Savannah Bay (MIG 58:103)

Late Spring
- 11 Jun 2003, Dyer Co. (MIG 74:130)
- 4 Jun 1986, Memphis (Robinson 1990)

Early Fall
- 18 Jun 1968, Columbia (MIG 39:64)
- 21 Jun 2003, Ensley (MIG 74:130)
- 21 Jun 2009, Ensley (MIG 80:124)
- 22 Jun 1996, Lake Co. (JRW, unpubl. data)
- 26 Jun 1971, Tennessee NWR (MIG 42:68)
- 26 Jun 1977, Amnicola Marsh (MIG 48:105)

High Counts – Spring
- 1,655 on 26 Apr 1992, Memphis SBC (MIG 63:47)
- 590 on 30 Apr 1995, Ensley (JRW, unpubl. data)
- 564 on 4 May 1995, Ensley (JRW, unpubl. data)

High Counts – Fall
- 15,000 on 16 Aug 2013, Ensley (SGS, pers. obs.)
- 4,400 on 4 Sep 2005, Ensley (MIG 77:24)
- 4,000 on 1 Sep 2002, Ensley (MIG 74:16)
- 3,551 on 10 Sep 1995, Ensley (MIG 67:18)
- 3,000 on 2 Oct 1999, Ensley (JRW, unpubl. data)

High Counts – Winter
- 860 on 4 Dec 2003, Ensley (MIG 75:73)
- 680 on 8 Dec 2004, Ensley (MT, pers. comm.)
- 600 on 18 Dec 1994, Memphis CBC (MIG 66:14)
- 544 on 3 Dec 1989, Ensley (MIG 61:57)
- 500 on 18 Dec 2004, Memphis CBC (MIG 76:65)
- 500 on 6 Dec 1994, Ensley (JRW, unpubl. data)

Substantiation: Specimen: LSUMZ, 75780

White-rumped Sandpiper, *Calidris fuscicollis*

Status and Abundance: Uncommon spring transient, rare fall transient
Habitat: Sandbars, mudflats, and edges of lakes and ponds
Spring Arrival: early May
Spring Departure: mid Jun
Fall Arrival: late Jul
Fall Departure: late Sep

Early Spring
- 26 Apr 1996, Ensley (JRW, unpubl. data)
- 26 Apr 1992, Ensley (JRW, unpubl. data)
- 27 Apr 1984, Sumner Co. (MIG 55:69)
- 27 Apr 1986, Memphis (MIG 57:66)
- 28 Apr 1979, Austin Springs (MIG 50:70)

Late Spring
- 19 Jun 1969, Austin Springs (MIG 40:70)
- 21 Jun 2008, Ensley (MIG 79:96)
- 23 Jun 1972, Gallatin Steam Plant (MIG 43:76)
- 26 Jun 2003, Lake Co. (MIG 74:130)

Early Fall
- 3 Jul 1975, Gallatin Steam Plant (MIG 46:88)
- 7 Jul 2009, Ensley (MIG 80:124)
- 10 Jul 2001, Ensley (MIG 72:123)
- 11 Jul 2003, Dyer Co. (MIG 74:130)
- 12 Jul 2003, Ensley (MIG 74:130)

Late Fall
- 5 Nov 2011, Eagle Creek, Henry Co. (SGS, pers. obs.)
- 1 Nov 1986, Shelby Co. (MIG 58:20)
- 25 Oct 1970, Hiwassee River Area (MIG 41:88)
- 19 Oct 2010, Rankin Bottoms (NAB 65(1):58)

High Counts – Spring
- 191 on 17 May 2003, Ensley (MIG 74:87)
- 164 on 4 Jun 2005, Ensley (MIG 76:144)
- 132 on 7 Jun 1982, Kingston Steam Plant (MIG 53:89)
- 120 on 4 Jun 1996, Lake Co. (JRW, unpubl. data)
- 100+ on 18 May 2003, Parker Road, Lake Co. (JRW, unpubl. data)
- 100+ on 26 May 2011, Dyer Co. (MIG 82:84)

High Counts – Fall
- 40 on 11 Sep 2011, Ensley (JRW, unpubl. data)
- 14 on 8 Sep 2011, Rankin Bottoms (MIG 82:156)

Substantiation: Photograph: 1 on 19 Oct 2010, Rankin Bottoms (NAB 65(1):58)

Buff-breasted Sandpiper, *Calidris subruficollis*
- Status and Abundance: Accidental spring transient, irregular (uncommon Mississippi Alluvial Valley) fall transient
- Habitat: Dry sandbars and exposed mudflats, often where some vegetation has begun to grow
- Fall Arrival: early Aug
- Fall Departure: late Sep
- Comments: All spring records are listed below
- Early Fall
    - 30 Jul 1994, Dyer Co. (MIG 65:62)
    - 31 Jul 1990, Ensley (JRW, unpubl. data)
    - 1 Aug 1976, Britton Ford (MIG 48:17)
    - 2 Aug 1986, Cross Creeks NWR (MIG 58:24)
- Late Fall
    - 22 Oct 1980, Kingston Steam Plant (MIG 52:25)
    - 17 Oct 1987, Shelby Co. (MIG 59:32)
- Spring Records
    - 4 Apr 1993, Shelby Farms (MIG 64:64)
    - 18 Apr 1993, UT Plant Science Farm, Knox Co. (MIG 64:88)
    - 26 Apr 1981, Memphis SBC (MIG 52:64)
    - 27 Apr 2011, Snow Bunting Peninsula (MIG 82:86)
    - 6 May 1997, Ensley (JRW, unpubl. data)
    - 14 May 1991, Ensley (MIG 62:110)
- High Counts – Fall
    - 65 on 6 Sep 1996, Ensley (JRW, unpubl. data)
    - 56 on 10 Sep 2000, Dyer Co. (MIG 72:38)
    - 42 on 30 Aug 2011, Rankin Bottoms (MIG 82:156)
    - 40 on 3 Sep 1989, Paris Landing SP (JRW, unpubl. data)
    - 31 on 10 Sep 1995, Ensley (JRW, unpubl. data)
- Substantiation: Photograph: 1 on 27 Apr 2011, Snow Bunting Peninsula (NAB 65(3):49)

Pectoral Sandpiper, *Calidris melanotos*
- Status and Abundance: Fairly common transient, very rare winter visitor
- Habitat: Sandbars, mudflats, and edges of lakes and ponds; more tolerant of emergent vegetation than other peeps except Least
- Spring Arrival: early Mar
- Spring Departure: late May
- Fall Arrival: early Jul
- Fall Departure: late Nov

Scolopacidae: Sandpipers, Phalaropes, and Allies

Early Spring
- 2 Feb 1957, Union City airfield (MIG 28:7)
- 11 Feb 1968, Knoxville (MIG 39:45)
- 19 Feb 1975, Tennessee NWR (MIG 46:44)

Late Spring
- 11 Jun 2003, Dyer Co. (MIG 74:130)
- 2 Jun 1988, Shelby Co. (Robinson 1990)
- 1 Jun 1989, Ensley (JRW, unpubl. data)
- 31 May 1987, Maury Co. (MIG 59:99)
- 31 May 2004, Dyer Co. (MIG 75:111)

Early Fall
- 20 Jun 1986, Kingston Steam Plant (MIG 57:113)
- 22 Jun 1985, Tennessee NWR (MIG 57:27)
- 22 Jun 2002, Ensley (MIG 73:111)
- 24 Jun 1993, Lake Co. (JRW, unpubl. data)
- 28 Jun 2003, Ensley (MIG 74:130)

Late Fall
- 30 Nov 1971, Hiwassee River Area (MIG 43:27)
- 29 Nov 1991, Ensley (MIG 63:52)

High Counts – Spring
- 4,800 on 14 Apr 2007, Ensley (MIG 78:99)
- 4,200 on 23 Apr 1989, Tennemo Levee, Dyer Co. (JRW, unpubl. data)
- 2,000+ on 8 Apr 1994, Lake Co. (MIG 65:51)
- 1,800 on 25 Apr 1992, Ensley (JRW, unpubl. data)
- 1,100 on 5 Apr 1987, Shelby Co. (MIG 58:92)

High Counts – Fall
- 6,484 on 24 Aug 1997, Ensley (MIG 69:41)
- 4,000 on 22 Aug 1991, Ensley (MIG 63:52)
- 3,000 on 21 Aug 1994, Ensley (JRW, unpubl. data)
- 2,500 on 17 Aug 1991, Ensley (JRW, unpubl. data)
- 2,500 on 23 Aug 2003, Ensley (MIG 75:24)

Summer Records
- 1 on 16 Jun 1995, Shelby Farms (MIG 66:66) (possibly an early southbound migrant?)

Winter Records
- 1 on 1 Jan 1976, Hiwassee River Area (MIG 47:48)
- 1 on 16 Dec 1979, Memphis CBC (MIG 51:32)
- 1 on 28 Jan 1987, Stewart Co. (MIG 58:56)
- 1 on 9 Dec 1990, Ensley (MIG 62:81)
- 1 on 18-24 Jan 1993, Ensley (MIG 64:47)
- 1 on 16 Dec 2000, Heloise (MIG 72:68)
- 1 on 17 Dec 2012, Reelfoot Lake CBC (MIG, in press)

1 on 4 Dec 2013, Britton Ford (MT, SGS, pers. obs.)
Substantiation: Specimen: LSUMZ, 75786

Semipalmated Sandpiper, *Calidris pusilla*
Status and Abundance: Fairly common transient, very rare winter visitor
Habitat: Sandbars, mudflats, and edges of lakes and ponds
Spring Arrival: mid Apr
Spring Departure: mid Jun
Fall Arrival: mid Jul
Fall Departure: late Oct
Early Spring
- 5 Mar 1986, Savannah Bay (MIG 57:84)
- 1 Apr 1991, Shelby Farms (MIG 62:110)
- 1 Apr 1992, Lake Co. (GC *fide* MAG)
- 6 Apr 1972, Buena Vista Marsh (MIG 43:50)

Early Fall
- 2 Jul 1994, Ensley (JRW, unpubl. data)
- 2 Jul 1996, Hwy 79W, Lake Co. (MIG 67:77)
- 4 Jul 1991, Ensley (JRW, unpubl. data)
- 5 Jul 1988, Cross Creeks NWR (Robinson 1990)
- 6 Jul 1981, Kingston Steam Plant (MIG 52:98)

Late Fall
- 28 Nov 1968, Cherokee Lake (MIG 40:22)
- 9 Nov 1970, Gallatin Steam Plant (MIG 42:19)
- 8 Nov 1998, Ensley (JRW, unpubl. data)
- 7 Nov 1959, Memphis (MIG 31:10)
- 5 Nov 1989, Ensley (JRW, unpubl. data)

High Counts – Spring
- 2,000 on 22 May 1983, Lake Co. (MIG 54:60)
- 389 on 20 May 1995, Ensley (JRW, unpubl. data)
- 262 on 15 May 2009, Ensley (MIG 80:87)

High Counts – Fall
- 564 on 17 Aug 2000, Ensley (MIG 72:38)
- 500 on 21 Aug 1994, Ensley (JRW, unpubl. data)
- 400 on 31 Jul 1994, Ensley (JRW, unpubl. data)
- 400 on 31 Aug 1980, Rankin Bottoms (MIG 52:25)
- 356 on 18 Jul 1998, Ensley (JRW, unpubl. data)

Summer Records
- 22 Jun 1985, Tennessee NWR (MIG 57:27)
- 22 Jun 1991, Lake Co. (JRW, unpubl. data)

Winter Records
- 1 on 8 Dec 2004, Ensley (MT, pers. comm.)

Scolopacidae: Sandpipers, Phalaropes, and Allies

Substantiation: Specimen: LSUMZ, 75772

Western Sandpiper, *Calidris mauri*
Status and Abundance: Uncommon transient
Habitat: Sandbars, mudflats, and edges of lakes and ponds
Spring Arrival: mid Apr
Spring Departure: late May
Fall Arrival: mid Jul
Fall Departure: early Nov
Early Spring
- 16 Mar 2004, Austin Springs (MIG 75:117)
- 3 Apr 1972, Buena Vista Marsh (MIG 43:50-51)
- 10 Apr 2004, Ensley (MIG 75:111)

Late Spring
- 8 Jun 2006, Ensley (MIG 77:143)
- 7 Jun 1996, Brainerd Levee (MIG 67:78)
- 4 Jun 1972, Gallatin Steam Plant (MIG 43:76)
- 28 May 1979, Kingston Steam Plant (MIG 54:60)

Early Fall
- 29 Jun 1986, Shelby Co. (MIG 57:103)
- 3-4 Jul 1994, Ensley (JRW, unpubl. data)
- 4 Jul 1985, Gallatin Steam Plant (MIG 57:27)
- 4 Jul 2000, Mud Lake, Lake Co. (MIG 71:119)
- 5 Jul 1997, Dyer Co. (JRW, unpubl. data)

Late Fall
- 26-29 Nov 1994, Ensley (JRW, unpubl. data)
- 25 Nov 1973, Buena Vista Marsh (MIG 45:21)
- 25 Nov 1994, Heloise (JRW, unpubl. data)
- 23 Nov 1968, Cherokee Lake (MIG 40:22)
- 22 Nov 1996, Ensley (JRW, unpubl. data)

High Counts – Spring
- 250 on 24 May 1997, Ensley (JRW, unpubl. data)
- 150 on 7 May 1997, Ensley (JRW, unpubl. data)

High Counts – Fall
- 276 on 18 Jul 1998, Ensley (MIG 69:186)
- 145 on 10 Aug 1997, Ensley (JRW, unpubl. data)
- 112 on 21 Aug 1994, Ensley (JRW, unpubl. data)
- 100+ on 3 Aug 2008, Ensley (MIG 80:23)
- 100 on 19-20 Jul 1996, Ensley (JRW, unpubl. data)
- 100 on 5 Sep 1937, Mud Lake, Shelby Co. (MIG 8:58)

Summer Records
- 21 Jun 2003, Ensley (MIG 74:130)

Winter Records
    1 on 12 Jan 1981, Dyer Co. (MIG 52:45)
    1 on 30 Jan 1983, Shelby Co. (MIG 54:40)
    2 on 16 Dec 1990, Ensley (MIG 62:81)
    1 on 18 Dec 1999, near Black Bayou WMA (JRW, unpubl. data)
    up to 3 on 1-9 Dec 2000, Everett Lake (MIG 72:68)
    1-2 on 11-12 Dec 2004, Ensley (JRW, unpubl. data)
Substantiation: Specimen: LSUMZ, 75777

Short-billed Dowitcher, *Limnodromus griseus*
Subspecies: *hendersoni*
Status and Abundance: Uncommon transient
Habitat: Sandbars, mudflats, and edges of lakes and ponds
Spring Arrival: late Apr
Spring Departure: mid May
Fall Arrival: mid Jul
Fall Departure: mid Sep
Comments: The Atlantic subspecies (*L. g. griseus*) has been photographed in Kentucky, so observers should be aware of the possibility that it could occur in Tennessee as a vagrant.
Early Spring
    16 Mar 2002, Brainerd Levee (MIG 73:61)
    19 Mar 1989, Ensley (JRW, unpubl. data)
    1 Apr 1990, Ensley (JRW, unpubl. data)
    2 Apr 2010, Walmart Dist. Center, Greene Co. (MIG 81:119)
    10 Apr 2005, Rankin Bottoms (MIG 76:101)
Late Spring
    21 May 1983, Kingston Steam Plant (MIG 54:65)
Early Fall
    28 Jun 1989, Lower Hatchie NWR (JRW, unpubl. data)
    29 Jun 1995, Island 13 (MIG 66:66)
    4 Jul 1986, Lake Co. (MIG 57:103)
    4 Jul 1991, Ensley (JRW, unpubl. data)
Late Fall
    27 Oct 1985, Gallatin Steam Plant (MIG 57:27)
    25 Oct 1980, Shelby Co. (MIG 52:22)
    22 Oct 1991, Ensley (JRW, unpubl. data)
    21 Oct 1994, Ensley (MIG 66:20)
High Counts – Spring
    112 on 13 May 2000, Greene Co. (MIG 71:52)
    102 on 30 Apr 2005, White Lake WMA (MIG 76:95)
    74 on 11 May 1996, Shelby Farms (MIG 67:60)

62 on 12 May 1984, Chattanooga (MIG 55:73)
High Counts – Fall
    55 on 9 Jul 1994, Ensley (JRW, unpubl. data)
    34 on 1 Sep 2006, Rankin Bottoms (MIG 78:39)
    26 on 18 Jul 1992, Ensley (JRW, unpubl. data)
High Counts – Summer
    22 Jun 2002, Ensley (MIG 73:111)
Substantiation: Specimen: LSUMZ, 75753

Long-billed Dowitcher, *Limnodromus scolopaceus*
Status and Abundance: Uncommon transient
Habitat: Sandbars, mudflats, and edges of lakes and ponds
Spring Arrival: mid Apr
Spring Departure: mid May
Fall Arrival: late Jul
Fall Departure: late Oct
Comments: This is the expected dowitcher species in October. Rare in east Tennessee.
Early Spring
    11 Mar 2010, Ensley (MIG 81:114)
    21-23 Mar 1991, Ensley (JRW, unpubl. data)
Late Spring
    19 May 1995, Shelby Forest (JRW, unpubl. data)
    14 May 1967, Knox Co. (Alsop and Wallace 1970)
Early Fall
    4 Jul 2005, Chickasaw NWR (MIG 76:144)
    10 Jul 1977, Sumner Co. (MIG 48:103)
    18 Jul 1995, Hwy 79, Lake Co. (MIG 66:66)
Late Fall
    24 Nov 1990, Pace Point (JRW, unpubl. data)
    21 Nov 1990, Ensley (JRW, unpubl. data)
    20 Nov 2004, Lauderdale Refuge (JRW, unpubl. data)
    19 Nov 2014, Thorny Cypress WMA, Dyer Co. (MAG, pers. comm.)
    13 Nov 2010, Lauderdale Refuge (MIG 81:154)
High Counts – Spring
    104 on 26 Apr 2008, Ensley (MIG 79:62)
    97 on 28 Apr 2009, Lake Co. (MIG 80:87)
    84 on 4 May 1995, Ensley (JRW, unpubl. data)
    78 on 17 Apr 2007, Dyer Co. (MIG 78:99)
    50 on 20 Apr 2005, White Lake WMA (MIG 76:95)
High Counts – Fall
    23 on 14 Nov 2002, Lauderdale Co. (MIG 74:16)

19 on 10 Oct 2009, Dyer Co. (MIG 81:50)
19 on 18 Oct 1996, Ensley (JRW, unpubl. data)
18 on 7 Oct 2000, Ensley (JRW, unpubl. data)

Winter Records
4 on 17 Dec 2005, Reelfoot Lake CBC (MIG 77:57)
3 on 1 Dec 1990, Lauderdale Refuge (JRW, unpubl. data)
3 on 2 Dec 1990, Pace Point (JRW, unpubl. data)
1 on 19 Feb 2005, Lauderdale Refuge (MIG 76:78)

Substantiation: Photograph: Todd, M.C. 2008. "Long-billed Dowitcher". <http://www.pbase.com/mctodd/image/96540064> Accessed 25 Sep 2014.

Wilson's Snipe, *Gallinago delicata*

Status and Abundance: Fairly common transient and winter resident; accidental summer resident

Habitat: Sandbars, mudflats, wet fields, and marshy edges of creeks, lakes and ponds, typically hidden in emergent vegetation and often not seen unless flushed

Spring Departure: mid May

Fall Arrival: mid Aug

Comments: There are several June records. Migrants arrive as early as early July.

Late Spring
27 May 1995, Reelfoot NWR (JRW, unpubl. data)
26 May 1979, Dyer Co. (MIG 50:86)
23 May 1961, Buena Vista Marsh (BNA:25)

Early Fall
5 Jul 1997, Black Bayou WMA (JRW, unpubl. data)
10 Jul 1975, Amnicola Marsh (MIG 46:90)
10 Jul 1977, Sumner Co. (MIG 48:103)
10 Jul 1993, Ensley (JRW, unpubl. data)
17 Jul 2004, Ensley (MIG 75:159)

High Counts – Spring
500 on 30 Mar 1996, Champey Pocket, Reelfoot Lake, Lake Co. (JRW, unpubl. data)
284 on 24 Mar 1990, Ensley (JRW, unpubl. data)
265 on 13 Mar 2013, Eagleville (SGS, pers. obs.)
235 on 16 Mar 1996, Eagle Lake WMA (MIG 67:60)
200 on 11 Apr 1996, Eagle Lake Refuge (JRW, unpubl. data)

High Counts – Fall
300 on 27 Nov 1998, Lauderdale Refuge (JRW, unpubl. data)
250 on 20 Nov 2014, Pond Creek Bottoms, Crockett Co. (MAG, pers.

comm.)
>165 on 29 Nov 1994, Lauderdale Refuge (JRW, unpubl. data)
>121 on 10 Nov 1993, Lake Co. (MIG 65:21)

High Counts – Summer
>2 on 16 Jun 2002, Mud Lake, Lake Co. (MIG 73:111)

High Counts – Winter
>340 on 1 Jan 1986, Hiwassee CBC (MIG 57:10)
>200 on 5 Dec 1990, Ensley (JRW, unpubl. data)
>144 on 17 Dec 2005, Reelfoot Lake CBC (MIG 77:43)
>142 on 30 Dec 2009, Savannah CBC (MIG 81:93)
>133 on 14 Dec 2002, Reelfoot Lake CBC (MIG 74:41)

Substantiation: Specimen: LSUMZ, 75751

American Woodcock, *Scolopax minor*

Status and Abundance: Uncommon permanent resident

Habitat: Lowland wooded areas, often adjacent to streams, marshes, or brushy fields; also in wooded thickets on and around high elevation balds

Comments: Generally undetected (although certainly present) during summer.

High Counts – Fall
>4 on 16 Sep 2006, Putnam Co. FBC (MIG 78:19)

High Counts – Winter
>23 on 30 Dec 1982, Duck River Reservoir CBC, near Columbia (MIG 56:7)
>22 on 3 Jan 2005, Savannah CBC (MIG 76:65)
>16 on 17 Dec 1967, Hardin Co. (MIG 39:19)

Substantiation: Specimen: UTM, 409

Wilson's Phalarope, *Phalaropus tricolor*

Status and Abundance: Irregular (uncommon Mississippi Alluvial Valley) transient

Habitat: Sandbars, mudflats, and edges of lakes and ponds

Spring Arrival: mid Apr

Spring Departure: mid May

Fall Arrival: late Jul

Fall Departure: mid Sep

Comments: More common during fall than during spring. Large invasion during spring 1978 brought high counts across the state.

Early Spring
>17 Mar 2003, Hardin Co. (MIG 74:87)
>1 Apr 1990, Ensley (JRW, unpubl. data)

4 Apr 2008, Dyer Co. (MIG 79:62)
9 Apr 2000, Brainerd Levee (MIG 71:92)

Late Spring
30 May 1985, Sumner Co. (MIG 56:76)
28 May 1988, Shelby Co. (Robinson 1990)

Early Fall
11 Jul 1975, Gallatin Steam Plant (MIG 46:88)
13 Jul 2003, Ensley (MIG 74:130)
20 Jul 1995, Ensley (JRW, unpubl. data)
23 Jul 1989, Cross Creeks NWR (MIG 60:106)
23 Jul 1994, Black Bayou WMA (JRW, unpubl. data)
23-31 Jul 2002, Ensley (MIG 73:111)

Late Fall
4/24 Nov 1989, Ensley (MIG 61:14)
9 Nov 1980, Douglas Lake (MIG 52:49)
16 Oct 2004, Ensley (JRW, unpubl. data)
14 Oct 1990, Ensley (MIG 62:48)
9 Oct 1938, Mud Lake, Shelby Co. (Coffey 1939)

High Counts – Spring
126-131 on 30 Apr-1 May 1997, Ensley (JRW, unpubl. data)
65 on 6 May 1978, Shelby Co. (MIG 49:66)
49 on 2 May 2010, Ensley (MIG 81:114)
41 on 29 Apr 2011, Ensley (SGS, pers. obs.)
40 on 5 May 1997, Ensley (MIG 68:107)

High Counts – Fall
101 on 5 Sep 2011, S. Holston Lake (MIG, in press)
10 on 25 Aug 2002, Ensley (MIG 74:16)

Substantiation: Specimen: LSUMZ, 3373

Red-necked Phalarope, *Phalaropus lobatus*

Status and Abundance: Rare transient
Habitat: Sandbars, mudflats, and edges of lakes and ponds
Fall Arrival: mid Aug
Fall Departure: late Sep
Comments: Over 60 records. Few spring records, but all are in mid- to late May.

Early Fall
5 Aug 1993, Dyer Co. (WC *fide* MAG)
5 Aug 2000, Ensley (MIG 72:39)
10 Aug 1992, Black Bayou WMA (MAG, pers. comm.)

Late Fall
1 Nov 1981, Cocke Co. (MIG 53:20)

21 Oct 1959, Bush Lake (Ogden 1959)
21 Oct 2007, Ensley (MIG 79:20)
High Counts – Spring
8 on 17 May 1980, Kingston Steam Plant (MIG 51:94)
2-4 on 26-27 May 1991, Limestone, Washington Co. (MIG 62:113)
High Counts – Fall
up to 6 on 14-21 Aug 1993, Ensley (MIG 65:21)
5 on 14 Aug 1993, Ensley (JRW, unpubl. data)
3 on 2 Sep 1991, Island 13 (MIG 63:53)
3 on 5 Sep 1998, Black Bayou WMA (MIG 70:47)
3 on 6-9 Sep 2011, Rankin Bottoms (MIG 82:156)
Substantiation: Photograph: 1 on 21 Sep 1983, Tennessee River, Knoxville (MIG 55:84)

Red Phalarope, *Phalaropus fulicarius*
Status and Abundance: Very rare fall transient and winter visitor
Habitat: Sandbars, mudflats, and edges of lakes and ponds; often in deeper water than other phalaropes
Comments: Over 30 records, mostly during fall. Nearly all sightings involve single birds.
Early Fall
14 Aug 1993, Ensley (Calhoon 1998)
19 Aug 2000, Ensley (JRW, unpubl. data)
19-22 Aug 2001, Ensley (MIG 72:39)
23/28 Aug 1998, Rankin (MIG 70:53)
1 Sep 1991, Island 13 (JRW, unpubl. data)
Late Fall
29 Nov 1959, Maryville, Blount Co. (Monroe 1959)
1-10 Nov 2003, Britton Ford (MIG 75:24)
5-9 Nov 2011, John Sevier Lake (MIG 82:156)
Winter Records
1 on 17 Dec 1944, GSMNP CBC (MIG 15:70)
1 on 4 Dec 1965, Woods Reservoir (McCrary and Wood 1966a, Calhoon 1998b)
1 on 12-13 Dec 1967, Savannah Bay (Dubke 1968)
1 on 16 Feb 1998, Brainerd Levee (Calhoon 1998b)
Substantiation: Photograph: 1 on 2 Oct 2010, Upper Douglas L., Cocke Co. (NAB 65(1):58)

Stercorariidae: Skuas and Jaegers. The three species of North American jaegers are accidental and could occur anywhere in the state, while the skua is accidental and the lone record is associated with the passing of a hurricane.

South Polar Skua, *Stercorarius maccormicki*
- Status and Abundance: Accidental fall visitor
- Habitat: Large rivers and lakes
- Comments: One remarkable record, seen during the passage of the remnants of Hurricane Katrina.
- Records
    (1) 1 on 30 Aug 2005, Pickwick Lake (MIG 76:24, Edwards 2012)
- Substantiation: Photograph: 1 on 30 Aug 2005, Pickwick Lake (NAB 60(1))

Pomarine Jaeger, *Stercorarius pomarinus*
- Status and Abundance: Accidental summer and fall visitor
- Habitat: Large rivers and lakes
- Comments: There are at least 8 records of unidentified jaegers from 1988-2011 (RLK, pers. comm.).
- Records
    (1) 1 subadult on 28 Jun-4 Sep 1987, Paris Landing SP (MIG 58:137, MIG 59:32). This bird was accompanied by a Long-tailed Jaeger during the last six days of the observation period.
    (2) 2 (1 ad, 1 imm) on 22-23 Sep 1989, Watauga Lake (MIG 61:21, Knight 1993, Knight 2008)
    (3) 1 dark morph imm on 8 Sep 1990, Island 13 (JRW, unpubl. data)
    (4) 1 on 6 Oct 1995, Nickajack Lake, Marion Co. (Greene 1997, MIG 67:22)
    (5) 1 on 23 Oct 2005, Mississippi River, Shelby Co. (MIG 76:24)
    (6) 1 on 7 Nov 2010, Pace Point (MIG 81:155)
    (7) 1 imm on 2 Sep 2012, Mud Island, Shelby Co. (JRW, unpubl. data)
- Substantiation: Photograph: 1 subadult on 15 Aug 1987, Paris Landing SP (TBRC Archives, UTK)

Parasitic Jaeger, *Stercorarius parasiticus*
- Status and Abundance: Accidental summer and fall visitor
- Habitat: Large rivers and lakes
- Comments: There are at least 8 records of unidentified jaegers from 1988-2011 (RLK, pers. comm.).
- Records
    (1) 1 on 16 Sep-27 Oct 1978, Woods Reservoir (MIG 50:21)

Stercorariidae: Skuas and Jaegers

(2) 1 on 6-22 Oct 1985, Pace Point (Stedman and Robinson 1986, Stedman and Robinson 1987)
(3) 1 ad on 22-23 Sep 1989, Watauga Lake (Knight 1993, Knight 2008, MIG 61:21)
(4) 1 on 7 Sep 1990, Ensley (JRW, unpubl. data)
(5) 1 ad, light phase on 11 Jul 2005, Pickwick Lake (MIG 76:14)
(6) 1 on 6 Sep 2011, Snow Bunting Peninsula, Old Hickory Lake (MIG 82:152)

Substantiation: Photograph: 1 in Oct 1985, Kentucky Lake, near Pace Point (TBRC Archives, UTK)

Long-tailed Jaeger, *Stercorarius longicaudus*

Status and Abundance: Accidental fall visitor

Habitat: Large rivers and lakes

Comments: There are at least 8 records of unidentified jaegers from 1988-2011 (RLK, pers. comm.).

Records

(1) 1 ad on 2-3 Sep 1984, Island 13 (Stedman 1985)
(2) 1 on 1 Sep 1985, Island 13 (JRW, unpubl. data)
(3) 1 on 29 Aug-5 Sep 1987, Paris Landing SP (Robinson 1990, previously reported as Parasitic, but photos show Long-tailed, MT, pers. comm.)
(4) 1 on 27 Aug 2000, Island 13 (MIG 72:39)
(5) 1 on 30 Aug 2005, Pickwick Lake (MIG 76:24, Edwards 2012)
(6) 1 imm on 3 Sep 2008, Paris Landing SP (MIG 80:23)
(7) 1 imm on 14 Sep 2008, Reelfoot Lake, Lake Co. (MIG 80:23)
(8) 1 imm on 14 Oct 2009, Eagle Bend Fish Hatchery (MIG 81:55)

Substantiation: 1 ad on 2-3 Sep 1984, Island 13 (Stedman 1985)

Alcidae: Auks, Murres, and Puffins. Only one species has been documented via one record.

Long-billed Murrelet, *Brachyramphus perdix*
Status and Abundance: *Unsubstantiated*

Comments: This species was an "expected" vagrant, but there are no photos to substantiate the record. TBRC accepted this as the first state record in 2014.

Records
(1) 1 on 14 Dec 2002, Reelfoot Lake, Lake Co. (NAB 57(2), MIG 74:49, 53)

Laridae: Gulls, Terns, and Skimmers. Twenty-seven species have been documented in Tennessee, with only one nesting species (Least Tern), nine regularly occurring species statewide, and 17 species rare to accidental. Several additional species (notably Slaty-backed Gull) could potentially occur as vagrants to Tennessee.

Black-legged Kittiwake, *Rissa tridactyla*
Status and Abundance: Very rare fall and winter visitor
Habitat: Large bodies of water, typically near dams or mudflats, beaches, or other adjacent flat, open resting areas
Records
- (1) 1 on 21-22 Aug 1971, J. Percy Priest Lake (Blunk 1984)
- (2) 4 on 7-13 Dec 1971, Chickamauga and Nickajack Lakes (MIG 43:27, Robinson 1990)
- (3) 1 first cycle on 10 Oct 1981, Cookeville (MIG 53:19)
- (4) 1 first cycle on 10-12 Dec 1983, Bard's Lake, Stewart Co. (Blunk 1984)
- (5) 1 first cycle on 15-17 Dec 1985, Fort Loudoun Lake (MIG 57:60-61)
- (6) 1 ad on 20 Nov 1988, Paris Landing SP (MIG 60:26)
- (7) 1 first cycle on 30 Nov 1988-26 Jan 1989, Ft. Loudoun Lake (MIG 60:33, 65)
- (8) 1 first cycle on 13-17 Nov 1991, Pickwick Dam (MIG 63:53)
- (9) 1 first cycle on 27 Nov 1993, Pickwick Dam (JRW, unpubl. data)
- (10) 1 first cycle (first cycle) on 23 Jan 1994, Pickwick Dam (JRW, unpubl. data)
- (11) 1 first cycle on 27 Dec 1995-1 Jan 1996, Boone Dam (MIG 67:9, 33)
- (12) 1 on 9 Feb 1996, Pickwick Dam (MIG 67:31)
- (13) 1 first cycle on 20 Oct 1999, Chota, Tellico Lake (MIG 71:39)
- (14) 1 ad on 19 Apr 2003, S. Holston Lake (MIG 74:95)
- (15) 1 first cycle on 26 Dec 2008, Boone Dam, Kingsport CBC (MIG 80:51, 60, 71)
- (16) 1 first cycle on 8-9 Dec 2008, Robco Lake (MIG 80:66)
- (17) 1 first cycle on 28-29 Oct 2013, S. Holston Lake (MIG, in press)

Substantiation: Photograph: 1 first cycle on 27 Dec 1995, Boone Dam (Knight 2008:55)

Ivory Gull, *Pagophila eburnea*
Status and Abundance: Accidental visitor
Comments: Known from one record of a first cycle individual on 10-21 Feb 1996 at Pickwick Lake (Greene 1997); eventually found wrapped in fishing line and thought to have died but specimen was evidently not

collected.

Records

(1) 1 first cycle on 10-21 Feb 1996 (Greene 1997)

Substantiation: Photograph: 1 first cycle on 10-21 Feb 1996, Pickwick Lake (NAB 50(2))

Sabine's Gull, *Xema sabini*

Status and Abundance: Very rare fall transient

Habitat: Large rivers and lakes

Comments: Probably occurs annually along Mississippi River.

Records

(1) 1 ad on 20 Sep 1988, Chickamauga Lake (Robinson 1990, Knight 1993)
(2) 1 on 1 Oct 1988, Ensley (JRW, unpubl. data)
(3) 2-8 on 16-18 Sep 1995, Island 13 (Criswell 1997a, Greene 1997)
(4) 1 first cycle on 3 Sep 2001, Mud Island (MIG 73:11)
(5) 1 first cycle on 17 Sep 2002, Mud Island (MIG 74:16)
(6) 1 on 7 Sep 2003, S. Holston Lake (Knight 2008)
(7) 2 first cycle on 10 Sep 2003, Island 13 (MIG 75:24)
(8) 1 ad on 21 Oct 2007, Mississippi River, Shelby Co. (MIG 79:20)
(9) 1 first cycle on 21 Oct 2007, Pace Point (MIG 79:20)
(10) 1 ad on 8 Oct 2008, Mississippi River, Shelby Co. (MIG 80:23) 199
(11) 1 ad on 13 Sep 2009, Loosahatchie Bar, Shelby Co. (MIG 81:50)
(12) 2 first cycle on 25 Sep 2009, Pickwick Dam (MIG 81:50)

Substantiation: Photograph: 1 on 7 Sep 2003, S. Holston Lake (NAB 58(1):87)

Bonaparte's Gull, *Chroicocephalus philadelphia*

Status and Abundance: Fairly common transient, uncommon winter resident

Habitat: Large bodies of water, typically near dams or mudflats, beaches, or other adjacent flat, open resting areas

Spring Departure: late Apr

Fall Arrival: mid Oct

Comments: Becomes less common during winter, but large numbers may be found.

Late Spring

1 Jun 1993, Ensley (JRW, unpubl. data)
30 May 1983, Shelby Co. (MIG 54:60)
12 May 2007, Davidson Co. NAMC (MIG 78:128)
10 May 1997, Lake Co. (JRW, unpubl. data)

10 May 2009, Old Hickory Lake (MIG 80:89)
Early Fall
 20 Aug 1978, Pace Point (MIG 50:19)
 30 Aug 1986, Pace Point (MIG 58:20)
 30 Aug 2011, Rankin Bottoms (MIG 82:156)
 6 Sep 2009, Rankin Bottoms (MIG 81:55)
 14 Sep 1996, Rankin Bottoms (MIG 68:29)
High Counts – Spring
 2,000 on 1 Apr 2001, Samburg (MIG 72:92)
 1,500 on 30 Mar 1996, Reelfoot Lake, Lake Co. (JRW, unpubl. data)
 1,300 on 4 Mar 1989, Chickamauga Lake, Hamilton Co. (MIG 60:89)
 1,000 on 20 Mar 1988, Shelby Co. (Robinson 1990)
 784 on 19 Mar 2011, Cherokee Lake (MIG 82:90)
High Counts – Fall
 3,500+ on 26 Nov 2000, Big Sandy Unit (MIG 72:39)
High Counts – Winter
 5,000 on 9 Jan 2005, Benton and Henry Co. (MIG 76:78)
 4,100 on 16 Dec 2006, Reelfoot Lake CBC (MIG 78:65)
 3,500 on 13 Feb 2010, Cook Recreation Area (MIG 81:101)
 2,900+ on 31 Jan 2012, Cook Recreation Area (MIG 83:23)
 2,000 on 13 Dec 1997, Cherokee Lake (MIG 69:111)
Substantiation: Specimen: APSU, 3374

Black-headed Gull, *Chroicocephalus ridibundus*

Status and Abundance: Accidental fall, winter, and spring visitor
Records
 (1) 1 ad on 13-22 Mar 1987, Hamilton Creek, J. Percy Priest Lake, Davidson Co. (MIG 58:97)
 (2) 1 ad on 1 May 1988, Kingston Steam Plant (MIG 59:101, Knight 1993)
 (3) 1 ad on 18 Nov 1995, Reelfoot Lake (JRW, unpubl. data)
 (4) 1 ad on 25 Jan 2004, Big Sandy Unit (MIG 75:73)
Substantiation: Photograph: 1 ad on 17 Mar 1987, Hamilton Creek, J. Percy Priest Lake, Davidson Co. (TBRC Archives, UTK)

Little Gull, *Hydrocoloeus minutus*

Status and Abundance: Very rare fall, winter, and spring visitor
Habitat: Large bodies of water, typically near dams or mudflats, beaches, or other adjacent flat, open resting areas
Comments: Possibly annual in late fall and winter on Reelfoot Lake.
Records
 (1) 1 on 5 Mar 1988, Ensley (JRW, unpubl. data)

(2) 1 ad on 4 Nov 1989, Pace Point (JRW, unpubl. data)
(3) 1 ad on 19 Jan-13 Feb 1994, Chickamauga Lake (MIG 65:44)
(4) 1 ad on 31 Mar 2001, Samburg (MIG 73:8, MIG 72:92)
(5) 2 (1 ad, 1 first cycle) on 19 Nov-4 Dec 2005, Blue Bank area, Reelfoot Lake (MIG 76:24, MIG 77:57)
(6) 1 first cycle on 19 Nov 2009, Lick Creek, Benton Co. (MIG 81:50)
(7) 2 (1 ad, 1 first cycle) on 21-27 Nov 2009-13 Dec 2009, Reelfoot Lake (MIG 81:50, NM, pers. comm.)
(8) 1 first cycle on 21 Nov 2010, Reelfoot Lake (MIG 81:154)
(9) 1 first cycle on 18-24 Nov 2011, Reelfoot Lake (MIG 82:150)
(10) 1 ad on 2-30 Dec 2011-5 Jan 2012, Reelfoot Lake, Lake Co. (MIG 83:21)
(11) 1 first cycle on 19 Nov 2014, Reelfoot Lake, Lake Co. (MAG, pers. comm.)

Substantiation: Photograph: 1 first cycle on 19 Nov 2009, Lick Creek, Benton Co. (NAB 64(1):53)

Laughing Gull, *Leucophaeus atricilla*

Status and Abundance: Irregular transient and winter visitor; accidental summer visitor

Habitat: Large bodies of water, typically near dams or mudflats, beaches, or other adjacent flat, open resting areas

Comments: Records from every month of the year. Sightings concentrated around early to mid-May and from mid-Aug through mid-Sep.

High Counts – Spring
21 on 17 Apr 2006, Reelfoot Lake (MIG 77:98)

High Counts – Fall
50+ on 30-31 Aug 2005, Pickwick Lake following Hurricane Katrina (MIG 77:24)
21 on 13 Sep 2005 (holdovers from Aug 2005), Pickwick Lake (MIG 77:24)
12 on 1 Oct 2005, Chickamauga Lake (MIG 77:30)
9 on 27 Sep 2003, Spring Creek, S. Holston Lake (Knight 2008)
1-7 on 30-31 Aug 2005, Old Hickory Lake (MIG 77:26)

Summer Records
1 on 2 Jun 1996, Tipton Co. (JRW, unpubl. data)
1 on 9-10 Jun 1996, Lake Co. (MIG 67:77)
1 on 19 Jun 1998, Dyer Co. (MIG 69:186)
1 on 12 Jul 2005, Gibson Co. (MIG 76:144)

High Counts – Winter
15 on 15 Dec 1971, Chickamauga Lake (MIG 43:27)

Substantiation: Photograph: 1 on 11 May 1983, Austin Springs (Knight

2008:54)

Franklin's Gull, *Leucophaeus pipixcan*
Status and Abundance: Rare spring transient, uncommon fall transient, and rare winter visitor in Mississippi Alluvial Valley and Southeastern Coastal Plain; very rare transient and winter visitor elsewhere; accidental summer visitor

Habitat: Large bodies of water, typically near dams or mudflats, beaches, or other adjacent flat, open resting areas

Spring Arrival: early Apr

Spring Departure: early May

Fall Arrival: early Oct

Fall Departure: mid Nov

Comments: Records from every month of the year. Sightings concentrated in Oct-Nov.

Early Spring
- 5 Mar 1988, Shelby Co. (Robinson 1990)
- 13 Mar 1988, Dover, Stewart Co. (Robinson 1990)
- 18 Mar 1995, Reelfoot (JRW, unpubl. data)
- 20 Mar 1991, Ensley (JRW, unpubl. data)

Late Spring
- 30 May 1983, Gallatin Steam Plant (MIG 54:62)
- 6 Jun 2010, Mississippi River, Shelby Co. (MIG 81:114)

Early Fall
- 14 Aug 1994, Island 10, Lake Co. (JRW, unpubl. data)
- 15 Sep 1963, Mud Island (MIG 34:50)

High Counts – Spring
- 5 on 18 May 1993, Dyer Co. (MIG 64:64)
- 3 on 7 Apr 2005, Lake Co. (MIG 76:95)

High Counts – Fall
- 3,145 on 2 Nov 2003, Mississippi River, Lake Co. (MIG 75:24)
- 1,600 on 31 Oct 2004, Henry Co. (MIG 76:28)
- 624 on 31 Oct 2004, Mississippi River, Shelby Co. (JRW, unpubl. data)
- 117+ on 30 Oct 2010, Reelfoot Lake (MIG 81:154)

Summer Records
- 1 on 2 Jul 1972, Tennessee NWR (MIG 43:75)
- 1 imm on 24 Jul 1989, Cross Creeks NWR (MIG 60:106)
- 4 on 5-7 Jun 1998, Dyer Co. (MIG 69:186)

High Counts – Winter
- 2 on 11 Dec 2012, Murfreesboro (SGS, pers. obs.)

Substantiation: Photograph: 3,145 on 2 Nov 2003, Mississippi River, Lake Co. (NAB 58(1):87)

Ring-billed Gull, *Larus delawarensis*

Status and Abundance: Common transient and winter resident, rare (locally uncommon) summer visitor

Habitat: Large bodies of water, typically near dams or mudflats, beaches, or other adjacent flat, open resting areas

Spring Departure: late May

Fall Arrival: mid Jul

Comments: Small numbers of nonbreeding birds may be found during summer on the larger lakes.

Early Fall
- 3 Aug 2003, Island 13 (MIG 75:24)
- 4 Aug 2002, Cherokee Lake, Jefferson Co. (MIG 74:23)
- 5 Aug 2002, S. Holston Lake (MIG 74:26)
- 8 Aug 1991, Island 13 (MIG 63:53)

High Counts – Spring
- 1,000 on 9 Apr 2001, S. Holston Lake (MIG 72:99)

High Counts – Winter
- 55,000 on 22 Jan 2011, Cook Recreation Area (SGS, pers. obs.)
- 35,395 on 17 Dec 2005, Reelfoot Lake CBC (MIG 77:43)
- 28,000 on 19 Jan 2012, Cook Recreation Area (MIG 83:23)
- 25,000 on 11 Feb 2011, Cook Recreation Area (SGS, pers. obs.)
- 23,000 on 13 Feb 2010, Cook Recreation Area (MIG 81:101)

Substantiation: Specimen: UTM, 301

California Gull, *Larus californicus*

Status and Abundance: Very rare winter visitor

Habitat: Large bodies of water, typically near dams or mudflats, beaches, or other adjacent flat, open resting areas

Records
- (1) 2 first cycle on 10-12 Dec 1990 and 12 Jan 1991, Pickwick Dam (JRW, unpubl. data)
- (2) 1-2 on 13 Jan-24 Feb 1996, Pickwick Dam (Greene 1997)
- (3) 1 first cycle on 10-18 Jan 2004, Pickwick Landing SP (MIG 75:73)
- (4) 1 ad on 25 Feb-9 Mar 2004, Big Sandy Unit (MIG 76:4, MIG 75:111, 77:4)
- (5) 1 on 23 Jan-20 Feb 2005, Lake Co. (MIG 76:78)
- (6) 1 first cycle on 11 Nov 2007-3 Jan 2008, Pace Point and Paris Landing SP (MIG 79:20, 51)
- (7) 2 (1 ad, 1 first cycle) on 31 Oct-2 Nov 2009, Pickwick Dam (MIG 81:50)
- (8) 1 first cycle on 21 Oct 2012, Eagle Creek, Henry Co. (MIG, in press)

Laridae: Gulls, Terns, and Skimmers

Substantiation: Photograph: NAB 64(1)

Herring Gull, *Larus argentatus*

Status and Abundance: Uncommon transient and winter resident, very rare summer visitor

Habitat: Large bodies of water, typically near dams or mudflats, beaches, or other adjacent flat, open resting areas

Spring Departure: early May

Fall Arrival: mid Sep

Comments: Summer records are of nonbreeding birds or lingering migrants.

Late Spring
- 31 May 1975, Old Hickory Lake (MIG 46:88)
- 18 May 2002, Champey Pocket, Reelfoot Lake, Lake Co. (JRW, unpubl. data)
- 14 May 1996, Ensley (JRW, unpubl. data)

Early Fall
- 20 Aug 2010, S. Holston Lake (MIG 81:163)
- 23 Aug 1986, Stewart Co. (MIG 58:24)
- 24 Aug 2002, Ensley (MIG 74:16)
- 6 Sep 1980, Pace Point (MIG 52:22)

High Counts – Spring
- 6 on 28 Apr 2001, Reelfoot Lake (MIG 72:92)

High Counts – Fall
- 400 on 20 Nov 2008, Pace Point (MIG 80:23)
- 50+ on 19 Sep 2010, Paris Landing SP (MIG 81:154)
- 20 on 18 Nov 2002, S. Holston Lake (MIG 74:26)

High Counts – Winter
- 258 on 29 Dec 1984, Highland Rim CBC (MIG 56:7)
- 76 on 22 Dec 1992, Reelfoot Lake CBC (MIG 64:7)
- 76 on 28 Dec 2010, Cross Creeks CBC (MIG 82:48)

Substantiation: Photograph: 1 on 16 Mar 2007, Erwindelete dash (Knight 2008:54)

Thayer's Gull, *Larus thayeri*

Status and Abundance: Accidental winter visitor (very rare along the western part of Tennessee River)

Habitat: Large bodies of water, typically near dams or mudflats, beaches, or other adjacent flat, open resting areas

Records
- (1) 1 on 27 Jan/3 Mar 1991, Pickwick Dam (JRW, unpubl. data)
- (2) 2 (1 first cycle, 1 second cycle) on 11-15 Feb 1996, Pickwick Dam

(JRW, unpubl. data)
(3) 1 second cycle on 10 Feb 2002, Pickwick Dam (JRW, unpubl. data)
(4) 2 first cycle on 25 Dec 2002, 23 Feb 2003, 2 Mar 2003, Pickwick Landing SP (MIG 74:53, 87)
(5) 1 first cycle on 9 Feb 2003, New Hope Landing, Benton Co. (JRW, unpubl. data)
(6) 1 first cycle on 9 Jan-21 Feb 2004, Pickwick Landing SP (MIG 75:73)
(7) 1-3 (evidently all first cycle) on 23 Jan-6 Mar 2005, Lake Co. (MIG 76:78, 95)
(8) 1 on 5 Feb 2006, Big Sandy Unit (MT, pers. comm.)
(9) 1 on 2-9 Dec 2006, 11 Feb 2007, Lake Co. (MIG 78:78)
(10) 1 ad on 11-18 Nov 2007, Pace Point (MIG 79:20)
(11) 1-2 (1 first cycle, no age for other) on 24 Oct-2 Nov 2009, Pickwick Dam (MIG 81:50)
(12) 2 (1 ad, 1 first cycle) on 26 Dec 2009, Pace Point (MIG 81:100)
(13) 1 imm on 28 Nov 2010, Pickwick Dam (MIG 81:154)
(14) 1 ad on 12 Feb 2011, Pace Point (MIG 82:57)
(15) 1 ad on 23 Jan 2014, Pickwick Dam (MT, pers. comm.)
Substantiation: Photograph: 1 on 13 Feb 2005, Lake Co. (NAB 59(2):277)

Iceland Gull, *Larus glaucoides*

Status and Abundance: Accidental winter visitor

Habitat: Large bodies of water, typically near dams or mudflats, beaches, or other adjacent flat, open resting areas

Records
(1) 1 imm on 27 Feb 1979, Old Hickory dam (MIG 50:42)
(2) 1 on 19 Dec 1992-11 Jan 1993, Chickamauga Lake (MIG 64:51)
(3) 1 first cycle on 7 Mar 1998, Lick Creek WMA, Benton Co. (MIG 69:162, Calhoon 1999)
(4) 1-3 (all first cycle) on 13-27 Feb 2005, 5 on 20 Feb 2005, Lake Co. (MIG 76:78) with 2 still on 6 Mar 2005, Lake Co. (MIG 76:96)
(5) 1 first cycle on 7 Feb 2007, Pace Point (MIG 78:78)
Substantiation: Photograph: 1 on 13 Feb 2005, Lake Co. (NAB 59(2):277)

Lesser Black-backed Gull, *Larus fuscus*

Status and Abundance: Irregular transient and winter resident (uncommon along western part of Tennessee River)

Habitat: Large bodies of water, typically near dams or mudflats, beaches, or other adjacent flat, open resting areas

Spring Departure: mid Apr

Fall Arrival: early Oct

Comments: First state record on 28 Dec 1990, Pickwick Lake (MIG 61:11,

Laridae: Gulls, Terns, and Skimmers

81, Knight 1993). Now found annually. Increase in occurrence likely related to expansion of wintering population across N. America with most birds likely coming from Greenland.

Late Spring
    8 Apr 2003, Paris Landing SP (MIG 74:87)
    2 Apr 2013, Pace Point (MIG, in press)
    31 Mar 2002, Pace Point (MIG 73:57)

Early Fall
    27 Aug-1 Sep 2011, Rankin Bottoms (MIG 82:156)
    3 Sep 2008, Paris Landing SP (MIG 80:23)
    7 Sep 2013, Upper Douglas Lake (MIG, in press)

High Counts – Spring
    4 on 2 Mar 2003, Pickwick Landing SP (MIG 74:87)

High Counts – Fall
    5 on 12 Oct 2010, Paris Landing SP (MIG 81:154)
    4 on 15 Nov 2009, Pickwick Dam (MIG 81:50)
    4 on 2 Oct 2014, Paris Landing SP (SGS, pers. obs.)

High Counts – Winter
    2 on 16 Feb 2002, Paris Landing SP (JRW, unpubl. data)
    2 on 26 Feb 2005, Lake Co. (MIG 76:79)

Substantiation: Photograph: Somershoe, S.G. 2011. "Lesser Black-backed Gull". <http://www.pbase.com/shoeman/image/137672782> Accessed 25 Sep 2014.

Glaucous Gull, *Larus hyperboreus*

Status and Abundance: Very rare winter resident

Habitat: Large bodies of water, typically near dams or mudflats, beaches, or other adjacent flat, open resting areas

Records
    (1) 1 first cycle on 18 Jan-2 Feb 1969, Old Hickory Lake (Parmer and Monk 1969)
    (2) 1 first cycle on 7-24 Mar 1971, Ft. Loudoun Lake (Nicholson and Morton 1972)
    (3) 1 first cycle on 12 Jan 1984, Paris Landing SP (MIG 55:43)
    (4) 1 first cycle on 19 Jan 1985, Chickamauga Dam (Robinson 1990)
    (5) 1 first cycle on 5-13 Mar 1988, Ensley and McKellar Lake, Shelby Co. (JRW, unpubl. data)
    (6) 1 first cycle on 7-26 Jan 1989, Woods Reservoir (MIG 60:62)
    (7) 1 first cycle on 21 Jan 1989, Ft. Loudoun Lake (JRW, unpubl. data)
    (8) 1 first cycle on 5 Jan 1991, Woods Reservoir (MIG 62:83)
    (9) 1 first cycle on 6-21 Jan 1991, Pickwick Landing SP (MIG 62:81, JRW, unpubl. data)

(10) 1 first cycle on 7 Jan 1991, Middle Point Landfill, Rutherford Co. (MIG 62:83)
(11) 1 first cycle 23 Jan 1994, Pickwick Dam (MIG 65:40)
(12) 1 first cycle on Jan 1998, Pennington Bend (MIG 69:109)
(13) 1 first cycle on 25-26 Feb 2001, Britton Ford (MIG 72:68), likely same bird on 4 Mar 2001, Paris Landing SP (MIG 72:92)
(14) 1 first cycle on 16 Mar 2002, Paris Landing SP (MIG 73:57)
(15) 1 first cycle 23 Feb 2003, Pickwick Landing SP (MIG 74:53), likely same bird on 2 Mar 2003, Pickwick Landing SP (MIG 74:87)
(16) 1 first cycle on 24 Dec 2005, Paris Landing SP (MIG 77:57)
(17) 1 first cycle on 25 Dec 2008, Shelby Farms (MIG 80:66)
(18) 1 first cycle on 25 Dec 2008, Robco Lake (MIG 80:66)
(19) 1 first cycle on 13 Dec 2009, Reelfoot Lake (MIG 81:100)
(20) 1 first cycle on 19/21 Feb 2011, Duck River Unit (MIG 82:58)
(21) 1 ad (first ad in TN) on 26 Nov 2011, Pickwick Dam (MIG 82:150)
(22) 1 first cycle on 3 Jan 2013, Pickwick Lake (MIG, in press)

Substantiation: Photograph: Wilson, J.R. 2008. "Glaucous Gull". <http://www.pbase.com/ol_coot/image/107447327> Accessed 15 Dec 2014.

Great Black-backed Gull, *Larus marinus*

Status and Abundance: Very rare winter resident; accidental fall visitor

Habitat: Large bodies of water, typically near dams or mudflats, beaches, or other adjacent flat, open resting areas

Comments: Over 35 records.

Substantiation: Photograph: Hollie, D. 2014. "Great Black-backed Gull". <http://s259.photobucket.com/user/featherbrain1/media/LBBG2_zpsd61ce9d8.jpg.html> Accessed 25 Sep 2014.

Sooty Tern, *Onychoprion fuscatus*

Status and Abundance: Accidental visitor

Comments: All records are associated with tropical storms.

Records
(1) 1 on 30 Jul 1926, GSMNP (Stupka 1963)
(2) 1 imm m on 20 Jun 1934, Knoxville (Ijams 1934)
(3) 1 on 28 Sep 2002, Nickajack Lake (MIG 74:23)
(4) 1 found dead on 29 Sep 2002, Blount Co. (MIG 74:23)
(5) 2 on 4 Oct 2002, Rocky Point, Big Sandy Unit, Henry Co. (MIG 74:16)
(6) 1 ad on 8-11 Sep 2004, S. Holston Lake (Knight 2008)
(7) 1 ad on 17 Sep 2004, Nickajack Dam, Marion Co. (MIG 76:92)
(8) 2 ad on 17 Sep 2004, Cherokee Dam (MIG 76:35)

Laridae: Gulls, Terns, and Skimmers

(9) 14 on 11 Jul 2005, Pickwick Lake (MIG 76:144)

(10) 1 ad on 12 Jul 2005, J. Percy Priest Lake, Davidson Co. (MIG 76:145)

(11) 1 ad found dead on 12 Jul 2005, western Putnam Co. (MIG 76:145)

(12) 4 ad on 11 Jul 2005 and 1 on 13 Jul 2005, Chickamauga Dam (MIG 76:146)

(13) 1 on 12 Jul 2005, Gibson Co. Lake (MIG 76:144)

(14) 6 (5 ad, 1 imm) on 30 Aug 2005, Tennessee River, Hamilton Co. (MIG 76:30)

(15) 1-3 ad on 29-30 Aug 2005, Pickwick Dam (MIG 77:25, Edwards 2012)

(16) 1 on 31 Aug 2005, Old Hickory Lake (MIG 76:26)

Substantiation: Photograph: 1 on 9 Sep 2004, S. Holston Lake (Knight 2008:55)

Bridled Tern, *Onychoprion anaethetus*

Status and Abundance: ***Unsubstantiated***

Comments: Both records were in connection with tropical storms, but neither has been submitted to the TBRC and no photographs are known to have been obtained. Bridled Terns are less prone than Sooty Terns to being entrained by tropical storms, so, in the absence of photos or convincing documentation, it is possible that these records are attributable to misidentified Sooty Terns.

Records

(1) 1 on 11 Jul 2005, Pickwick Dam (MIG 76:144)

(1) 1 on 31 Aug 2005, Tennessee River, Hamilton Co. (MIG 77:30)

Least Tern, *Sternula antillarum*

Subspecies: *athalassos*

Status and Abundance: Fairly common spring transient and locally common summer resident in Mississippi Alluvial Valley, rare transient elsewhere

Habitat: Found along rivers and oxbows, nests on exposed sandbars, or in nearby agricultural fields if water levels are high

Spring Arrival: mid May

Fall Departure: mid Sep

Comments: This subspecies, often referred to as the Interior Least Tern, is listed as an Endangered Species under the Endangered Species Act of 1973. Nesting occurs almost exclusively on sandbars in the Mississippi River.

Early Spring

30 Mar 1969, near Nashville (MIG 40:46)

25 Apr 1997, Shelby Farms (MIG 68:107)
1 May 1994, Dyer Co. (JRW, unpubl. data)
2 May 1986, Columbia SBC (MIG 57:67)
Late Fall
19 Sep 2009, Shelby Co. FBC (MIG 81:43)
25 Sep 2004, Shelby Co. (MIG 76:28)
29 Sep 1974, Knoxville (MIG 46:22)
17 Oct 1983, Austin Springs (MIG 55:25)
High Counts – Spring
400 on 22 May 2011, Mooring, Lake Co. (MIG 82:85)
300 on 31 May 2002, Lake Co. (MIG 73:57)
180 on 25 May 2011, Robinson Bayou Road, Lake Co. (SGS, pers. obs.)
103 on 13 May 2000, Lake Co. NAMC (MIG 71:52)
High Counts – Fall
555 on 16 Aug 2013, Tiptonville Bar (SGS, pers. obs.)
55 on 1 Aug 2010, Mississippi River, Shelby Co. (MIG 81:154)
High Counts – Summer
600+ on 12 Jun 2004, Tipton Co. (MIG 75:159)
265 on 1 Jun 2002, Lake and Dyer Co. (MIG 73:111)
224 on 3 Jul 1984, Lauderdale Co. (MIG 55:88)
Substantiation: Specimen: LSUMZ, 75799

Gull-billed Tern, *Gelochelidon nilotica*
Status and Abundance: **Unsubstantiated**
Comments: Accepted by the TBRC on the basis of written documentation.
Records
(1) 1 on 22 May 2004, Hwy 103 near Great River Road, Dyer Co. (MIG 75:111)
(2) 1 ad on 26-27 May 2006, Kingston Steam Plant (Witt 2006, MIG 76:4)

Caspian Tern, *Hydroprogne caspia*
Status and Abundance: Uncommon transient, rare summer visitor, accidental winter visitor
Habitat: Large bodies of water and large exposed mudflats
Spring Arrival: early Apr
Spring Departure: mid May
Fall Arrival: mid Jul
Fall Departure: mid Oct
Comments: Birds may occur throughout June and July. They may be late spring transients, early fall transients, or nonbreeding birds as some appear to spend the summer in the state.

Early Spring
- 22 Mar 2003, Nickajack Lake (MIG 74:93)
- 26 Mar 1988, J. Percy Priest Lake (MIG 59:97)
- 28 Mar 2013, Pace Point (CF, pers. comm.)
- 29 Mar 2009, Nickajack Lake, Marion Co. (MIG 80:93)
- 30 Mar 2011, Pickwick Dam (JRW, unpubl. data)

Early Fall
- 29 Jun 1979, Kingston Steam Plant (MIG 50:89)
- 29 Jun 1995, Ensley (JRW, unpubl. data)
- 30 Jun 2002, Tiptonville Bar (JRW, unpubl. data)
- 2 Jul 1994, Black Bayou WMA (JRW, unpubl. data)
- 4 Jul 1991, Ensley (JRW, unpubl. data)

Late Fall
- 10 Nov 1984, Hiwassee River Area (MIG 56:25)
- 25 Oct 2007, S. Holston Lake (MIG 79:28)
- 24 Oct 2009, Pickwick Dam (MIG 81:50)
- 22 Oct 1976, Shelby Co. (MIG 48:17)
- 22 Oct 2011, Paris Landing SP (SGS, CAS, pers. obs)

High Counts – Spring
- 15 on 25 Apr 2000, Kingsport (MIG 71:92)
- 12 on 27 Apr 1990, Ensley (JRW, unpubl. data)
- 11 on 15 Apr 1990, Pickwick Dam (JRW, unpubl. data)
- 10 on 12 May 1996, Ensley (JRW, unpubl. data)
- 10 on 20 Apr 2011, Old Hickory Lake, Davidson Co. (SGS, pers. obs.)

High Counts – Fall
- 189+ on 22 Sep 2008, Paris Landing SP (MIG 80:23)
- 130 on 5 Sep 1964, Boone Lake (MIG 35:106)
- 130+ on 18 Aug 2012, Duck River Unit (SGS, pers. obs.)
- 110 on 5 Sep 2007, Pace Point (MIG 79:20)
- 100 on 17 Sep 1956, Memphis (MIG 27:67)

Summer Records
- 3 on 16 Jun 1963, Old Hickory Lake (Dubke 1963)
- 1 on 14 Jun 1977, Austin Springs (MIG 48:105)
- 15 Jun 1996, Island 13 (JRW, unpubl. data)
- 22 Jun 1996, Ridgely, Lake Co. (JRW, unpubl. data)
- 3 on 13 Jun 1997, Old Hickory Lake (MIG 68:135)
- 17 Jun 2001, Ensley (JRW, unpubl. data)
- 5 on 30 Jun 2002, Tiptonville Bar (JRW, unpubl. data)

Winter Records
- 1 on 3 Dec 1972, Nickajack Lake (MIG 44:26)
- 1 on 22 Jan 1993, Chickamauga Lake (MIG 64:51)
- 2 on 2 Jan 2006, Hatchie NWR (MIG 77:57)

Substantiation: Photograph: 5 on 9 Sep 2004, Musick's Campground (Knight 2008:56)

Black Tern, *Chlidonias niger*
Status and Abundance: Uncommon transient
Habitat: Large rivers and lakes
Spring Arrival: early May
Spring Departure: early Jun
Fall Arrival: mid Jul
Fall Departure: mid Sep
Comments: There are several mid-June records of uncertain migratory status.
Early Spring
    11 Apr 1976, Savannah Bay (MIG 47:78)
    13 Apr 1978, Shelby Co. (MIG 49:66)
    14 Apr 1928, Radnor Lake (BNA:27)
Late Spring
    15 Jun 2002, Paris Landing SP (MIG 73:111)
    13 Jun 2003, White Lake WMA (MIG 74:130)
    11 Jun 1989, Shelby Forest WMA (JRW, unpubl. data)
    9 Jun 1996, Reelfoot Lake (JRW, unpubl. data)
    8 Jun 1997, Mississippi River, Dyer Co. (JRW, unpubl. data)
Early Fall
    30 Jun 1987, Cross Creeks NWR (MIG 59:36)
    1 Jul 1962, Lake Co. (MIG 33:47)
    1 Jul 2007, Dacus Bar (MIG 78:140)
    6 Jul 2007, Dacus Bar (MIG 78:140)
    8 Jul 2004, Shelby Farms (MIG 75:159)
Late Fall
    14 Oct 1976, Shelby Co. (MIG 48:17)
    5 Oct 1995, Boone Lake (MIG 67:22)
    1 Oct 1964, Bluff City, Sullivan Co. (MIG 35:104)
High Counts – Spring
    75 on 18 May 2002, Dyer Co. (MIG 73:57)
    67 on 18 May 2002, Mud Lake, Lake Co. (JRW, unpubl. data)
    57 on 14 May 1995, Ensley (JRW, unpubl. data)
    53 on 19 May 1995, Shelby Farms (JRW, unpubl. data)
    52 on 13 May 2000, Lake Co. NAMC (MIG 71:52)
High Counts – Fall
    700 on 17 Aug 2002, Lake and Dyer Co. (MIG 74:16)
    230 on 30 Aug 1955, Nashville (MIG 26:48)
    100+ on 30-31 Aug 2005, Pickwick Lake (MIG 77:25)

117 on 25 Jul 2009, Mississippi River, Shelby Co. (MIG 80:124)
60 on 29 Jul 2006, Mud Island (MIG 77:143)
Substantiation: Specimen: LSUMZ, 75802

Common Tern, *Sterna hirundo*
Status and Abundance: Uncommon transient
Habitat: Large rivers and lakes
Spring Arrival: mid Apr
Spring Departure: mid May
Fall Arrival: mid Aug
Fall Departure: early Oct
Comments: There are several June records of uncertain migratory status.
Early Spring
31 Mar 2012, Kentucky Lake, Henry Co. (TW, CS, pers. comm.)
1 Apr 1972, Cherokee Lake (MIG 43:53)
Late Spring
4 Jun 1996, Hwy 79W, Lake Co. (MIG 67:77)
4 Jun 1996, Island 13 (MIG 67:77)
3 Jun 1968, Columbia (MIG 39:64)
3 Jun 1972, Tennessee NWR (MIG 43:75)
Early Fall
28 Jun 1993, S. Holston Lake (MIG 64:88)
2 Jul 1972, Tennessee NWR (MIG 43:75)
4 Jul 1972, Old Hickory Lake (MIG 43:76)
5 Jul 2003, Great River Road (MIG 74:130)
7 Jul 1984, Savannah Bay (MIG 55:94)
Late Fall
9 Nov 1991, Nolichucky Waterfowl Sanctuary, Greene Co. (MIG 63:55)
9 Nov 1997, Middlebrook Lake, Sullivan Co. (MIG 69:49)
3 Nov 1984, Rutherford Co. (MIG 56:21)
31 Oct 2007, Eagle Creek, Henry Co. (MIG 79:20)
29 Oct 1980, Austin Springs (MIG 52:25)
High Counts – Spring
18 on 10 May 1997, Jefferson Co. NAMC (MIG 68:99)
5 on 12 May 2001, Lake Co. NAMC (MIG 72:16)
5 on 17 May 2001, S. Holston Lake (MIG 72:99)
High Counts – Fall
100 on 6 Sep 2011, Old Hickory Lake, Davidson Co. (SGS, pers. obs.)
100+ on 17 Sep 2004, Cherokee Dam (MIG 76:34)
96 on 24 Sep 1988, Ft. Loudoun Lake (MIG 60:33)
91 on 15 Sep 2002, Boone Lake (MIG 74:23)
66 on 19 Sep 2006, S. Holston Lake (MIG 78:42)

High Counts – Summer
- 6 on 25 Jul 1994, Burnt Woods Road (MIG 65:62)
- 6 on 3 Jun 2012, Woods Reservoir (MIG 83:103)

Substantiation: Photograph: Somershoe, S.G. 2011. "Common Tern" <http://www.pbase.com/image/157564231> Accessed 25 Sep 2014.

Arctic Tern, *Sterna paradisaea*

Status and Abundance: ***Unsubstantiated***

Comments: Accepted by the TBRC on the basis of written documentation. An evaluation of the first record by Cardiff and Dittman (1991) concluded that the description was generally consistent with Arctic Tern and that the timing was reasonable for a vagrant Arctic Tern, but they also noted several points of concern. No details on the second record have ever been published. This is a tricky identification issue, especially for observers not familiar with the species (as was the case with both of these records).

Records
- (1) 1 on 6 Jul 1990, Island 13 (Criswell 1991, Knight 1993)
- (2) 1 on 14-15 Jun 2003, Champey Pocket to Bo's Landing, Reelfoot Lake, Lake Co. (JRW, GC, pers. comm.)

Forster's Tern, *Sterna forsteri*

Status and Abundance: Fairly common transient; irregular winter resident
Habitat: Large rivers and lakes; mudflats
Spring Arrival: early Apr
Spring Departure: mid May
Fall Arrival: mid Jul
Fall Departure: mid Nov

Comments: There are several June records of uncertain migratory status. Records exist for every month of the year. Fall birds may linger late into winter. All winter records have occurred since 1983.

Early Spring
- 10 Mar 2002, Mud Island, Shelby Co. (JRW, unpubl. data)
- 16 Mar 1990, Mud Lake, Shelby Co. (JRW, unpubl. data)
- 26 Mar 1988, J. Percy Priest Lake (MIG 59:97-98)
- 27 Mar 2011, Duck River Unit (MIG 82:86)
- 1 Apr 1988, Paris Landing SP (Robinson 1990)

Late Spring
- 15 Jun 1991, Reelfoot Lake (JRW, unpubl. data)
- 10 Jun 1996, Hwy 79W, Lake Co. (MIG 67:77)
- 8-9 Jun 1991, Reelfoot Lake (JRW, unpubl. data)
- 7 Jun 1986, Lawrence Co. (MIG 57:79)

3 Jun 1972, Tennessee NWR (MIG 43:75)
Early Fall
    2 Jul 1972, Tennessee NWR (MIG 43:75)
    3 Jul 1975, Old Hickory Lake (BNA:26)
    7 Jul 1984, Savannah Bay (MIG 55:94)
Late Fall
    28 Nov 2009, Robco Lake (MIG 81:50)
    26 Nov 1993, Shelby Farms (JRW, unpubl. data)
    19 Nov 1985, Britton Ford (MIG 57:23)
High Counts – Spring
    180 on 1 May 1994, Dyer Co. (JRW, unpubl. data)
    56 on 2 May 1989, Island 13 (MIG 60:83)
    45 on 28 Apr 1996, Reelfoot Lake (JRW, unpubl. data)
    26 on 12 May 2001, Lake Co. NAMC (MIG 72:16)
    23 on 9 May 1992, Chattanooga SBC (MIG 63:48)
High Counts – Fall
    200+ on 11 Oct 2008, Reelfoot Lake (MIG 80:23)
    200+ on 31 Oct 2007, Eagle Creek, Henry Co. (MIG 79:20)
    152 on 12 Oct 2006, Henry Co. (MIG 78:33)
    75+ on 3 Nov 2012, Eagle Creek, Henry Co. (MIG 83:148)
    50+ on 22-24 Sep 1989, Watauga Lake (MIG 61:21)
High Counts – Winter
    50 on 3 Dec 2006, Lick Creek WMA, Benton Co. (MIG 78:78)
    8 on 24 Feb 2001, Robco Lake (JRW, unpubl. data)
    7 on 17 Feb 2001, Robco Lake (JRW, unpubl. data)
    5 on 4 Dec 2005, Lick Creek WMA, Benton Co. (MIG 77:57)
    5 on 9 Jan 2005, Lick Creek WMA, Benton Co. (MIG 76:79)
Substantiation: Specimen: LSUMZ, 75797

Royal Tern, *Thalasseus maximus*

Status and Abundance: Accidental summer and fall visitor

Habitat: Large rivers and lakes

Comments: All records except the last were associated with tropical storms.

Records
    (1) 2 on 22 Sep 1989, Roan Creek section of Watauga Lake (MIG 61:21, Knight 1993)
    (2) 1 on 12 Jul 2005, Pickwick Lake (MIG 76:144)
    (3) 1 on 1 Sep 2005, Dacus Bar (MIG 76:25)
    (4) 1 on 2 Sep 2005, Pickwick Lake (MIG 76:25)
    (5) 1 on 26 Jul 2008, Dacus Bar (MIG 79:97)

Substantiation: Photograph: 1 on 1 Sep 2005, Dacus Bar (NAB 62(4))

Black Skimmer, *Rynchops niger*
Status and Abundance: Accidental fall visitor

Habitat: Large rivers and lakes

Comments: All records are associated with thepassage of tropical storms systems.

Records
- (1) 1 found dead in 1890 in Obion Co. after a severe storm (Rhoads 1895). Specimen was placed in Albert Ganier's collection (Alsop 1972), but its current location is unknown.
- (2) 1 on 5 Oct 1995, Tennessee River, Marion Co. (Greene 1997)
- (3) 1 on 30 Aug 2005, Pickwick Lake (MIG 76:25, Edwards 2012)
- (4) 1 on 2 Sep 2005, Tennessee River, Hamilton Co. (MIG 76:30)
- (5) 1 on 17 Sep 2005, Dacus Bar (MIG 76:25)

Substantiation: Photograph: 1 on 2 Sep 2005, Tennessee River, Hamilton Co. (NAB 60(1):82)

Columbidae: Pigeons and Doves

Columbidae: Pigeons and Doves. Eight species represent this varied group of birds in Tennessee, although one is extinct. Three species are statewide and common to uncommon year round residents, with two of these species being non-native.

Rock Pigeon, *Columba livia*
Status and Abundance: Common permanent resident
Habitat: Urban areas, farmlots, under bridges and on cliff walls
Comments: A domesticated Old World species introduced into the U.S.
High Counts
 3,200 on 17 Dec 1994, Chattanooga CBC (MIG 66:14)
 1,773 on 18 Dec 2004, Chattanooga CBC (MIG 76:64)
 1,589 on 30 Apr 2011, Elizabethton SBC (MIG 82:69)
 1,578 on 20 Dec 1998, Memphis CBC (MIG 70:14)
 1,438 on 28 Dec 1996, Chattanooga CBC (MIG 68:21)
Substantiation: Specimen: APSU, 1232

Band-tailed Pigeon, *Patagioenas fasciata*
Status and Abundance: *Unsubstantiated*
Comments: One well-described bird on 9 Apr 1974, near Nashville (Fintel 1974). TBRC lists it as provisional because the origin of the bird was in doubt (Nicholson 1983). In the opinion of the authors, that bird was more likely a natural vagrant.
Records
 (1) 1 on 9 Apr 1974, near Nashville (Fintel 1974)

Eurasian Collared-Dove, *Streptopelia decaocto*
Status and Abundance: Locally uncommon to common permanent resident; introduced
Habitat: Suburban areas, agricultural lands and adjacent industrial complexes
Comments: First record was on 23 May 1994, Shelby Co. (JRW, unpubl. data). Consistent with the trend across North America, this species has steadily increased over the past 20 years. Records exist from nearly all counties in Tennessee.
High Counts
 3,000 on 1 Dec 2007, President's Island (MIG 79:51)
 624 on 15 Jan 2004, President's Island (MIG 75:73)
 515 on 20 Dec 2009, Memphis CBC (MIG 81:93)
 473 on 5 Oct 2003, Presidents Island (MIG 75:24)
 351 on 16 Dec 2007, Memphis CBC (MIG 79:37)

Substantiation: Photograph: Somershoe, S.G. 2008. "Eurasian Collared-Dove" <http://www.pbase.com/shoeman/image/157564157> Accessed 25 Sep 2014.

Passenger Pigeon, *Ectopistes migratorius*
Status and Abundance: Extinct
Comments: No nest records known for Tennessee (Ganier 1933a). Last sighting was possibly 8 birds shot near Brownsville in 1893 (Rhoads 1895).

Inca Dove, *Columbina inca*
Status and Abundance: Accidental spring, fall, and winter visitor
Records
  (1) 1 on 21-22 May 2005, Ensley (MIG 77:5) (not submitted to TBRC)
  (2) 1 on 28 Aug 2005, near Chickamauga Dam, Hamilton Co. (MIG 77:5)
  (3) 1 on 24 Nov-7 Dec 2005, Fayette Co. (Graham 2012) (first accepted TBRC record in TN)
  (4) 1 on 18 Oct-16 Dec 2006, Morristown (MIG 78:39, MIG 78:82, Edwards 2012)
  (5) 1 on 25 Aug 2010, Cates Landing (MIG 81:155)
Substantiation: Photograph: 1 on 22 May 2005, Ensley (NAB 59(3):445)

Common Ground-Dove, *Columbina passerina*
Status and Abundance: Very rare visitor
Comments: Over 30 records. Most records during fall and winter. Few spring records and few recent records.
High Counts – Spring
  2 on 13 Mar 1987, Hardin Co. (MIG 58:93)
  2 on 3 Mar 2008, Moss Island WMA (MIG 81:100)
High Counts – Fall
  3 on 14 Nov 1992, Ensley (JRW, unpubl. data)
Substantiation: Specimen: UTM, 406

White-winged Dove, *Zenaida asiatica*
Status and Abundance: Very rare spring and fall visitor; accidental summer resident
Habitat: Fields, farms, and agricultural areas
Comments: Appears to have bred on President's Island in 2011 and appears to be occurring with increasing frequency. No records before 2000.

Records
- (1) 1 on 25-27 Jun 2000, Shelby Co. (Purrington 2000) (not submitted to TBRC)
- (2) 1 on 25 May 2001, Clarksville (MIG 76:4) (photo submitted to TBRC but without written documentation)
- (3) 1 on 9-10 Jul 2005, Tipton Co. (MIG 76:4)
- (4) 1 on 19 May 2008, McKenzie, Carroll Co. (MIG 79:62)
- (5) 1 on 18 Apr 2009, Butcher Valley, Hawkins Co. (MIG 80:93)
- (6) 2 on 22 May 2009, President's Island (MIG 80:88)
- (7) 1 on 18 Jun 2010, Memphis (MIG 81:125)
- (8) up to 5 (incl. imm birds): 2 on 30 Apr 2011, 3 on 23-28 Aug 2011, 5 on 3 Sep 2011, President's Island, (MIG 82:85, MIG 82:150, JRW, unpubl. data)
- (9) 3 on 23-28 Aug 2011, Mud Island (MIG 82:150)
- (10) 1 on 29 Apr 2012, near Pikeville, Bledsoe Co. (MIG 83:71)
- (11) 1 on 5 May 2012, White Co. (MIG 83:66)
- (12) 1-2 on 6-16 May and 10 Jun 2012, President's Island (MIG 83:65, MIG 83:103)
- (13) 2 on 14 Dec 2012, Shelby Co. (MIG, in press)
- (14) 1 on 18-20 Apr 2013, Nashville (MIG, in press)
- (15) 1 on 25 Apr 2013, DeKalb Co. (MIG, in press)
- (16) 1 on 29 Apr 2013, Shelby Co. (MIG, in press)
- (17) 1 on 8-9 Jul 2013, Standifer Gap Marsh (MIG, in press)

Substantiation: Photograph: 2 on 30 Apr 2011, President's Island (NAB 65(3):50)

Mourning Dove, *Zenaida macroura*

Status and Abundance: Common permanent resident

Habitat: Fields, farms, open areas; common urban and suburban resident

High Counts
- 5,000 on 1 Jan 1958, Lebanon CBC (MIG 28:65)
- 1,288 on 21 Dec 1991, Kingsport CBC (MIG 63:14)
- 1,128 on 18 Dec 1993, Jackson CBC (MIG 65:17)
- 1,059 on 17 Dec 1994, Chattanooga CBC (MIG 66:14)
- 1,027 on 14 Dec 2003, Memphis CBC (MIG 75:59)

Substantiation: Specimen: LSUMZ, 75803

Cuculidae: Cuckoos, Roadrunners, and Anis. Three species occur in Tennessee, one is a widespread breeding species, one is rare and a very local breeding species, and one is accidental. Greater Roadrunner is a possible vagrant to Tennessee.

Yellow-billed Cuckoo, *Coccyzus americanus*
    Status and Abundance: Fairly common transient and summer resident
    Habitat: Found in river bottoms, hedgerows, and woodland edges
    Spring Arrival: mid Apr
    Fall Departure: late Oct
    Early Spring
        29 Mar 1967, Reelfoot Lake (MIG 38:47)
        3 Apr 1985, Nashville (MIG 56:77)
    Late Fall
        25 Nov 1973, Old Hickory Lake (MIG 45:21)
        6 Nov 1977, Dyersburg (MIG 49:41)
        5 Nov 1980, Austin Springs (MIG 52:49)
    High Counts – Spring
        61 on 11 May 2002, Nashville SBC (MIG 73:105)
        58 on 11 May 2002, Shelby Co. NAMC (MIG 73:96)
        43 on 8 May 2004, Nashville SBC (MIG 75:105)
        36 on 30 Apr 1961, Knoxville SBC (MIG 32:31)
    High Counts – Fall
        59 on 18 Sep 2010, Shelby Co. FBC (MIG 81:143)
        17 on 15 Sep 2001, Shelby Co. FBC (MIG 73:31)
        12 on 21 Sep 2003, Shelby Co. FBC (MIG 73:51)
        9 on 17 Sep 2005, Shelby Co. FBC (MIG 77:17)
    High Counts – Summer
        13 on 30 Jun 1996, Carter Co. (MIG 67:79)
    Winter Records
        1 on 23 Dec 1941, Memphis (MIG 13:20)
        1 on 9 Dec 1953, Memphis (MIG 25:15)
        1 on 25 Feb 1961, Nashville (MIG 32:5)
    Substantiation: Specimen: LSUMZ, 75811

Black-billed Cuckoo, *Coccyzus erythropthalmus*
    Status and Abundance: Irregular transient; rare summer resident
    Habitat: Found in shrubby open areas and in woodlands
    Spring Arrival: mid Apr
    Fall Departure: early Oct
    Comments: One of Tennessee's most enigmatic and unpredictable species.

Nesting has been documented across Tennessee, but is rare. June birds may be late spring migrants or post-breeding birds. Nest with recent fledglings confirmed at Hampton Creek Cove on 24 May 2011 (MIG 82:94), so birds in June may also be local breeders.

Early Spring
 8 Apr 1965, Elizabethton (MIG 36:65)

Late Fall
 3 Nov 1974, near Erwin (MIG 46:24)
 27 Oct 1957, Shelby Co. (MIG 29:7)
 26 Oct 1997, Shelby Forest SP (MIG 69:41)
 22 Oct 1973, Old Hickory Lake (MIG 44:100)

High Counts – Spring
 9 on 4 May 1958, Kingsport SBC (MIG 29:31)
 9 on 7 May 1950, Elizabethton SBC (MIG 21:26)
 7 on 14 May 2005, Montgomery Co. NAMC (MIG 76:129)
 5 on 13 May 2008, Hampton Creek Cove (SGS, pers. obs., m.ob.)

High Counts – Fall
 2 on 25 Sep 2010, Elizabethton FBC (MIG 81:143)

Substantiation: Specimen: LSUMZ, 75815

Groove-billed Ani, *Crotophaga sulcirostris*

Status and Abundance: Accidental visitor

Records
 (1) 1 on 29 Nov 1968, north of Dyersburg (Leggett 1969)
 (2) 1 on 17 Oct 1985, Tigrett WMA (Criswell 1986)

Substantiation: Specimen: LSUMZ, 75817

Tytonidae: Barn Owls. One species occurs and is an uncommon permanent resident statewide.

Barn Owl, *Tyto alba*
  Status and Abundance: Uncommon permanent resident
  Habitat: Found in open areas, incl. riparian, woodland edge, pasture/agricultural areas and in towns and cities
  High Counts – Spring
    9 on 8 May 2004, Hamilton Co. NAMC (MIG 75:94)
    7 on 10 May 2003, Hamilton Co. NAMC (MIG 74:115)
    6 on 13 May 2000, Greene Co. NAMC (MIG 71:52)
    6 on 25 Apr 1998, Greeneville NAMC (MIG 69:151)
  High Counts – Winter
    4 on 17 Dec 2005, Columbia CBC (MIG 77:42)
    4 on 2 Jan 2005, Fayette Co. CBC (MIG 76:64)
  Substantiation: Specimen: LSUMZ, 75818

Strigidae: Typical Owls. Seven species occur in Tennessee, with four resident species, two species found wintering statewide, and one species accidental. Burrowing Owl is a possible vagrant to Tennessee.

Eastern Screech-Owl, *Megascops asio*
> Status and Abundance: Fairly common permanent resident
> Habitat: Found in wooded areas
> Comments: Less common in bottomland hardwood forests that are regularly inundated by floodwaters.
> High Counts – Spring
>> 18 on 18 Mar 2010, Davidson Co. (SGS, pers. obs.)
>> 14 on 13 May 2000, Hamilton Co. NAMC (MIG 71:52)
>> 12 on 5 May 1991, Elizabethton SBC (MIG 62:36)
>> 11 on 5 May 1991, Knoxville SBC (MIG 62:36)
>
> High Counts – Fall
>> 29 on 4 Oct 2009, White Co. FBC (MIG 81:43)
>> 26 on 25 Sep 2010, Elizabethton FBC (MIG 81:143)
>> 24 on 25 Sep 2010, DeKalb Co. FBC (MIG 81:143)
>> 22 on 15 Sep 2008, Putnam Co. FBC (MIG 79:14)
>> 22 on 5 Oct 2002, Elizabethton FBC (MIG 73:51)
>
> High Counts – Winter
>> 31 on 20 Dec 1981, Knoxville CBC (MIG 53:7)
>> 25 on 26 Dec 2004, Bristol CBC (MIG 76:64)
>> 24 on 28 Dec 1998, Bristol CBC (MIG 70:15)
>
> Substantiation: Specimen: LSUMZ, 75823

Great Horned Owl, *Bubo virginianus*
> Status and Abundance: Fairly common permanent resident
> Habitat: Found in wooded areas
> High Counts – Spring
>> 16 on 12 May 2001, Maury Co. NAMC (MIG 72:16)
>> 16 on 30 May 1989, Knoxville SBC (MIG 60:49)
>> 7 on 1 May 2005, Lincoln Co. SBC (MIG 76:139)
>
> High Counts – Fall
>> 10 on 4 Oct 2009, White Co. FBC (MIG 81:43)
>> 9 on 18 Oct 2010, White Co. FBC (MIG 81:143)
>> 7 on 21 Sep 2002, Putnam Co. FBC (MIG 73:51)
>> 7 on 9 Oct 2010, Nashville FBC (MIG 81:143)
>
> High Counts – Winter
>> 22 on 31 Dec 1995, Bristol CBC (MIG 67:9)
>> 19 on 17 Dec 1994, Nashville CBC (MIG 66:14)

19 on 2 Jan 1995, Columbia CBC (MIG 66:14)
19 on 28 Dec 1996, Bristol CBC (MIG 68:21)
18 on 27 Dec 1986, Bristol CBC (MIG 58:3)
Substantiation: Specimen: LSUMZ, 75832

Snowy Owl, *Bubo scandiacus*

Status and Abundance: Very rare irruptive winter visitor
Habitat: Found in fields, pastures, farmland, and other wide open areas
Records
(1) 1 shot on 3 Feb 1918, Paris, Henry Co. (MIG 2:7)
(2) 1 shot on 3 Dec 1930, Reelfoot Lake (MIG 2:7)
(3) 1 shot on 21 Dec 1930, Paris, Henry Co. (Thompson 1930)
(4) 1 shot on 31 Dec 1930, Johnson City (MIG 2:7)
(5) 1 killed during winter 1930-31, Sullivan Co. (Coffey 1964)
(6) 1 on 11 Nov 1954, Eagle Creek Bay, Henry Co., later shot in mid-Dec. in Benton Co. (Cypert 1955a)
(7) 1 on 1 Dec 1956, Cumberland/White Co. line (Kellberg 1956)
(8) 1 on 18 Dec 1960-26 Feb 1961, Nashville (Munro 1961)
(9) 1 shot in Jan 1961, Telford, Washington Co. (Knight 2008)
(10) 1 on 5 Jan-6 Feb 1987, Barkley WMA, Stewart Co. (MIG 58:56-57)
(11) 1 on 11 Dec 2001, Cherokee Lake (MIG 73:39)
(12) 1 on 16 Jan-15 Feb 2009, Spring Hill, Maury Co., seen as early as 3 Dec 2008 (MIG 80:68)
Substantiation: Specimen: CSM, AV-324

Barred Owl, *Strix varia*

Status and Abundance: Uncommon permanent resident in Ridge and Valley and Southern Blue Ridge; fairly common permanent resident elsewhere
Habitat: Found in wooded areas, especially bottomland woods and wooded swamps
High Counts – Spring
20 on 7 May 2011, Nashville SBC (MIG 82:69)
11 on 13 May 2006, Nashville SBC (MIG 77:123)
11 on 8 May 2004, Montgomery Co. NAMC (MIG 75:95)
9 on 14 May 2005, Montgomery Co. NAMC (MIG 76:129)
8 on 12 May 2001, Lake Co. NAMC (MIG 72:16)
High Counts – Fall
14 on 20 Sep 2008, Putnam Co. FBC (MIG 80:16)
11 on 19 Sep 2009, Putnam Co. FBC (MIG 81:43)
7 on 18 Oct 2010, White Co. FBC (MIG 81:143)
7 on 5 Oct 2002, Elizabethton FBC (MIG 73:51)

Strigidae: Typical Owls

High Counts – Winter
    24 on 17 Dec 2005, Reelfoot Lake CBC (MIG 77:43)
    24 on 19 Dec 1981, Lebanon CBC (MIG 54:13)
    22 on 16 Dec 2006, Reelfoot Lake CBC (MIG 78:65)
    17 on 20 Dec 1986, Reelfoot Lake CBC (MIG 58:3)
Substantiation: Specimen: LSUMZ, 75835

Long-eared Owl, *Asio otus*
Status and Abundance: Rare winter resident
Habitat: Found in coniferous woods and mixed coniferous/deciduous woods
Spring Departure: mid Mar
Fall Arrival: mid Nov
Comments: Probably annual and uncommon, with most individuals undetected.
Late Spring
    10 Apr 1975, Bristol (MIG 46:70)
    9 Apr 1958, Memphis (Irwin 1958)
    6 May 1989, Cades Cove (MIG 60:91)
    3 Apr 1954, Memphis (Landis 1955)
Early Fall
    7 Nov 2010, Pace Point area (MIG 81:155)
    4 Nov 1972, Lawrence Co. (MIG 44:23)
High Counts – Fall
    5 on 26 Nov 2000, Hop-In WMA (MIG 72:39)
    3 on 27 Nov 1998, West Sandy WMA, Henry Co. (JRW, unpubl. data)
Substantiation: Specimen: LSUMZ, 75838

Short-eared Owl, *Asio flammeus*
Status and Abundance: Locally uncommon transient and winter resident
Habitat: Found in open areas, especially open, brushy fields
Spring Departure: late Mar
Fall Arrival: mid Nov
Late Spring
    25 May 1997, Fayette Co. (MIG 68:72)
    5 May 1955, Buena Vista Marsh (BNA:30)
    5 May 1956, Nashville SBC (MIG 27:33)
    17 Apr 1954, Nashville (Ganier 1954)
    17 Apr 1954, Shelby Farms (Coffey 1955)
Early Fall
    2 Oct 1988, Metro Center, Nashville (MIG 60:29)
    12 Oct 1955, Memphis (MIG 27:16)

13 Oct 2006, Big Bald Mtn. (MIG 78:42)
13 Oct 2006, Smith Co. (MIG 78:35)
25 Oct 1930, Knox Co. (Howell and Monroe 1958)
25 Oct 1990, Lake Co. (KM *fide* MAG)

High Counts – Spring
25 on 5 Apr 1954, Nashville (Ganier 1954)

High Counts – Fall
5 on 25 Oct 1990, Lake Co. (KM *fide* MAG)

High Counts – Winter
17 on 6 Feb 2001, Dyer Co. (MIG 72:69)
15 on 9 Dec 1990, Ensley (MIG 62:81)
13 on 18 Dec 2010, Reelfoot Lake CBC (MIG 82:50)
10 on 23 Dec 1988, Savannah CBC (MIG 60:16)
7 on Feb 1998, Wolf River WMA (MIG 69:107)

Substantiation: Specimen: LSUMZ, 75837

Northern Saw-whet Owl, *Aegolius acadicus*

Status and Abundance: Rare late fall and early spring transient and winter resident; locally uncommon permanent resident in Southern Blue Ridge

Habitat: Breeds in dense spruce and fir forests and deciduous hardwood forests generally above 3500 ft in SBR; during winter and migration, coniferous forests and thickets and mixed conifer/hardwood forests

Comments: Possibly the most underdetected species in Tennessee relative to its likely abundance; banding data in Alabama suggests good numbers pass through middle Tennessee, but are rarely detected. Nesting documented on Roan Mtn., Unaka Mountain, GSMNP, and likely occurs at Whigg Meadow, Cherokee NF. See Knight (2010) for a summary of nesting on Roan Mtn. Two ad with 2 recently fledged young on 8-11 May 1988 in Claiborne Co. (McKinney and Owen 1989).

Late Spring
2 Mar 1989, Mud Island (MIG 60:83)

Early Fall
29 Oct 2011, Chapel Hill, Marshall Co. (MIG 82:152)
7 Nov 2010, Seven Islands Wildlife Refuge (MIG 81:160)
8 Nov 2007, Warner Parks (MIG 79:22)

High Counts – Fall
4 banded on 10 Nov 2007, Seven Islands Wildlife Refuge (MIG 79:26)

Substantiation: Specimen: UTM, 410

Caprimulgidae: Goatsuckers. Three species occur statewide in Tennessee, all as breeding residents and transients where preferred habitat is available. Lesser Nighthawk could potentially occur as a vagrant.

Common Nighthawk, *Chordeiles minor*

Status and Abundance: Fairly common transient and summer resident; very rare early winter resident

Habitat: Urban areas (nesting on flat rooftops), particularly areas with lots of nighttime lights. Also found nesting in cedar glades, on exposed limestone, and other similar habitats

Spring Arrival: late Apr

Fall Departure: late Oct, possible lingering into Nov and into winter

Comments: Large numbers can be observed migrating in the fall, usually from late Aug to early Sep. Over 10 winter records, primarily from Nashville and Knoxville, although overwintering has not been established. These early winter records are likely lingering transients or residents feeding on insects attracted to well-lit parking lots and stadiums, and they either die or migrate further south when freezing temperatures reduce the supply of insects. Approximately 6 lingered into Dec 1999, Knoxville (MIG 71:37).

Early Spring
- 4 Mar 1985, Nashville (MIG 56:77)
- 20 Mar 2004, Kingsport (MIG 75:117)
- 31 Mar 1968, Greeneville (MIG 39:45)
- 16 Apr 1978, Memphis (MIG 49:66)

Late Fall
- 30 Nov 1983, Davidson Co. (MIG 55:21)
- 25 Nov 2008, Knoxville (MIG 80:29)
- 11 Nov 1979, Chattanooga (MIG 51:42)
- 4 Nov 1988, Johnson City (MIG 60:33)
- 1 Nov 1986, Reelfoot Lake (MIG 58:21)

High Counts – Spring
- 150 on 8 May 1996, Reelfoot Lake (JRW, unpubl. data)
- 100 on 5 May 1996, Ensley (JRW, unpubl. data)
- 40 on 26 Apr 1992, Elizabethton SBC (MIG 63:48)
- 39 on 13 May 2000, Shelby Co. NAMC (MIG 71:53)
- 24 on 13 May 2006, Montgomery Co. NAMC (MIG 77:133)

High Counts – Fall
- 4,000 on 26 Aug 1978, Fentress Co. (MIG 50:21)
- 3,500 on 8 Sep 1971, Nashville (MIG 42:92)

2,500 on 5 Oct 1956, Chickamauga Lake dam (MIG 27:50)
834 on 30 Aug 1993, Johnson City (Knight 2008)
Winter Records
1 on 1 Dec 1992, Nashville (MIG 64:49)
1 on 3 Dec 1992, Memphis (JRW, unpubl. data)
2 on 6 Jan 1998, Memphis (MIG 69:107)
1 on 25 Feb 1999, Maury Co. (MIG 70:70)
up to 6 into Dec 1999, Knoxville (MIG 71:37)
1 on 7 Dec 2004, Nashville (MIG 76:80)
Substantiation: Specimen: LSUMZ, 8704

Chuck-wills-widow, *Antrostomus carolinensis*

Status and Abundance: Uncommon transient; locally common summer resident statewide except in Mississippi Alluvial Valley and higher elevations of the Southern Blue Ridge

Habitat: Open deciduous and coniferous wooded areas, including cedar glades

Spring Arrival: mid Apr

Fall Departure: mid Sep, difficult to detect during fall

Early Spring
29 Mar 1953, Decatur Co. (Nicholson 1980)
5 Apr 1965, Bristol (MIG 36:66)
6 Apr 1939, Clarksville (MIG 10:32)

Late Fall
5 Oct 1984, Knox Co. (MIG 56:25)
23 Sep 1934, Nashville (MIG 5:45)

High Counts – Spring
157 on 30 May 1988, McNairy Co. (MIG 59:124)
149 on 30 May 1988, Chester Co. (MIG 59:124)

High Counts – Summer
138 on 7 Jun 1979, Fayette Co. (Coffey and Coffey 1980)
111 on 6 Jun 2012, Wilson and Rutherford Co. (MIG 83:104)
75 on 3 Jun 2012, Wilson Co. (MIG 83:104)

Substantiation: Specimen: LSUMZ, 75843

Eastern Whip-poor-will, *Antrostomus vociferus*

Status and Abundance: Fairly common transient; fairly common summer resident

Habitat: Wooded areas (typically somewhat less open than Chuck-wills-widow)

Spring Arrival: late Mar

Fall Departure: late Sep

Caprimulgidae: Goatsuckers

Early Spring
- 7 Mar 1954, Signal Mtn. (MIG 25:34)
- 9 Mar 1974, Hardin Co. (MIG 45:20)
- 19 Mar 1997, Tennessee River Gorge, Marion Co. (MIG 68:111)

Late Fall
- 25 Nov 1968, Memphis (MIG 40:19)
- 27 Oct 1979, Williamson Co. (MIG 51:16)
- 18 Oct 2010, White Co. FBC (MIG 81:144)

High Counts – Spring
- 171 on 30 May 1988, Chester Co. (MIG 59:124)
- 112 on 30 May 1969, Holston Mtn., Sullivan and Carter Co. (Bridgforth 1969)
- 98 on 30 May 1988, McNairy Co. (MIG 59:124)
- 83 on 12 May 2007, Hamilton Co. NAMC (MIG 78:128)
- 63 on 7 May 2011, Cumberland Co. SBC (MIG 82:69)

High Counts – Summer
- 69 on 6 Jun 2012, Wilson and Rutherford Co. (SGS, pers. obs.)

Substantiation: Specimen: LSUMZ, 75851

Apodidae: Swifts. One species occurs as a common transient and summer resident statewide. Vaux's Swift occurs regularly on the Gulf Coast during fall and winter, and its possible occurrence as a vagrant in Tennesssee should not be ruled out.

Chimney Swift, *Chaetura pelagica*
  Status and Abundance: Common transient and summer resident
  Habitat: Aerial insectivore; widespread over urban and suburban areas and a wide variety of other habitats; almost entirely limited to manmade structures for nesting and roosting
  Spring Arrival: late Mar
  Fall Departure: late Oct
  Comments: There are two winter reports: 1 on 5 Dec 1972, Daus, Sequatchie Co. (MIG 44:26); 28 Nov 1989, Chattanooga (MIG 61:19). The authors have not been able to find any supporting documentation for either record that would rule out a vagrant Vaux's Swift. Vaux's Swift will almost certainly be documented in Tennessee at some point, and late November to early December would be the most likely time period based on that species' pattern of vagrance on the Gulf Coast.
  Early Spring
    1 Mar 1991, Chattanooga (MIG 62:113)
    7 Mar 1944, Clarksville (MIG 15:17)
    10 Mar 1989, Johnson City (MIG 60:90)
    18 Mar 1945, Memphis (MIG 16:11)
  Late Fall
    17 Nov 1984, Memphis (MIG 56:17)
    13 Nov 1977, Radnor Lake (MIG 49:42)
    31 Oct 1972, Knoxville (MIG 43:102)
  High Counts – Spring
    1,023 on 12 May 2012, Anderson Co. SBC (MIG 83:55)
    770 on 3-4 May 1997, Murfreesboro SBC (MIG 68:58)
    391 on 1 May 1994, Knoxville SBC (MIG 65:33)
    373 on 9 May 1992, Chattanooga SBC (MIG 63:48)
    340 on 5 May 1991, Knoxville SBC (MIG 62:36)
  High Counts – Fall
    11,700 on 11 Sep 2013, Nashville (MIG, in press)
    10,000 on 11 Oct 1933, Nashville (MIG 4:49)
    9,000 on 7 Sep 2013, Tullahoma (RL, pers. comm.)
    6,800 on 9 Sep 2012, Tullahoma (RL, pers. comm.)
    2,000 on 15 Oct 2004, Elizabethton (MIG 76:38)

Apodidae: Swifts

High Counts – Summer
    400 on 28 Jun 2003, Davidson Co. (MIG 74:131)
Substantiation: Specimen: LSUMZ, 75856

Trochilidae: Hummingbirds. One abundant and widespread species, while seven additional species are uncommon to accidental fall and winter visitors. Several additional species could potentially occur as vagrants.

Green Violetear, *Colibri thalassinus*
Status and Abundance: Accidental visitor
Comments: Unfortunately for the state's birders, the state's only record did not come to light until the host submitted the photo at a hummingbird festival a year later!
Records
  (1) 1 on 15 Sep 2007, Shelby Co. (NAB 63(1):59)
Substantiation: Photograph: 1 on 15 Sep 2007, Shelby Co. (Photograph: NAB 63(1):59)

Ruby-throated Hummingbird, *Archilochus colubris*
Status and Abundance: Fairly common spring transient and early summer resident; very common late summer and fall transient; very rare early winter resident
Habitat: Suburban and rural residential areas; open hardwood forest, forest edge, shrubby fields
Spring Arrival: early Apr
Fall Departure: late Oct
Early Spring
  24 Mar 2000, Pennington Bend (MIG 71:89)
  24 Mar 1979, Nashville (MIG 50:69)
  25 Mar 1954, Shelby Co. (MIG 25:51)
Late Fall
  24 Nov 1973, Nashville (MIG 45:21)
  7 Nov 2010, DeKalb Co. (MIG 81:156)
  4 Nov 1968, Reelfoot Lake (MIG 40:19)
High Counts – Spring
  51 on 12 May 2007, Putnam Co. NAMC (MIG 78:129)
  42 on 12 May 2007, Shelby Co. NAMC (MIG 78:129)
  38 on 29 Apr 2001, Elizabethton SBC (MIG 72:28)
  35 on 13 May 2000, Shelby Co. NAMC (MIG 71:53)
  34 on 12 May 2007, Hamilton Co. NAMC (MIG 78:128)
High Counts – Fall
  245 on 17 Sep 2005, Shelby Co. FBC (MIG 77:17)
  138 on 20 Sep 2008, Putnam Co. FBC (MIG 80:16)
  123 on 15 Sep 2008, Shelby Co. FBC (MIG 79:14)

121 on 15 Sep 2008, Putnam Co. FBC (MIG 79:14)
High Counts – Winter
2 on 18 Dec 2004, Columbia CBC (MIG 76:65)
Substantiation: Specimen: LSUMZ, 75862

Black-chinned Hummingbird, *Archilochus alexandri*
Status and Abundance: Accidental late fall and winter visitor
Records
- (1) 1 m (banded) on 20 Oct 1990-14 Jan 1991, Chattanooga (Sargent and Sargent 1993, MIG 62:86)
- (2) 1 ad m on 4 Sep 1997, Oak Ridge (MIG 69:46)
- (3) 1 imm f (banded) on 14 Dec 1997-24 Feb 1998, Franklin (MIG 69:109)
- (4) 1 ad f (banded) on 3-31 Dec 1998 (maybe into 1999), Williamson Co. (MIG 70:70, Calhoon 1999)
- (5) 1 imm m through winter season 1999-2000 (banded 3 Dec 1999), Hamilton Co. (MIG 71:45)
- (6) 1 imm f (banded) on 8 Dec 2001, Cleveland (MIG 73:39)

Substantiation: Unpublished photographs

Anna's Hummingbird, *Calypte anna*
Status and Abundance: Accidental winter visitor
Records
- (1) 1 banded on 6 Jan 1995 (present for weeks before and after banding), Nashville (Knight 1996, MIG 66:42)

Substantiation: Photograph: Sargent, B. 1995. "Anna's Hummingbird". <http://www.pbase.com/shoeman/image/157564308> Accessed 25 Sep 2014.

Calliope Hummingbird, *Selasphorus calliope*
Status and Abundance: Accidental late fall and winter visitor
Records
- (1) 1 imm f (banded) on 2 Dec 1997-1 Apr 1998, Nashville (MIG 69:109, MIG 69:164), bird returned during winters 1998-99, 1999-2000 (MIG 70:50, 70, MIG 71:43)
- (2) 1 imm m (banded) on 25 Nov-19 Dec 2000, Monterey, Putnam Co. (MIG 72:44, MIG 72:72)
- (3) 1 (banded) on 22-28 Jan 2001, Hamilton Co. (MIG 73:7, MIG 72:72)
- (4) 1 ad m (with a band, attempts to capture it failed) on 28 Oct-5 Nov 2003, Louisville, Blount Co. (MIG 75:31)
- (5) 1 imm m (banded) on 14-18 Nov 2007, Woodbury, Cannon Co. (MIG 79:22)

(6) 1 on 31 Oct 2008, Johnson City (MIG 80:29)

(7) 1 imm m (banded) on Oct 2012-April 2013, Nashville (CAS, SGS, m.ob.), returned during fall 2013 and was last seen 5 Jan 2014 during extremely cold weather

Substantiation: 1 ad m on 30 Oct 2003, Louisville, Blount Co. (MIG 75:31)

Photograph: NAB 58(1):88

Rufous Hummingbird, *Selasphorus rufus*

Status and Abundance: Irregular late summer and fall transient and winter resident

Spring Departure: early Apr

Fall Arrival: early Aug

Comments: The "expected" winter hummingbird. Five to 15 reported most years, almost always from feeders. More are reported in east Tennessee than middle Tennessee, and more in middle Tennessee than west, but this may be more a function of urban density and observer awareness than of actual distribution.

High Counts – Fall

3 banded at one feeder on 4 Nov 2012, Mountain City, Johnson Co. (MIG 83:157)

High Counts – Winter

4 on 3 Jan 2004, Knoxville CBC (MIG 75:59)

Substantiation: Photograph: 1 on 6-8 Sep 1983, Murfreesboro (TBRC Archives, UTK)

Allen's Hummingbird, *Selasphorus sasin*

Status and Abundance: Accidental late fall and winter visitor

Records

(1) 1 (banded) on 30 Oct 1993-5 Jan 1994, Chattanooga (MIG 65:44, Knight 1996)

(2) 1 (banded) on 29 Oct-29 Dec 1996, Knoxville (Pardue 1997)

(3) 1 (banded) on 17 Jan 1997, Monroe Co. (Calhoon 1998a)

(4) 1 (banded) on 17 Nov-16 Dec 1997, Johnson City (Calhoon 1998a, Knight 2008)

(5) 1 imm m (banded) on 26 Jan 2003, Elmwood, Smith Co. (MIG 74:55)

(6) 1 ad f (banded) on 5 Dec 2004, Williamson Co. (MIG 76:80)

(7) 1 imm m (banded) on 17 Dec 2007-2 Jan 2008, found dead on 3 Jan 2008, Mountain City, Johnson Co. (MIG 79:56)

(8) 1 m (banded) late Oct-1 Dec 2011, Russellville, Hamblen Co. (MA, pers. comm.), returned during winter 2011-12 (MIG 82:157, MIG

Trochilidae: Hummingbirds

83:154)

Substantiation: Photograph: Knight 2008

Broad-tailed Hummingbird, *Selasphorus platycerus*

Status and Abundance: Accidental late fall and winter visitor

Records

(1) 1 on 9-12 Nov 2002 (banded on 9 Nov by CAS), Nashville (Todd 2004)

(2) 1 imm m (banded 3 Dec by CAS) on 24 Nov-12 Dec 2005, Signal Mtn., Hamilton Co. (MIG 76:31)

Substantiation: Photograph: 1 on 9 Nov 2002, Nashville (NAB 57(1):70)

Alcedinidae: Kingfishers. One species is a permanent resident statewide.

Belted Kingfisher, *Megaceryle alcyon*
    Status and Abundance: Fairly common permanent resident
    Habitat: Creeks and streams and along the edges of lakes, ponds, and rivers
    High Counts – Spring
        28 on 9 May 1992, Chattanooga SBC (MIG 63:48)
        21 on 24 Apr 2004, Elizabethton SBC (MIG 75:105)
        18 on 5 May 1991, Knoxville SBC (MIG 62:36)
        16 on 13 May 2000, Hamilton Co. NAMC (MIG 71:53)
    High Counts – Fall
        33 on 26 Sep 2009, Elizabethton FBC (MIG 81:43)
        31 on 25 Sep 2010, Elizabethton FBC (MIG 81:144)
        30 on 24 Sep 2005, Elizabethton FBC (MIG 77:10)
        30 on 29 Sep 2012, Elizabethton FBC (MIG 83:139)
    High Counts – Winter
        60 on 18 Dec 1982, Knoxville CBC (MIG 54:13)
        52 on 2 Jan 2011, Knoxville CBC (MIG 82:51)
        50 on 1 Jan 1992, Hiwassee CBC (MIG 63:15)
        49 on 18 Dec 1994, Knoxville CBC (MIG 66:14)
        48 on 30 Dec 2006, Knoxville CBC (MIG 78:65)
    Substantiation: Specimen: LSUMZ, 75865

Picidae: Woodpeckers and Allies. Eight species have been documented in Tennessee, with seven common, statewide, year round residents or winter residents and one extirpated species.

Red-headed Woodpecker, *Melanerpes erythrocephalus*
Status and Abundance: Locally uncommon permanent resident in Central Hardwoods, Cumberland Plateau, Ridge and Valley, Southern Blue Ridge; fairly common permanent resident in Mississippi Alluvial Valley, Southeastern Coastal Plain

Habitat: Open woods, wooded swamps, clear cuts with many dead snags, and river bottoms

Comments: Numbers increase locally during winter with migrants. Fall migrants often seen at ridge-top hawk watches.

High Counts – Spring
  75 on 7-8 May 1966, Crossville SBC (MIG 37:37)
  65 on 13 May 2000, Lake Co. NAMC (MIG 71:52)

High Counts – Fall
  341 on 30 Oct 1983, Shelby Co. (MIG 55:18)
  157 on 27 Oct 1991, Shelby Forest SP (MIG 63:53)
  132 on 29 Oct 1978, Shelby Co. (MIG 50:19)

High Counts – Winter
  199 on 17 Dec 1983, Reelfoot Lake CBC (MIG 55:9)
  56 on 30 Dec 2009, Savannah CBC (MIG 81:93)

Substantiation: Specimen: LSUMZ, 75924

Red-bellied Woodpecker, *Melanerpes carolinus*
Status and Abundance: Common permanent resident

Habitat: Forest, generally absent from high elevation (4,000+ ft)

High Counts
  177 on 17 Dec 1989, Memphis CBC (MIG 61:4)
  155 on 19 Dec 1999, Memphis CBC (MIG 71:16)
  153 on 20 Dec 1998, Memphis CBC (MIG 70:15)
  150 on 5 Jan 2002, Knoxville CBC (MIG 72:117)
  137 on 18 Dec 1994, Memphis CBC (MIG 66:14)

Substantiation: Specimen: LSUMZ, 75895

Yellow-bellied Sapsucker, *Sphyrapicus varius*
Status and Abundance: Fairly common transient and winter resident; rare summer resident in Southern Blue Ridge

Habitat: Forest

Spring Departure: mid May

Fall Arrival: late Sep

Comments: The southern Appalachian mountain form has sometimes been treated as a separate subspecies (*S. v. appalachiensis*); in Tennessee, it is a rare breeding bird of high elevation forests in east Tennessee from Johnson Co. south to Monroe Co. This form may be more common, but underreported.

Late Spring
- 29 May 1972, Knox Co. (MIG 43:79)
- 19 May 1980, Montgomery Co. (MIG 51:56)

Early Fall
- 25 Aug 1975, Memphis (MIG 47:17)
- 27 Aug 1977, Savannah Bay (MIG 49:21)
- 9 Sep 1980, Nashville (BNA:30)

High Counts – Fall
- 27 on 9 Oct 2010, Nashville FBC (MIG 81:144)

High Counts – Summer
- 2 on 8 Jun 2010, Ripshin Lake (MIG 81:129)

High Counts – Winter
- 73 on 2 Jan 2010, Knoxville CBC (MIG 81:93)
- 69 on 26 Dec 1977, Nashville CBC (MIG 49:7)
- 61 on 21 Dec 1975, Memphis CBC (MIG 47:36)

Substantiation: Specimen: LSUMZ, 75953

Downy Woodpecker, *Picoides pubescens*

Status and Abundance: Common permanent resident

Habitat: Forest, forest edge, urban and suburban yards

High Counts
- 107 on 9 Oct 2010, Nashville FBC (MIG 81:144)
- 148 on 26 Dec 1977, Nashville CBC (MIG 49:7)
- 147 on 27 Dec 1980, Nashville CBC (MIG 52:14)
- 131 on 2 Jan 2005, Knoxville CBC (MIG 76:65)
- 92 on 8 Oct 2005, Nashville FBC (MIG 77:10)

Substantiation: Specimen: LSUMZ, 76013

Hairy Woodpecker, *Picoides villosus*

Status and Abundance: Fairly common permanent resident

Habitat: Forest

High Counts
- 53 on 16 Dec 1979, Knoxville CBC (MIG 51:32)
- 28 on 26 Dec 1977, Nashville CBC (MIG 49:6)
- 27 on 4 May 1952, Greeneville SBC (MIG 23:27)
- 26 on 17 Dec 1989, Memphis CBC (MIG 61:4)

19 on 3 Oct 2009, Nashville FBC (MIG 81:43)
Substantiation: Specimen: LSUMZ, 75965

Red-cockaded Woodpecker, *Picoides borealis*
Status and Abundance: Extirpated
Comments: Formerly found locally across the state in areas with mature pine forest (e.g. Catoosa WMA and Cherokee NF). The last known birds were seen in the wild on 19 Aug 1994, Polk Co. (KAC, pers. comm.) and 1 m on 18 Nov 1994, Polk Co. (JRW, unpubl. data).
Substantiation: Specimen: LSUMZ, 76015

Northern Flicker, *Colaptes auratus*
Subspecies: *auratus*
Status and Abundance: Fairly common permanent resident
Habitat: Open forest and forest edge; also at times in corn and other agricultural fields
Comments: More abundant as a transient and during winter. Yellow-shafted Flicker (ssp. *auratus*) is the expected subspecies, but there are a handful of poorly documented reports of Red-shafted Flickers (ssp. *cafer*). An apparent hybrid was in Memphis 25 Dec 1959-1 Jan 1960 (MIG 30:60).
High Counts – Spring
  72 on 9 May 1992, Chattanooga SBC (MIG 63:48)
  43 on 27 Apr 1997, Knox Co. SBC (MIG 68:58)
  41 on 30 May 2005, Elizabethton SBC (MIG 76:139)
High Counts – Fall
  83 on 9 Oct 2010, Nashville FBC (MIG 81:144)
  59 on 1 Oct 2011, Nashville FBC (MIG 82:134)
  57 on 25 Sep 2010, DeKalb FBC (MIG 81:144)
  53 on 8 Oct 2005, Nashville FBC (MIG 77:10)
  52 on 4 Oct 2009, White Co. FBC (MIG 81:43)
High Counts – Winter
  221 on 21 Dec 1975, Memphis CBC (MIG 47:36)
  198 on 17 Dec 1989, Memphis CBC (MIG 61:5)
  184 on 20 Dec 1998, Memphis CBC (MIG 70:15)
  167 on 16 Dec 2006, Reelfoot Lake CBC (MIG 78:65)
  164 on 18 Dec 1988, Memphis CBC (MIG 60:16)
Substantiation: Specimen: LSUMZ, 75872

Pileated Woodpecker, *Dryocopus pileatus*
Status and Abundance: Fairly common permanent resident
Habitat: Mature forest

High Counts
>   60 on 18 Dec 1982, Reelfoot Lake CBC (MIG 54:13)
>   55 on 28 Dec 2003, Cades Cove CBC (MIG 75:60)
>   48 on 1 May 1994, Elizabethton SBC (MIG 65:33)
>   46 on 10 May 2008, Putnam Co. NAMC (MIG 79:76)
>   46 on 9 May 2009, Putnam Co. NAMC (MIG 80:107)

Substantiation: Specimen: LSUMZ, 75889

Ivory-billed Woodpecker, *Campephilus principalis*

Status and Abundance: **Unsubstantiated**; extinct

Comments: There are no definitive records of this iconic woodpecker from Tennessee, but it seems a virtual certainty that it occurred in bottomland hardwood forests in west Tennessee. Audubon (1929) reported them from a boat on the Mississippi River along the Tennessee border in the winter of 1820-21, but he did not state specifically that he saw them on the Tennessee side of the river. There are also records from Fulton Co., Kentucky, which borders Tennessee (U.S. Fish and Wildlife Service 2010). This species is almost certainly extinct, but reports have persisted from the Hatchie River bottoms at least through January 2006 (U.S. Fish and Wildlife Service 2010). Repeated organized efforts to verify those reports failed to obtain any conclusive evidence (U.S. Fish and Wildlife Service 2010).

Falconidae: Caracaras and Falcons. Five species have been documented in Tennessee, of which three occur annually statewide, and two are rare visitors or accidental. Crested Caracara is a possible vagrant to Tennessee.

American Kestrel, *Falco sparverius*
　　Status and Abundance: Fairly common permanent resident
　　Habitat: Open fields, roadsides, urban and suburban areas
　　High Counts – Spring
　　　　23 on 26 Apr 1997, Elizabethton SBC (MIG 68:57)
　　　　22 on 1 May 2010, White Co. SBC (MIG 82:6)
　　　　11 on 12 May 2007, Putnam Co. NAMC (MIG 78:127)
　　High Counts – Fall
　　　　57 on 30 Sep 2006, Macon FBC (MIG 78:26)
　　　　52 on 4 Oct 2009, White Co. FBC (MIG 81:42)
　　　　26 on 16 Sep 2006, Putnam Co. FBC (MIG 78:19)
　　High Counts – Winter
　　　　118 on 21 Dec 2004, White Co. CBC (MIG 76:63)
　　　　96 on 17 Dec 1991, Cookeville CBC (MIG 63:14)
　　　　90 on 4 Jan 1992, Murfreesboro CBC (MIG 63:14)
　　　　85 on 27 Dec 1986, Murfreesboro CBC (MIG 58:3)
　　　　80 on 2 Jan 1993, Murfreesboro CBC (MIG 64:7)
　　Substantiation: Specimen: LSUMZ, 75711

Merlin, *Falco columbarius*
　　Status and Abundance: Irregular (uncommon in Mississippi Alluvial Valley) transient; irregular (locally uncommon) winter resident; accidental summer visitor
　　Habitat: Forest and forest edge, typically near larger bodies of water
　　Spring Departure: early May
　　Fall Arrival: early Sep
　　Comments: Most records of single birds, generally not relocated. Small numbers linger through winter across the state.
　　Late Spring
　　　　2 Jun 2009, Carver's Gap (Knight 2010)
　　　　23 May 2006, Washington Co. (MIG 77:103)
　　　　20 May 1995, Ensley (JRW, unpubl. data)
　　　　14 May 2005, Hamilton Co. Spring NAMC (MIG 76:126)
　　　　13 May 1957, Knoxville (MIG 28:43)
　　Early Fall
　　　　31 Jul 2002, Gibson Co. (MIG 73:110)

6 Aug 1989, Cross Creeks NWR (JRW, unpubl. data)
12 Aug 1999, Shelby Bottoms Park (MIG 71:33)
17 Aug 2004, S. Holston Lake (MIG 76:38)
21 Aug 1985, Eagle Bend Fish Hatchery (MIG 57:32)
21 Aug 2001, Erwin (MIG 72:46)

High Counts – Fall
5 on 18 Sep 1992, Ensley (JRW, unpubl. data)

High Counts – Winter
3 on 1 Jan 2000, Hickory-Priest CBC (MIG 71:16)
3 on 2 Jan 2006, Savannah CBC (MIG 77:43)
3 on 29 Dec 2008, Savannah CBC (MIG 80:51)

Substantiation: Specimen: LSUMZ, 75709

Gyrfalcon, *Falco rusticolus*

Status and Abundance: **Unsubstantiated**

Comments: Accepted by the TBRC on the basis of written documentation. The published description is convincing, although questions or provenance will always remain.

Records
(1) 1 white morph bird on 13 Jan 1978, Jefferson Co. (Koella 1985)

Peregrine Falcon, *Falco peregrinus*

Status and Abundance: Irregular (uncommon in Mississippi Alluvial Valley) transient and winter visitor, rare local summer resident

Habitat: Open areas and along lakes, rivers, and bluffs; also urban areas where they occasionally nest on large buildings, bridges, or similar structures

Comments: One to 2 known nesting pairs in state from 1997-2013, both in GSMNP (SGS *fide* PS). Winter records mostly limited to Dec with few in Jan and Feb, although this may be the result of increased observer effort associated with Christmas Bird Counts. Nesting occurred historically, but was extirpated by the 1940s. Cliff-nesting occurred in the Southern Blue Ridge, Ridge and Valley, and Cumberland Plateau with the only tree nesting occurring at Reelfoot Lake. Restoration by means of hacking captive-bred young in Tennessee of birds with unknown genetic origin (mostly likely hybrids of western and tundra subspecies and not of the native eastern population) began in 1984 and continued through 1993 with 44 young hacked at two mountain sites. Additional young were hacked at Chattanooga and Memphis in 1993. The first modern nests were discovered in 1997 at a cliff in the GSMNP and on a railroad bridge in Chattanooga (Knight and Hatcher 1997). The GSMNP site remains active. Possible breeding has been reported from additional sites in the GSMNP, near Roan Mtn. and in the Doe River Gorge, Carter Co. Continued increases in nesting should be expected.

Late Spring
> 26 May 1984, Reelfoot Lake (MIG 55:67)

Early Fall
> 19 Jul 2009, Ensley (MIG 80:124)
> 4 Aug 1972, J. Percy Priest Lake (MIG 43:99)
> 7 Aug 1994, Ensley (JRW, unpubl. data)
> 11 Aug 1985, Shelby Co. (MIG 57:22)

High Counts – Fall
> 7 on 24 Sep 1995, Ensley (JRW, unpubl. data)
> 5 on 26 Sep 2004, Ensley (JRW, unpubl. data)
> 4 on 24 Sep 2005, Soddy Mtn. Hawk Watch (MIG 77:29)
> 4 on 26 Sep 1993, Ensley (JRW, unpubl. data)

High Counts – Winter
> 2 on 18 Dec 2004, Chattanooga CBC (MIG 76:64)
> 2 on 30 Dec 2009, Paris Landing SP (MIG 81:99)

Substantiation: Specimen: LSUMZ, 75706

Prairie Falcon, *Falco mexicanus*

Status and Abundance: **Unsubstantiated**; very rare fall and winter visitor in Mississippi Alluvial Valley; accidental elsewhere

Habitat: Large open fields

Records
> (1) 1 on 5 Oct 1958, Memphis (Coffey 1981)
> (2) 1 on 12 Oct 1980, Memphis (Coffey 1981)
> (3) 1 on 15/19 Oct 1984, Island 13 (MIG 56:17)
> (4) 1 on 6 Sep 1986, Mound City, TN/ARK state line (MIG 58:19)
> (5) 1 on 11 Sep 1987, Island 10, Lake Co. (Robinson 1990)
> (6) 1 on 11 Mar 1989, Ensley (JRW, unpubl. data)
> (7) 1 on 13 Sep 1992, Ensley (MIG 64:4)
> (8) 1 on 2 Nov 1997, Fairview, Williamson Co, flew over car at close range (MIG 69:42)
> (9) 1 on 16-17 Dec 1997, Long Point, Reelfoot Lake, KY, and Phillippy, Lake Co. (MIG 69:107)
> (10) 1 on 4 Apr 2000, n. Memphis (MIG 71:87), same bird likely seen on 29 Apr 2000, Shelby Farm (MIG 71:87)
> (11) 1 on 4 Dec 2001-26 Jan 2002, last seen on 17 Mar 2002, Lake Co. (MIG 73:35, MIG 73:56)
> (12) 1 on 8 May 2011, Ensley (MIG 82:84)
> (13) 1 on 20 Dec 2013, Obion Co. (MAG, pers. comm.)

Psittacidae: Lories, Parakeets, Macaws, and Parrots. This family is represented by only a single, extinct species, but several introduced species could occur as escapees or strays from established populations elsewhere.

Carolina Parakeet, *Conuropsis carolinensis*
    Status and Abundance: Extinct
    Comments: Range was apparently restricted to river bottoms in middle and west Tennessee.

Tyrannidae: Tyrant Flycatchers. Fifteen species of flycatchers have been documented in Tennessee. Nine species breed in the state; however some species breed statewide while others are regional or very local breeders. Two species are transients (one of which bred historically) and four other species are rare winter or accidental winter visitors.

Olive-sided Flycatcher, *Contopus cooperi*
>Status and Abundance: Irregular transient; very rare summer resident in Southern Blue Ridge
>Habitat: Forest and forest edge; usually on an exposed perch
>Spring Arrival: early May
>Spring Departure: early Jun
>Fall Arrival: mid Aug
>Fall Departure: late Sep
>Comments: Formerly more common in GSMNP, where a nest has been documented (Williams 1976, Knight 2010).
>Early Spring
>>11 Apr 1965, near Greeneville (MIG 36:64)
>>21 Apr 2001, Memphis (MIG 72:93)
>>21 Apr 2001, Green Mtn., Greene Co. (MIG 72:99)
>>24 Apr 1965, Radnor Lake (BNA:31)
>>24 Apr 1992, Lake Co. (GC *fide* MAG)
>
>Late Spring
>>4 Jun 1998, Big South Fork NRRA (MIG 69:167)
>>1 Jun 1991, Haywood Co. (MIG 63:21)
>>31 May 1986, Hickman Co. (MIG 57:79)
>
>Early Fall
>>26 Jul 1969, Heaton Creek, Carter Co. (MIG 40:70)
>>30 Jul 1974, Grundy Co. (MIG 45:102)
>>1 Aug 1992, Ensley (JRW, unpubl. data)
>>8 Aug 1943, Memphis (MIG 14:52)
>>8 Aug 1977, Island 13 (GJ *fide* MAG)
>
>Late Fall
>>9 Oct 2001, Shelby Bottoms Park (MIG 73:13)
>>9 Oct 2006, Knox Co. (MIG 78:39)
>>5 Oct 2003, Erwin (MIG 75:34)
>>5 Oct 2010, Cades Cove (MIG 81:163)
>>1 Oct 1989, Decatur Co. (MIG 61:14)
>
>High Counts – Spring
>>7 on 9 May 1993, Reelfoot Lake area (4 in Lake Co., 3 in Obion Co.)

(JRW, unpubl. data)
4 on 24 May 1986, Overton Co. (MIG 57:79)
3 on 8 May 1999, Nashville SBC (MIG 70:120)
3 on 9 May 1998, Shelby Co. NAMC (MIG 69:152)
2 on 13 May 2000, Lake Co. NAMC (MIG 71:52)
High Counts – Fall
3 on 25 Aug 2000, Island 13 and vicinity (MIG 72:39)
Substantiation: Specimen: APSU, 1216

Eastern Wood-Pewee, *Contopus virens*
Status and Abundance: Common spring transient and summer resident; fairly common fall transient
Habitat: Forest
Spring Arrival: mid Apr
Fall Departure: mid Oct
Early Spring
27 Mar 1997, Memphis (MIG 68:107)
31 Mar 1968, Reelfoot Lake (MIG 39:42)
1 Apr 1975, Knoxville (MIG 46:68)
Late Fall
20 Nov 1967, Elizabethton (MIG 38:101)
20 Nov 2002, Nashville (MIG 74:19)
6 Nov 2004, Johnson City (MIG 76:35)
4 Nov 2002, Shelby Bottoms Park (MIG 74:18)
High Counts – Spring
126 on 13 May 2006, Putnam Co. NAMC (MIG 77:133)
124 on 10 May 2008, Putnam Co. NAMC (MIG 79:91)
101 on 13 May 2006, Montgomery Co. NAMC (MIG 77:133)
100 on 13 May 2000, Putnam Co. NAMC (MIG 71:53)
99 on 12 May 2007, Putnam Co. NAMC (MIG 78:131)
99 on 12 May 2007, Shelby Co. NAMC (MIG 78:131)
High Counts – Fall
59 on 19 Sep 2009, Putnam Co. FBC (MIG 81:43)
58 on 18 Sep 2010, Shelby Co. FBC (MIG 81:144)
57 on 16 Sep 2006, Putnam Co. FBC (MIG 78:20)
52 on 30 Sep 2006, Nashville FBC (MIG 78:27)
Substantiation: Specimen: LSUMZ, 76083

Yellow-bellied Flycatcher, *Empidonax flaviventris*
Status and Abundance: Irregular transient
Habitat: Forest and forest edge
Spring Arrival: mid May

Spring Departure: late May
Fall Arrival: early Sep
Fall Departure: late Sep
Comments: Care should be taken during fall to differentiate this species from fresh immatures of other Empidonax flycatchers, which can have a fairly extensive yellowish wash across the breast and belly.
Early Spring
    24 Apr 1991, Memphis (MIG 62:111)
    3 May 1983, Memphis (MIG 54:60)
Late Spring
    3 Jun 2000, Nashville (MIG 71:120)
Early Fall
    8 Aug 1936, Nashville (BNA:31)
    25 Aug 2002, Cocklebur Lake (JRW, unpubl. data)
    26 Aug 1989, Pace Point (JRW, unpubl. data)
Late Fall
    17 Oct 2000, Nashville (MIG 72:41)
    14 Oct 1961, Nashville (Laskey 1962)
    12 Oct 2000, Lewis Co. (banded) (MIG 72:41)
    10 Oct 1981, Norris (MIG 53:20)
    7 Oct 1995, Island 13 (MAG, pers. comm.)
High Counts – Spring
    3 on 26 May 1997, Walnut Log Road, Obion Co. (JRW, unpubl. data)
High Counts – Fall
    4, found dead, on 6 Oct 1954, Chattanooga (MIG 25:67)
    2 on 18 Sep 2010, Shelby Co. FBC (MIG 81:144)
Substantiation: Specimen: LSUMZ, 76060

Acadian Flycatcher, *Empidonax virescens*
Status and Abundance: Common transient and summer resident
Habitat: Mature forest, especially in ravines and bottomland hardwood forests
Spring Arrival: mid Apr
Fall Departure: mid Oct
Early Spring
    3 Mar 1990, Fall Creek Falls SP (MIG 61:77)
    10 Apr 2006, GSMNP (MIG 77:107)
    11 Apr 1972, Nashville (MIG 43:51)
Late Fall
    25 Oct 1998, Shelby Forest SP (MIG 70:48)
    18 Oct 1972, Nashville (MIG 43:100)
    16 Oct 1967, Nashville (MIG 38:95)

High Counts – Spring
  110 on 10 May 2003, Shelby Co. NAMC (MIG 74:116)
  104 on 8 May 2004, Shelby Co. NAMC (MIG 75:97)
  98 on 12 May 2007, Shelby Co. NAMC (MIG 78:131)
  98 on 20 May 2004, western Putnam Co. (MIG 75:113)
  87 on 10 May 2008, Shelby Co. NAMC (MIG 79:76)
High Counts – Fall
  44 on 15 Sep 2001, Shelby Co. FBC (MIG 73:31)
  42 on 17 Sep 2005, Shelby Co. FBC (MIG 77:17)
  38 on 13 Sep 2008, Shelby Co. FBC (MIG 80:16)
  37 on 18 Sep 2010, Shelby Co. FBC (MIG 81:144)
  36 on 16 Sep 2006, Shelby Co. FBC (MIG 78:20)
High Counts – Summer
  39 on 21 Jun 1980, Hatchie NWR SBC (MIG 51:56)
Substantiation: Specimen: LSUMZ, 76070

Alder Flycatcher, *Empidonax alnorum*

Status and Abundance: Fairly common summer resident at Roan Mtn; uncommon transient elsewhere
Habitat: Forest edge, secondary growth or other open areas with small trees or large shrubs; breeds in alder thickets at Roan Mtn.
Spring Arrival: mid May
Spring Departure: late May
Fall Arrival: mid Aug
Fall Departure: late Sep
Comments: Fall occurrence is less well-documented due to difficulty distinguishing from Willow other than by voice.
Early Spring
  1 May 2012, Roan Mtn. (MIG, in press)
  3 May 2008, Ensley (MIG 79:62)
  7 May 2010, Carver's Gap (MIG 81:122)
  8 May 2011, Bells Bend (SGS, CAS, ES, pers. obs.)
  9 May 2008, Radnor Lake (MIG 79:64)
Early Fall
  17 Aug 2000, Carver's Gap (MIG 72:46)
  26 Aug 2010, Cates Landing (MIG 81:155)
  26 Aug 2012, Duck River Unit (SGS, CAS, pers. obs.)
Late Fall
  20 Sep 2006, Radnor Lake (MIG 78:35)
  18 Sep 2010, Shelby Co. FBC (MIG 81:144)
High Counts – Fall
  3 on 26 Aug 2012, Duck River Unit (MIG 83:150)

Tyrannidae: Tyrant Flycatchers

High Counts – Summer
    15 on 20 Jun 2002, Roan Mtn. (Knight 2008)
Substantiation: Specimen: LSUMZ, 8769

Willow Flycatcher, *Empidonax traillii*

Status and Abundance: Uncommon transient; locally uncommon summer resident
Habitat: Shrubby areas, usually near water or willow thickets
Spring Arrival: early May
Fall Departure: mid Sep
Comments: Difficult or impossible to distinguish from Alder Flycatcher by sight when not singing during fall, complicating efforts to identify departure dates.
Early Spring
    20 Apr 1986, Stewart Co. (MIG 57:79)
    22 Apr 2000, Freel's Bend, Oak Ridge (MIG 71:93)
    23 Apr 2010, Hampton Creek Cove SNA (MIG 81:122)
Late Fall
    7-8 Oct 1995, Ensley (JRW, unpubl. data)
    17 Sep 2005, Shelby Co. FBC (MIG 76:17)
High Counts – Spring
    16 on 22 May 2009, Shady Valley (MIG 80:96)
    11 on 30 May 1987, Cross Creeks NWR (Robinson 1990)
    10 on 23 May 1987, Britton Ford (MIG 58:93)
High Counts – Fall
    2 on 26 Aug 2012, Duck River Unit (MIG 83:150)
High Counts – Summer
    19 on 2-3 Jun 1989, Mountain City, Johnson Co. (MIG 60:109)
    9 on 19 Jun 1995, Ensley (JRW, unpubl. data)
    5 on 18 Jun 1988, Ensley (MIG 59:124)
    4 banded on 9 Jul 2006, Seven Islands Wildlife Refuge (MIG 77:146)
Substantiation: Specimen: LSUMZ, 76074

Least Flycatcher, *Empidonax minimus*

Status and Abundance: Uncommon transient; locally fairly common summer resident in Southern Blue Ridge
Habitat: Brushy habitats; forest and forest edge
Spring Arrival: late Apr
Spring Departure: late May
Fall Arrival: late Aug
Fall Departure: early Oct

Early Spring
    14 Apr 2004, Radnor Lake (MIG 75:113)
    19 Apr 1968, Hardin Co. (MIG 39:42)
    24 Apr 2000, Cove Lake SP (MIG 71:93)
Early Fall
    3 Jul 1996, Shelby Forest SP (MIG 67:77)
    24 Jul 1996, Prentice Cooper WMA, Marion Co. (MIG 67:79)
    2 Aug 1998, Black Bayou WMA (MIG 70:48)
    12 Aug 2000, Shelby Bottoms Park (MIG 72:41)
Late Fall
    20 Oct 1999, Ensley (MIG 71:32)
    9 Oct 1990, Lewis Co. (MIG 62:50)
High Counts – Spring
    32 on 2 May 1954, Roan Mtn. SBC (MIG 25:30)
High Counts – Fall
    5 on 1 Sep 1996, Tennemo Levee, Dyer Co. (JRW, unpubl. data)
High Counts – Summer
    21 on 4 Jun 2011, Carter Co. (MIG 82:123)
Substantiation: Specimen: LSUMZ, 76081

Eastern Phoebe, *Sayornis phoebe*

Status and Abundance: Fairly common summer resident and spring and fall transient, uncommon winter resident

Habitat: Found along creeks and woodland edges, usually near water; also along cliffs and rock outcroppings, and cave openings.

High Counts – Spring
    124 on 9 May 2009, Putnam Co. NAMC (MIG 80:107)
    107 on 10 May 2008, Putnam Co. NAMC (MIG 79:77)
    99 on 12 May 2007, Putnam Co. NAMC (MIG 78:131)
    86 on 14 May 2005, Putnam Co. NAMC (MIG 76:129)
    77 on 13 May 2006, Putnam Co. NAMC (MIG 77:133)
    77 on 8 May 2004, Putnam Co. NAMC (MIG 75:97)
High Counts – Fall
    127 on 19 Sep 2009, Putnam Co. FBC (MIG 81:43)
    115 on 20 Sep 2008, Putnam Co. FBC (MIG 80:16)
    113 on 16 Sep 2006, Putnam Co. FBC (MIG 78:20)
High Counts – Winter
    52 on 2 Jan 2010, Buffalo River CBC (MIG 81:94)
    42 on 30 Dec 2009, Savannah CBC (MIG 81:95)
    37 on 21 Dec 2009, White Co. CBC (MIG 81:95)
    35 on 2 Jan 2010, Knoxville CBC (MIG 81:95)
    29 on 1 Jan 2010, Hiwassee CBC (MIG 81:95)

Tyrannidae: Tyrant Flycatchers

Substantiation: Specimen: LSUMZ, 76043

Say's Phoebe, *Sayornis saya*
Status and Abundance: Accidental fall, winter, and spring visitor
Records
- (1) 1 on 27-30 Sep 1984, Radnor Lake, not confirmed by TBRC (Robinson 1990)
- (2) 1 on 29 Sep 1985, Metro Center, Nashville (MIG 57:28)
- (3) 1 on 7 May 1994, Phillippy, Lake Co. (Knight 1996)
- (4) 1 on 25 Nov 1994, Lauderdale Refuge (JRW, unpubl. data)
- (5) 1 on 14 Feb 1995, Halls, Lauderdale Co. (Knight 1996) (possibly the same individual as the previous record)
- (6) 1 on 27 Dec 2003, Brandywine Island, Tipton Co. (MIG 75:73)
- (7) 1 on 29 Nov 2005, near Reelfoot Lake SP (MIG 76:25)
- (8) 1 on 2 Feb 2009, Lincoln Co. (DS, pers. comm., not submitted to TBRC)
- (9) 1 on 29 Jan-18 Feb 2012, Hatchie NWR (MIG 83:6)
- (10) 1 on 19-24 Dec 2013, Hall Griffin Road, Obion Co. (MIG, in press)
- (11) 1 on 25 Nov-31 Dec 2013, Phillippy (BL, pers. comm.)

Substantiation: Photograph: Somershoe, S.G. 2012. "Say's Phoebe". <http://www.pbase.com/shoeman/image/141260250> Accessed 15 Dec 2014.

Vermilion Flycatcher, *Pyrocephalus rubinus*
Status and Abundance: Very rare spring, fall, and winter visitor
Comments: Nearly all records along major rivers, with most along the Mississippi River floodplain.
Records
- (1) 1 on 14 May 1960, Reelfoot Lake (Leggett 1969a)
- (2) 1 on 15 Oct 1961, Reelfoot Lake (Smith 1965)
- (3) 1 in Dec 1961, Reelfoot Lake (Leggett 1969a)
- (4) 1 on 21-22 Oct 1964, Knoxville (Owen 1965)
- (5) 1 on 28 Dec 1966, Reelfoot Lake (Leggett 1969a)
- (6) 1 on 27 Dec 1967, Reelfoot Lake (Hogg 1968)
- (7) 1 on 23 Nov-8 Dec 1968, Reelfoot Lake (MIG 40:19)
- (8) 1 on 12 May 1970, Dyersburg (MIG 41:68)
- (9) 1 on 30 Sep 1973, Lauderdale Co. (MIG 44:99)
- (10) 1 on 1 Dec 1984, Shelby Co. (MIG 56:48)
- (11) 1 on 20 Sep 1987, Island 13 (MIG 59:32)
- (12) 1 on 26-28 Sep 1987, Austin Springs (MIG 59:41)
- (13) 1 on 17 Oct 1993, Shelby Farms (MIG 65:22)
- (14) 1 on 14 Oct 1997, Phillippy (MIG 69:41)

(15) 1 on 5 Dec 2003-26 Jan 2004, Airpark Inn, Reelfoot Lake, Lake Co. (MIG 75:73)
(16) 1 on 22 Feb-13 Mar 2004, Hatchie NWR (MIG 75:74, MIG 75:111)
(17) 1 on 28 Nov-14 Dec 2004, Hatchie NWR (MIG 76:28, MIG 76:79)
(18) 1 f on 21 Nov 2009, Tigrett WMA (MIG 81:50)
(19) 1 m on 29 Dec 2009, Savannah CBC (MIG 81:101)
(20) 1 f on 1 May 2014, Gibson Co. (MAG, pers. comm.)

Substantiation: Photograph: 1 on 27 Sep 1987, Austin Springs (Knight 2008:66)

Ash-throated Flycatcher, *Myiarchus cinerascens*

Status and Abundance: Accidental winter visitor

Records
(1) 22 Dec 1985, Kingsport CBC (Nicholson and Stedman 1988)
(2) 11 Dec 2002, Ensley (MIG 74:53)
(3) 14 Nov 2009, Woods Reservoir, at dam (MIG 81:52)
(4) 29 Jan 2012-12 Jan 2013, Shelby Forest WMA (SNM, pers. comm., m.ob.)
(5) 1 on 9-14 Oct 2013, Nickajack Cave, Marion Co. (MIG, in press)

Substantiation: Photograph: 1 on 14 Nov 2009, Woods Reservoir (NAB 64(1):89)

Great Crested Flycatcher, *Myiarchus crinitus*

Status and Abundance: Fairly common summer resident and spring and early fall transient

Habitat: Deciduous forest and forest edge

Spring Arrival: mid Apr

Fall Departure: late Sep

Comments: Birds found in late fall or winter should be examined closely as vagrant Myiarchus flycatchers occasionally occur in the eastern United States during winter.

Early Spring
27 Mar 1954, Shelby Co. (MIG 25:51)
31 Mar 2012, Hamilton Co. (BH, pers. comm.)
2 Apr 1967, Rutherford Co. (DeVore 1975)
4 Apr 1994, Sullivan Co. (MIG 65:54)

Late Fall
30 Nov-5 Dec 1997, Mosheim, Greene Co. (MIG 69:47)
8 Nov 1974, Woodbury, Cannon Co. (MIG 46:71)
3 Oct 1993, Holston Mtn., Carter Co. (MIG 65:26)

High Counts – Spring
80 on 8 May 2004, Putnam Co. NAMC (MIG 75:97)

71 on 12 May 2007, Shelby Co. NAMC (MIG 78:131)
71 on 13 May 2000, Montgomery Co. NAMC (MIG 71:53)
70 on 9 May 2009, Putnam Co. NAMC (MIG 80:107)
65 on 10 May 1997, Chattanooga SBC (MIG 68:58)

High Counts – Fall
4 on 17 Sep 2005, Shelby Co. FBC (MIG 77:17)
4 on 25 Sep 2010, DeKalb Co. FBC (MIG 81:144)

Substantiation: Specimen: LSUMZ, 76041

Variegated Flycatcher, *Empidonomus varius*

Status and Abundance: Accidental visitor

Records
(1) 1 on 13-15 May 1984, east side of Reelfoot Lake, Obion Co. (Calhoon 2000)

Substantiation: Photograph: 1 on 13-15 May 1984, east side of Reelfoot Lake, Obion Co. (Birding 16(5):back cover)

Western Kingbird, *Tyrannus verticalis*

Status and Abundance: Very rare (uncommon in Shelby Co.) transient; locally uncommon summer resident in Shelby Co.

Habitat: Fields and other open areas; uses adjacent man-made structures (e.g. power poles and substations) for nesting

Spring Arrival: early May

Fall Departure: late Sep

Comments: The status of this species has changed significantly in the last 15 years. Since breeding was first documented in Shelby Co. in 1999, this species has steadily increased as a breeding resident in that county and is now relatively easy to find there. A high count of 19 nests was documented in 2011 (MIG 82:120). Multiple nests involving hybridization between this species and Scissor-tailed Flycatcher have also been documented (JRW, unpubl. data).

Early Spring
1 Mar 1992, Hickman Co. (MIG 63:74)
15 Apr 1948, Reelfoot Lake area (GW *fide* MAG)
23 Apr 2003, Ensley (MIG 74:87)
28 Apr 2011, Shelby Co. (MIG 82:85)
29 Apr 2001, Ensley (MIG 72:93)

Late Fall
1 Nov 1988, Ensley (MW, pers. comm.)
30 Oct 2003, Memphis (MIG 75:25)
25 Oct 2007, Oak Ridge (MIG 79:26)
29 Sep 1988, Shelby Co. (MIG 60:26)

27 Sep 1998, Ensley (CB, pers. comm.)
High Counts – Spring
   3 on 12 May 2001, Shelby Co. NAMC (MIG 72:17)
   3 on 9 May 2009, Shelby Co. NAMC (MIG 80:107)
High Counts – Fall
   4 on 2 Jul 1995, President's Island (JRW, unpubl. data)
   1 on 21 Aug 1997, Horns Bluff Refuge (MIG 69:41)
High Counts – Summer
   13 (6 ad, 7 young) on 23 Jun 2002, Ensley (JRW, unpubl. data)
   4 ad on 17 Jun 2001, Ensley (JRW, unpubl. data)
Substantiation: Photograph: 1 with nest on 3 Jul 1999, Ensley (NAB 53(4):396)

Eastern Kingbird, *Tyrannus tyrannus*

Status and Abundance: Fairly common transient and summer resident
Habitat: Fields and other open areas; forest edges
Spring Arrival: early Apr
Fall Departure: mid Sep
Early Spring
   11 Mar 2002, Fayette Co. (MIG 73:57)
   12 Mar 2004, Warren Co. (MIG 75:113)
   12 Mar 1961, Nashville (MIG 32:5)
   13 Mar 1991, Baileyton, Greene Co. (MIG 62:113)
   17 Mar 1964, Bristol (MIG 35:41)
Late Fall
   13 Nov 1971, Tennessee NWR (MIG 43:25)
   22 Oct 1972, Austin Springs (MIG 43:102)
   17 Oct 1993, Greeneville (MIG 65:25)
   13 Oct 1974, Lawrence Co. (MIG 46:20)
High Counts – Spring
   322 on 15 May 1955, Memphis (MIG 26:47)
   130 on 10 May 2008, Putnam Co. NAMC (MIG 79:77)
   122 on 8 May 1999, Hamilton Co. NAMC (MIG 70:40)
   116 on 13 May 2006, Lake Co. NAMC (MIG 77:133)
High Counts – Fall
   5,000 on 5 Sep 1937, Mud Lake, Shelby Co. (MIG 8:57)
   1,000 on 28 Aug 1980, Memphis (MIG 52:23)
Substantiation: Specimen: LSUMZ, 76029

Scissor-tailed Flycatcher, *Tyrannus forficatus*

Status and Abundance: Rare (locally uncommon) transient and summer resident

Habitat: Fields and other open areas
Spring Arrival: mid Apr
Fall Departure: early Oct
Comments: Small numbers now nest locally across the state. Several individuals have nested and hybridized with Western Kingbirds in Shelby Co.

Early Spring
- 31 Mar 2012, Florence Road, Rutherford Co. (SGS, pers. comm.)
- 8 Apr 1975, Shelby Co. (MIG 46:65)
- 8 Apr 2011, Murfreesboro (SGS, pers. obs.)
- 15 Apr 2012, Rutherford Co. (SGS, pers. obs.)

Late Fall
- 15 Nov 1982, Lake Co. (MIG 54:20)
- 31 Oct 2004, Ensley (MIG 76:28)
- 9 Oct 2010, Rutherford Co. on Nashville FBC (MIG 81:156)

High Counts – Spring
- 8 on 9 May 2008, Rutherford Co. (SGS, pers. obs.)

High Counts – Fall
- 8 on 26 Aug 2012, Bedford Co. (MIG 83:150)
- 5 on 29 Sep 2012, Rutherford Co. (MIG 83:150)

High Counts – Summer
- 10 at 5 sites on 24 Jul 2011, Bledsoe Co. (MIG 82:122)

Substantiation: Photograph: Somershoe, S.G. 2010. "Scissor-tailed Flycatcher". <http://www.pbase.com/shoeman/image/124067125> Accessed 15 Dec 2014.

Laniidae: Shrikes.
Two species have been documented in Tennessee with one being an uncommon statewide resident, and the other species being an accidental visitor known from one record.

Loggerhead Shrike, *Lanius ludovicianus*
Status and Abundance: Permanent resident, uncommon in Mississippi Alluvial Valley, locally uncommon to rare elsewhere
Habitat: Fields and other open areas; often with overgrown fencerows
Comments: Usually found singly or in pairs. Populations have declined dramatically since 1966, according to the Breeding Bird Survey (Sauer et al. 2012).
High Counts – Spring
17 on 13 May 2000, Lake Co. NAMC (MIG 71:56)
12 on 4-5 May 1991, Clarksville SBC (MIG 62:37)
High Counts – Winter
53 on 21 Dec 1941, Memphis CBC (MIG 13:20)
29 on 26 Dec 1988, Nashville CBC (MIG 60:16)
29 on 3 Jan 1999, Fayette CBC (MIG 70:16)
28 on 29 Dec 1998, Buffalo River CBC (MIG 70:16)
25 on 17 Dec 1991, Reelfoot Lake CBC (MIG 63:16)
Substantiation: Specimen: LSUMZ, 9001

Northern Shrike, *Lanius excubitor*
Status and Abundance: Accidental visitor
Comments: This species will likely occur again in late fall or winter.
Records
(1) 1 on 9-10 Nov 1964 (collected 10 Nov 1964), Bristol (Coffey 1964a)
Substantiation: Specimen: LSUMZ, 76523

Vireonidae: Vireos. Seven species occur in Tennessee, with six being common to uncommon breeding species in appropriate deciduous forest habitat statewide, while one species appears at present to be restricted to Fort Campbell in the northern part of the Central Hardwoods.

White-eyed Vireo, *Vireo griseus*
Status and Abundance: Fairly common transient and summer resident; very rare winter visitor
Habitat: Scrubby forest edges, dense forest undergrowth, and second growth areas
Spring Arrival: late Mar
Fall Departure: mid Oct
Early Spring
   6 Mar 1988, Warner Parks (Robinson 1990)
   6 Mar 2006, Hamilton Co. (MIG 77:104)
Late Fall
   30 Nov 1991, Conklin, Washington Co. (MIG 63:56)
   25 Nov 2003, Knox Co. (MIG 75:31)
   21 Nov 1967, Nashville (MIG 38:96)
High Counts – Spring
   277 on 26 Apr 2008, Jackson Co. SBC (MIG 79:91)
   250 on 12 May 2007, Putnam Co. NAMC (MIG 78:131)
   184 on 25-26 Apr 1997, Columbia SBC (MIG 68:59)
   166 on 10 May 2008, Putnam Co. NAMC (MIG 79:77)
   149 on 12 May 2001, Putnam Co. NAMC (MIG 72:19)
High Counts – Fall
   148 on 17 Sep 2005, Shelby Co. FBC (MIG 77:17)
   146 on 18 Sep 2010, Shelby Co. FBC (MIG 81:145)
   140 on 16 Sep 2006, Shelby Co. FBC (MIG 78:20)
High Counts – Winter
   4 on 29 Dec 1989, Clarksville CBC (MIG 62:19)
Substantiation: Specimen: LSUMZ, 76533

Bell's Vireo, *Vireo bellii*
Status and Abundance: Very rare local summer resident in west Tennessee; locally uncommon summer resident at Ft. Campbell
Habitat: Shrubby areas lacking a tall forest canopy
Spring Arrival: early May
Fall Departure: mid Sep
Comments: Annual at Ft. Campbell since mid-2000s and population has

been increasing in recent years. No records in east Tennessee.
Early Spring
 29 Apr 2015, Ft. Campbell, Montgomery Co. (DM, pers. comm.)
 6 May 2014, Ft. Campbell, Montgomery Co. (DM, pers. comm.)
 6 May 2005, Black Bayou Refuge (MIG 76:96)
 7 May 2004, Lake Co. NAMC (MIG 75:97, MAG, pers. comm.)
Late Fall
 14 Oct 2004, Black Bayou Refuge (MIG 76:28)
 15 Sep 2012, Ft. Campbell, Montgomery Co. (MIG 83:150)
 11 Sep 1998, Shelby Forest SP (MIG 70:48)
 11 Sep 2004, Gray's Landing, Stewart Co. (MIG 76:30)
High Counts – Spring
 3 on 18 May 2010, Ft. Campbell, Montgomery (DM, pers. comm.)
 2 on 7-12 May 2003, Black Bayou WMA (MT, pers. comm.)
High Counts – Fall
 1-2 on 27 Aug-10 Sep 2002, Black Bayou WMA (MIG 74:17)
High Counts – Summer
 6 m during spring/summer 2012, Ft. Campbell, 3 in Montgomery Co., 3 in Stewart Co. (DM, pers. comm.)
 2 on 24-30 Jun 1935, Memphis (Coffey 1935a)
Substantiation: Photograph: Todd, M.C. 2010. "Bell's Vireo". <http://www.pbase.com/mctodd/image/124797169> Accessed 25 Sep 2014.

Yellow-throated Vireo, *Vireo flavifrons*
Status and Abundance: Fairly common transient and summer resident
Habitat: Hardwood forest
Spring Arrival: early Apr
Fall Departure: mid Oct
Early Spring
 28 Mar 1933, Memphis (MIG 4:8)
 28 Mar 1997, Radnor Lake (MIG 68:109)
 30 Mar 1975, Old Hickory Lake (MIG 46:66)
Late Fall
 29 Oct 1987, Claiborne Co. (MIG 59:41)
 27 Oct 1984, Arrow Lake, Maury Co. (MIG 56:21)
 26 Oct 1984, Murfreesboro (MIG 56:21)
High Counts – Spring
 66 on 10 May 2008, Putnam Co. NAMC (MIG 79:77)
 50 on 13 May 2000, Putnam Co. NAMC (MIG 71:57)
 48 on 8 May 1999, Putnam Co. NAMC (MIG 70:41)
 39 on 12 May 2001, Shelby Co. NAMC (MIG 72:19)

36 on 27 Apr 1958, Knoxville SBC (MIG 29:32)
High Counts – Fall
29 on 16 Sep 2006, Putnam Co. FBC (MIG 78:20)
27 on 18 Oct 2010, White Co. FBC (MIG 81:145)
20 on 20 Sep 2008, Putnam Co. FBC (MIG 80:17)
18 on 19 Sep 2009, Putnam Co. FBC (MIG 81:44)
Substantiation: Specimen: LSUMZ, 76552

Blue-headed Vireo, *Vireo solitarius*

Status and Abundance: Uncommon (fairly common Cumberland Plateau, Ridge and Valley, Southern Blue Ridge) transient statewide; fairly common summer resident in Cumberland Plateau, Ridge and Valley, Southern Blue Ridge (rare Central Hardwoods); accidental winter visitor

Habitat: Hardwood forest

Spring Arrival: mid Mar

Spring Departure: mid May

Fall Arrival: late Sep

Fall Departure: early Nov

Comments: Few winter records, most in Mississippi Alluvial Valley but scattered across state. Spring arrival is one to two weeks earlier in eastern mountains.

Early Spring
3 Mar 2005, Bartlett, Shelby Co. (MIG 76:96)
9 Mar 2004, Tremont, GSMNP (MIG 75:119)
11 Mar 1974, GSMNP (MIG 45:26)
11 Mar 2001, S. Holston Dam (MIG 72:99)
13 Mar 2005, Foothills WMA (MIG 76:103)
13 Mar 1997, Putnam Co. (MIG 68:109)

Late Spring
27 May 2010, Cheatham WMA (MIG 81:116)
21 May 1937, Nashville (BNA:35)

Early Fall
29 Aug 1942, Nashville (MIG 13:46)
31 Aug 1998, Shelby Farms (MIG 70:48)
9 Sep 1992, Shelby Forest SP (MIG 64:17)
12 Sep 1995, Shelby Forest SP (MIG 67:19)

Late Fall
30 Nov 1985, Sullivan Co. (MIG 57:34)
24 Nov 1995, Rhea Co. (MIG 67:23)
23 Nov 1985, Woods Reservoir (MIG 57:28)

High Counts – Spring
    93 on 1 May 1994, Elizabethton SBC (MIG 65:34)
    88 on 29 Apr 1995, Elizabethton SBC (MIG 66:35)
    56 on 26 Apr 1992, Elizabethton SBC (MIG 63:49)
    56 on 30 Apr 2005, Elizabethton SBC (MIG 76:139)
High Counts – Fall
    48 on 26 Sep 2004, Elizabethton FBC (MIG 76:21)
    24 on 24 Sep 2011, Elizabethton FBC (MIG 82:135)
    23 on 24 Sep 2005, Elizabethton FBC (MIG 77:10)
    23 on 27 Sep 2003, Elizabethton FBC (MIG 75:16)
High Counts – Summer
    54 on 7 Jun 2014, Carter Co. Summer Count (*fide* RLK)
    18 on 2 Jun 2002, Frozen Head SP (MIG 73:114)
Winter Records
    3 on 15 Dec 2002, Memphis CBC (MIG 74:48)
    2 on 31 Dec 1999, Nickajack CBC (MIG 71:45)
Substantiation: Specimen: LSUMZ, 76562

Warbling Vireo, *Vireo gilvus*
    Status and Abundance: Fairly common spring transient and summer resident, rare in Ridge and Valley and Southern Blue Ridge; uncommon fall transient, rare in Ridge and Valley and Southern Blue Ridge
    Habitat: Open riparian forest and forest edge; particularly cottonwoods and sycamores
    Spring Arrival: mid Apr
    Fall Departure: late Sep
    Comments: No summer records in southeast Tennessee. Rare during spring and fall in southeast Tennessee.
    Early Spring
        29 Mar 1997, Hamilton Co. (MIG 68:111)
        30 Mar 2010, Shelby Co. (MIG 81:114)
        1 Apr 1975, Shelby Co. (MIG 46:65)
        2 Apr 2012, Williamson Co. (MW, pers. comm.)
        5 Apr 1921, Nashville (BNA:35)
        5 Apr 2003, Duck River Unit (MIG 74:89)
    Late Fall
        13 Nov 1949, Carter Co. (MIG 22:19)
        15 Oct 1964, Nashville (Laskey 1964)
        11 Oct 1998, Shelby Farms (MIG 70:48)
        10 Oct 1939, Knoxville (MIG 10:76)

High Counts – Spring
    114 on 8 May 2004, Lake Co. NAMC (MIG 75:97)
    94 on 13 May 2000, Lake Co. NAMC (MIG 71:56)
    85 on 10 May 2003, Lake Co. NAMC (MIG 74:116)
    54 on 12 May 2001, Lake Co. NAMC (MIG 72:18)
Substantiation: Specimen: LSUMZ, 76579

Philadelphia Vireo, *Vireo philadelphicus*
Status and Abundance: Uncommon transient
Habitat: Forest and forest edge
Spring Arrival: late Apr
Spring Departure: mid May
Fall Arrival: early Sep
Fall Departure: mid Oct
Early Spring
    31 Mar 1945, Memphis (MIG 16:11)
    7 Apr 1940, Knox Co. (Howell and Monroe 1957)
Late Spring
    28 May 2001, Putnam Co. (MIG 72:95)
    24 May 1954, Nashville (BNA:35)
Early Fall
    19 Aug 2006, Shelby Forest SP (MIG 78:34)
    28 Aug 1972, Hiwassee River Area (MIG 43:102)
    2 Sep 1998, Shelby Forest SP (MIG 70:48)
    3 Sep 1976, Old Hickory Lake (BNA:35)
Late Fall
    30 Oct 1964, Columbia (MIG 35:101)
    30 Oct 2002, Nashville (MIG 74:19)
High Counts – Spring
    11 on 11 May 2002, Nashville SBC (MIG 73:105)
    8 on 12 May 2007, Davidson Co. NAMC (MIG 78:130)
High Counts – Fall
    37 killed at airport tower on 7 Oct 1951, Nashville (Laskey 1951)
    28 on 19 Sep 2012, Shelby Forest SP (MIG 83:148)
    27 killed at airport tower on 6 Oct 1954, Chattanooga (MIG 25:68)
    24 on 5 Oct 2002, Nashville FBC (MIG 73:52)
    19 on 22 Sep 2004, Shelby Forest SP (MIG 76:28)
Substantiation: Specimen: LSUMZ, 76570

Red-eyed Vireo, *Vireo olivaceus*
Status and Abundance: Common transient and summer resident
Habitat: Hardwood forest

Spring Arrival: mid Apr
Fall Departure: mid Oct
Early Spring
- 24 Mar 1993, Shelby Farms (MIG 64:64)
- 25 Mar 2005, Radnor Lake (MIG 76:98)
- 30 Mar 1945, Nashville (MIG 16:14)
- 31 Mar 1991, Buffalo Mtn., Washington Co. (MIG 62:115)
- 1 Apr 2003, Royal Blue WMA (MIG 74:93)

Late Fall
- 9 Nov 1963, Kingsport (MIG 34:76)
- 9 Nov 1995, Greeneville (MIG 67:23)
- 30 Oct 1964, Columbia (MIG 35:101)
- 27 Oct 1984, Arrow Lake, Maury Co. (MIG 56:21)

High Counts – Spring
- 691 on 13 May 2006, Putnam Co. NAMC (MIG 77:134)
- 672 on 10 May 2008, Putnam Co. NAMC (MIG 79:77)
- 666 on 12 May 2001, Putnam Co. NAMC (MIG 72:19)
- 625 on 12 May 2007, Putnam Co. NAMC (MIG 78:131)
- 612 on 9 May 1998, Putnam Co. NAMC (MIG 69:154)

High Counts – Fall
- 53 on 18 Sep 2010, Shelby Co. FBC (MIG 81:145)
- 48 on 19 Sep 2009, Shelby Co. FBC (MIG 81:44)
- 34 on 5 Oct 2002, Nashville FBC (MIG 73:52)
- 22 on 16 Sep 2006, Putnam Co. FBC (MIG 78:20)

High Counts – Summer
- 327 on 22 Jun 2000, Big South Fork NRRA, Twin Arches area (Stedman and Stedman 2002)
- 75 on 8 Jun 1999, Watauga Lake (MIG 70:134)
- 73 on 15 Jun 1996, Marion Co. (MIG 67:79)

Substantiation: Specimen: LSUMZ, 76568

Corvidae: Jays and Crows. Four species occur regularly. Two species are common statewide permanent residents, one species is limited to the higher elevations of the eastern mountains, and one species is primarily limited to the Mississippi River Valley and tributaries and the Tennessee River valley in the southern half of the state.

Blue Jay, *Cyanocitta cristata*
  Status and Abundance: Common permanent resident
  Habitat: Open forest and forest edge; urban and suburban yards
  High Counts – Spring
    941 on 26 Apr 1998, Soddy Mtn. (MIG 69:166)
    763 on 25 Apr 1998, Soddy Mtn. (MIG 69:166)
    459 on 7 May 2005, Nashville SBC (MIG 76:140)
    440 on 27 Apr 1998, Soddy Mtn. (MIG 69:166)
    415 on 27 Apr 2003, Knoxville SBC (MIG 74:124)
  High Counts – Fall
    1,000 on 22 Sep 2004, Benton Co. (MIG 76:28)
    880 on 10 Oct 1982, near Chattanooga (MIG 54:25)
    770 on 4 Oct 2009, White Co. FBC (MIG 81:44)
    707 on 26 Sep 2004, Knoxville FBC (MIG 76:21)
    441 on 4 Oct 2011, Gray's Landing, Stewart Co. (MIG 82:150)
  High Counts – Winter
    601 on 20 Dec 1998, Memphis CBC (MIG 70:15)
    551 on 21 Dec 2009, White Co. CBC (MIG 81:95)
    510 on 22 Dec 1996, Knoxville CBC (MIG 68:21)
    499 on 30 Dec 2009, Savannah CBC (MIG 81:95)
    485 on 2 Jan 2005, Knoxville CBC (MIG 76:67)
  Substantiation: Specimen: LSUMZ, 76162

American Crow, *Corvus brachyrhynchos*
  Status and Abundance: Common permanent resident
  Habitat: Pastures, fields, urban and suburban areas, and forest edge
  High Counts – Spring
    559 on 29 Apr 2001, Elizabethton SBC (MIG 72:29)
    405 on 1 May 1994, Elizabethton SBC (MIG 65:33)
    391 on 9 May 1992, Chattanooga SBC (MIG 63:48)
    388 on 26 Apr 1992, Elizabethton SBC (MIG 63:48)
  High Counts – Fall
    885 on 26 Sep 2009, Elizabethton FBC (MIG 81:44)
    731 on 8 Oct 2005, Nashville FBC (MIG 77:11)

645 on 30 Sep 2006, Elizabethton FBC (MIG 78:28)

High Counts – Winter
50,000+ on 26 Jan 1990, Jackson (MIG 61:58)
42,812 on 2 Jan 1999, Jackson CBC (MIG 70:69)
35,000 on 26 Dec 1965, Nashville CBC (MIG 36:89)
30,000 on 28 Dec 1996, Jackson CBC (MIG 68:21)
27,500 on 26 Dec 1988, Nashville CBC (MIG 60:16)

Substantiation: Specimen: LSUMZ, 19160

Fish Crow, *Corvus ossifragus*

Status and Abundance: Fairly common transient and summer resident in Mississippi Alluvial Valley and tributaries (Hatchie River, Forked Deer River); uncommon winter resident in Mississippi Alluvial Valley (Hatchie River, Forked Deer River); uncommon transient and summer resident in Hamilton Co.; rare visitor (resident?) along Tennessee River in Hardin and up through Roane and Knox Co.

Habitat: Pastures, fields, urban and suburban areas, and forest edge near large rivers and lakes

Comments: Status of populations along the Tennessee River in Hardin and from Hamilton through Roane and Knox needs further study. Immature American Crows have nasal calls that are similar to Fish Crow; accordingly, out-of-range reports from late summer and fall merit very careful documentation.

Early Spring
150+ on 21 Mar 1990, Heloise (MAG, pers. comm.)

High Counts – Spring
100+ 17 Mar 2009, Obion Co. (MIG 80:88)
89 on 12 May 2001, Lake Co. NAMC (MIG 72:18)
36 on 11 May 2002, Lake Co. NAMC (MIG 73:97)
17 on 26 Apr 1992, Memphis SBC (MIG 63:48)

High Counts – Fall
46 on 8 Aug 1991, Shelby Forest SP (MIG 63:53)

High Counts – Winter
960 on 21 Dec 1987, Lauderdale Co. (MIG 59:65)
51 on 29 Dec 2001, Jackson CBC (MIG 72:119)

Substantiation: Specimen: LSUMZ, 76205

Common Raven, *Corvus corax*

Status and Abundance: Locally uncommon permanent resident in Southern Blue Ridge

Habitat: Mountains, typically above 3,000 ft during summer, spreading into lower elevations during winter

Corvidae: Jays and Crows

Comments: Occasionally found at lower elevations in northern counties of Ridge and Valley, North Cumberland WMA, and Frozen Head SP. Research on wintering Golden Eagles documented ravens almost daily visiting bait sites on North Cumberland WMA, Campbell Co. (SGS, pers. comm.)

High Counts – Spring
- 24 on 29 Apr 2001, Elizabethton SBC (MIG 72:29)
- 14 on 24 Apr 2004, Elizabethton SBC (MIG 75:106)
- 13 on 26 Apr 1992, Elizabethton SBC (MIG 63:48)

High Counts – Fall
- 45 on 27 Sep 1991, Roan Mtn. (MIG 63:57)
- 23 on 5 Oct 2002, Elizabethton FBC (MIG 73:52)
- 22 on 25 Sep 2004, Elizabethton FBC (MIG 76:21)
- 22 on 7 Nov 1990, Roan Mtn. (MIG 62:54)

High Counts – Winter
- 23 on 23 Feb 1990, Roan Mtn. (MIG 61:63)
- 20+ on 15 Dec 1991, Elizabethton (MIG 63:63)
- 17 on 28 Dec 1985, Bristol CBC (MIG 57:11)

Substantiation: Specimen: LSUMZ, 76202

Alaudidae: Larks. Only one species occurs in Tennessee.

Horned Lark, *Eremophila alpestris*
>   Status and Abundance: Fairly common permanent resident in Mississippi Alluvial Valley and locally in Southeastern Coastal Plain; uncommon to locally common summer resident, transient, and winter resident elsewhere
>   Habitat: Cultivated, bare, and short grass fields
>   High Counts – Spring
>>   502 on 13 May 2000, Lake Co. NAMC (MIG 71:52)
>>   248 on 12 May 2001, Lake Co. NAMC (MIG 72:18)
>>   165 on 10 May 2003, Lake Co. NAMC (MIG 74:116)
>   High Counts – Fall
>>   30 on 6 Sep 2014, Eagleville, Rutherford Co. (SGS, pers. obs.)
>>   26 on 15 Nov 2002, Obion Co. (MAG, pers. comm.)
>>   20 on 14 Sep 2010, Robertson Co. (MIG 81:156)
>   High Counts – Winter
>>   2,500 on 4 Jan 2003, Savannah Bottoms (MAG, pers. comm.)
>>   2,000 on 30 Jan 1978, Coffee Co. (MIG 49:43)
>>   1,518 on 15 Dec 2001, Reelfoot Lake CBC (MIG 72:119)
>>   1,503 on 18 Dec 1999, Reelfoot Lake CBC (MIG 71:18)
>>   1,354 on 16 Dec 2001, Reelfoot Lake CBC (MIG 72:69)
>   Substantiation: Specimen: LSUMZ, 76109

Hirundinidae: Swallows. Eight species have been documented in Tennessee with five common breeding species statewide, one uncommon or locally common transient with few known breeding sites, and two vagrant species.

Purple Martin, *Progne subis*
- Status and Abundance: Common spring and early fall transient and summer resident
- Habitat: Open and semi-open areas, frequently near water or where nesting structures have been erected
- Spring Arrival: late Feb
- Fall Departure: early Sep
- Comments: Roosts of migrant Purple Martins in late summer are often visible on Doppler radar and may contain hundreds of thousands of individuals; look for rapidly expanding reflective "donuts" (which are birds dispersing from the roost) around dawn on otherwise clear mornings.
- Early Spring
    - 30 Jan 2001, Cove Lake SP (MIG 72:72)
    - 2 Feb 1964, Chattanooga (MIG 35:16)
    - 8 Feb 1987, Memphis (MIG 58:53)
    - 15 Feb 2003, Cates Landing (JRW, unpubl. data)
- Late Fall
    - 23 Oct 1968, Reelfoot Lake (MIG 39:89)
    - 17 Oct 2010, Ensley (MIG 81:155)
    - 1 Oct 1983, Ashland City (BNA:32)
    - 30 Sep 1989, Davidson Co. (MIG 61:16)
    - 25 Sep 2010, Tiptonville Ferry Landing, Lake Co. (MIG 81:155)
- High Counts – Spring
    - 237 on 8 May 2004, Hamilton Co. NAMC (MIG 75:96)
    - 230 on 10 May 2008, Putnam Co. NAMC (MIG 79:77)
    - 217 on 5 May 1991, Memphis SBC (MIG 62:36)
    - 183 on 10 May 2003, Hamilton Co. NAMC (MIG 74:116)
    - 168 on 10 May 1997, Putnam Co. SBC (MIG 68:58)
- High Counts – Fall
    - 1,000,000 on 26 Aug 1994, Island 10, Lake Co. (MAG, JRW, unpubl. data)
    - 850,000+ on 29 Aug 1994, Island 10, Lake Co. (MIG 66:21)
    - 500,000 on 14 Aug 1999, Island 18, Dyer Co. (MIG 71:32)
    - 250,000 on 14 Aug 1994, Island 10, Lake Co. (MIG 66:21)
    - 120,000 on 17 Aug 2011, Nashville (MIG 82:152)

High Counts – Summer
    80,000+ on 18 Jul 2012, Nashville (MIG 83:104)
    10,000 on 29 Jun 2011, Nashville (SGS, pers. obs.)
    4,000+ on 23 Jul 1992, Island 10, Lake Co. (MIG 63:96)
Substantiation: Specimen: LSUMZ, 76144

Tree Swallow, *Tachycineta bicolor*

Status and Abundance: Fairly common transient and summer resident; rare winter visitor

Habitat: Near or over open ponds, lakes, marshes, rivers, or other bodies of water

Spring Arrival: mid Feb

Fall Departure: mid Nov

Comments: This species has increased significantly as a breeder in the past 20 years.

Early Spring
    2 Feb 2013, Chickamauga Lake (MIG, in press)
    8 Feb 2003, Cherokee Dam (MIG 74:57)
    10 Feb 1975, Tennessee NWR (MIG 46:44)
    10 Feb 1990, Chickamauga Lake (MIG 61:62)

Late Fall
    29 Dec 1992, Shelby Farms (MIG 64:16)
    15 Dec 2004, Old Hickory Lake, Sumner Co. (MIG 76:80)
    13 Dec 2008, Old Hickory Lake, Sumner Co. (MIG 80:68)
    28 Nov 1971, Reelfoot Lake (MIG 43:23)
    28 Nov 2002, S. Holston Lake (MIG 74:27)

High Counts – Spring
    968 on 24 Apr 2005, Knoxville SBC (MIG 76:140)
    500 on 24 Mar 1996, Reelfoot Lake (MAG, pers. comm.)

High Counts – Fall
    500,000 on 18 Oct 1970, Reelfoot Lake (MIG 41:83)
    80,000 on 18 Oct 1936, Shelby Co. (MIG 7:98)
    25,000 on 5 Nov 1991, Reelfoot Lake (MIG 63:53)
    11,000 on 12 Oct 1968, Reelfoot Lake (MIG 39:89)

High Counts – Summer
    2,850 on 31 Jul 2009, Greene Co. (MIG 80:127)
    1,000+ on 23 Jun 2005, Rankin Bottoms (MIG 76:146)

High Counts – Winter
    50 on 24 Feb 2002, Kyker Bottoms WMA (MIG 73:39)

Substantiation: Specimen: LSUMZ, 76119

Violet-green Swallow, *Tachycineta thalassina*
Status and Abundance: **Unsubstantiated**
Comments: Accepted by the TBRC on the basis of written documentation.
Records
(1) 1 on 27 Mar 1994, Austin Springs (Knight 1996)

Northern Rough-winged Swallow, *Stelgidopteryx serripennis*
Status and Abundance: Common transient and summer resident; very rare winter visitor
Habitat: Near or over open ponds, lakes, marshes, rivers, or other bodies of water; sometimes other open areas with access to burrows or crevices in dirt banks, rock banks, or artificial structures providing potential nest sites
Spring Arrival: mid Mar
Fall Departure: late Oct
Early Spring
  1 Mar 1984, Maury Co. (MIG 55:70)
  5 Mar 2005, Greene Co. (MIG 76:101)
Late Fall
  25 Nov 1983, Cross Creeks NWR (MIG 55:21)
  15 Nov 1995, Nickajack Lake (MIG 67:22)
  9 Nov 1995, Hiwassee River Area, Meigs Co. (MIG 67:22)
  6 Nov 2007, S. Holston Lake (MIG 79:29)
  5 Nov 1995, Watauga River (MIG 67:24)
High Counts – Spring
  1,050 on 25 Apr 1987, Elizabethton SBC (MIG 58:82)
  201 on 1 May 1994, Elizabethton SBC (MIG 65:33)
High Counts – Fall
  3,000 on 17 Aug 1997, Island 13 (MIG 69:41)
  2,000 on 23 Aug 1997, Rankin Bottoms (MIG 69:47)
  2,000 on 28 Aug 1968, Reelfoot Lake (MIG 39:89)
Winter Records
  2 on 8 Dec 1994, Black Bayou WMA (MIG 66:41)
  1-2 on 1 Jan 2009, Cherokee Dam (MIG 80:71)
  1 on 31 Dec 2011, Jackson CBC (MAG, pers. comm., photo)
  1 on 3 Jan 2013, Robco Lake (MIG, in press)
  1 on 1 Jan 2014, Hiwassee CBC (KAC, m.ob., pers. comm.)
Substantiation: Specimen: LSUMZ, 19511

Bank Swallow, *Riparia riparia*
Status and Abundance: Uncommon transient, rare to locally uncommon

summer resident

Habitat: Breeds along rivers with exposed dirt embankments or limestone and zinc mine tailings; congregates with other swallows over large bodies of water in migration

Spring Arrival: late Apr

Fall Departure: late Sep

Early Spring
- 21 Mar 1965, Coleman Lake, Davidson Co. (BNA:32)
- 31 Mar 1989, Austin Springs (MIG 60:90)
- 5 Apr 1997, Ensley (JRW, unpubl. data)
- 5 Apr 2003, Lake Co. (MIG 74:88)
- 9 Apr 1972, Erwin (MIG 43:54)

Late Fall
- 26 Oct 1976, Shelby Co. (MIG 48:18)
- 14 Oct 1959, Bush Lake (MIG 31:11)

High Counts – Spring
- 300 on 23 May 1998, Fulton, Lauderdale Co. (JRW, MAG, unpubl. data)
- 300 on 28 May 2001, Hwy 79W, Lake Co. (MIG 72:93)
- 103 on 13 May 2000, Lake Co. NAMC (MIG 71:52)
- 100 on 23 Apr 1996, Eagle Lake WMA (MIG 67:61)
- 82 on 5 May 1991, Memphis SBC (MIG 62:36)

High Counts – Fall
- 5,000+ on 10 Aug 2010, Bessie Bend, Lake Co. (MIG 81:155)
- 3,000 on 17 Aug 1997, Island 13 (MIG 69:41)
- 2,500+ on 29 Aug 2009, Island 13 (SGS, pers. obs.)
- 2,250 on 9 Sep 1980, Douglas Lake (MIG 52:25)
- 2,000 on 13 Aug 1998, Lower Hatchie NWR (JRW, unpubl. data)

High Counts – Summer
- 5,000 on 27 Jul 1968, Reelfoot Lake (MIG 39:64)
- 3,000 on 31 Jul 1978, Reelfoot Lake (MIG 49:91)
- 1,200+ on 18 Jul 1990, Midway, Dyer Co. (MIG 62:23)
- 1,000+ on 30 Jul 2001, Greene Co. (MIG 72:126)
- 800+ on 21 Jul 2007, Greene Co. (MIG 78:142)

Substantiation: Specimen: LSUMZ, 76124

Cliff Swallow, *Petrochelidon pyrrhonota*

Status and Abundance: Fairly common transient and summer resident

Habitat: Rivers, lakes, and other open bodies of water; nests colonially under bridges

Spring Arrival: late Mar

Fall Departure: mid Sep

Early Spring
>   6 Mar 1974, Tennessee NWR (MIG 45:20)
>   10 Mar 1987, Chattanooga (MIG 58:104)
>   10 Mar 2011, Bennett Lake, Marion Co. (MIG 82:91)

Late Fall
>   24 Oct 1958, Bush Lake (Palmer 1959)
>   23 Oct 1949, Memphis (MIG 20:68)
>   21 Oct 2000, Mud Island (JRW, unpubl. data)

High Counts – Spring
>   2,000 on 17 Apr 2013, Tennessee River and I-40, Humphreys Co. (SGS, pers. obs.)
>   807 on 8 May 2004, Nashville SBC (MIG 75:106)
>   775 on 8 May 2004, Cheatham Co. NAMC (MIG 75:96)
>   634 on 4-5 May 1991, Clarksville SBC (MIG 62:36)
>   606 on 7-8 May 1994, Montgomery SBC (MIG 65:33)

High Counts – Fall
>   2,000 on 26 Aug 1936, Campbell Co. (MIG 7:73)

High Counts – Summer
>   1,890 on 16 Jun 2012, Mississippi River bridge, Dyer Co. (MIG 83:103)

Winter Records
>   1 on 17 Dec 1991, Reelfoot Lake CBC (MIG 63:15)

Substantiation: Specimen: LSUMZ, 19515

Cave Swallow, *Petrochelidon fulva*

Status and Abundance: Accidental visitor

Records
>   (1) 2 on 30 Sep 2006, Mud Island, Shelby Co. (NAB 61(1):81)
>   (2) 1 on 17 Sep 2011, Memphis (MIG 82:150)
>   (3) 1 on 18-19 Sep 2011, Tiptonville Bar (MIG 82:150)
>   (4) 2 on 24 Apr 2012, Mississippi River, Shelby Co. (MIG 83:65)
>   (5) 2 on 7 Nov 2012, Musick's Campground (Knight 2012)

Substantiation: Photograph: 1 on 30 Sep 2006, Mud Island, Shelby Co. (NAB 61(1):81)

Barn Swallow, *Hirundo rustica*

Status and Abundance: Common transient and summer resident; rare winter visitor

Habitat: Fields, pastures, other open areas or edges, often near water

Spring Arrival: mid Mar

Fall Departure: late Oct

Early Spring
>   13 Feb 2005, Hamilton Co. (MIG 76:82)

5 Mar 1986, Lawrence Co. (MIG 57:79)

8 Mar 2006, Shelby Farms (MIG 77:99)

Late Fall

19 Nov 1961, near Mud Lake, Shelby Co. (MIG 33:12)

18 Nov 1983, Woods Reservoir (MIG 55:21)

3 Nov 1979, Savannah Bay (MIG 51:42)

High Counts – Spring

1,080 on 25 Apr 1987, Elizabethton SBC (MIG 58:82)

428 on 11 May 2002, Shelby Co. NAMC (MIG 73:97)

Winter Records

1 on 18 Dec 1976, Lebanon CBC (MIG 48:32)

1 on 22-23 Dec 1978, Samburg (MIG 50:41)

1 on 13 Jan 1993, Paris Landing SP (MIG 64:48)

1 on 21 Jan 1995, Bradley Co. (MIG 66:43)

1 on 13 Dec 1998, Williamson Co. (MIG 70:70)

Substantiation: Specimen: LSUMZ, 76129

Paridae: Chickadees and Titmice. Three species are found in Tennessee with two being common permanent residents statewide and the third being found almost exclusively in the GSMNP.

Carolina Chickadee, *Poecile carolinensis*
- Status and Abundance: Common permanent resident
- Habitat: Forest, forest edge, parks, suburban areas, and other semi-open habitats
- High Counts – Spring
    - 237 on 9 May 1992, Chattanooga SBC (MIG 63:48)
    - 193 on 10 May 1997, Chattanooga SBC (MIG 68:58)
    - 182 on 7 May 2005, Nashville SBC (MIG 76:140)
- High Counts – Fall
    - 457 on 8 Oct 2005, Nashville FBC (MIG 77:11)
    - 404 on 30 Sep 2006, Nashville FBC (MIG 78:28)
- High Counts – Winter
    - 602 on 2 Jan 2005, Knoxville CBC (MIG 76:67)
    - 600 on 16 Dec 2006, Nashville CBC (MIG 78:67)
    - 546 on 31 Dec 2005, Knoxville CBC (MIG 77:45)
    - 495 on 21 Dec 1985, Chattanooga CBC (MIG 57:11)
    - 450 on 4 Jan 2003, Knoxville CBC (MIG 74:43)
- Substantiation: Specimen: LSUMZ, 76221

Black-capped Chickadee, *Poecile atricapillus*
- Status and Abundance: Uncommon permanent resident in Southern Blue Ridge
- Habitat: Mountain forests, typically above 4,500 feet in breeding season, possibly lower during winter
- Comments: Found primarily in GSMNP, but occurs south to Whigg Meadow, Cherokee NF (SGS, pers. comm.). Knight (2010) summarizes occurrences in the mountains of eastern Tennessee. Evidently there is no known hybridization with Carolina Chickadees due to apparent elevational separation during spring and summer.
- High Counts – Winter
    - 186 on 29 Dec 1991, GSMNP CBC (MIG 63:15)
    - 79 on 27 Dec 1998, GSMNP CBC (MIG 70:74)
- Substantiation: Specimen: USNM, 351088

Tufted Titmouse, *Baeolophus bicolor*
- Status and Abundance: Common permanent resident
- Habitat: Forest, forest edge, parks, suburban areas, and other semi-open

habitats

High Counts – Spring
    254 on 9 May 1992, Chattanooga SBC (MIG 63:48)
    236 on 10 May 2008, Putnam Co. NAMC (MIG 79:77)
    221 on 12 May 2007, Putnam Co. NAMC (MIG 78:131)
    172 on 7 May 2005, Nashville SBC (MIG 76:140)

High Counts – Fall
    246 on 18 Oct 2010, White Co. FBC (MIG 81:145)
    232 on 25 Sep 2010, DeKalb Co. FBC (MIG 81:145)
    215 on 15 Sep 2008, Putnam Co. FBC (MIG 79:14)
    206 on 8 Oct 2005, Nashville FBC (MIG 77:11)
    173 on 4 Oct 2009, White Co. FBC (MIG 81:44)

High Counts – Winter
    417 on 28 Dec 1985, Clarksville CBC (MIG 57:11)
    392 on 2 Jan 2010, Knoxville CBC (MIG 81:95)
    370 on 2 Jan 2005, Knoxville CBC (MIG 76:67)

Substantiation: Specimen: LSUMZ, 76254

Sittidae: Nuthatches. The family is represented by three species, with one species being an uncommon resident statewide, one species being resident in certain parts of the state, and the third being a breeder in the higher elevations of the eastern mountains and, at times, a common winter resident across the state in some years.

Red-breasted Nuthatch, *Sitta canadensis*
Status and Abundance: Irruptive (rare to fairly common) transient and winter resident; locally uncommon permanent resident in Southern Blue Ridge

Habitat: Breeds in high-elevation spruce-fir forest or pines at mid-elevation; during winter, conifer and mixed forest and forest edge

Spring Departure: early May

Fall Arrival: mid Sep

Comments: Permanent resident that breeds in the higher elevations of the eastern mountains, but is a spring and fall transient and winter resident in rest of state. Nested in June 2002, Big South Fork NRRA, Scott Co. (Renfrow and Stedman 2003).

Late Spring
- 20 May 1978, Nashville (MIG 49:92)
- 15 May 2002, Tipton Co. (MIG 73:57)
- 14 May 1986, Knoxville (MIG 57:85)

Early Fall
- 25 Aug 1968, Chattanooga (MIG 39:93-94)
- 28 Aug 1968, Nashville (BNA:33)
- 1 Sep 1997, Byrdstown, Pickett Co. (MIG 69:43))
- 6 Sep 1997, Memphis (MIG 69:41)
- 9 Sep 1975, Memphis (MIG 47:17)

High Counts – Spring
- 8 on 26 Apr 1992, Elizabethton SBC (MIG 63:48)

High Counts – Fall
- 122 on 21 Oct 1977, Roan Mtn. (MIG 49:23)
- 30+ on 19 Nov 1999, Big South Fork NRRA (MIG 71:37)
- 19 on 30 Sep 2006, Elizabethton FBC (MIG 78:28)

High Counts – Winter
- 175 on 1 Jan 1950, GSMNP CBC (MIG 20:62)
- 128 on 30 Dec 1981, Roan Mtn. CBC (MIG 53:8)
- 71 on 17 Dec 2006, GSNMP CBC (MIG 78:67)

Substantiation: Specimen: LSUMZ, 76290

White-breasted Nuthatch, *Sitta carolinensis*
Subspecies: *carolinensis*
Status and Abundance: Fairly common permanent resident
Habitat: Forest (mainly hardwood) and forest edge
High Counts – Spring
    68 on 9 May 1992, Chattanooga SBC (MIG 63:48)
    57 on 10 May 2008, Putnam Co. NAMC (MIG 79:77)
    45 on 12 May 2007, Putnam Co. NAMC (MIG 78:131)
High Counts – Fall
    115 on 4 Oct 2008, White Co. FBC (MIG 80:17)
    109 on 18 Oct 2010, White Co. FBC (MIG 81:145)
    103 on 15 Sep 2008, Putnam Co. FBC (MIG 79:14)
    103 on 25 Sep 2010, DeKalb Co. FBC (MIG 81:145)
    91 on 20 Sep 2008, Putnam Co. FBC (MIG 80:17)
High Counts – Winter
    136 on 23 Dec 2009, Crossville CBC (MIG 81:95)
    136 on 23 Dec 2010, Crossville CBC (MIG 82:50)
    126 on 26 Dec 2005, Buffalo River CBC (MIG 77:44)
    115 on 23 Dec 2006, Crossville CBC (MIG 78:66)
    112 on 22 Dec 1984, Nashville CBC (MIG 56:8)
Substantiation: Specimen: LSUMZ, 76263

Brown-headed Nuthatch, *Sitta pusilla*
Status and Abundance: Locally fairly common permanent resident, primarily along Tennessee River in e. Tennessee, but also Hardin Co.
Habitat: Open stands of mature pines
Comments: Expanded range into Tennessee with first record consisting of 2 birds on 14 Dec 1968 in Hamilton Co. (Basham 1969). Populations appear to be expanding in areas of open pine. Populations are concentrated in Hamilton Co. and vicinity, Roane, Loudon, Knox, Blount, and Anderson Counties, with recent records in Franklin, Polk, Putnam, Van Buren, Greene, Coffee and Scott counties. A small population is resident at Pickwick Dam in Hardin Co.
High Counts – Spring
    28 on 9 May 1992, Chattanooga SBC (MIG 63:48)
    20 on 14 May 2005, Hamilton Co. NAMC (MIG 76:130)
High Counts – Fall
    7 on 2 Nov 2009, Pickwick Dam (MIG 81:50)
High Counts – Summer
    20 on 21 Jul 2002, Dayton, Rhea Co. (MIG 73:114)

High Counts – Winter
    46 on 1 Jan 2000, Hiwassee CBC (MIG 71:19)
    40 on 18 Dec 2010, Chattanooga CBC (MIG 82:50)
    34 on 1 Jan 1999, Hiwassee CBC (MIG 70:16)
    34 on 20 Dec 1997, Chattanooga CBC (MIG 69:23)
    31 on 19 Dec 2009, Chattanooga CBC (MIG 81:94)
Substantiation: Photograph: 1 on 12 Apr 1981, Hamilton Co. (MIG 52(4):81)

Certhiidae: Creepers. Only one species occurs, a transient and winter resident across the state with a small breeding population in the high elevations of the eastern mountains and possibly west Tennessee river bottoms.

Brown Creeper, *Certhia americana*
    Status and Abundance: Uncommon late fall and early spring transient and winter resident; locally uncommon summer resident in Southern Blue Ridge; very rare summer resident in Mississippi Alluvial Valley
    Habitat: Forest
    Spring Departure: early Apr
    Fall Arrival: mid Oct
    Comments: Breeding birds are found primarily in GSMNP and in the Unaka Mountains, but small numbers likely breed over permanent water in Mississippi Alluvial Valley and Southeastern Coastal Plain (Ford 1987). Nest was documented at Radnor Lake on 13-17 May 1976 (Bierly 1978).
    Late Spring
        21 May 1969, Elizabethton (MIG 40:70)
        9 May 1998, Shelby Co. (MIG 69:162)
    Early Fall
        29 Aug 1986, Knoxville (MIG 58:29)
        12 Aug 1982, Nashville (MIG 54:22)
    High Counts – Spring
        7 on 24 Apr 2010, Unaka Mtn., Unicoi Co. (MIG 81:122)
    High Counts – Fall
        11 on 7 Nov 1998, Big South Fork NRRA (MIG 70:53)
    High Counts – Winter
        36 on 26 Dec 1936, Memphis CBC (MIG 8:8)
        31 on 30 Dec 1962, GSMNP CBC (MIG 33:69)
        26 on 20 Dec 2003, Reelfoot Lake CBC (MIG 75:61)
    Substantiation: Specimen: LSUMZ, 76301

Troglodytidae: Wrens. Seven species have been documented in Tennessee, with five being regular and common or uncommon in appropriate habitat, one almost extirpated as a permanent resident, and one accidental. The status, distribution, and identification criteria for Pacific Wren are still somewhat unclear, so birders should be aware of the possibility that this newly-split species could occur in Tennessee.

Rock Wren, *Salpinctes obsoletus*
  Status and Abundance: Accidental visitor
  Records
    (1) 1 on 23 Dec 1956, Memphis CBC (MIG 27:69)
    (2) 1 on 5 Nov 1965, Chattanooga Point Park (Bierly 1980)
  Substantiation: Specimen: LSUMZ, 76384

House Wren, *Thryomanes aedon*
  Status and Abundance: Uncommon transient; fairly common summer resident in Cumberland Plateau, Ridge and Valley, Southern Blue Ridge; uncommon summer resident in Central Hardwoods; uncommon in Southeastern Coastal Plain; rare summer resident in Mississippi Alluvial Valley; rare winter resident
  Habitat: Dense shrubby fields, hedgerows, suburban yards
  Spring Arrival: mid Apr
  Fall Departure: mid Dec
  Comments: Breeding range has expanded across most of east and middle Tennessee in recent decades. Regularly detected through CBC period and then few reports until spring.
  Early Spring
    5 Mar 1999, Nashville (MIG 70:99)
  High Counts – Spring
    65 on 14 May 2005, Shelby Co. NAMC (MIG 76:131)
    50 on 8 May 1988, Elizabethton SBC (Robinson 1990)
    48 on 29 Apr 2001, Elizabethton SBC (MIG 72:29)
  High Counts – Fall
    31 on 20 Sep 2008, Putnam Co. FBC (MIG 80:17)
    11 on 25 Sep 2010, Elizabethton FBC (MIG 81:145)
    11 on 28 Sep 2008, Knoxville FBC (MIG 80:17)
    8 on 24 Sep 2006, Knoxville FBC (MIG 78:28)
  High Counts – Winter
    9 on 16 Dec 2006, Reelfoot Lake CBC (MIG 78:67)
    6 on 17 Dec 1994, Reelfoot Lake CBC (MAG, pers. comm.)
    5 on 1 Jan 2004, Hiwassee CBC (MIG 75:61)

3 on 17 Dec 1989, Memphis CBC (MIG 61:58)
Substantiation: Specimen: LSUMZ, 76311

Winter Wren, *Troglodytes troglodytes*
Status and Abundance: Fairly common early spring and late fall transient and winter resident; common summer resident in Southern Blue Ridge
Habitat: Forest with underbrush, particularly bottomland forest and along woodland creeks
Spring Departure: mid Apr
Fall Arrival: early Oct
Late Spring
24 May 1999, Putnam Co. (MIG 70:99)
13 May 1961, Kingsport SBC (MIG 32:31)
7 May 1974, Nashville (BNA:33)
Early Fall
10 Sep 2004, Radnor Lake (MIG 76:30)
14 Sep 1972, Nashville (MIG 43:100)
21 Sep 1968, Hamilton Co. (MIG 39:94)
High Counts – Spring
9 on 1 May 1994, Elizabethton SBC (MIG 65:34)
High Counts – Fall
13 on 13 Nov 1999, Big South Fork NRRA (MIG 71:37)
High Counts – Winter
60 on 24 Dec 1971, Reelfoot Lake CBC (MIG 43:12)
43 on 1 Jan 2003, Hickory-Priest CBC (MIG 74:42)
42 on 16 Dec 2006, Reelfoot Lake CBC (MIG 78:67)
Substantiation: Specimen: LSUMZ, 76316

Sedge Wren, *Cistothorus platensis*
Status and Abundance: Uncommon transient; rare summer resident; rare winter visitor
Habitat: Shrubby or grassy fields, wet meadows, marsh grasslands
Spring Arrival: late Apr
Spring Departure: mid May
Fall Arrival: mid Jul
Fall Departure: late Oct
Comments: This species is known to make a partial migration in late summer and then resume breeding; it may breed in Tennessee more regularly than records suggest. First confirmed breeding in Tennessee on 9 Sep 2003 at Ft. Campbell with 2 young in nest (MIG 75:48). Confirmed nesting at Heritage Marsh, White Co. and nine singing

males on 14 Aug 2004, adult with young on 25 Sep 2004 (MIG 76:30). Up to 14 singing, territorial males found and one pair with empty nest at Duck River Unit on 26 Aug 2012 (SGS, CAS, pers. obs.).

Early Spring
   29 Mar 1997, Ensley (JRW, unpubl. data)
   6 Apr 1977, Memphis (MIG 48:75)

Late Spring
   2 Jun 1972, Knox Co. (MIG 43:79)

Early Fall
   3 Jul 1966, Amnicola Marsh (MIG 37:55)
   2 Aug 1998, Orchard Bog (MIG 70:55)

Late Fall
   25 Nov 1942, GSMNP (Stupka 1963)
   9 Nov 1975, Buena Vista Marsh (MIG 47:46)

High Counts – Spring
   5 on 26 Apr 1992, Elizabethton SBC (MIG 63:48)

High Counts – Fall
   25+ on 29 Sep 1993, Big Sandy Unit (MIG 65:22)
   24 on 7 Aug 1936, Clarksville (Coffey et al. 1942)
   17 on 29 Sep 2012, Nashville FBC (MIG 83:141)
   15 on 22 Sep 1990, Iris Hill, Shelby Co. (MIG 62:48)

High Counts – Summer
   1 on 26 Jun 1993, Hwy 79W, Lake Co. (JRW, unpubl. data)

High Counts – Winter
   6 on 1 Jan 2003, Hickory-Priest CBC (MIG 74:42)
   3 on 3 Jan 2004, Fayette Co. CBC (MIG 75:60)
   3 on 8 Dec 2004, Montgomery Co. (MIG 76:80)

Substantiation: Specimen: LSUMZ, 76382

Marsh Wren, *Cistothorus palustris*

Status and Abundance: Uncommon transient; rare winter visitor

Habitat: Shrubby or grassy fields, wet meadows, marsh grasslands; also dense cattails

Spring Arrival: mid Apr

Spring Departure: mid May

Fall Arrival: mid Sep

Fall Departure: early Nov

Comments: Some birds may linger into winter, but few records after completion of the CBC count period.

Early Spring
   29 Mar 1997, Ensley (JRW, unpubl. data)
   12 Apr 1975, Cheatham Lake, Cheatham Co. (MIG 46:66)

Late Spring
    28 May 1985, Britton Ford (MIG 56:74)
    26 May 1940, GSMNP (Coffey et al. 1942)
    26 May 1975, Cheatham Lake (MIG 46:88)
Early Fall
    25 Aug 2001, Kingston Steam Plant (MIG 73:17)
    8 Sep 1976, Austin Springs (MIG 48:107)
Late Fall
    17 Nov 1989, Ensley (JRW, unpubl. data)
    16 Nov 1986, Monroe Co. (MIG 58:31)
    11 Nov 1978, Maury Co. (MIG 50:43)
High Counts – Fall
    30+ on 25 Sep 1999, near Black Bayou WMA (JRW, unpubl. data)
    26 on 1 Oct 1978, Nashville (MIG 50:21)
    15 on 29 Sep 1993, Big Sandy Unit (MIG 65:23)
High Counts – Winter
    7 on 30 Dec 1996, Savannah CBC (MIG 68:22)
    6 on 16 Dec 1995, Reelfoot Lake CBC (MAG, pers. comm.)
    4 on 19 Dec 1998, Reelfoot Lake CBC (MAG, pers. comm.)
Substantiation: Specimen: LSUMZ, 76369

Carolina Wren, *Thryothorus ludovicianus*
Status and Abundance: Common permanent resident
Habitat: Forest, forest edge, shrubland, urban and suburban yards
High Counts – Spring
    288 on 14 May 2005, Putnam Co. NAMC (MIG 76:131)
    282 on 12 May 2007, Putnam Co. NAMC (MIG 78:131)
    244 on 30 Apr 1972, Knoxville SBC (MIG 43:46)
    228 on 13 May 2006, Putnam Co. NAMC (MIG 77:135)
High Counts – Fall
    287 on 8 Oct 2005, Nashville FBC (MIG 77:11)
    245 on 18 Oct 2010, White Co. FBC (MIG 81:145)
    242 on 19 Sep 2009, Putnam Co. FBC (MIG 81:44)
High Counts – Winter
    467 on 2 Jan 2005, Knoxville CBC (MIG 76:67)
    295 on 31 Dec 2005, Knoxville CBC (MIG 77:45)
    279 on 14 Dec 2002, Nashville CBC (MIG 74:43)
    271 on 2 Jan 2010, Knoxville CBC (MIG 81:95)
    270 on 2 Jan 2011, Knoxville CBC (MIG 82:51)
Substantiation: Specimen: LSUMZ, 76364

Bewick's Wren, *Troglodytes bewickii*

Status and Abundance: Rare local summer (permanent?) resident primarily in Rutherford and Wilson Co.

Habitat: Dry, brushy, often rocky open areas and adjacent rural and suburban habitats, often very "junky" areas with old trailers, cars, and outbuildings

Comments: General population began to decline in the 1940s. The cause of the decline is not well understood and predated the arrival and establishment of nesting House Wrens in the state. Formerly, Bewick's Wrens were more common in west and east Tennessee; however the only known breeding population consists of a few birds in Rutherford and Wilson counties. In April-May 2010, four singing males were located in Rutherford and Wilson Co. (MIG 81:116, SGS, pers. obs.). One nest was located and a second singing male was paired (pair seen together) (MIG 81:116, SGS, pers. obs). Surveys in the 1990s occasionally found individuals on recent hardwood (not pine) clearcuts along the Tennessee River in w. Tennessee (D. Simbeck, pers. comm.), so a small population could conceivably linger there as well, although there are no recent reports.

High Counts – Spring
- 28 on 14 May 1955, Nashville SBC (MIG 26:30)
- 26 on 5 May 1968, Savannah SBC (MIG 39:35)
- 13 on 3 May 1953, Kingsport SBC (MIG 24:37)
- 5 (4 m, 1 f) on 29 Apr 2010, Wilson and Rutherford Co. (SGS, pers. obs.)

High Counts – Fall
- 3 on 25 Sep 1993, Wilson Co. FBC (MIG 65:23)
- 3 on 30 Sep 1990, Cross Creeks NWR (JRW, unpubl. data)

Substantiation: Specimen: LSUMZ, 76337

Polioptilidae: Gnatcatchers and Gnatwrens.
One species occurs across Tennessee as a common transient and summer resident.

Blue-gray Gnatcatcher, *Polioptila caerulea*
Status and Abundance: Common transient and summer visitor; rare winter visitor
Habitat: Forest and forest edge
Spring Arrival: late Mar
Fall Departure: early Oct
Comments: Several November and winter records.
Early Spring
  6 Mar 1986, Pickett Co. (MIG 57:79)
  6 Mar 2010, Knox Co. (MIG 81:120)
  12 Mar 2003, Knoxville (MIG 74:93)
  17 Mar 2003, Shelby Forest SP (MIG 74:88)
Late Fall
  29 Nov 1989, Knoxville (MIG 61:19)
  28 Nov 2004, Knox Co. (MIG 76:35)
  28 Nov 2009, Pace Point (MIG 81:50)
  27 Nov 2004, Shelby Farms (MIG 76:28)
High Counts – Spring
  297 on 9 May 2009, Putnam Co. NAMC (MIG 80:109)
  226 on 10 May 2008, Putnam Co. NAMC (MIG 79:78)
  192 on 12 May 2007, Putnam Co. NAMC (MIG 78:131)
  191 on 13 May 2000, Putnam Co. NAMC (MIG 71:53)
  185 on 26 Apr 1959, Knoxville SBC (MIG 30:23)
High Counts – Fall
  14 on 19 Sep 2009, Putnam Co. FBC (MIG 81:45)
  11 on 17 Sep 2005, Blount Co. FBC (MIG 77:17)
Winter Records
  1 on 14 Dec 1998, Brainerd Levee (MIG 70:73)
  1 on 18 Dec 2004, Shelby Bottoms Park (MIG 76:80)
  1 on 10 Dec 2006 and 17 Jan 2007, Knox Co. (MIG 78:82)
Substantiation: Specimen: LSUMZ, 9619

Regulidae: Kinglets. Two species occur statewide in Tennessee as transients and winter residents, and one is an uncommon breeding bird in the higher elevations of the eastern mountains.

Golden-crowned Kinglet, *Regulus satrapa*

Status and Abundance: Fairly common late fall and early spring transient; common winter resident; fairly common summer resident in Southern Blue Ridge

Habitat: Forest and forest edge; breeds in high elevation spruce-fir forest

Spring Departure: mid Apr

Fall Arrival: early Oct

Comments: Occasional summer records in mid-elevation ravines with hemlocks.

Late Spring
- 6 May 1984, Montgomery Co. SBC (MIG 55:60)
- 5 May 1951, Kingsport SBC (MIG 22:25)
- 5 May 1984, Radnor Lake (BNA:33)

Early Fall
- 13 Sep 1952, Nashville (BNA:33)
- 22 Sep 1966, Chattanooga (MIG 37:83)
- 22 Sep 1967, Hardin Co. (MIG 38:94)

High Counts – Spring
- 26 on 26 Apr 1997, Elizabethton SBC (MIG 68:58)

High Counts – Fall
- 115 on 7 Nov 1998, Big South Fork NRRA (MIG 70:53)
- 87 on 13 Nov 1999, Big South Fork NRRA (MIG 71:37)
- 53 on 22 Oct 1995, Scott Co. (MIG 67:23)

High Counts – Summer
- 42 on 7 Jul 2006, Roan Mtn. (MIG 77:148)
- 26 on 5 Jun 1999, Roan Mtn. (MIG 70:134)
- 16 on 24 Jun 1996, Roan Mtn. (MIG 67:80)

High Counts – Winter
- 375 on 1 Jan 1992, Hiwassee CBC (MIG 63:15)
- 353 on 19 Dec 1998, Reelfoot Lake CBC (MIG 70:16)
- 221 on 29 Dec 1991, GSMNP CBC (MIG 63:15)
- 118 on 11 Jan 2000, Big South Fork NRRA, Twin Arches area (Stedman and Stedman 2002)

Substantiation: Specimen: LSUMZ, 76480

Ruby-crowned Kinglet, *Regulus calendula*

Status and Abundance: Fairly common transient; common winter resident;

accidental summer visitor in Southern Blue Ridge

Habitat: Forest and forest edge

Spring Departure: mid May

Fall Arrival: mid Sep

Comments: There is no evidence to suggest that the three summer records were breeding individuals. Given that no established breeding populations are near the state, those individuals are more likely to have been post-breeding wanderers or non-breeding individuals.

Late Spring
- 24 May 2000, Nashville (MIG 71:89)
- 17 May 1938, Nashville (BNA:33)

Early Fall
- 1 Sep 1976, Iron Gap, Unicoi Co. (Robinson 1990)
- 5 Sep 1997, Knoxville (MIG 69:47)

High Counts – Spring
- 30 on 29 Apr 1990, Knoxville BC (MIG 61:52)
- 28 on 27 Apr 1997, Knox Co. SBC (MIG 68:58)
- 27 on 26 Apr 1992, Elizabethton SBC (MIG 63:49)

High Counts – Fall
- 50 on 9 Oct 2010, Nashville FBC (MIG 81:145)
- 24 on 30 Sep 2006, Nashville FBC (MIG 78:28)
- 23 on 8 Oct 2005, Nashville FBC (MIG 77:11)

Summer Records
- 1 on 13 Jun 1993, Holston Mtn. (MIG 64:89)
- 1 on 21 Jul 1972, GSMNP (MIG 43:80)
- 1 on 21 Jun 1988, Roan Mtn. (MIG 59:130)

High Counts – Winter
- 585 on 19 Dec 1998, Reelfoot Lake CBC (MIG 70:16)
- 131 on 1 Jan 2000, Hiwassee CBC (MIG 71:19)
- 124 on 21 Dec 1975, Memphis CBC (MIG 47:37)
- 121 on 28 Dec 2010, Crossville CBC (MIG 82:50)
- 115 on 28 Dec 1991, Savannah CBC (MIG 63:15)

Substantiation: Specimen: LSUMZ, 76484

Turdidae: Thrushes. Nine species have been documented in Tennessee. Seven are found statewide and are relatively common or uncommon in appropriate forested habitat as breeding birds or transients, while two species are vagrants. Mountain Bluebird is also a possible vagrant to Tennessee.

Eastern Bluebird, *Sialia sialis*
> Status and Abundance: Common permanent resident
> Habitat: Open and semi-open areas, including fields, pastures, and roadsides; occasionally found in mature forest
> High Counts – Spring
>> 360 on 9 May 1992, Chattanooga SBC (MIG 63:49)
>> 342 on 10 May 2008, Putnam Co. NAMC (MIG 79:78)
>> 307 on 12 May 2001, Putnam Co. NAMC (MIG 72:19)
>
> High Counts – Fall
>> 514 on 20 Sep 2008, Putnam Co. FBC (MIG 80:18)
>> 360 on 16 Sep 2006, Putnam Co. FBC (MIG 78:21)
>> 355 on 4 Oct 2009, White Co. FBC (MIG 81:45)
>> 291 on 1 Oct 2005, White Co. FBC (MIG 77:11)
>
> High Counts – Winter
>> 573 on 19 Sep 2009, Putnam Co. FBC (MIG 81:45)
>> 535 on 21 Dec 2006, White Co. CBC (MIG 78:67)
>> 494 on 14 Dec 2002, Cookeville CBC (MIG 74:42)
>> 430 on 2 Jan 2010, Buffalo River CBC (MIG 81:94)
>
> Substantiation: Specimen: LSUMZ, 76472

Townsend's Solitaire, *Myadestes townsendi*
> Status and Abundance: Accidental visitor
> Records
>> (1) 1 on 20 Nov 2005, Seven Islands Wildlife Refuge (Mooney and Mooney 2006)
>> (2) 1 on 19-21 Jan 2008, Union Co. (MIG 79:55)
>> (3) 1 on 20-21 Apr 2008, Herb Parson's Lake, Fayette Co. (MIG 79:62)
>> (4) 1 on 10 Apr 2014, Frozen Head SP (MW, pers. comm.)
>
> Substantiation: Photograph: 1 on 20 Apr 2008, Herb Parson's Lake, Fayette Co. NAB 62(3):48

Veery, *Catharus fuscescens*
> Status and Abundance: Uncommon transient; common summer resident in higher elevations of Southern Blue Ridge and upper Cumberland Plateau

Habitat: Forest
Spring Arrival: late Apr
Spring Departure: mid May
Fall Arrival: early Sep
Fall Departure: early Oct
Comments: Locally common breeding at higher elevations of Southern Blue Ridge. Also found in small numbers breeding in upper Cumberland Plateau, North Cumberland WMA, and at Frozen Head SP.

Early Spring
    11 Apr 1972, Nashville (MIG 43:51)

Late Spring
    7 Jun 1998, Macon Co. (MIG 69:188)
    30 May 1986, Knoxville (MIG 57:85)
    28 May 1958, Nashville (BNA:34)

Early Fall
    18 Aug 1971, Davidson Co. (MIG 42:93)
    24 Aug 1969, Two Jays (MIG 40:90)

Late Fall
    4 Nov 2006, Britton Ford (MIG 78:34)
    11 Oct 1952, Radnor Lake (BNA:34)
    11 Oct 1954, Nashville (BNA:34)
    10 Oct 1984, Chattanooga (MIG 56:25)

High Counts – Spring
    27 on 5 May 1991, Elizabethton SBC (MIG 62:37)

High Counts – Fall
    102, most via nocturnal flight call, on 26 Sep 2010, Knoxville FBC (MIG 81:146)
    6 on 27 Sep 2009, Knoxville FBC (MIG 81:45)

High Counts – Summer
    40 on 28 Jun 1987, Roan Mtn. (Robinson 1990)
    33 on 21 Jun 1996, Unaka Mtn. (MIG 67:80)
    25 on 12 Jun 2000, Unaka Mtn. (MIG 71:123)

Substantiation: Specimen: LSUMZ, 8875

Gray-cheeked Thrush, *Catharus minimus*
    Status and Abundance: Uncommon transient
    Habitat: Forest
    Spring Arrival: late Apr
    Spring Departure: late May
    Fall Arrival: early Sep
    Fall Departure: mid Oct

Early Spring
    3 Apr 1995, Shelby Co. (JRW, unpubl. data)
    6 Apr 1939, Clarksville (MIG 10:32)
    12 Apr 1987, Greeneville SBC (MIG 58:83)
Late Spring
    16 Jun 1949, Nashville (BNA:34)
    4 Jun 1994, Morgan Co. (MIG 65:64)
    26 May 1963, Memphis (MIG 34:49)
    26 May 1963, Nashville (MIG 34:50)
Early Fall
    27 Aug 1985, Tennessee River Gorge (MIG 57:34)
    4 Sep 1980, Nashville (BNA:34)
Late Fall
    13 Nov 1994, Memphis (MIG 66:21)
    8 Nov 1984, Nashville (MIG 56:21)
    30 Oct 1972, Nashville (Goodpasture 1974)
High Counts – Spring
    23 on 29 Apr 1984, Memphis SBC (MIG 55:60)
High Counts – Fall
    75 on 16 Sep 2006, Greene Co. FBC (MIG 78:21)
    58 killed on 24 Sep 1955, Smyrna airport, Rutherford Co. (Laskey 1956)
    54 on 26 Sep 2010, Knoxville FBC (MIG 81:146)
Substantiation: Specimen: LSUMZ, 76454

Swainson's Thrush, *Catharus ustulatus*

Status and Abundance: Common transient; accidental summer visitor (resident?) in Southern Blue Ridge
Habitat: Forest and forest edge
Spring Arrival: mid Apr
Spring Departure: late May
Fall Arrival: early Sep
Fall Departure: late Oct
Comments: Recent summer expansion south to mountains in western North Carolina and a few sites on the Tennessee border.
Early Spring
    30 Mar 2007, Haywood Co. (MIG 78:101)
    2 Apr 1972, Roan Mtn. (MIG 43:55)
    3 Apr 2007, Elizabethton (MIG 78:107)
    6 Apr 1986, Nashville (MIG 57:79-80)
    6 Apr 2010, Obion Co. (MIG 81:115)

Late Spring
    3 Jun 1940, Nashville (BNA:34)
    3 Jun 1995, Shelby Forest SP (JRW, unpubl. data)
    3 Jun 2003, Ft. Campbell (MIG 74:90)
    1 Jun 1992, Radnor Lake (MIG 63:97)
    1 Jun 1997, Shelby Co. (MIG 68:135)
    30 May 1971, Savannah (MIG 42:68)
Early Fall
    19 Aug 2006, Shelby Forest SP (MIG 78:34)
    25 Aug 2006, Roan Mtn. (MIG 78:42)
    27 Aug 1955, Ashland City Marsh (BNA:34)
    28 Aug 2011, Knoxville (MIG 82:157)
Late Fall
    26 Nov 1966, Knox Co. (Alsop 1967)
    23 Nov 1975, Old Hickory Lake (MIG 47:46)
High Counts – Spring
    578 on 10 May 2008, Shelby Co. NAMC (MIG 79:78)
    150 on 7 May 1978, Knoxville SBC (MIG 49:57)
    125 on 7 May 2011, Nashville SBC (MIG 82:70)
High Counts – Fall
    635 (morning flight) on 13 Sep 2011, Whigg Meadow, Monroe Co. (MIG 82:160)
    601 on 16 Sep 2006, Greene Co. FBC (MIG 78:21)
    500 nocturnal flight calls on 26 Sep 2010, Knoxville (MIG 81:160)
    253 on 26 Sep 2010, Knoxville FBC (MIG 81:146)
    199 on 27 Sep 1980, Elizabethton FBC (*fide* RLK)
Summer Records
    1 on 29 Jun 2008, Mt. LeConte (Knight 2010)
    1 on 14 Jul 2009, Mt. LeConte (MIG 80:129)
Winter Records
    1 on 29 Dec 1965, Reelfoot Lake CBC (MIG 36:84)
    1 on 18 Dec 1994, Elizabethton CBC (MIG 66:15)
Substantiation: Specimen: LSUMZ, 76451

Hermit Thrush, *Catharus guttatus*
    Status and Abundance: Uncommon early spring and late fall transient; common winter resident; rare local summer resident in Southern Blue Ridge
    Habitat: Forest and forest edge; dense hedges and shrubs
    Spring Departure: late Apr
    Fall Arrival: early Oct
    Comments: Breeding inferred from capture of dependent immatures on

Roan Mtn. (Knight 2010). Summer records also from Unaka Mtn., GSMNP, and Roger's Ridge in Johnson Co.

Late Spring
 14 May 1981, Knoxville (MIG 52:74)
 8 May 2004, Davidson Co. (MIG 75:114)

Early Fall
 20 Sep 1970, Memphis (MIG 41:83)
 23 Sep 2005, Bedford Co. (MIG 76:26)
 27 Sep 1931, Radnor Lake (BNA:34)
 27 Sep 1980, Roan Creek (MIG 52:27)

High Counts – Fall
 130 on 1 Nov 2005, Holston Valley (MIG 77:33)

High Counts – Summer
 11+ thru Jun 2000, Mt. LeConte (MIG 71:123)
 5 on 12 Jun 2002, Roan Mtn. (MIG 73:115)

High Counts – Winter
 105 on 22 Dec 2008, White Co. CBC (MIG 80:53)
 69 on 30 Dec 1995, Nickajack CBC (MIG 67:10)
 66 on 24 Dec 1939, Memphis CBC (MIG 11:22)
 52 on 30 Dec 2003, DeKalb Co. CBC (MIG 75:60)

Substantiation: Specimen: LSUMZ, 76440

Wood Thrush, *Hylocichla mustelina*

Status and Abundance: Fairly common transient and summer resident; accidental winter visitor

Habitat: Forest (usually relatively mature)

Spring Arrival: mid Apr

Fall Departure: mid Oct

Early Spring
 1 Apr 1969, Savannah (MIG 40:45)
 1 Apr 1955, Gatlinburg (Stupka 1963)
 1 Apr 2012, Nashville (CAS, pers. obs.)
 2 Apr 2004, Shelby Forest SP (MIG 75:111)
 3 Apr 1929, near Nashville (BNA:34)

Late Fall
 27 Nov 1994, Johnson City (MIG 66:25)
 13 Nov 1990, Johnson City (MIG 62:52)
 10 Nov 1966, Memphis (MIG 37:80)
 6 Nov 1962, Nashville (MIG 34:9)
 5 Nov 1976, Knoxville (MIG 48:50)

High Counts – Spring
 177 on 30 Apr 1972, Knoxville SBC (MIG 43:46)

140 on 27 Apr 1997, Knox Co. SBC (MIG 68:59)
125 on 12 May 2007, Putnam Co. NAMC (MIG 78:131)
High Counts – Fall
28 on 26 Sep 2010, Knoxville FBC (MIG 81:146)
15 on 30 Sep 2006, Elizabethton FBC (MIG 78:28)
High Counts – Summer
35 on 28 May 1998, Big South Fork NRRA (MIG 69:168)
Winter Records
1 on 17 Dec 1978-1 Jan 1979, Memphis (MIG 50:41)
1 on late Nov-17 Dec 2009, City Lake, Putnam Co. (MIG 81:101)
1 on 16 Feb-31 Mar 2013, Johnson City (NAB 67(2):283, MIG, in press)
Substantiation: Specimen: LSUMZ, 9688

American Robin, *Turdus migratorius*
Status and Abundance: Common permanent resident
Habitat: Wide variety of urban, suburban, rural, open and woodland habitats
High Counts – Spring
1,033 on 26 Apr 1992, Elizabethton SBC (MIG 63:49)
940 on 1 May 1994, Elizabethton SBC (MIG 65:34)
804 on 9 May 2009, Putnam Co. NAMC (MIG 80:109)
722 on 24 Apr 2010, Elizabethton SBC (MIG 82:8)
662 on 9 May 1992, Chattanooga SBC (MIG 63:49)
High Counts – Fall
1,096 on 29 Sep 2012, Elizabethton FBC (MIG 83:142)
611 on 27 Sep 2003, Nashville FBC (MIG 75:17)
536 on 9 Oct 2010, Nashville FBC (MIG 81:146)
523 on 24 Sep 2005, Elizabethton FBC (MIG 77:11)
High Counts – Winter
1,000,000 on 5 Jan 2009, Hohenwald, Lewis Co. (MIG 80:68)
800,000 on 31 Dec 1960, Nashville CBC (MIG 31:76)
500,000 on 1 Jan 2009, Hohenwald, Lewis Co. (MIG 80:68)
500,000 on 29 Dec 1962, Nashville CBC (MIG 33:69)
Substantiation: Specimen: LSUMZ, 9247

Varied Thrush, *Ixoreus naevius*
Status and Abundance: Accidental winter and early spring visitor
Records
(1) 1 at same location on 13 Dec 1990-12 Mar 1991 and 11-12 Feb 1992, Walden, Hamilton Co. (Edwards 1991, Knight 1993, MIG 63:62)
(2) 1 m on 13-17 Apr 1996, Oak Ridge (Cushman and Cushman 1997)
(3) 1 on 2 Apr 2006, Martin (MIG 77:99, MIG 83:60)

Turdidae: Thrushes

Substantiation: Unpublished photograph

Mimidae: Mockingbirds and Thrashers.
Four species have occurred in Tennessee, with three regular and statewide in distribution and one vagrant.

Gray Catbird, *Dumetella carolinensis*
Status and Abundance: Fairly common transient; uncommon summer resident; rare winter visitor

Habitat: Shrubby second growth, forest undergrowth, forest edge

Spring Arrival: mid Apr

Fall Departure: late Oct

Comments: A few individuals each year linger into mid-winter.

Early Spring
- 9 Mar 1972, Johnson City (MIG 43:27)
- 10 Mar 2000, Pennington Bend (MIG 71:90)
- 10 Mar 2004, Shelby Farms (MIG 75:112)
- 20 Mar 1990, Ed Jones Lake, Obion Co. (MAG, pers. comm.)
- 20 Mar 2004, Nashville (MIG 75:114)

Late Fall
- 29 Nov 1931, Memphis (MIG 3:9)
- 29 Nov 2003, Sullivan Co. (MIG 75:35)
- 26 Nov 1961, Chattanooga (MIG 33:15)
- 23 Nov 1985, Stewart Co. (MIG 57:28)

High Counts – Spring
- 118 on 7 May 1950, Elizabethton SBC (MIG 21:27)
- 94 on 1 May 1994, Elizabethton SBC (MIG 65:34)
- 47 on 30 Apr 2011, Elizabethton SBC (MIG 82:70)
- 37 on 11 May 2002, Putnam Co. NAMC (MIG 73:98)
- 36 on 13 May 2006, Putnam Co. NAMC (MIG 77:135)

High Counts – Fall
- 124 on 26 Sep 2010, Knoxville FBC (MIG 81:146)
- 123 on 18 Sep 2010, Shelby Co. FBC (MIG 81:146)
- 96 on 28 Sep 2008, Knoxville FBC (MIG 80:18)
- 77 on 27 Sep 2009, Knoxville FBC (MIG 81:45)
- 75 on 8 Oct 2005, Nashville FBC (MIG 77:11)

High Counts – Winter
- 3 on 17 Dec 2005, Elizabethton CBC (MIG 77:44)
- 2 on 14 Dec 2003, Elizabethton CBC (MIG 75:60)

Substantiation: Specimen: LSUMZ, 76393

Brown Thrasher, *Toxostoma rufum*
Status and Abundance: Fairly common permanent resident

Habitat: Hedges, shrubby thickets

Comments: Birds withdraw from breeding grounds and may participate in a short distance migration during winter. Becomes more common in early March.

High Counts – Spring
- 157 on 26 Apr 1964, Knoxville SBC (MIG 35:47)
- 92 on 9 May 2009, Putnam Co. NAMC (MIG 80:109)
- 83 on 10 May 1997, Hamilton Co. NAMC (MIG 68:102)
- 82 on 12 May 2007, Putnam Co. NAMC (MIG 78:133)
- 79 on 11 May 2002, Putnam Co. NAMC (MIG 73:98)

High Counts – Fall
- 69 on 25 Sep 2005, Knoxville FBC (MIG 77:11)
- 61 on 29 Sep 2012, Nashville FBC (MIG 83:142)
- 59 on 26 Sep 2010, Knoxville FBC (MIG 81:146)

High Counts – Winter
- 46 on 30 Dec 1995, Nickajack CBC (MIG 67:10)
- 41 on 20 Dec 1997, Chattanooga CBC (MIG 69:25)
- 40 on 20 Dec 1998, Memphis CBC (MIG 70:16)
- 38 on 1 Jan 1990, Hiwassee CBC (MIG 61:5)
- 35 on 16 Dec 2006, Chattanooga CBC (MIG 78:66)

Substantiation: Specimen: LSUMZ, 76401

Sage Thrasher, *Oreoscoptes montanus*

Status and Abundance: Accidental visitor

Records
- (1) 1 on 8 Nov 2003-17 Feb 2004, Knox Co. (MIG 75:32, 79, Hoyle 2011)

Substantiation: Photograph: 1 on 10 Nov 2003, Knoxville (NAB 58(1):173)

Northern Mockingbird, *Mimus polyglottos*

Status and Abundance: Common permanent resident

Habitat: Open and semi-open areas, hedgerows and shrubby thickets in a variety of urban, suburban, and rural habitats

High Counts – Spring
- 500 on 26 Apr 1959, Knoxville SBC (MIG 30:23)
- 245 on 11 May 2002, Montgomery Co. NAMC (MIG 73:98)
- 213 on 9 May 2009, Putnam Co. NAMC (MIG 80:109)

High Counts – Fall
- 251 on 4 Oct 2008, White Co. FBC (MIG 80:18)
- 179 on 30 Sep 2012, Knoxville FBC (MIG 83:142)
- 157 on 29 Sep 2002, Knoxville FBC (MIG 73:52)
- 156 on 26 Sep 2010, Knoxville FBC (MIG 81:146)

High Counts – Winter
    388 on 2 Jan 2005, Knoxville CBC (MIG 76:67)
Substantiation: Specimen: LSUMZ, 9095

Sturnidae: Starlings. This family is represented by one non-native, widespread, and abundant species.

European Starling, *Sturnus vulgaris*
> Status and Abundance: Common permanent resident; introduced
> Habitat: Urban and suburban areas; fields and pastures
> High Counts – Spring
>> 2,022 on 9 May 2009, Putnam Co. NAMC (MIG 80:109)
>> 1,189 on 14 May 2005, Putnam Co. NAMC (MIG 76:131)
>
> High Counts – Fall
>> 6,268 on 19 Sep 2009, Putnam Co. FBC (MIG 81:45)
>> 4,887 on 25 Sep 2010, DeKalb Co. FBC (MIG 81:146)
>> 3,024 on 20 Sep 2003, Putnam Co. FBC (MIG 75:11)
>> 2,660 on 29 Sep 2012, Elizabethton FBC (MIG 83:142)
>> 2,529 on 17 Sep 2005, Putnam Co. FBC (MIG 77:17)
>
> High Counts – Winter
>> 2,004,966 on 19 Dec 1993, Knoxville CBC (MIG 65:18)
>> 2,000,000 on 29 Dec 1962, Nashville CBC (MIG 33:69)
>> 1,000,000 on 30 Dec 1961, Reelfoot Lake CBC (MAG, pers. comm.)
>> 500,000 on 30 Dec 2000, Jackson CBC (MIG 72:69)
>> 500,000 on 6 Jan 1990, Murfreesboro CBC (MIG 61:5)
>
> Substantiation: Specimen: LSUMZ, 6833

Motacillidae: Wagtails and Pipits. Two species represent this family in Tennessee with one being a regular winter resident and the other an accidental winter visitor.

American Pipit, *Anthus rubescens*
> Subspecies: *rubescens*
> Status and Abundance: Uncommon transient and winter resident; accidental summer visitor
> Habitat: Pastures and agricultural fields with little or no vegetation; sometimes mudflats and shorelines
> Spring Departure: mid Apr
> Fall Arrival: early Oct
> Late Spring
>> 20 May 1984, Roan Mtn. (MIG 55:75)
>> 11 May 1989, Ensley (MIG 60:83)
>> 11 May 2002, Lake Co. NAMC (MIG 73:98)
>> 10 May 1958, Reelfoot Lake SBC (MIG 29:32)
>> 10 May 2003, Shelby Co. NAMC (MIG 74:117)
>
> Early Fall
>> 23 Aug 1984, Hiwassee River Area (MIG 56:26)
>> 5 Sep 1998, Black Bayou WMA (MAG, pers. comm.)
>> 11 Sep 1937, Warner Parks (BNA:34)
>> 18 Sep 2004, Kingston Steam Plant (MIG 76:35)
>> 19 Sep 1993, Ensley (JRW, unpubl. data)
>
> High Counts – Spring
>> 600 on 22 Mar 1998, Tri-Cities Airport (MIG 69:168)
>> 150 on 5 May 1997, Phillippy (JRW, unpubl. data)
>> 150+ on 24 Mar 1996, Airpark Inn, Reelfoot Lake, Lake Co. (MIG 67:61)
>> 100+ on 24 Mar 1999, U.T. Plants Science Farm, Knox Co. (MIG 70:102)
>> 95 on 26 Apr 1992, Elizabethton SBC (MIG 63:49)
>
> High Counts – Fall
>> 350+ on 19 Nov 2010, Limestone, Washington Co. (MIG 81:160)
>> 200+ on 15 Nov 2003, Greene Co. (MIG 75:32)
>> 200+ on 22 Nov 2003, Scott Co. (MIG 75:32)
>> 200+ on 5 Nov 2003, Washington Co. (MIG 75:32)
>> 120+ on 25 Nov 2000, Holston Valley (MIG 72:47)
>
> Summer Records
>> 1 on 12 Jun 1987, Round Bald (MIG 61:79)
>
> High Counts – Winter
>> 746 on 1 Jan 1986, Hiwassee CBC (MIG 57:11)
>> 677 on 28 Dec 2000, Savannah CBC (MIG 72:69)

610 on 2 Jan 1998, Savannah CBC (MIG 69:24)
492 on 21 Dec 1985, Knoxville CBC (MIG 57:11)
400+ on 2 Jan 1998, Hardin Co. (MIG 69:107)
Substantiation: Specimen: LSUMZ, 76488

Sprague's Pipit, *Anthus spragueii*

Status and Abundance: Accidental visitor; formerly rare winter visitor mainly in Mississippi Alluvial Valley

Habitat: Large, open fields with relatively short grass (particularly *Aristida* spp.)

Comments: Possibly undetected due in part to its secretive nature and little focused observer effort. Found nearly annually in Shelby Co. from 1953-1959, range of dates 12 Oct-21 Apr. Only subsequent records: 31 Jan 1976, near Golddust, Lauderdale Co. (MIG 47:45); 27 Oct 1991, grassy balds on Roan Mtn. (Knight 1992); 9 Jan 2004, Hardin Co. (MIG 75:75); 2 on 29 Mar 2005, Gibson Co. (MAG, pers. comm.); 1 on 28 Nov 2007, Gibson Co. (MAG, pers. comm).

High Counts – Winter
7 on 23 Dec 1956, Memphis CBC (MIG 27:73)
Substantiation: Specimen: LSUMZ, 76489

Bombycillidae: Waxwings. One species represents this family in Tennessee and it can be found across the state.

Cedar Waxwing, *Bombycilla cedrorum*
Status and Abundance: Fairly common (sometimes common) transient and winter resident; uncommon summer resident in Cumberland Plateau, Ridge and Valley, Southern Blue Ridge; rare summer resident in Central Hardwoods, Southeastern Coastal Plain, Mississippi Alluvial Valley

Habitat: Open forest and forest edge; yards and parks with fruiting trees

High Counts – Spring
- 1,000+ on 22 Apr 2002, Knoxville (MIG 73:62)
- 991 on 9 May 2009, Hamilton Co. NAMC (MIG 80:109)
- 792 on 1 May 1994, Knoxville SBC (MIG 65:34)
- 619 on 13 May 2006, Davidson Co. NAMC (MIG 77:135)
- 600+ on 11 Apr 2009, Bells Bend (MIG 80:90)

High Counts – Fall
- 330 on 9 Nov 2004, Carver's Gap (MIG 76:39)
- 262 on 30 Sep 2006, Elizabethton FBC (MIG 78:28)
- 243 on 25 Sep 2010, Elizabethton FBC (MIG 81:146)

High Counts – Summer
- 110 on 1 Jun 2005, Shelby Bottoms Park (MIG 76:145)
- 55 on 1 Jun 2001, Shelby Bottoms Park (MIG 72:124)

High Counts – Winter
- 2,830 on 31 Dec 2000, Bristol CBC (MIG 72:74)
- 2,500 on 28 Feb 1986, Memphis (MIG 57:51)
- 2,000 on 15 Mar 1980, Davidson Co. (MIG 51:39-40)
- 1,715 on 3 Jan 2009, Knoxville CBC (MIG 80:53)
- 1,608 on 3 Jan 2004, Knoxville CBC (MIG 75:61)

Substantiation: Specimen: LSUMZ, 76494

Calcariidae: Longspurs and Snow Buntings.

Five species have been documented in Tennessee, with Lapland Longspur being the only regularly occurring species, although Smith's Longspur formerly occurred regularly. All species occur in late fall through early spring and prefer open fields, farmland, or have preferences for certain types of grasslands.

Lapland Longspur, *Calcarius lapponicus*

Status and Abundance: Rare spring and late fall transient and winter resident, mainly Mississippi Alluvial Valley, Southeastern Coastal Plain; irregular in Central Hardwoods, Cumberland Plateau, Ridge and Valley, and Southern Blue Ridge

Habitat: Open fields, particularly fallow or stubbly agricultural fields and pastures

Spring Departure: early Mar

Fall Arrival: mid Nov

Late Spring
- 13 May 2000, Greene Co. NAMC (MIG 71:58)
- 9 Apr 2006, Lincoln Co. (MIG 77:126)

Early Fall
- 16 Oct 1993, Ensley (JRW, unpubl. data)
- 23 Oct 1982, Austin Springs (MIG 54:26)
- 25 Oct 1987, Cross Creeks NWR (MIG 59:37)
- 30 Oct 2010, Lake Co. (MIG 81:155)

High Counts – Fall
- 400+ on 27 Nov 1998, Bessie Bend, Lake Co. (MIG 70:48)
- 300+ on 17 Nov 2000, Lake Co. (MIG 73:12)

High Counts – Winter
- 8,550 on 20 Dec 2008, Reelfoot Lake CBC (MIG 80:55)
- 6,845 on 20 Dec 2014, Reelfoot Lake CBC (*fide* MAG)
- 6,000 on 27 Jan 2014, Van Works Road, Lake Co. (MAG, pers. comm.)
- 5,700 on 28 Dec 2002, Dyer and Lake Co. (MIG 74:54)

Substantiation: Specimen: LSUMZ, 8988

Chestnut-collared Longspur, *Calcarius ornatus*

Status and Abundance: Accidental visitor

Records
- (1) 3 on 19 Dec 2008, Lake Co. (NAB 63:2)
- (2) 1 f on 14 Nov 2012, Ensley (MIG 83:148)
- (3) 1 m on 27 Jan 2014, Van Works Road, Lake Co. (MAG, pers. comm.)

Substantiation: Photograph: Wilson, J.R. 2012. "Chestnut-collared Longspur". <http://www.pbase.com/ol_coot/image/147329278> Accessed 25 Sep 2014.

Smith's Longspur, *Calcarius pictus*
Status and Abundance: Accidental winter resident
Habitat: Grassy fields dominated by Aristida grass
Spring Departure: mid Mar
Fall Arrival: early Nov
Comments: Nearly all records from Shelby Co. from 1953-1958. Few records because the specific habitat is very rare. Recent records concentrated at Ft. Campbell and in the Cates Landing area, although the Cates Landing habitat appears to have since been destroyed by development.
Late Spring
  16 Apr 1989, Ensley (MIG 60:83)
  2 Apr 2001, Cates Landing (MIG 72:94)
Early Fall
  25 Oct 1990, Ensley (JRW, unpubl. data)
High Counts – Spring
  1 on 28 Mar 1975, Gallatin, Sumner Co. (BNA:41)
High Counts – Fall
  8 on 25 Nov 1989, Shelby Farms (MIG 61:14)
High Counts – Winter
  37 on 27 Dec 1953, Memphis CBC (MIG 24:79)
  30 on 3 Dec 1989, Shelby Co. (MIG 61:58)
  8 on 9 Dec 2000, Cates Landing (JRW, unpubl. data)
Substantiation: Specimen: LSUMZ, 77510

McCown's Longspur, *Calcarius mccownii*
Status and Abundance: Accidental visitor
Records
  (1) 1 on 28 Nov 1998, Pace Point (Calhoon 1999)
  (2) 1 on 23 Mar 2013, Camp Jordan, Hamilton Co. (NAB 67(3):455)
Substantiation: Photograph: 1 on 23 Mar 2013, Camp Jordan, Hamilton Co. (NAB 67(3):544)

Snow Bunting, *Plectrophenax nivalis*
Status and Abundance: Very rare visitor from late fall through winter into early spring
Habitat: Open fields, particularly fallow or stubbly agricultural fields and pastures; in mountains, occurs on high grassy balds; also occasionally

Calcariidae: Longspurs and Snow Buntings

grassy or rocky edges of lakes

Spring Departure: mid Feb

Fall Arrival: mid Nov

Comments: Most records are from Roan Mtn. and Big Bald Mtn. Very few records in recent years.

Late Spring
- 14 Mar 1965, Hump Mtn., Carter Co. (Behrend 1965)
- 2 Mar 1979, Roan Mtn. (MIG 50:47)

Early Fall
- 24 Oct 1954, Big Bald Mtn. (Behrend 1955)
- 1 Nov 2000, Windrock Mtn., Anderson Co. (MIG 72:45)
- 1 Nov 2005, Big Bald Mtn. (MIG 76:34)
- 2 Nov 1960, Memphis (Irwin 1961)

High Counts – Winter
- 15 on 25 Dec 1960, Roan Mtn. (MIG 31:78)
- 15 on 28 Dec 1969, Cherokee Lake (Etnier 1971)

Substantiation: Unpublished photographs

Parulidae: Wood-Warblers. Forty-one species of warbler occur in Tennessee, of which 25 species are uncommon to common breeding birds across the state, while another 16 are transients or vagrants. Warblers occur in nearly all types of field, woody wetland, and upland forest habitats. On a good migration day during spring, it is possible to see over 30 species of warbler in one day in Tennessee.

Ovenbird, *Seiurus aurocapilla*
- Status and Abundance: Common to fairly common transient; common summer resident in Cumberland Plateau, Ridge and Valley, Southern Blue Ridge; uncommon summer resident in Central Hardwoods, Southeastern Coastal Plain; rare summer resident in Mississippi Alluvial Valley; rare winter visitor
- Habitat: Forest and forest edge in migration; breeds in mature hardwood forest
- Spring Arrival: mid Apr
- Fall Departure: mid Oct
- Comments: All fall high counts from ceilometer or transmission tower kills.
- Early Spring
    - 6 Mar 2000, Shelby Bottoms Park (MIG 71:90)
    - 30 Mar 2012, Sullivan Co. (MIG 83:75)
    - 31 Mar 1945, Memphis (MIG 16:11)
    - 1 Apr 1928, Nashville (BNA:38)
- Late Fall
    - 2 Dec 2003, Nashville (MIG 75:76)
    - 30 Nov 1959, GSMNP (Stupka 1963)
    - 30 Nov 1999, Elizabethton (MIG 71:39)
    - 26 Nov 1920, Davidson Co. (BNA:38)
- High Counts – Spring
    - 183 on 7 May 2011, Nashville SBC (MIG 82:70)
    - 175 on 9 May 1998, Putnam Co. NAMC (MIG 69:155)
    - 169 on 3 May 2008, Cumberland Co. SBC (MIG 79:92)
    - 167 on 12 May 2007, Putnam Co. NAMC (MIG 78:133)
    - 157 on 24 Apr 2004, Elizabethton SBC (MIG 75:107)
- High Counts – Fall
    - 625 killed at transmission tower on 28 Sep 1970, Nashville (MIG 41:86)
    - 387 on 7 Oct 1951, Knoxville (Howell and Tanner 1951)
    - 220 on 14 Oct 1969, Nashville (Laskey 1969)
    - 187 on 24 Sep 1955, Smyrna (Laskey 1956)

Parulidae: Wood-Warblers

High Counts – Summer
    98 on 3 Jun 2007, Frozen Head SP (MIG 78:142)
    71 on 4 Jun 1998, Big South Fork NRRA (MIG 69:189)
    55 on 10 Jun 1996, Holston Mtn., Sullivan Co. (MIG 67:80)
Winter Records
    1 on 15 Dec 1976, Watauga Lake (MIG 48:51)
    1 on 14 Dec 1978-8 Jan 1979, Nashville (BNA:38)
    1 on 21 Dec 1985, Chattanooga (MIG 57:11)
    1 on 20 Dec 2003, Cookeville CBC (MIG 75:60)
    1 on 13 Jan 2009, Johnson City (MIG 80:71)
Substantiation: Specimen: LSUMZ, 76775

Worm-eating Warbler, *Helmitheros vermivorum*

Status and Abundance: Uncommon to fairly common transient; uncommon to locally fairly common summer resident except in Mississippi Alluvial Valley, where rare
Habitat: Hilly hardwood forest, usually near ravines
Spring Arrival: mid Apr
Fall Departure: late Sep
Early Spring
    27 Mar 1954, Shelby Co. (MIG 25:51)
    30 Mar 2012, near S. Holston Lake (MIG 83:75)
    3 Apr 2005, Ensley (MIG 76:96)
    5 Apr 1986, Knoxville (MIG 57:86)
    5 Apr 2012, Beaman Park (MIG 83:67)
Late Fall
    25 Oct 1989, Shelby Farms (MIG 61:14)
    18 Oct 1972, Nashville (MIG 43:100)
    18 Oct 1993, Madison Co. (MIG 65:22)
    6 Oct 1954, Johnson City (MIG 25:68)
High Counts – Spring
    35 on 14 May 2005, Shelby Co. NAMC (MIG 76:131)
    35 on 29 Apr 2001, Elizabethton SBC (MIG 72:31)
    31 on 26 Apr 1987, Knoxville SBC (MIG 58:83)
High Counts – Fall
    7 on 15 Sep 2006, Shelby Forest SP (MIG 78:34)
High Counts – Summer
    15 on 4 Jun 1993, Frozen Head SP (MIG 64:88)
Substantiation: Specimen: LSUMZ, 76825

Louisiana Waterthrush, *Parkesia motacilla*

Status and Abundance: Fairly common spring and summer resident; rare

early fall transient; accidental winter visitor
Habitat: Wooded streams and creeks
Spring Arrival: mid Mar
Fall Departure: mid Aug
Comments: Often among the earliest returning migrants in the spring. Very early fall migrant departing by mid-August. Few records after August. One well described winter record.
Early Spring
  3 Mar 1986, Cherokee NF (MIG 57:87)
  9 Mar 2000, Radnor Lake (MIG 71:90)
  10 Mar 2000, Putnam Co. (MIG 71:90)
  13 Mar 2007, Shelby Forest SP (MIG 78:100)
  13 Mar 2007, Williamson Co. (MIG 78:102)
  13 Mar 2012, Signal Mtn. (CBl, pers. comm.)
Late Fall
  9 Oct 2010, Nashville FBC (MIG 81:147)
  5 Oct 1974, Erwin (MIG 46:23)
  5 Oct 2002, Nashville FBC (MIG 73:53)
  4 Oct 2005, Ellington Ag Center (MIG 76:26)
  26 Sep 1970, Williamson Co. (BNA:38)
High Counts – Spring
  39 on 29 Apr 1961, Nashville SBC (MIG 32:33)
  34 on 29 Apr 2001, Elizabethton SBC (MIG 72:31)
  23 on 14 May 2005, Montgomery Co. NAMC (MIG 76:133)
High Counts – Fall
  4 on 26 Aug 2012, Duck River Unit (MIG 83:150)
Winter Records
  1 on 8 Dec 1954-25 Jan 1955, Gatlinburg (Stupka 1963)
Substantiation: Specimen: LSUMZ, 76802

Northern Waterthrush, *Parkesia noveboracensis*
Status and Abundance: Uncommon transient; rare winter visitor
Habitat: Riparian forest and forest edge
Spring Arrival: mid Apr
Spring Departure: mid May
Fall Arrival: late Aug
Fall Departure: mid Oct
Early Spring
  1 Apr 1967, Nashville (MIG 38:49)
  1 Apr 2004, Nashville (MIG 75:114)
Late Spring
  13 Jun 1994, Radnor Lake (MIG 65:64)

27 May 2009, Laurel Bloomery, Johnson Co. (MIG 80:96)
26 May 2007, Holston Valley (MIG 78:107)
25 May 1997, Holston Valley (MIG 68:114)

Early Fall
12 Jul 2003, Signal Mtn., Hamilton Co. (MIG 74:133)
8 Aug 1962, Elizabethton (MIG 33:51)
19 Aug 1971, Nashville (MIG 42:93)
21 Aug 1987, Reelfoot Lake (Robinson 1990)

Late Fall
23 Nov 1982, Austin Springs (MIG 54:26)
6 Nov 1994, Memphis (MIG 66:22)
28 Oct 1984, Tennessee NWR (MIG 56:22)

High Counts – Spring
13 on 29 Apr 1972, Nashville SBC (MIG 43:47)
13 on 29 Apr 2011, Bells Bend (MIG 82:88)
11 on 9 May 1992, Chattanooga SBC (MIG 63:49)
9 on 10 May 1997, Hamilton Co. NAMC (MIG 68:103)

High Counts – Fall
9 on 18 Sep 2010, Blount Co. FBC (MIG 81:147)
7 on 25 Sep 2010, Greeneville FBC (MIG 81:147)
6 on 19 Sep 2009, Blount Co. FBC (MIG 81:46)
6 on 3 Oct 2004, Greene Co. (MIG 76:36)

Winter Records
1 on 24 Dec 1971, Reelfoot Lake CBC (MIG 43:13)
1 on 23 Dec 1972, Reelfoot Lake CBC (MIG 44:12)
1 on 20 Dec 1980, Reelfoot Lake CBC (MIG 52:14)
1 on 20 Dec 2003, Reelfoot Lake CBC (MIG 75:61)
1 on 2 Jan 2005, Knoxville CBC (MIG 76:67)

Substantiation: Specimen: LSUMZ, 76793

Golden-winged Warbler, *Vermivora chrysoptera*

Status and Abundance: Uncommon transient; uncommon summer resident in Cumberland Plateau, Southern Blue Ridge

Habitat: Forest edge and shrubby second growth

Spring Arrival: mid Apr

Spring Departure: mid May

Fall Arrival: early Sep

Fall Departure: early Oct

Comments: Migrants found across the state, but nests mainly in two known locations: North Cumberland WMA and Hampton Creek Cove (including adjacent Roan Mtn.). Formerly nested in other locations on the Cumberland Plateau. See Blue-winged Warbler account for discussion of hybridization.

Early Spring
    9 Apr 2004, near Scott/Campbell Co. line (MIG 75:118)
    9 Apr 1986, Stewart Co. (MIG 57:80)
    12 Apr 1947, Shelby Co. (MIG 18:62)
    14 Apr 2001, Davidson Co. (MIG 72:95)

Late Spring
    26 May 1935, Putnam Co. (Crook 1936)
    22 May 1977, Radnor Lake (MIG 48:104)

Early Fall
    14 Aug 1969, Nashville (MIG 40:91)
    17 Aug 1979, Nashville (MIG 51:16)
    17 Aug 2004, Shelby Bottoms Park (MIG 76:31)

Late Fall
    10 Oct 1990, Jackson (MIG 62:49)
    11 Oct 1990, WSMV Towerkill, Nashville (MIG 62:50)
    15 Oct 1969, Nashville (Laskey 1969)

High Counts – Spring
    19 on 25 Apr 1971, Knoxville SBC (MIG 42:38)
    18 on 25 May 2001, Cross Mtn. (MIG 72:98)
    17 on 29 Apr 2000, Elizabethton SBC (MIG 71:68)
    16 on 1 May 2010, Hampton Creek Cove (MIG 81:122)
    14 on 12 May 1990, Chattanooga SBC (MIG 61:52)

High Counts – Fall
    8 on 15 Sep 2006, Shelby Forest SP (MIG 78:34)
    6 on 15 Sep 2012, Perry Co. FBC (MIG 83:142)
    6 on 17 Sep 2011, Shelby Forest WMA (MIG 82:150)
    5 on 15 Sep 1997, Radnor Lake (MIG 69:44)
    5 on 22 Sep 2004, Shelby Forest SP (MIG 76:28)

High Counts – Summer
    5 on 13 Jun 1999, Anderson Co. (MIG 70:132)

Substantiation: Specimen: LSUMZ, 76586

Blue-winged Warbler, *Vermivora pinus*

Status and Abundance: Uncommon transient; uncommon summer resident in Central Hardwoods, Cumberland Plateau, Ridge and Valley, Southern Blue Ridge; accidental winter visitor

Habitat: Forest edge and shrubby second growth

Spring Arrival: early Apr

Fall Departure: mid Oct

Comments: A hybrid Blue-winged x Golden-winged nest has been documented in Hampton Creek Cove (SGS, pers. obs.), and hybrids are regularly, if infrequently, documented as transients and occasionally breeders.

Early Spring
    3 Mar 2000, Nashville (MIG 71:90)
    19 Mar 2001, Lake Co. (MIG 72:93)
    27 Mar 1954, Shelby Co. (MIG 25:51)
    2 Apr 2012, Bells Bend (FF, pers. comm.)

Early Fall
    28 Jul 2004, Shelby Forest SP (MIG 75:159)
    10 Aug 1991, Ensley (JRW, unpubl. data)
    12 Aug 2004, Shelby Forest SP (MIG 76:28)
    19 Aug 1991, Shelby Farms (MIG 63:53)

Late Fall
    31 Oct 1981, Elizabethton (MIG 53:23)
    14 Oct 1968, Radnor Lake (MIG 39:90)

High Counts – Spring
    33 on 30 Apr 1983, Columbia SBC (MIG 54:53)
    30 on 13 May 2000, Putnam Co. NAMC (MIG 71:57)
    28 on 12 May 2007, Putnam Co. NAMC (MIG 78:133)
    26 on 12 May 2001, Putnam Co. NAMC (MIG 72:21)

High Counts – Fall
    8 on 17 Aug 2004, Shelby Bottoms Park (MIG 76:31)
    6 on 16 Sep 2006, Shelby Co. FBC (MIG 78:21)
    6 on 18 Oct 2010, White Co. FBC (MIG 81:146)
    5 on 25 Sep 2010, DeKalb Co. FBC (MIG 81:146)

High Counts – Winter
    1 on 14 Dec 2003, Memphis CBC (MIG 75:61)

Substantiation: Specimen: LSUMZ, 76594

Black-and-white Warbler, *Mniotilta varia*

Status and Abundance: Fairly common transient; fairly common summer resident in Cumberland Plateau, Ridge and Valley, Southern Blue Ridge; uncommon summer resident in Central Hardwoods, Southeastern Coastal Plain; rare summer resident in Mississippi Alluvial Valley; accidental winter visitor

Habitat: Forest

Spring Arrival: late Mar

Fall Departure: mid Oct

Comments: Less than 10 winter records, with no records after early January which suggests that the winter records are attributable to lingering fall transients.

Early Spring
    15 Mar 2000, Pennington Bend (MIG 71:90)
    18 Mar 1922, Radnor Lake (BNA:37)
Late Spring
    15 Jun 1990, Big Cypress Tree SNA, Weakley Co. (MAG, pers. comm.)
    15 Jun 1990, Shelby Farms (JRW, unpubl. data)
    14 Jun 2004, Shelby Farms (MIG 75:159)
Early Fall
    4 Jul 2008, Shelby Co. (MIG 79:97)
Late Fall
    9 Nov 1958, Kingsport (MIG 30:11)
    6 Nov 1954, Radnor Lake (BNA:37)
    1 Nov 1986, Shelby Co. (MIG 58:21)
High Counts – Spring
    126 on 9 May 1998, Putnam Co. NAMC (MIG 69:155)
    108 on 11 May 2002, Putnam Co. NAMC (MIG 73:99)
    108 on 8 May 1999, Putnam Co. SBC (MIG 70:123)
    107 on 24 Apr 2004, Elizabethton SBC (MIG 75:107)
High Counts – Fall
    29 on 15 Sep 2001, Putnam Co. FBC (MIG 73:32)
    25 on 20 Sep 2008, Putnam Co. FBC (MIG 80:19)
    20 on 30 Sep 2006, Nashville FBC (MIG 78:29)
    20 on 5 Oct 2002, Nashville FBC (MIG 73:53)
High Counts – Summer
    24 on 12 Jun 1999, Walnut Mtn., Carter Co. (MIG 70:134)
High Counts – Winter
    2 on 29 Dec 1989, Clarksville CBC (MIG 62:19)
Substantiation: Specimen: LSUMZ, 6920

Prothonotary Warbler, *Protonotaria citrea*
Status and Abundance: Uncommon spring and early fall transient and summer resident in Cumberland Plateau, Ridge and Valley, Southern Blue Ridge; fairly common spring and early fall transient and summer resident in Central Hardwoods, Southeastern Coastal Plain, Mississippi Alluvial Valley
Habitat: Wooded swamps; forest edges of lakes, ponds, and other wetlands
Spring Arrival: early Apr
Fall Departure: mid Sep
Early Spring
    27 Mar 1977, Fayette Co. (MIG 48:75)
    28 Mar 2003, Cheatham Co. (MIG 74:90)

Late Fall
- 24 Oct 1980, Nashville (BNA:38)
- 24 Oct 1989, S. Holston Lake (MIG 61:21)
- 19 Oct 1943, Elizabethton (Herndon 1944)

High Counts – Spring
- 87 on 29 Apr 1967, Reelfoot Lake SBC (MIG 38:34)
- 68 on 13 May 2000, Lake Co. NAMC (MIG 71:56)
- 51 on 12 May 2007, Shelby Co. NAMC (MIG 78:133)

High Counts – Summer
- 44 on 6 Jun 2009, Rankin Bottoms (MIG 80:127)
- 39 on 19 Jun 2005, Rankin Bottoms (MIG 76:146)

Substantiation: Specimen: LSUMZ, 76832

Swainson's Warbler, *Limnothlypis swainsonii*

Status and Abundance: Uncommon spring and early fall transient and summer resident in Mississippi Alluvial Valley, Southeastern Coastal Plain, Cumberland Plateau, Ridge and Valley, Southern Blue Ridge; rare spring and early fall transient and summer resident in Central Hardwoods

Habitat: In Mississippi Alluvial Valley and Southeastern Coastal Plain, wooded swamps with canebrakes or thick woody understory; in Cumberland Plateau, Ridge and Valley, and Southern Blue Ridge in forest with Rhododendron thickets

Spring Arrival: mid Apr

Fall Departure: early Sep

Comments: Fall migration poorly known. Species generally not detected after males stop singing in June and July. Inaccessibility of occupied habitat also influences low detection rate.

Early Spring
- 1 Apr 1972, Sequatchie Co. (MIG 43:54)
- 6 Apr 1998, Shelby Forest SP (MIG 69:163)
- 11 Apr 1977, Memphis (MIG 48:75)
- 14 Apr 1992, Ripshin Lake (MIG 63:78)

Late Fall
- 15 Oct 1969, Savannah (MIG 40:88)
- 7 Oct 1951, Knoxville (Howell and Tanner 1951)
- 3 Oct 1993, Shelby Bottoms Park (MIG 65:23)
- 29 Sep 1996, Roan Creek (MIG 68:31)
- 28 Sep 1970, Nashville (BNA:38)

High Counts – Spring
- 14 on 31 May 1986, Haywood Co. (MIG 57:74)
- 10 on 24 Apr 1994, Memphis SBC (MIG 65:35)

10 on 8 May 1999, Shelby Forest SP (MIG 70:98)
8 on 26 Apr 1992, Memphis SBC (MIG 63:49)
7 on 10 May 1981, Shady Valley (Knight 2008)

High Counts – Fall
9 killed at transmission tower on 30 Sep 1972, Holston Mtn. (Knight 2008)

High Counts – Summer
8 on 7 Jul 1992, Shelby Forest SP (MIG 63:96)
5 on 6 Jun 1991, Shelby Farms SP (MAG, pers. comm.)
3 on 24 Jun 1988, Pine Creek, Big South Fork NRRA, Scott Co. (MIG 59:128)
3 on 9 Jun 1988, Citico Creek, Monroe Co. (MIG 59:130)

Substantiation: Specimen: LSUMZ, 76813

Tennessee Warbler, *Oreothlypis peregrina*

Status and Abundance: Common transient; accidental winter visitor
Habitat: Forest and forest edge
Spring Arrival: mid Apr
Spring Departure: mid May
Fall Arrival: late Aug
Fall Departure: late Oct
Comments: The authors have not reviewed the documentation for any of the winter records. It is possible that some were confused with the more expected Orange-crowned Warbler. The specimen listed as substantiation is the type specimen collected by Alexander Wilson on a visit to Nashville in April 1810 (see Nicholson 1986).

Early Spring
4 Apr 1975, Memphis (MIG 46:65)
9 Apr 1986, Stewart Co. (MIG 57:80)
10 Apr 1999, Radnor Lake (MIG 70:99)
11 Apr 1965, Chattanooga (MIG 36:64)

Late Spring
9 Jun 2008, Radnor Lake (MIG 79:97)
4 Jun 2001, Memphis (MIG 72:123)
28 May 1997, Radnor Lake (MIG 68:109)
26 May 1979, Nashville (BNA:36)

Early Fall
2 Aug 1980, Nashville (BNA:36)
3 Aug 2000, Pennington Bend (MIG 72:41)
8 Aug 1994, Nashville (MIG 66:23)
9 Aug 1969, near Roan Mtn. (MIG 40:93)

Late Fall
- 1 Dec 1991, Dyer Co. (MIG 63:53)
- 1 Dec 2003, Nashville (MIG 75:76)
- 28 Nov 1961, Nashville (BNA:36)
- 27 Nov 1991, Shelby Farms (MIG 63:53)
- 23 Nov 2003, Roane Co. (MIG 75:32)

High Counts – Spring
- 219 on 8 May 2004, Shelby Co. NAMC (MIG 75:99)
- 205 on 10 May 1997, Shelby Co. NAMC (MIG 68:102)
- 175 on 8 May 1999, Shelby Co. NAMC (MIG 70:42)
- 163 on 7 May 2011, Nashville SBC (MIG 82:70)
- 151 on 10 May 2008, Shelby Co. NAMC (MIG 79:78)

High Counts – Fall
- 1000+ on 6 Sep 2001, Carver's Gap (MIG 73:19)
- 372 on 24 Sep 2011, Elizabethton FBC (MIG 82:136)
- 325 killed at transmitter tower on 30 Sep 1972, Holston Mtn. (Herndon 1973)
- 300+ on 9 Sep 2000, Carver's Gap (MIG 72:47)
- 254 killed at transmission tower on 14 Oct 1969, Nashville (Laskey 1969)

Winter Records
- 1 on 17 Nov 1935-2 Jan 1935, Nashville (Mayfield 1935)
- 1 on 3 Jan 1936, Knoxville (MIG 7:24)
- 1 on 28 Jan 1950, Nashville (Laskey 1950)
- 1 on 15-19 Dec 1991, Dyer Co. (GC *fide* MAG)
- 1 on 26 Dec 1991, Dyer Co. (MIG 63:61)
- 1 on 28 Jan 2002, Davidson Co. (MIG 73:37)
- 1 on 17 Dec 2006, Memphis CBC (MIG 78:67)

Substantiation: Specimen: Peale Museum, 7787 (This museum no longer exists and the current location of this specimen is unknown.)

Orange-crowned Warbler, *Oreothlypis celata*

Status and Abundance: Uncommon transient; uncommon winter resident in Mississippi Alluvial Valley, irregular to rare winter resident in rest of state

Habitat: Forest and forest edge

Spring Arrival: early Apr

Spring Departure: late Apr

Fall Arrival: late Sep

Fall Departure: mid Nov

Comments: Rare winter resident from all regions of the state, becoming regular in Mississippi Alluvial Valley, especially in Memphis area.

Birds observed before the last week of September should be studied thoroughly to avoid confusion with Yellow, Tennessee, or Cape May Warblers.

Early Spring
- 2 Mar 1987, Shelby Farms (MIG 58:93)
- 4 Mar 2005, Shelby Bottoms Park (MIG 76:98)
- 5 Mar 1950, Elizabethton (MIG 21:15)

Late Spring
- 20 May 1949, Clarksville (Clebsch 1950)
- 15 May 1981, Johnson City (MIG 52:74)
- 15 May 1994, Roan Mtn. (MIG 65:56)
- 11 May 1997, Nashville (MIG 68:109)
- 11 May 2002, Lake Co. NAMC (MIG 73:98)

Early Fall
- 29 Aug 1992, Big Hill Pond SP (MIG 64:17)
- 7 Sep 1987, Radnor Lake (MIG 59:37)
- 9 Sep 1999, Radnor Lake (MIG 71:34)
- 13 Sep 1999, Greene Co. (MIG 71:38)

Late Fall
- 25 Nov 1978, Nashville (BNA:36)
- 19 Nov 1967, Greeneville (MIG 38:100)

High Counts – Fall
- 7 on 26 Oct 1996, Ensley (JRW, unpubl. data)
- 5 on 16 Oct 1975, Williamson Co. (Goodpasture 1977)
- 5 on 2 Oct 2004, Nashville FBC (MIG 76:22)
- 5 on 6 Oct 2012, Henry and Stewart Co. (MIG 83:148)
- 4 on 2 Nov 2007, Lewis Co. (MIG 79:22)

High Counts – Winter
- 6 on 21 Dec 2008, Memphis CBC (MIG 80:53)
- 5 on 19 Dec 1999, Memphis CBC (MIG 71:18)
- 3 on 17 Dec 2000, Memphis CBC (MIG 72:69)
- 3 on 18 Dec 2004, Memphis CBC (MIG 76:67)
- 3 on 18 Dec 2010, Chattanooga CBC (MIG 82:61)

Substantiation: Specimen: LSUMZ, 76601

Nashville Warbler, *Oreothlypis ruficapilla*

Status and Abundance: Fairly common transient; accidental winter visitor
Habitat: Forest and forest edge
Spring Arrival: mid Apr
Spring Departure: mid May
Fall Arrival: early Sep
Fall Departure: late Oct

Comments: The specimen listed as substantiation is the type specimen collected by Alexander Wilson on a visit to Nashville in Apr 1810 (see Nicholson 1986).

Early Spring
- 1 Apr 1978, Ashland City (MIG 49:68)
- 1 Apr 2002, Memphis (MIG 73:57)

Late Spring
- 26 May 1997, Putnam Co. (MIG 68:109)

Early Fall
- 18 Aug 1939, Hardeman Co. (Calhoun 1941)
- 27 Aug 2002, Wilbur Lake (MIG 74:27)
- 28 Aug 1968, Carter Co. (MIG 39:96)
- 28 Aug 2001, Shelby Bottoms Park (MIG 73:13)

Late Fall
- 27 Nov 1991, Shelby Farms (MIG 63:53)
- 24 Nov 1977, Dyersburg (MIG 49:41)
- 17 Nov 1981, Radnor Lake (BNA:36)
- 17 Nov 2005, Knox Co. (MIG 76:31)

High Counts – Spring
- 44 on 30 Apr 1972, Knoxville SBC (MIG 43:47)

High Counts – Fall
- 30 on 26 Sep 1992, Ensley (JRW, unpubl. data)
- 24 on 30 Sep 2006, Nashville FBC (MIG 78:29)
- 7 on 17 Sep 2005, Shelby Co. FBC (MIG 77:17)

Winter Records
- 1 on 30 Dec 1994, Savannah CBC (MIG 66:16)
- 1 on 9-10 Dec 2006, Knox Co. (MIG 78:83)

Substantiation: Specimen: Peale Museum, 7789 (This museum no longer exists and the current location of this specimen is unknown.)

Connecticut Warbler, *Oporornis agilis*

Status and Abundance: Irregular to rare spring and very rare fall transient

Habitat: Shrubby thickets and dense undergrowth in forest and forest edge

Spring Arrival: mid May

Spring Departure: late May

Fall Arrival: mid Sep

Fall Departure: early Oct

Comments: Observers should be cautious of early "heard only" records due to possible confusion with singing Northern Waterthrush, which can sound surprisingly similar. Any April report of this species should be thoroughly documented. There is no documentation (of which the authors are aware) to support any April sighting of this species (although it is reported in April with some frequency), and the authors believe it likely that some or all of those records are attributable to misidentified singing Northern Waterthrushes.

Late Spring
  13 Jun 1976, Alcoa Marsh (MIG 47:102)
  5 Jun 2000, Warner Parks (MIG 71:120)
  1 Jun 1997, Tennessee River Gorge, Marion Co. (MIG 68:137)

Early Fall
  1 Aug 2009, Greeneville (MIG 81:57)
  18 Aug 2000, Craven's House (MIG 72:45)
  21 Aug 2008, Greene Co. (MIG 80:30)
  23 Aug 2007, Hamilton Co. (MIG 79:27)
  29 Aug 1999, Shelby Co. (MIG 71:32)

Late Fall
  19 Oct 1975, Washington Co. (MIG 47:24)
  17 Oct 1946, Nashville (BNA:38)
  15 Oct 1988, Ensley (MIG 60:26)
  15 Oct 1988, Shelby Farms (MIG 60:26)
  15 Oct 1998, Nashville (MIG 70:50)

High Counts – Spring
  4 on 16 May 1943, Nashville (Abernathy 1943)

Substantiation: Specimen: LSUMZ, 76896

MacGillivray's Warbler, *Geothlypis tolmiei*

Status and Abundance: Accidental visitor

Records
  (1) 1 on 25 Oct-19 Nov 2003, Radnor Lake (Shaw 2004)

Substantiation: Photograph: 1 on 25 Oct-19 Nov 2003, Radnor Lake (Shaw 2004)

Mourning Warbler, *Geothlypis philadelphia*

Status and Abundance: Uncommon transient, accidental summer visitor in Southern Blue Ridge

Habitat: Shrubby thickets and dense undergrowth in forest and forest edge

Spring Arrival: early May

Spring Departure: late May

Fall Arrival: early Sep

Fall Departure: late Sep

Comments: Likely overlooked or misidentified during fall. One male on Roan Mtn. during summer 2001 and 2002 indicated possible nesting

(Trently 2003).

Early Spring
- 15 Apr 1990, Shelby Forest SP (MIG 61:72)
- 16 Apr 1954, Shelby Co. (MIG 25:52)
- 18 Apr 1999, Overton Park (MIG 70:98)
- 19 Apr 1989, Shelby Farms (MIG 60:83)
- 21 Apr 1972, Johnson City (MIG 43:54)

Late Spring
- 6 Jun 2003, Big South Fork NRRA (MIG 74:94)
- 4 Jun 1936, Centennial Park, Nashville (Parmer 1963)
- 4 Jun 2005, Nashville (MIG 76:145)
- 2 Jun 1998, Holston Valley (MIG 69:191)
- 2 Jun 2004, Edwin Warner Park (MIG 75:114)

Early Fall
- 8 Aug 1998, Kingston Steam Plant (MIG 70:54)
- 11 Aug 2000, Radnor Lake (MIG 72:41)
- 11 Aug 2008, Putnam Co. (MIG 80:26)
- 18 Aug 1933, White Co. (MIG 4:39)
- 19 Aug 1944, Shelby Co. (Tucker 1950)

Late Fall
- 2 Nov 1986, Shelby Farms (MIG 58:21)
- 31 Oct 2003, Cove Lake SP (MIG 75:32)
- 31 Oct 2003, Radnor Lake (MIG 75:28)
- 28 Oct 1959, Nashville (Laskey 1960)
- 27 Oct 1996, Eagle Lake WMA (MIG 68:27)

High Counts – Spring
- 7 on 19 May 1993, Radnor Lake (MIG 64:67)
- 2 on 28 May 2001, Shelby Bottoms Park (MIG 72:95)

High Counts – Fall
- 5 on 9 Sep 1973, Two Jays (MIG 44:100)

Summer Records
- 1 on 25 Jun 1985, Putnam Co. (MIG 56:111)
- 1 m on 23 Jun-4 Jul 2001, Roan Mtn. (Trently 2003)
- 1 m on 6-29 Jun 2002, Roan Mtn. (Trently 2003)

Substantiation: Specimen: LSUMZ, 76903

Kentucky Warbler, *Geothlypis formosus*

Status and Abundance: Fairly common spring transient and summer resident; uncommon early fall transient

Habitat: Mature forest with developed understory growth

Spring Arrival: mid Apr

Fall Departure: mid Sep

Early Spring
    20 Mar 2008, Moss Island WMA (MIG 79:62)
    25 Mar 1954, Shelby Co. (MIG 25:51)
Late Fall
    29 Oct 1983, Nashville (MIG 55:22)
    9 Oct 1982, Knoxville (MIG 54:26)
High Counts – Spring
    99 on 10 May 2008, Putnam Co. NAMC (MIG 79:77)
    89 on 13 May 2000, Putnam Co. NAMC (MIG 71:57)
    83 on 9 May 1998, Putnam Co. NAMC (MIG 69:155)
    80 on 8 May 2004, Putnam Co. NAMC (MIG 75:99)
    78 on 10 May 2003, Putnam Co. NAMC (MIG 74:118)
    78 on 12 May 2001, Putnam Co. NAMC (MIG 72:21)
High Counts – Fall
    4 on 17 Sep 2005, Shelby Co. FBC (MIG 77:17)
    3 on 18 Sep 2010, Shelby Co. FBC (MIG 81:147)
Substantiation: Specimen: LSUMZ, 76888

Common Yellowthroat, *Geothlypis trichas*
    Status and Abundance: Common transient and summer resident; rare winter visitor
    Habitat: Marshes and marshy edges to lakes and ponds; brushy fields and similar second growth areas
    Spring Arrival: early Apr
    Fall Departure: late Oct
    Early Spring
        3 Mar 1957, Chattanooga (MIG 28:9)
        5 Mar 2000, Cheatham Co. (MIG 71:90)
        19 Mar 1975, Memphis (MIG 46:65)
    Late Fall
        29 Nov 1985, Nashville (MIG 57:29)
    High Counts – Spring
        409 on 12 May 2001, Putnam Co. NAMC (MIG 72:21)
        295 on 9 May 1998, Putnam Co. NAMC (MIG 69:155)
        285 on 26 Apr 2008, Jackson Co. SBC (MIG 79:93)
        281 on 13 May 2000, Putnam Co. NAMC (MIG 71:57)
        256 on 12 May 2007, Putnam Co. NAMC (MIG 78:133)
    High Counts – Fall
        67 on 29 Sep 2012, Nashville FBC (MIG 83:142)
        67 on 8 Oct 2005, Nashville FBC (MIG 77:12)
        55 on 26 Sep 2004, Knoxville FBC (MIG 76:23)

High Counts – Winter
>	5 on 1 Dec 2000, Black Bayou WMA (MIG 72:69)
>	3 on 15 Jan 1986, Tigrett WMA (MIG 57:51)
>	3 on 17 Dec 2005, Reelfoot Lake CBC (MIG 77:45)

Substantiation: Specimen: LSUMZ, 76857

Hooded Warbler, *Setophaga citrina*

Status and Abundance: Fairly common transient and summer resident

Habitat: Hillsides and ravines in mature forests, also bottomland hardwood forests

Spring Arrival: early Apr

Fall Departure: mid Oct

Early Spring
>	23 Mar 1991, Hamilton Co (MIG 62:114)
>	25 Mar 2008, Moss Island WMA (MIG 79:62)
>	29 Mar 1977, Memphis (MIG 48:102)

Late Fall
>	29 Nov 1955, GSMNP (Stupka 1963)
>	29 Oct 1972, Lawrence Co. (MIG 43:100)
>	27 Oct 2008, Shelby Farms (MIG 80:24)

High Counts – Spring
>	188 on 26 Apr 2008, Cumberland Co. (MIG 79:93)
>	168 on 7 May 2011, Cumberland Co. SBC (MIG 82:71)
>	167 on 29 Apr 1995, Elizabethton SBC (MIG 66:36)
>	164 on 5 May 2010, Cumberland Co. SBC (MIG 82:9)
>	154 on 24 Apr 2004, Elizabethton SBC (MIG 75:107)
>	154 on 30 Apr 2005, Elizabethton SBC (MIG 76:141)

High Counts – Fall
>	27 on 20 Sep 2008, Putnam Co. FBC (MIG 80:19)
>	17 on 16 Sep 2006, Putnam Co. FBC (MIG 78:22)
>	17 on 19 Sep 2009, Putnam Co. FBC (MIG 81:46)

High Counts – Summer
>	119 on 4 Jun 2011, Carter Co. (*fide* RLK)
>	117 on 11 Jun 2006, Carter Co. (*fide* RLK)
>	73 on 22 Jun 2000, Big South Fork NRRA, Twin Arches area (Stedman and Stedman 2002)
>	38 on 10 Jun 1996, Holston Mtn., Sullivan Co. (MIG 67:80)
>	30 on 6 Jun 1993, Frozen Head SP (MIG 64:88)

Substantiation: Specimen: LSUMZ, 76911

American Redstart, *Setophaga ruticilla*

Status and Abundance: Fairly common transient; uncommon to locally common summer resident in Cumberland Plateau, Ridge and Valley, Southern Blue Ridge; locally uncommon summer resident in Central Hardwoods, Southeastern Coastal Plain, Mississippi Alluvial Valley; accidental winter visitor

Habitat: Forest and forest edge; breeds primarily in bottomland forest

Spring Arrival: mid Apr

Fall Departure: mid Oct

Comments: Breeding populations tend to be isolated in some areas, whereas other areas that appear suitable are unoccupied. Breeding populations most common along the Hatchie and Mississippi River drainages, upper Cumberland Plateau and Cumberland Mountains, and Southern Blue Ridge.

Early Spring
- 28 Mar 1997, Nashville (MIG 68:110)
- 28 Mar 1995, Nashville (MIG 66:53)
- 1 Apr 1967, Williamson Co. (MIG 38:49)
- 3 Apr 1967, Tennessee River Gorge (MIG 38:52)
- 6 Apr 2000, Pennington Bend (MIG 71:90)
- 6 Apr 2002, Knoxville (MIG 73:62)

Late Spring
- 6 Jun 2000, Radnor Lake (MIG 71:120)

Late Fall
- 27 Nov 2009, Osceola Island, Sullivan Co. (MIG 81:59)
- 18 Nov 1969, Nashville (BNA:38)
- 12 Nov 1953, Gatlinburg (Stupka 1963)

High Counts – Spring
- 95 on 12 May 2001, Shelby Co. NAMC (MIG 72:21)
- 72 on 20 May 2010, western Putnam Co. (MIG 81:117)
- 68 on 8 May 2004, Putnam Co. NAMC (MIG 75:99)
- 60 on 11 May 2002, Shelby Co. NAMC (MIG 73:99)
- 55 on 10 May 1997, Putnam Co. NAMC (MIG 68:59)

High Counts – Fall
- 75 on 24 Sep 2011, Elizabethton FBC (MIG 82:136)
- 57 on 28 Sep 2003, Knoxville FBC (MIG 75:18)
- 51 on 27 Sep 2003, Nashville FBC (MIG 75:18)
- 48 on 25 Sep 2010, DeKalb Co. FBC (MIG 81:147)
- 48 on 5 Oct 2002, Nashville FBC (MIG 73:53)

High Counts – Summer
- 81 on 4 Jun 1995, Frozen Head SP (MIG 66:67)
- 75 on 2 Jun 2002, Frozen Head SP (MIG 73:114)
- 73 on 4 Jun 1999, Frozen Head SP (MIG 70:133)

Winter Records
> 1 imm m on 29 Dec 1995, Kingsport (MIG 67:33)
> 2 on 15 Dec 1998, GSMNP (MIG 70:74)
> 1 on 1 Dec 2007, Cove Island, Knox Co. (MIG 79:55)
> 1 on 10 Dec 2011, Hiwassee Refuge (MIG, in press)

Substantiation: Specimen: LSUMZ, 9665

Kirtland's Warbler, *Setophaga kirtlandii*

Status and Abundance: **Unsubstantiated**; accidental

Comments: One well-described bird was seen on 28 Sep 1956 at Greeneville, Greene Co. (Darnell 1956). TBRC placed it on the provisional list of Tennessee bird species in 1983 (Nicholson 1983) on the basis of written documentation. A well-described color-banded bird was found 13 May 1997 at Eastern State WMA (now Forks of the River WMA) (Skelton and Kays 1997).

Records
> (1) 1 on 28 Sep 1956, Greeneville (Darnell 1956)
> (2) 1 on 13 May 1997, Eastern State WMA (Skelton and Kays 1997)

Cape May Warbler, *Setophaga tigrina*

Status and Abundance: Fairly common spring transient and uncommon to fairly common fall transient in Cumberland Plateau, Ridge and Valley, Southern Blue Ridge; uncommon spring transient and rare fall transient in Mississippi Alluvial Valley, Southeastern Coastal Plain, Central Hardwoods; accidental winter visitor

Habitat: Forest and forest edge

Spring Arrival: mid Apr

Spring Departure: mid May

Fall Arrival: early Sep

Fall Departure: mid Oct

Comments: Generally more common in eastern third of the state, incl. Cumberland Plateau, Ridge and Valley, Southern Blue Ridge, esp. during fall. At least eight winter records scattered across the state.

Early Spring
> 1 Apr 2010, Knox Co. (MIG 81:120)
> 7 Apr 1974, Bristol (MIG 45:80)

Late Spring
> 2 Jun 1946, Pickett Co. (Spofford 1948)
> 30 May 1963, Knoxville (MIG 34:52)

Early Fall
> 18 Aug 2007, Carver's Gap (MIG 79:29)
> 18 Aug 2011, Roan Mtn. (MIG 82:160)

20 Aug 1941, Memphis (MIG 12:58)
25 Aug 2006, Carver's Gap (MIG 78:43)
26 Aug 2009, Roan Mtn. (MIG 81:59)

Late Fall
22 Nov 1975, Knoxville (MIG 47:48)
26 Oct 1982, Elizabethton (MIG 54:27)

High Counts – Spring
20 on 30 May 1989, Knoxville SBC (MIG 60:50)
20 on 7 May 2011, Cumberland Co. SBC (MIG 82:70)
19 on 5 May 1991, Knoxville SBC (MIG 62:38)
18 on 9 May 1998, Nashville NAMC (MIG 69:154)
17 on 9 May 1998, Hamilton Co. NAMC (MIG 69:154)

High Counts – Fall
80 on 27 Sep 1980, Elizabethton FBC (*fide* RLK)
72 on 29 Sep 1994, Elizabethton FBC (*fide* RLK)
66 on 24 Sep 2011, Elizabethton FBC (MIG 82:136)
55 on 26 Sep 1998, Elizabethton FBC (*fide* RLK)

Winter Records
1 on 2 Jan 2000, Knoxville CBC (MIG 71:45)
1 on 4 Feb 1995, Pickwick Landing SP (MIG 66:41)

Substantiation: Specimen: LSUMZ, 76704

Cerulean Warbler, *Setophaga cerulea*

Status and Abundance: Uncommon spring and early fall transient; locally common summer resident in Cumberland Plateau; uncommon to rare summer resident in rest of state

Habitat: River or creek bottoms adjacent to steep forested slopes in west Tennessee, bottomland hardwood forests in the Mississippi Alluvial Valley, and in upland mature deciduous forests and riparian areas in large forested tracts in middle and east Tennessee

Spring Arrival: mid Apr

Fall Departure: early Sep

Comments: Locally abundant breeding bird in the Cumberland Mountains (e.g. North Cumberland WMA and Frozen Head SP). Also found in moderate numbers in other areas of the western escarpment of the Cumberland Plateau (SJS, pers. comm.). Small breeding populations are found at Shelby Forest SP and WMA, Reelfoot NWR, Cheatham WMA, and Edgar Evins SP. Small scattered populations of breeding birds may be found, but many former nesting areas (e.g. Natchez Trace Parkway, Warner Parks in Nashville) are no longer used by breeding Cerulean Warblers. Birds leave nesting areas in July and August. Fall migration is poorly known and most birds have departed

by late August.
Early Spring
: 15 Mar 2000, Pennington Bend (MIG 71:90)
: 29 Mar 1985, Williamson Co. (MIG 56:77)
: 29 Mar 2000, Warner Parks (MIG 71:90)
: 3 Apr 2012, DeKalb Co. (MIG 83:67)
: 4 Apr 2003, Shelby Forest SP (MIG 74:88)
: 4 Apr 2005, Narrows of the Harpeth SP (MIG 76:99)

Early Fall
: 21 Jul 2002, Craven's House (MIG 73:114)
: 25 Jul 2004, Craven's House (MIG 75:161)
: 27 Jul 2003, Craven's House (MIG 74:133)
: 28 Jul 1991, Signal Mtn., Hamilton Co. (MIG 63:23)
: 31 Jul 1991, Rivermont Park, Hamilton Co. (MIG 63:23)

Late Fall
: 13 Oct 1990, Pace Point (JRW, unpubl. data)
: 11 Oct 1995, Tipton Co. (MIG 67:20)
: 9 Oct 1989, Norris Lake (MIG 61:19)
: 6 Oct 1979, Nashville (BNA:37)
: 4 Oct 1975, Washington Co. (MIG 47:22)

High Counts – Spring
: 55 on 29 Apr 1973, Knoxville SBC (MIG 44:47)
: 53 on 20 May 2010, western Putnam Co. (MIG 81:117)
: 49 on 12 May 2001, Putnam Co. NAMC (MIG 72:21)
: 47 on 14 May 2005, Putnam Co. NAMC (MIG 76:131)

High Counts – Fall
: 3 on 6 Sep 2005, Craven's House (MIG 77:31)

High Counts – Summer
: 106 on 4 Jun 1994, Frozen Head SP (MIG 65:64)
: 87 on 4 Jun 1995, Frozen Head SP (MIG 66:67)
: 85 on 6 Jun 1997, Frozen Head SP (MIG 68:136)
: 74 on 4 Jun 1999, Frozen Head SP (MIG 70:133)

Substantiation: Specimen: LSUMZ, 7935

Northern Parula, *Setophaga americana*

Status and Abundance: Uncommon to fairly common transient and summer resident; accidental winter visitor
Habitat: Wooded swamps and riparian areas in lowland forests
Spring Arrival: late Mar
Fall Departure: mid Oct
Early Spring
: 23 Mar 1975, Shelby Co. (MIG 46:65)

21 Mar 1999, Radnor Lake (MIG 70:100)
17 Mar 2003, Shelby Forest SP (MIG 74:88)

Early Fall
20 Jun 2003, Craven's House (MIG 74:133)

Late Fall
28 Nov 2006, Elizabethton (MIG 78:43)
3 Nov 1984, Nashville (MIG 56:21)

High Counts – Spring
104 on 29 Apr 1990, Memphis SBC (MIG 61:52)
98 on 18 Apr 1971, Memphis SBC (MIG 42:39)
94 on 12 May 2007, Shelby Co. NAMC (MIG 78:133)
88 on 8 May 2004, Shelby Co. NAMC (MIG 75:99)
85 on 26 Apr 1992, Memphis SBC (MIG 63:49)

High Counts – Fall
51 on 18 Sep 2010, Shelby Co. FBC (MIG 81:146)
29 on 21 Sep 2002, Shelby Co. FBC (MIG 73:52)
29 on 29 Sep 2012, Shelby Co. FBC (MIG 83:143)
27 on 17 Sep 2005, Shelby Co. FBC (MIG 77:17)
25 on 18 Sep 2004, Shelby Co. FBC (MIG 76:17)

High Counts – Summer
25 on 8 Jun 1999, Watauga Lake (MIG 70:134)

Winter Records
1 on 27 Dec 2013, Elizabethton (MIG, in press)

Substantiation: Specimen: LSUMZ, 19591

Magnolia Warbler, *Setophaga magnolia*

Status and Abundance: Fairly common transient; uncommon local summer resident in Southern Blue Ridge

Habitat: Forest and forest edge

Spring Arrival: mid Apr

Spring Departure: late May

Fall Arrival: late Aug

Fall Departure: late Oct

Comments: Uncommon summer resident in higher elevations in eastern mountains, almost exclusively on Unaka and Roan Mtns., but may occur elsewhere in the Southern Blue Ridge.

Early Spring
10 Mar 1951, Elizabethton (MIG 22:18)
13 Apr 1944, Nashville (MIG 15:32)

Late Spring
4 Jun 1979, Shelby Co. (MIG 50:86)
4 Jun 1997, Radnor Lake (MIG 68:135)

3 Jun 1963, Nashville (MIG 34:50)

Early Fall
- 2 Aug 2000, Humboldt, Gibson Co. (MIG 72:40)
- 7 Aug 2002, Shelby Forest SP (MIG 74:17)
- 12 Aug 2008, City Lake, Putnam Co. (MIG 80:25)
- 12 Aug 2009, Shelby Bottoms (MIG 81:52)
- 13 Aug 1958, Kingsport (MIG 29:58)

Late Fall
- 14 Nov 1989, Johnson City (MIG 61:19)
- 6 Nov 1938, Nashville (MIG 9:98)
- 31 Oct 1956, Elizabethton (MIG 28:13)

High Counts – Spring
- 77 on 11 May 2002, Nashville SBC (MIG 73:106)
- 63 on 11 May 2002, Davidson Co. NAMC (MIG 73:99)
- 24 on 9 May 1992, Chattanooga SBC (MIG 63:49)

High Counts – Fall
- 167 on 5 Oct 2002, Nashville FBC (MIG 73:53)
- 141 on 28 Sep 2008, Knoxville FBC (MIG 80:18)
- 121 on 27 Sep 2003, Nashville FBC (MIG 75:17)
- 117 on 4 Oct 2008, White Co. FBC (MIG 80:18)
- 116 on 6 Oct 2008, Nashville FBC (MIG 79:7)

High Counts – Summer
- 11 during summer 1991, Unaka Mtn. (MIG 63:24)
- 6 on 6 Jun 2008, Roan Mtn. (MIG 2010)
- 5 on 3 Jun 2009, Unaka Mtn. (MIG 80:129)
- 3 on 10 Jun 2007, Roan Mtn. (MIG 78:143)

Substantiation: Specimen: LSUMZ, 6798

Bay-breasted Warbler, *Setophaga castanea*

Status and Abundance: Fairly common transient
Habitat: Forest
Spring Arrival: late Apr
Spring Departure: mid May
Fall Arrival: early Sep
Fall Departure: late Oct

Early Spring
- 3 Apr 1995, Shelby Co. (JRW, unpubl. data)
- 18 Apr 1988, Murfreesboro (Robinson 1990)

Late Spring
- 28 May 1982, Radnor Lake (BNA:37)

Early Fall
- 13 Aug 1953, Nashville (BNA:37)

20 Aug 1984, Van Buren Co. (MIG 56:21)
31 Aug 1998, Shelby Farms (MIG 70:48)

Late Fall
21 Nov 1925, Nashville (BNA:37)
7 Nov 1974, Memphis (MIG 46:44)

High Counts – Spring
60 on 12 May 1973, Kingsport SBC (MIG 44:47)
26 on 9 May 1998, Putnam Co. NAMC (MIG 69:155)

High Counts – Fall
206 killed at ceilometer/transmission tower on 14 Oct 1969, Nashville (Laskey 1969)
138 on 28 Sep 1985, Elizabethton FBC (*fide* RLK)
63 killed at ceilometer/transmission tower on 7 Oct 1951, Knoxville (Howell and Tanner 1951)
58 on 5 Oct 1997, Big South Fork NRRA (MIG 69:47)

Substantiation: Specimen: LSUMZ, 76760

Blackburnian Warbler, *Setophaga fusca*

Status and Abundance: Uncommon transient; locally fairly common to uncommon summer resident in upper Cumberland Plateau, Southern Blue Ridge

Habitat: Forest and forest edge; breeds in coniferous and mixed coniferous-deciduous forest and deciduous forest

Spring Arrival: mid Apr

Spring Departure: late May

Fall Arrival: late Aug

Fall Departure: mid Oct

Early Spring
9 Apr 2001, Nashville (MIG 72:95)
8 Apr 1977, Shelby Co. (MIG 48:75)
7 Apr 2003, Nashville (MIG 74:90)
4 Apr 1935, near Knoxville (MIG 6:38)

Late Spring
4 Jun 1994, Cheatham Co. (MIG 65:63)

Early Fall
28 Jul 1996, Signal Mtn., Hamilton Co. (MIG 67:79)
4 Aug 1955, Chattanooga (MIG 25:50)
4 Aug 1960, Nashville (BNA:37)

Late Fall
5 Nov 2006, near Milligan College, Carter Co. (MIG 78:43)
30 Oct 1964, Nashville (MIG 35:102)
30 Oct 1991, Jackson (MIG 63:53)

High Counts – Spring
    41 on 27 Apr 1958, Knoxville SBC (MIG 29:32)
High Counts – Fall
    11 on 26 Sep 2010, Knoxville FBC (MIG 81:147)
    9 on 5 Oct 2002, Nashville FBC (MIG 73:53)
    8 on 27 Sep 2009, Knoxville FBC (MIG 81:45)
High Counts – Summer
    21 on 10-12 Jun 2011, Shady Valley (Knight 2011a)
    11 on 3 Jun 2007, Frozen Head SP (MIG 78:142)
Substantiation: Specimen: LSUMZ, 76713

Yellow Warbler, *Setophaga petechia*

Status and Abundance: Fairly common transient; rare summer resident in Mississippi Alluvial Valley and Southeastern Coastal Plain; uncommon summer resident in Central Hardwoods; fairly common summer resident elsewhere; accidental winter visitor

Habitat: Forest edge and in open areas with scattered trees (particularly willows), usually near water

Spring Arrival: mid Apr

Fall Departure: late Sep

Early Spring
    27 Mar 1938, Knox. Co. (Howell and Monroe 1957)
    30 Mar 1988, Cheatham Co. (Robinson 1990)
    31 Mar 2013, Seven Islands Wildlife Refuge (KB, pers. comm.)
    5 Apr 2000, Basin Spring, Williamson Co. (MIG 71:90)

Late Fall
    14 Nov 2004, Celina, Clay Co. (MIG 76:31)
    10 Oct 2007, S. Holston Lake (MIG 79:29)
    9 Oct 1959, Nashville (MIG 31:11)

High Counts – Spring
    131 on 1 May 1949, Elizabethton SBC (MIG 20:36)
    104 on 9 May 1998, Putnam Co. NAMC (MIG 69:154)
    91 on 1 May 1994, Elizabethton SBC (MIG 65:34)
    82 on 10 May 2008, Putnam Co. NAMC (MIG 79:78)

High Counts – Fall
    3 on 26 Sep 2009, Elizabethton FBC (MIG 81:45)

Winter Records
    1 on 17 Nov-11 Dec 1985, Knoxville (MIG 57:61)
    1 on 1 Jan 2014, Anderson Road Rec. Area, Davidson Co. (SGS, pers. obs.)

Substantiation: Specimen: LSUMZ, 76619

Chestnut-sided Warbler, *Setophaga pensylvanica*

Status and Abundance: Fairly common transient; fairly common local summer resident in Southern Blue Ridge and upper Cumberland Plateau, rare elsewhere in Cumberland Plateau

Habitat: Forest, forest edge, shrubby second growth

Spring Arrival: mid Apr

Spring Departure: mid May

Fall Arrival: late Aug

Fall Departure: mid Oct

Comments: Locally common nesting bird on Frozen Head SP and North Cumberland WMA and in the higher elevations of the Southern Blue Ridge. Occasionally found elsewhere on the Cumberland Plateau, but very local and unexpected, possibly unreported due to low observer density in the area.

Early Spring
- 2 Apr 1981, Radnor Lake (MIG 52:72)

Late Spring
- 31 May 1949, Nashville (Parmer 1963)
- 26 May 1963, Memphis (MIG 34:49)

Early Fall
- 20 Jul 2003, Craven's House (MIG 74:133)
- 2 Aug 2000, Humboldt, Gibson Co. (MIG 72:40)
- 11 Aug 2004, Cane Creek Park (MIG 76:31)
- 13 Aug 1994, Shelby Forest SP (MIG 66:21)
- 15 Aug 1998, Ensley (JRW, unpubl. data)

Late Fall
- 2 Nov 1974, Old Hickory Lake (MIG 46:71)
- 21 Oct 1941, Memphis (MIG 12:71)

High Counts – Spring
- 86 on 5 May 1991, Elizabethton SBC (MIG 62:38)
- 79 on 27 Apr 2002, Elizabethton SBC (MIG 73:106)
- 75 on 1 May 1994, Elizabethton SBC (MIG 65:34)
- 63 on 29 Apr 1995, Elizabethton NAMC (MIG 66:35)
- 55 on 24 Apr 1976, Elizabethton SBC (MIG 47:92)

High Counts – Fall
- 115 killed at transmission tower on 14 Oct 1969, Nashville (Laskey 1969)
- 34 on 16 Sep 2006, Putnam Co. FBC (MIG 78:21)
- 24 on 5 Oct 2002, Nashville FBC (MIG 73:53)

Substantiation: Specimen: LSUMZ, 76623

Parulidae: Wood-Warblers

Blackpoll Warbler, *Setophaga striata*
Status and Abundance: Fairly common spring transient, rare fall transient
Habitat: Forest
Spring Arrival: mid Apr
Spring Departure: late May
Comments: Fall migration is primarily along the Atlantic coast and offshore. Fall Blackpoll Warblers should be identified with care.
Early Spring
  27 Mar 1954, Chattanooga (MIG 25:54)
  10 Apr 1952, Nashville (BNA:37)
  10 Apr 2000, Shady Valley (MIG 71:95)
Late Spring
  7 Jun 1997, Nashville (MIG 68:135)
  4 Jun 2001, Hardeman Co. (MIG 72:123)
  2 Jun 1942, Nashville (MIG 13:46)
  2 Jun 1968, Gatlinburg (MIG 39:67)
  2 Jun 2002, Humboldt (MIG 73:112)
High Counts – Spring
  422 on 7 May 2011, Nashville SBC (MIG 82:70)
  59 on 11 May 2002, Davidson Co. NAMC (MIG 73:99)
  57 on 9 May 1998, Putnam Co. NAMC (MIG 69:155)
  35 on 10 May 1997, Obion Co. (JRW, unpubl. data)
Substantiation: Specimen: LSUMZ, 76749

Black-throated Blue Warbler, *Setophaga caerulescens*
Status and Abundance: Fairly common transient in Cumberland Plateau, Ridge and Valley, Southern Blue Ridge; rare transient elsewhere; uncommon summer resident in upper Cumberland Plateau, rare summer resident in rest of Cumberland Plateau; fairly common summer resident in Southern Blue Ridge; accidental winter visitor
Habitat: Deciduous and mixed deciduous-coniferous forest
Spring Arrival: late Apr
Spring Departure: mid May
Fall Arrival: early Sep
Fall Departure: mid Oct
Comments: Early fall records are for areas away from known breeding sites in east Tennessee. Only known breeding area away from the Southern Blue Ridge is at Frozen Head SP in the Cumberland Mountains.
Early Spring
  3 Apr 1982, GSMNP (MIG 53:71)

7 Apr 1973, Reelfoot Lake (MIG 44:50)
11 Apr 1972, Nashville (MIG 43:51)
11 Apr 2004, Ramsey Cascade, GSMNP (MIG 75:119)

Late Spring
30 May 1976, Center Hill Lake (MIG 47:100)
16 May 1978, Warren Co. (MIG 49:92)
12 May 1960, Nashville (MIG 31:45)

Early Fall
24 Aug 2010, Shelby Forest (MIG 81:155)
6 Sep 2000, Pennington Bend (MIG 72:41)
9 Sep 1981, Nashville (MIG 53:17)
11 Sep 1994, Ensley (JRW, unpubl. data)

Late Fall
24 Nov 1981, Watauga Lake (MIG 53:23)
4 Nov 2003, Memphis (MIG 75:25)
29 Oct 2004, Radnor Lake (MIG 76:31)
27 Oct 1985, Shelby Co. (MIG 57:23)
26 Oct 2005, Shelby Forest SP (MIG 76:25)

High Counts – Spring
169 on 1 May 1994, Elizabethton SBC (MIG 65:34)
120 on 30 Apr 2011, Elizabethton SBC (MIG 82:70)
116 on 26 Apr 2008, Elizabethton SBC (MIG 79:92)
95 on 24 Apr 2004, Elizabethton SBC (MIG 75:107)
84 on 29 Apr 2001, Elizabethton SBC (MIG 72:30)

High Counts – Fall
150+ on 5 Sep 2001, Carver's Gap (MIG 73:19)
105 killed at transmission tower on 30 Sep 1972, Holston Mtn. (Herndon 1973)
100+ on 9 Sep 2000, Carver's Gap (MIG 72:47)

Winter Records
1 m on 3 Dec 1996, Cookeville (MIG 68:64)
1 on 15 Dec 1991, Elizabethton CBC (MIG 63:16)

Substantiation: Specimen: LSUMZ, 76638

Palm Warbler, *Setophaga palmarum*

Subspecies: See comments
Status and Abundance: Fairly common transient; uncommon winter resident
Habitat: Forest edge; shrubby second growth; brushy fields
Spring Arrival: mid Apr
Spring Departure: mid May
Fall Arrival: mid Sep

Fall Departure: late Oct

Comments: Small numbers can be found during winter, but are generally absent from most areas. Western Palm Warblers (ssp. *palmarum*) are substantially more common than Yellow Palm Warblers (ssp. *hypochrysea*).

Early Spring
- 7 Mar 1987, Blount Co. (MIG 58:104)
- 28 Mar 2000, Sycamore Shoals SP (MIG 71:95)
- 30 Mar 1963, near Nashville (MIG 34:50)
- 1 Apr 1975, Shelby Farms (MIG 46:65)

Late Spring
- 7 Jun 1998, Macon Co. (MIG 69:188)
- 4 Jun 1988, Nashville (Robinson 1990)
- 1 Jun 2000, Pennington Bend (MIG 71:120)
- 31 May 1937, Cades Cove (MIG 8:41)

Early Fall
- 7 Sep 1999, Pennington Bend (MIG 71:34)
- 5 Sep 1976, Cannon Co. (MIG 48:19)
- 29 Aug 1992, Big Hill Pond SP (MIG 64:17)
- 24 Aug 2003, Hwy 78, Dyer Co. (MIG 75:25)
- 13 Aug 1975, Radnor Lake (MIG 47:19)

Late Fall
- 25 Nov 1966, Nashville (MIG 37:81)
- 25 Nov 1984, Jefferson Co. (MIG 56:26)

High Counts – Spring
- 157 on 5 May 1968, Chattanooga SBC (MIG 39:33)
- 110 on 27-28 Apr 1990, Columbia SBC (MIG 61:52)

High Counts – Fall
- 239 on 26 Sep 2010, Knoxville FBC (MIG 81:147)
- 161 on 24 Sep 2011, Elizabethton FBC (MIG 82:136)
- 127 on 30 Sep 2006, Elizabethton FBC (MIG 78:29)
- 120 on 28 Sep 2010, Cades Cove (MIG 81:164)
- 117 on 9 Oct 2010, Nashville FBC (MIG 81:147)

High Counts – Winter
- 30 on 3 Jan 2004, Knoxville CBC (MIG 75:61)
- 16 on 16 Dec 2006, Chattanooga CBC (MIG 78:66)
- 15 on 29 Dec 1963, GSMNP CBC (MIG 34:84)
- 12 on 2 Jan 1982, Hickory-Priest CBC (MIG 53:8)

Substantiation: Specimen: LSUMZ, 76736

Pine Warbler, *Setophaga pinus*

Status and Abundance: Fairly common resident

Habitat: Coniferous forest (or conifer stands within mixed coniferous-deciduous forest)

High Counts – Spring
    45 on 8 May 2004, Putnam Co. NAMC (MIG 75:99)
    36 on 3 May 2008, Cumberland Co. SBC (MIG 79:92)
    35 on 12 May 2007, Putnam Co. NAMC (MIG 78:133)
    34 on 11 May 2002, Putnam Co. NAMC (MIG 73:99)
    32 on 12 May 2007, Hamilton Co. NAMC (MIG 78:132)

High Counts – Fall
    30 on 10 Aug 1934, Reelfoot Lake area (USFWS *fide* MAG)
    28 on 20 Sep 2003, Putnam Co. FBC (MIG 75:11)
    26 on 16 Sep 2006, Putnam Co. FBC (MIG 78:22)
    26 on 20 Sep 2008, Putnam Co. FBC (MIG 80:18)
    25 on 10 Oct 1995, Shelby Farms (MIG 67:20)

High Counts – Winter
    64 on 1 Jan 1992, Hiwassee CBC (MIG 63:16)
    63 on 13 Mar 1987, Hardin Co. (MIG 58:93)
    57 on 1 Jan 1987, Hiwassee CBC (MIG 58:4)

Substantiation: Specimen: LSUMZ, 76656

Yellow-rumped Warbler, *Setophaga coronata*

Subspecies: *coronata*

Status and Abundance: Common transient; fairly common winter resident; accidental summer visitor (resident?) in Southern Blue Ridge

Habitat: Forest and forest edge

Spring Departure: mid May

Fall Arrival: late Sep

Comments: Occasional reports of summering birds at the high elevations of the eastern mountains along the TN/NC state line. At least a dozen summer records of one to two males singing on Roan Mtn. since 1994 indicate possible nesting (Knight 2010, Knight 2011). A pair and unoccupied nest, possibly of Yellow-rumped Warblers, found 18 Jun 2002 on Unaka Mtn. (MIG 73:115). While Myrtle Warbler (*S. c. coronata*) is the expected subspecies, there are ten unsubstantiated records of Audubon's Warbler (*S. c. auduboni*):

(1) 1 on 1 Jun 1952, Johnson City (Knight 2008)
(2) 1 on 15 Mar 1987, LBL, Stewart Co. (Robinson 1988b)
(3) 1 on 14 Apr 2001, Amnicola Marsh (MIG 72:98)
(4) 1 on 14 Dec 2002, Norris CBC (MIG 74:57)
(5) 1 on 16 Feb 2008, Putnam Co. (MIG 79:53)
(6) 1 m on 18 Apr 2008, Knoxville (MIG 79:68)
(7) 1 m on 27 Apr 2008, LBL, Stewart Co. (MIG 79:64)

(8) 1 on 27 Oct 2008, Knoxville (MIG 80:29)
(9) 1 on 12 Jan 2009, Tigrett WMA (MIG 80:125)
(10) 1 on 25 Jan 2010, Knoxville (MIG 81:104)

Late Spring
1 Jun 1994, Coffee Co. (MIG 65:63)
28 May 1997, Nashville (MIG 68:109)
24 May 1976, Nashville (MIG 47:100)

Early Fall
11 Aug 1955, Chattanooga (MIG 26:50)

High Counts – Spring
522 on 28 Apr 1968, Knoxville SBC (MIG 39:33)
200 on 29 Apr 1995, Ensley (JRW, unpubl. data)

High Counts – Fall
204 on 9 Oct 2010, Nashville FBC (MIG 81:147)
145 on 8 Oct 2005, Nashville FBC (MIG 77:12)

Summer Records
1 on 28 Jun 1977, Nashville (MIG 48:104)
1 on 26 Jul 1984, Lawrence Co. (MIG 56:21)
1 on 18 Jun 2000, Hatchie NWR (MIG 71:119)
2 on 26 May 2005, Roan Mtn. (MIG 76:146)
5 on 2 Jun 2014, Roan Mtn. (MIG, in press)

High Counts – Winter
626 on 1 Jan 2004, Hiwassee CBC (MIG 75:61)
581 on 5 Jan 2002, Savannah CBC (MIG 72:119)
564 on 3 Jan 2004, Knoxville CBC (MIG 75:61)
543 on 17 Dec 2005, Chattanooga CBC (MIG 77:44)
540 on 31 Dec 2005, Knoxville CBC (MIG 77:45)

Substantiation: Specimen: LSUMZ, 76723

Yellow-throated Warbler, *Setophaga dominica*

Status and Abundance: Fairly common transient and summer resident; accidental winter visitor

Habitat: Forest and forest edge, usually riparian; prefers pines, sycamores and cypress trees

Spring Arrival: late Mar

Fall Departure: mid Oct

Comments: At least 8 winter records.

Early Spring
15 Mar 1977, Tennessee River Gorge (MIG 48:50)
16 Mar 2003, Sewanee (MIG 74:93)
19 Mar 1933, Memphis (MIG 4:8)
19 Mar 2012, Sevier Co. (MIG 83:75)

20 Mar 1997, Radnor Lake (MIG 68:109)
22 Mar 1997, Cades Cove (MIG 68:113)
22 Mar 2000, Big South Fork NRRA, Morgan Co. (Stedman and Stedman 2002)

Late Fall
10 Nov 1997, Kingston Steam Plant (MIG 69:47)
5 Nov 1970, Columbia (MIG 42:19)
28 Oct 1984, Knoxville (MIG 56:26)

High Counts – Spring
88 on 5 May 2010, Cumberland Co. SBC (MIG 82:9)
69 on 10 May 2008, Putnam Co. NAMC (MIG 79:77)
56 on 7 May 2011, Cumberland Co. SBC (MIG 82:70)
41 on 3 May 2008, Cumberland Co. SBC (MIG 79:92)
40 on 8 May 2004, Putnam Co. NAMC (MIG 75:99)

High Counts – Fall
6 on 15 Sep 2001, Putnam Co. NAMC (MIG 73:32)
6 on 18 Oct 2010, White Co. FBC (MIG 81:147)
5 on 30 Sep 2006, Nashville FBC (MIG 78:29)

High Counts – Summer
34 on 8 Jun 1999, Watauga Lake (MIG 70:134)

Substantiation: Specimen: LSUMZ, 9413

Prairie Warbler, *Setophaga discolor*

Status and Abundance: Fairly common spring transient; uncommon fall transient and summer resident; rare summer resident in Mississippi Alluvial Valley; accidental winter visitor

Habitat: Shrubby second growth

Spring Arrival: early Apr

Fall Departure: late Sep

Early Spring
6 Mar 2000, Maury Co. (MIG 71:90)
21 Mar 1972, Sequatchie Co. (MIG 43:54)
30 Mar 2012, Bells Bend (ES, pers. comm.)

Late Fall
18 Nov 2000, Cane Creek Park (MIG 72:41)
7 Nov 1999, Shelby Bottoms Park (MIG 71:34)
19 Oct 1968, Knoxville (MIG 39:94)
19 Oct 1984, Percy Warner Park (MIG 56:21)

High Counts – Spring
141 on 3 May 2008, Cumberland Co. SBC (MIG 79:92)
131 on 11 May 2002, Putnam Co. NAMC (MIG 73:99)
117 on 13 May 2000, Putnam Co. NAMC (MIG 71:57)

Parulidae: Wood-Warblers

    116 on 5 May 2010, Cumberland Co. SBC (MIG 82:9)
    111 on 10 May 2008, Putnam Co. NAMC (MIG 79:79)
High Counts – Fall
    6 on 19 Sep 2009, Putnam Co. FBC (MIG 81:45)
    6 on 25 Sep 2010, DeKalb Co. FBC (MIG 81:147)
    5 on 21 Sep 2002, Putnam Co. FBC (MIG 73:53)
Winter Records
    1 on 16 Dec 1998, Putnam Co. (MIG 70:71)
    1 on 16 Dec 1999, Cherokee Dam (MIG 70:73)
    1 on 28 Dec 2002, Nickajack CBC (MIG 74:57)
    1 on 20 Dec 2008, Chattanooga CBC (MIG 80:52)
Substantiation: Specimen: LSUMZ, 76700

Black-throated Gray Warbler, *Setophaga nigrescens*
Status and Abundance: Accidental visitor
Records
    (1) 1 ad m found dead on 2 Oct 1972 at the weather station on Holston Mtn. after tower kill on night of 30 Sep 1972 (Herndon 1972)
Substantiation: Specimen: LSUMZ 182658

Townsend's Warbler, *Setophaga townsendi*
Status and Abundance: **Unsubstantiated**; accidental visitor
Comments: Accepted by the TBRC on the basis of written documentation.
Records
    (1) 1 on 3 Dec 1994, Blount Co. (Knight 1996)
    (2) 1 on 30 Dec 1994, Pickwick Landing SP (Knight 1996)
    (3) 1 ad m on 13 Jan 2004, Wilbur Lake (Knight 2005)
    (4) 1 imm f on 23 Aug 2006, Wilson Co. (Edwards 2012)

Black-throated Green Warbler, *Setophaga virens*
Status and Abundance: Fairly common transient; fairly common to uncommon summer resident in Cumberland Plateau, Ridge and Valley, Southern Blue Ridge; accidental summer visitor in Central Hardwoods
Habitat: Forest and forest edge
Spring Arrival: late Mar
Spring Departure: mid May
Fall Arrival: late Aug
Fall Departure: late Oct
Early Spring
    13 Mar 1967, Tennessee River Gorge (MIG 38:52)
    19 Mar 1933, Memphis (MIG 4:8)

22 Mar 2003, Knoxville (MIG 74:93)
24 Mar 2004, Cane Creek Park (MIG 75:114)

Late Spring
9 Jun 1992, Narrows of the Harpeth (MIG 63:97)
7 Jun 2002, Overton Park (MIG 73:111)
6 Jun 2000, Cheatham Co. (MIG 71:120)
4 Jun 1987, Benton Co. (MIG 58:138)
3 Jun 1995, Eagle Lake WMA (JRW, unpubl. data)

Early Fall
1 Aug 1992, Ensley (JRW, unpubl. data)
1 Aug 2001, Memphis (MIG 73:11)
2 Aug 1960, Nashville (MIG 31:46)
2 Aug 1986, Memphis (MIG 58:21)
7 Aug 1937, Memphis (MIG 8:58)

Late Fall
24 Nov 2012, Jefferson Co. (MIG 83:155)
12 Nov 1979, Nashville (MIG 51:40)
9 Nov 1975, Memphis (MIG 47:45)
9 Nov 2002, Radnor Lake (MIG 74:19)
31 Oct 1996, Washington Co. (MIG 68:28)

High Counts – Spring
156 on 24 Apr 2004, Elizabethton SBC (MIG 75:107)
149 on 26 Apr 2008, Elizabethton SBC (MIG 79:92)
132 on 29 Apr 2001, Elizabethton SBC (MIG 72:30)
130 on 20 Apr 1999, Big South Fork NRRA, Scott Co. (MIG 70:102)
109 on 24 Apr 2010, Elizabethton SBC (MIG 82:8)

High Counts – Fall
50 on 29 Sep 2001, Davidson Co. FBC (MIG 73:32)
47 on 4 Oct 2008, Nashville FBC (MIG 80:18)
45 on 1 Oct 2011, Nashville FBC (MIIG 82:137)
43 on 9 Oct 2010, Nashville FBC (MIG 81:147)
38 on 29 Sep 2012, Nashville FBC (MIG 83:143)

High Counts – Summer
17 on 30 Jun 1996, Hamilton Co. (MIG 67:79)

Substantiation: Specimen: LSUMZ, 76689

Canada Warbler, *Cardellina canadensis*
Status and Abundance: Uncommon transient; locally common summer resident in Cumberland Plateau and higher elevations in Southern Blue Ridge
Habitat: Forest and forest edge, typically with some undergrowth
Spring Arrival: late Apr

Spring Departure: late May
Fall Arrival: late Aug
Fall Departure: late Sep
Comments: Locally uncommon nesting bird in Cumberland Co. on Frozen Head SP and vicinity.

Early Spring
- 14 Apr 2001, Big South Fork NRRA, Scott Co. (MIG 72:98)
- 15 Apr 2001, Alum Cave Bluff trail, GSMNP (MIG 72:99)
- 17 Apr 1969, Tennessee River Gorge (MIG 40:50)
- 19 Apr 2005, Putnam Co. (MIG 76:99)

Late Spring
- 16 Jun 1998, Greeneville (MIG 69:189)
- 31 May 1954, Knoxville (MIG 25:55)
- 30 May 1997, Marion Co. (MIG 68:112)
- 27 May 2005, Cookeville (MIG 76:99)

Early Fall
- 30 Jul 1994, Radnor Lake (MIG 65:64)
- 31 Jul 1938, Nashville (MIG 9:52)
- 1 Aug 1993, Frozen Head SP (MIG 65:25)
- 5 Aug 1964, Knoxville (MIG 35:63)
- 11 Aug 1941, Memphis (MIG 12:58)

Late Fall
- 21 Oct 1979, Knoxville (MIG 51:19)
- 13 Oct 1990, Shelby Co. (MIG 62:49)
- 12 Oct 1976, Giles Co. (MIG 48:19)

High Counts – Spring
- 59 on 28 Apr 2012, Elizabethton SBC (*fide* RLK)
- 44 on 30 Apr 2011, Elizabethton SBC (*fide* RLK)
- 36 on 10 May 1953, Roan Mtn. SBC (MIG 24:39)

High Counts – Fall
- 25 on 9 Aug 1934, Reelfoot Lake (Crook 1935)
- 3 on 25 Sep 2010, DeKalb Co. FBC (MIG 81:147)
- 2 on 5 Oct 2002, Nashville FBC (MIG 73:53)

High Counts – Summer
- 44 on 9 Jun 2012, Carter Co. (*fide* RLK)
- 29 on 13 Jun 1992, Carter Co. (*fide* RLK)
- 28 on 21 Jun 1996, Unaka Mtn. (MIG 67:80)
- 24 on 13 Jun 2008, Unaka Mtn. (MIG 79:101)

Substantiation: Specimen: LSUMZ, 76923

Wilson's Warbler, *Cardellina pusilla*

Status and Abundance: Uncommon transient; accidental winter visitor

Habitat: Forest and forest edge; shrubby second growth
Spring Arrival: late Apr
Spring Departure: mid May
Fall Arrival: late Aug
Fall Departure: mid Oct
Early Spring
    15 Apr 1976, Johnson City (MIG 47:78)
    17 Apr 1954, Lebanon SBC (MIG 25:32)
Late Spring
    30 May 2001, Williamson Co. (MIG 72:95)
    29 May 1981, Nashville (BNA:39)
Early Fall
    4 Aug 1980, Nashville (BNA:39)
    4 Aug 2007, Warren Co. (MIG 79:23)
    10 Aug 1995, Hamilton Co. (MIG 67:23)
    12 Aug 1939, Knoxville (MIG 11:76)
Late Fall
    2 Nov 1971, Memphis (MIG 43:23)
    24 Oct 1966, Nashville (Laskey 1966)
High Counts – Spring
    15 on 22 May 1983, Radnor Lake (MIG 54:62)
    5 on 11 May 2002, Davidson Co. NAMC (MIG 73:99)
High Counts – Fall
    4 on 24 Sep 2011, Shelby Forest SP (MIG 82:150)
    3 on 15 Sep 2001, Shelby Co. FBC (MIG 73:33)
    3 on 23 Sep 2005, Hamilton Co. (MIG 77:31)
Winter Records
    1 on 26 Dec 1991, Greeneville (MIG 63:62)
    1 on 25 Dec 1993-3 Jan 1994, Greeneville (MIG 65:12, 44)
Substantiation: Specimen: LSUMZ, 5775

Yellow-breasted Chat, *Icteria virens*

Status and Abundance: Common to fairly common transient and summer resident; rare winter visitor
Habitat: Shrubby fields and similar second growth areas, regenerating clearcuts and burns
Spring Arrival: mid Apr
Fall Departure: late Sep
Comments: At least 13 winter records (Stedman and Hawkins 2003).
Early Spring
    8 Apr 1953, Nashville (BNA:39)

Late Fall
- 19 Nov 1991, Memphis (MIG 63:53)
- 15 Nov 1981, Nashville (MIG 53:17)
- 9 Nov 2009, Radnor Lake (MIG 81:53)
- 25 Oct 2006, Watauga Lake (MIG 78:43)

High Counts – Spring
- 153 on 5 May 2010, Cumberland Co. SBC (MIG 82:9)
- 147 on 13 May 2000, Putnam Co. NAMC (MIG 71:57)
- 114 on 12 May 2001, Putnam Co. NAMC (MIG 72:21)
- 112 on 11 May 2002, Putnam Co. NAMC (MIG 73:99)
- 70+ on 28 May 2009, Bark Camp Barrens WMA (MIG 80:90)

High Counts – Fall
- 5 on 18 Sep 2010, Blount Co. FBC (MIG 81:147)
- 3 on 25 Sep 2010, DeKalb Co. FBC (MIG 81:147)

Substantiation: Specimen: LSUMZ, 9668

Emberizidae: Sparrows. Twenty-six species of sparrows have been documented in Tennessee. Ten species are breeding birds with few as permanent residents, while ten species are transients and/or winter residents. Six occur only as vagrants.

Green-tailed Towhee, *Pipilo chlorurus*
Status and Abundance: ***Unsubstantiated***; accidental visitor
Records
(1) 1 on 21-25 Dec 1952, Memphis (Smith 1952)
(2) 1 on 23 Dec 1956, Memphis (MIG 27:73)
(3) 1 on 24 Mar-26 Apr 1957, trapped and banded in Elizabethton (Herndon 1957)

Spotted Towhee, *Pipilo maculates*
Status and Abundance: Accidental visitor
Records
(1) 1 on 20 Dec-28 Apr 1952-53, Shelby Co. (Seahorn 1953)
(2) 1 on 19 Nov 1955, Shelby Co. (MIG 27:16)
(3) 1 on 12-25 Dec 1975, Shelby Co. (MIG 47:45)
(4) 1 on 3 Dec-19 Mar 1976-77, Shelby Co. (MIG 48:45)
(5) 1 on 12 Jan-26 Feb 1978, Reelfoot Lake (MIG 49:41)
(6) 1 on 13 Nov 1988-21 Apr 1989, Dyersburg (MIG 60:83)
(7) 1 on 26 Jan/18 Apr 1992 (possibly same bird), Ensley (JRW, unpubl. data)
(8) 1 on 13 Nov 1993, Ensley (MAG, pers. comm.)
(9) 1 on 12 Apr 1996, Ensley (JRW, unpubl. data)
(10) 1 on 18 Apr 1996, Eagle Lake WMA (MIG 67:61)
(11) 1 on 11-13 Feb 2000, Pace Point (MIG 71:43)
(12) 1 on 17 Feb 2002, Dyer Co. (JRW, unpubl. data)
(13) 1 on 15 Dec 2002, Reelfoot Lake (MAG, pers. comm.)
(14) 1 on 11-23 Jan 2011, Gibson Co. (MIG 82:57)
(15) 1 on 15 Dec 2012, Reelfoot Lake CBC (MIG, in press)
(16) 1 on 20 Dec 2013, Obion Co., (MIG, in press)
(17) 1 on 17-25 Mar 2013, Shelby Co. (DP, pers. comm.)
(18) 1 on 27 Mar 2014, Collierville, Shelby Co. (eBird, photo by Jude Vickery)
Substantiation: Photograph: Wilson, J.R. 1993. "Spotted Towhee". <http://www.pbase.com/ol_coot/image/28466180> Accessed 25 Sep 2014.

Eastern Towhee, *Pipilo erythrophthalmus*

Status and Abundance: Fairly common to common permanent resident
Habitat: Forest edge, shrubby thickets, second growth
High Counts – Spring
    394 on 29 Apr 1962, Knoxville SBC (MIG 33:31)
    248 on 12 May 2007, Putnam Co. NAMC (MIG 78:133)
    238 on 10 May 2008, Putnam Co. NAMC (MIG 79:79)
    166 on 9 May 2009, Hamilton Co. NAMC (MIG 80:111)
    161 on 11 May 2002, Putnam Co. NAMC (MIG 73:100)
High Counts – Fall
    85 on 9 Oct 2010, Nashville FBC (MIG 81:147)
    62 on 30 Sep 2006, Nashville FBC (MIG 78:29)
    61 on 16 Sep 2006, Putnam Co. FBC (MIG 78:22)
    59 on 8 Oct 2005, Nashville FBC (MIG 77:11)
High Counts – Winter
    199 on 2 Jan 2005, Knoxville CBC (MIG 76:67)
    171 on 16 Dec 2006, Chattanooga CBC (MIG 78:66)
    163 on 31 Dec 2005, Knoxville CBC (MIG 77:45)
Substantiation: Specimen: LSUMZ, 77192

Bachman's Sparrow, *Peucaea aestivalis*

Status and Abundance: Uncommon local summer resident
Habitat: Open woods or old fields with interspersion of bare ground and herbaceous cover, generally either adjacent to pine forest or clear-cut areas replanted to pine until understory becomes too thick
Spring Arrival: early Apr
Fall Departure: mid Aug
Comments: Current known distribution is almost exclusively from Ft. Campbell, but individuals are found in other places. Likely more are present on clearcuts managed by timber companies, particularly in the counties of southern middle and west Tennessee, but are not found due to lack of observer effort. Fall migration/departure poorly known.
Early Spring
    4 Mar 1921, Nashville (BNA:40)
    9 Mar 1960, Chattanooga (MIG 31:15)
    11 Mar 1961, Hardeman Co. (MIG 32:4)
Late Fall
    17 Oct 1920, Nashville (BNA:40)
    30 Sep 2011, Lewis Co. (MIG 82:153)
    25 Sep 1970, Elizabethton (MIG 41:89)

15 Sep 2012, Montgomery Co. FBC (MIG 83:144)

High Counts – Spring
15 on 28 May 1988, Hardin Co. (Robinson 1990)

Substantiation: Specimen: LSUMZ, 77321

American Tree Sparrow, *Spizelloides arborea*

Status and Abundance: Rare winter resident; irruptive

Habitat: Shrubby or brushy fields and forest edges; sometimes visits feeders

Spring Departure: mid Mar

Fall Arrival: mid Nov

Comments: Annual in northwest Lake Co.

Late Spring
10 May 2008, Wilson Co. NAMC (MIG 79:77)
8 May 1999, Montgomery Co. NAMC (MIG 70:43)
21 Apr 1990, Greeneville SBC (MIG 61:53)
19 Apr 1996, Jackson (MIG 67:61)

Early Fall
6 Oct 2001, Davidson Co. (MIG 73:14)
19 Oct 1969, Reelfoot Lake (MIG 40:89)
20 Oct 2012, Lewis Co. (MIG 83:151)
23 Oct 1998, Orchard Bog, Johnson Co. (MIG 70:55)
28 Oct 1969, near Roan Mtn. (MIG 40:93)

High Counts – Winter
200 on 17 Jan 1977, Cheatham Co. (MIG 48:48)
68 on 14 Jan 2001, Lake and Dyer Co. (JRW, unpubl. data)
55+ on 26 Dec 1991, Airpark Inn, Reelfoot Lake, Lake Co. (MIG 63:61)
50 on 1 Jan 2001, Hickory-Priest CBC (MIG 72:70)
50 on 10 Feb 2001, Dyer Co. (MIG 72:69)

Substantiation: Specimen: LSUMZ, 7273

Chipping Sparrow, *Spizella passerina*

Status and Abundance: Fairly common transient and summer resident; uncommon winter resident in southern half of state, while nearly absent from northern half of state

Habitat: Open woodlands; yards; thickets and shrubs

High Counts – Spring
270 on 14 May 2005, Putnam Co. NAMC (MIG 76:133)
267 on 10 May 2008, Putnam Co. NAMC (MIG 79:77)
241 on 12 May 2001, Putnam Co. NAMC (MIG 72:21)
201 on 11 May 2002, Putnam Co. NAMC (MIG 73:100)
187 on 12 May 2007, Putnam Co. NAMC (MIG 78:133)

Emberizidae: Sparrows

High Counts – Fall
222 on 4 Oct 2008, White Co. FBC (MIG 80:19)
210 on 19 Sep 2009, Putnam Co. FBC (MIG 81:46)
196 on 20 Sep 2008, Putnam Co. FBC (MIG 80:19)
177 on 24 Sep 2011, Bledsoe Co. FBC (MIG 82:137)
152 on 25 Sep 2010, DeKalb Co. FBC (MIG 81:147)

High Counts – Winter
315 on 4 Jan 2003, Savannah CBC (MIG 74:43)
311 on 1 Jan 2006, Hiwassee CBC (MIG 77:61)
168 on 17 Dec 2005, Chattanooga CBC (MIG 77:61)
132 on 3 Jan 2004, Savannah CBC (MIG 75:61)

Substantiation: Specimen: LSUMZ, 77377

Clay-colored Sparrow, *Spizella pallida*

Status and Abundance: Very rare transient; accidental winter visitor

Records
(1) 1 on 30 Apr-2 May 1933, Johnson City (Tyler 1933)
(2) 1 banded on 17 Oct 1969, near Savannah (Patterson and Patterson 1969)
(3) 1 on 18 Oct 1997, Levee Road, Lake Co. (JRW, unpubl. data)
(4) 1 on 4 May 2002, Tiptonville Ferry Road (MIG 73:57)
(5) 2 on 1 Oct 2002, Standifer Gap Marsh (MIG 74:24)
(6) 1 on 11 Oct 2003, Kyker Bottoms Refuge (MIG 75:32)
(7) 1 on 18 Sep 2004, Blount Co. NAMC (MIG 76:12)
(8) 1 on 10 Oct 2007, Standifer Gap Marsh (MIG 79:27)
(9) 1 on 29 Nov-15 Dec 2008, near Lake Tansi, Cumberland Co. (MIG 80:30)
(10) 1 on 26 Apr 2009, Knox Co. (MIG 80:94)
(11) 1 on 16 Oct 2009, DeKalb Co. (MIG 81:53)
(12) 1 on 18 Dec 2011, Memphis CBC (MIG 83:17)
(13) 1 on 6 Oct 2012, Big Sandy Unit (MIG 83:148)
(14) 1 m (singing) on 11-13 May 2013, Sycamore Shoals SP (MIG, in press)

Substantiation: Specimen: LSUMZ, 77386

Field Sparrow, *Spizella pusilla*

Status and Abundance: Common permanent resident
Habitat: Brushy fields

High Counts – Spring
259 on 10 May 2008, Putnam Co. NAMC (MIG 79:80)
174 on 11 May 2002, Putnam Co. NAMC (MIG 73:100)
174 on 14 May 2005, Putnam Co. NAMC (MIG 76:133)

162 on 8 May 2010, Nashville SBC (MIG 82:9)
149 on 7 May 2005, White Co. SBC (MIG 76:141)
High Counts – Fall
133 on 9 Oct 2010, Nashville FBC (MIG 81:147)
125 on 1 Oct 2011, Nashville FBC (MIG 82:137)
101 on 29 Sep 2012, Nashville FBC (MIG 83:144)
94 on 20 Sep 2008, Putnam Co. FBC (MIG 80:19)
88 on 4 Oct 2008, White Co. FBC (MIG 80:19)
High Counts – Winter
647 on 1 Jan 1983, Hiwassee CBC (MIG 54:14)
617 on 19 Dec 1981, Ashland City CBC (MIG 53:9)
598 on 2 Jan 1993, Savannah CBC (MIG 64:9)
512 on 21 Dec 1941, Memphis CBC (MIG 13:20)
Substantiation: Specimen: LSUMZ, 77394

Vesper Sparrow, *Pooecetes gramineus*
Status and Abundance: Uncommon transient; locally uncommon summer resident in Southern Blue Ridge; rare winter resident
Habitat: Weedy, stubbly, or fallow fields; breeds in grass fields including high elevation balds
Spring Departure: late Apr
Fall Arrival: mid Oct
Comments: Only breeds in the mountains primarily in a few spots on high elevation balds on Roan Mtn., Shady Valley, and other sites in Carter and Johnson Co.
Late Spring
20 May 2004, Ft. Campbell (MIG 75:115)
13 May 2005, Kingston Steam Plant (MIG 76:102)
12 May 2007, Montgomery Co. NAMC (MIG 78:135)
11 May 2002, Lake Co. NAMC (MIG 73:100)
8 May 1988, Lebanon SBC (MIG 60:51)
Early Fall
17 Sep 2011, Blount Co FBC (MIG 82: 137)
18 Sep 1991, Blount Co. (MIG 63:56)
22 Aug 1971, Savannah Bay (MIG 42:95)
High Counts – Spring
41 on 27 Mar 1993, Ensley (JRW, unpubl. data)
23 on 3 Mar 1997, Shady Valley (MIG 68:114)
High Counts – Fall
29 on 8 Nov 2003, Cades Cove (MIG 75:35)
14 on 14 Nov 1999, Williamsport Lakes WMA (MIG 71:35)
11 on 25 Oct 1991, Britton Ford (MIG 63:53)

High Counts – Winter
>   34 on 30 Dec 1998, Savannah CBC (MIG 70:17)
>   25 on 3 Dec 1999, Cross Creeks CBC (MIG 70:17)
>   22 on 4 Jan 2008, Savannah CBC (MIG 79:41)
>   21 on 3 Jan 2004, Savannah CBC (MIG 75:63)
>   20 on 15 Dec 2007, Chattanooga CBC (MIG 79:55)

Substantiation: Specimen: LSUMZ, 77312

Lark Sparrow, *Chondestes grammacus*

Status and Abundance: Rare transient; uncommon local summer resident; rare winter resident

Habitat: Cedar glades; fields or pastures with sparse vegetation

Spring Arrival: mid Apr

Fall Departure: mid Sep

Comments: In Central Hardwoods, found breeding mostly in Wilson and Rutherford Co. Modest numbers can be found across west Tennessee. At least a half dozen winter records, all from Central Hardwoods and Ridge and Valley.

Early Spring
>   9 Mar 1957, Lebanon (MIG 28:9)
>   22 Mar 1980, Knoxville (MIG 51:63)

Late Fall
>   21 Nov 1992, Jefferson Co. (MIG 64:21)
>   9 Nov 1986, Shelby Farms (MIG 58:21)
>   7 Nov 1970, Williamson Co. (MIG 42:20)

High Counts – Spring
>   10 on 7 May 2005, Nashville SBC (MIG 76:141)
>   5 on 13 May 2014, Loop Road, Gibson Co. (MAG, pers. obs.)

High Counts – Summer
>   12 on 9 Jul 1955, Wilson Co. (Ogden 1955)

Substantiation: Specimen: LSUMZ, 77319

Black-throated Sparrow, *Amphispiza bilineata*

Status and Abundance: Accidental visitor

Records
>   (1) 1 on 29 Nov 2005-9 Apr 2006, Elora, Lincoln Co. (Edwards 2012)

Substantiation: Photograph: 1 on 29 Nov 2005-9 Apr 2006, Elora, Lincoln Co. (Edwards 2012:35)

Lark Bunting, *Calamospiza melanocorys*

Status and Abundance: Accidental visitor

Records
>   (1) 1 f on 1-22 Apr 1966, Woodbury, Cannon Co. (McCrary and Wood 1966a)
>   (2) 1 m near Elizabethton, 26 Apr 1980 (MIG 51:64)

Substantiation: Specimen: LSUMZ, 77224

Savannah Sparrow, *Passerculus sandwichensis*

Status and Abundance: Fairly common transient; fairly common to uncommon winter resident; rare local summer resident

Habitat: Grassy, stubbly, or fallow fields

Spring Departure: late May

Fall Arrival: mid Sep

Comments: Rare breeding bird in Tennessee, but small numbers have been found in June and July on Cumberland Plateau, Ridge and Valley and Southern Blue Ridge. One singing bird found 5 Jul 1992, Fayette Co. (MIG 63:96). Nesting documented in Hawkins Co. in 1973 (Alsop 1978) and in Washington Co. in 1987 (MIG 58:146, MIG 74:133). Likely recent nesting in central Cumberland Co. (2009-2013, EL, pers. comm.) and in Washington, Johnson, Greene Co., plus summer records in Hamblen, Carter, and Bledsoe Co.

Late Spring
>   30 May 2000, Greene Co. (MIG 71:93)
>   29 May 2010, Cates Landing (SGS, pers. obs.)
>   29 May 2005, Orchard Bog (MIG 76:104)
>   28 May 1957, Two Jays (BNA:40)

Early Fall
>   11 Sep 1990, Austin Springs (MIG 62:53)

High Counts – Spring
>   101 on 11 May 2002, Lake Co. NAMC (MIG 73:100)
>   94 on 1 May 2005, Lincoln Co. SBC (MIG 76:141)

High Counts – Fall
>   50+ on 31 Oct 2000, Quarry Bog (MIG 72:47)
>   48 on 9 Oct 2010, Nashville FBC (MIG 81:147)
>   44 on 2 Nov 2011, Warren Co. (MIG 82:153)

High Counts – Summer
>   7 on 3 Jul 1991, Doe Valley, Johnson Co. (MIG 63:24)

High Counts – Winter
>   950 on 4 Jan 2003, Savannah CBC (MIG 74:45)
>   735 on 30 Dec 1998, Savannah CBC (MIG 70:17)
>   522 on 18 Dec 2010, Reelfoot Lake CBC (MIG 82:52)

Substantiation: Specimen: LSUMZ, 77223

Emberizidae: Sparrows

Grasshopper Sparrow, *Ammodramus savannarum*
> Status and Abundance: Uncommon to fairly common spring transient and summer resident; uncommon fall transient; rare winter visitor
> Habitat: Grassy fields and meadows; typically with some taller plants (e.g. thistle) for song perches
> Spring Arrival: mid Apr
> Fall Departure: mid Oct
> Comments: Occurs during fall through mid-Oct, but inconspicuous and rarely detected after August.
> Early Spring
>> 31 Mar 1923, Nashville (BNA:40)
>> 1 Apr 2012, Limestone, Washington Co. (MIG 83:72)
>> 2 Apr 1994, Ensley (MIG 65:52)
>> 2 Apr 2012, Duck River Unit (MIG 83:68)
>> 3 Apr 2012, Greene Co. (DMi, pers. comm.)
>
> Late Fall
>> 14 Nov 1988, Nashville (MIG 60:30)
>> 13 Nov 1966, Nashville (Laskey 1966)
>> 13 Nov 1989, Shelby Farms (JRW, unpubl. data)
>> 13 Nov 1993, Ensley (MIG 65:22)
>> 10 Nov 1968, Boone Lake (MIG 40:23)
>
> High Counts – Spring
>> 150 on 10 May 2003, Lake Co. (MIG 74:88)
>> 100+ on 11 May 2002, Lake Co. (MIG 73:58)
>> 60 on 13 May 2000, Lake Co. NAMC (MIG 71:58)
>> 60 on 2 May 1954, Knoxville SBC (MIG 25:33)
>
> High Counts – Fall
>> 28 on 3 Aug 1991, Savannah Bottoms (MIG 63:53)
>
> High Counts – Summer
>> 17 on 21 Jun 2009, Bledsoe Co. (MIG 80:128)
>
> Winter Records
>> 1 on 26 Dec 1955, Reelfoot Lake CBC (MIG 26:63)
>> 1 on 6 Dec 1989, Britton Ford (JRW, unpubl. data)
>> 1 on 14 Dec 1991, Chattanooga CBC (MIG 63:16)
>> 1 on 30 Dec 1994, White Lake WMA (MIG 66:41)
>> 1 on 14 Dec 2009, Bogota WMA (MIG 81:115)
>
> Substantiation: Specimen: LSUMZ, 77262

Henslow's Sparrow, *Ammodramus henslowii*
> Status and Abundance: Rare (locally common) spring transient and locally common summer resident; rare fall transient; accidental winter visitor

Habitat: Fairly dense grassy fields, almost brushy
Spring Arrival: late Mar
Fall Departure: mid Oct
Comments: Breeds locally in the barrens of Coffee Co. and on Ft. Campbell. A moderate sized population bred on the Cumberland Plateau in Cumberland Co. in recent years. Small colonies have also been documented from a number of other counties in the last ten years, but in most cases those colonies did not persist. Becomes inconspicuous after August and fall migration poorly known. First breeding record from Stewart Co. in 1997.
Early Spring
    1 Mar 1970, Memphis (MIG 41:42)
    10 Mar 2007, Maury Co. (MIG 78:102)
    15 Mar 2012, Montgomery Co. (MIG 83:68)
Late Fall
    23 Nov 2002, Shelby Bottoms Park (MIG 74:20)
    22 Nov 1990, Boothspoint Road, Dyer Co. (JRW, unpubl. data)
    10 Nov 2009, Brainerd Levee (MIG 81:57)
    9 Nov 1997, Hamilton Co. (MIG 69:47)
    7 Nov 1994, Shelby Farms (JRW, unpubl. data)
High Counts – Spring
    43 on 30 May 2006, Bark Camp Barrens WMA (MIG 77:144)
    30 on 11 May 2002, Montgomery Co. NAMC (MIG 73:100)
    20 on 25 Apr 2009, Bridgestone-Firestone WMA, White Co. (MIG 80:94)
    17 on 8 May 2004, Montgomery Co. NAMC (MIG 75:101)
    15+ on 10 Apr 2002, Ft. Campbell, Montgomery Co. (MIG 73:60)
High Counts – Fall
    12 on 14 Aug 2012, Ft. Campbell, Montgomery Co. (MIG 83:151)
High Counts – Summer
    97 (76 singing, 21 silent) on 15 Jul 2006, Mayland, Cumberland Co. (MIG 77:147)
    29 on 1 Jun 2006, Bark Camp Barrens WMA (SGS, per. obs.)
Winter Records
    1 on 3 Dec 1988, Ensley (JRW, unpubl. data)
    1 on 30 Dec 1995, Savannah CBC (MIG 67:11)
Substantiation: Photograph: 1 on 1 May 2004, Limestone, Washington Co. (Knight 2008:89)

Le Conte's Sparrow, *Ammodramus leconteii*

Status and Abundance: Rare transient; uncommon winter resident
Habitat: Grassy fields, usually damp or adjacent to wetlands, typically

featuring panacum or similar "blonde" grasses that form mats and drop small seeds underneath

Spring Departure: late Mar

Fall Arrival: late Oct

Comments: Most easily found in Mississippi Alluvial Valley, esp. around Reelfoot Lake, but there is a reasonable chance of finding this species anywhere that its fairly particular habitat requirements are present.

Late Spring
- 21 May 2006, Chickasaw NWR (MIG 77:99)
- 12 May 2007, Blount Co. (MIG 78:136)
- 8 May 1996, Ensley (MIG 67:61)
- 5 May 1998, Black Bayou WMA (MIG 69:163)
- 1 May 2004, Columbia SBC (MIG 75:107)

Early Fall
- 25 Sep 1929, Nashville (Mayfield 1932a)
- 15 Oct 2010, North Treatment Plant, Shelby Co. (MIG 81:155)
- 19 Oct 2002, Shady Valley (MIG 74:27)

High Counts – Fall
- 12 on 20 Nov 1999, Big Sandy Unit (MIG 71:32)
- 11 on 18 Nov 2012, Shelby Farms (MIG 83:148)
- 10+ on 22 Oct 2011, Big Sandy Unit (MIG 82:151)
- 9 on 17 Nov 1989, Shelby Farms (JRW, unpubl. data)
- 6 on 6 Nov 2006, Henry Co. (MIG 78:34)

High Counts – Winter
- 55 on 15 Dec 1991, Memphis CBC (MIG 63:61)
- 28 on 6 Dec 1998, Britton Ford (JRW, unpubl. data)
- 25 on 16 Dec 2012, Memphis CBC (MIG, in press)
- 18 on 18 Dec 2010, Reelfoot Lake CBC (MIG 82:52)
- 14 on 7 Dec 1943, Memphis (MIG 14:77)

Substantiation: Specimen: LSUMZ, 77284

Nelson's Sparrow, *Ammodramus nelsoni*

Status and Abundance: Rare (mostly fall) transient

Habitat: Grassy fields, usually damp or adjacent to wetlands; often in fields that host or could host Le Conte's Sparrows

Spring Arrival: late Apr

Spring Departure: mid May

Fall Arrival: late Sep

Fall Departure: early Nov

Comments: Probably occurs more frequently than records suggest, occupies specialized habitat that is scarce and is not searched frequently.

Early Spring
    19 Mar 2004, Big Sandy Unit (MIG 75:112)
    13 Apr 1979, Alcoa Marsh (MIG 50:71)
    22 Apr 1988, Ensley (JRW, unpubl. data)
Late Spring
    24 May 2001, Quarry Bog (MIG 72:99)
Early Fall
    16 Sep 2014, Proctor City Road, Lake Co. (MAG, pers. comm.)
    25 Sep 1999, near Black Bayou WMA (JRW, unpubl. data)
Late Fall
    5 Dec 1999, Phipps Bend (MIG 71:45)
    13 Nov 1989, Shelby Farms (JRW, unpubl. data)
    12 Nov 1970, Knoxville (MIG 42:21)
    12 Nov 2005, Hatchie NWR (MIG 76:25)
High Counts – Spring
    7 on 11 May 1996, Austin Springs (MIG 67:64)
High Counts – Fall
    4 on 4 Oct 1987, Henry Co. (3) and Stewart Co. (1) (Robinson 1990)
Substantiation: Specimen: LSUMZ, 77290

Fox Sparrow, *Passerella iliaca*
Subspecies: *iliaca*
Status and Abundance: Uncommon transient and winter resident
Habitat: Shrubby fields and forest edge
Spring Departure: late Mar
Fall Arrival: mid Oct
Comments: "Red Fox Sparrow" (*P. i. iliaca*) is the subspecies found here. There is no evidence to suggest that other Fox Sparrow subspecies (which are likely to be split into several species in the next few years) are likely to occur as vagrants here.
Late Spring
    31 May 1976, Lawrence Co. (Williams 1978)
    8 May 1993, Putnam Co. (MIG 64:67)
    7 May 1995, Austin Springs (MIG 66:54)
    30 Apr 1967, Chattanooga SBC (MIG 38:35)
    30 Apr 1989, Murfreesboro SBC (MIG 60:51)
Early Fall
    1 Oct 1965, Knoxville (MIG 36:96)
    4 Oct 1965, Two Jays (MIG 36:94)
High Counts – Fall
    40+ on 5 Nov 2010, Bells Bend (MIG 81:157)
    15 on 27 Nov 2004, Seven Islands Wildlife Refuge (MIG 76:36)

High Counts – Winter
- 186 on 21 Dec 1980, Memphis CBC (MIG 52:14)
- 173 on 26 Dec 1965, Memphis CBC (MIG 36:90)
- 169 on 24 Dec 1939, Memphis CBC (MIG 11:22)
- 71 on 16 Dec 2000, Reelfoot Lake CBC (MIG 72:69)

Substantiation: Specimen: LSUMZ, 6827

Song Sparrow, *Melospiza melodia*

Status and Abundance: Common permanent resident in Cumberland Plateau, Ridge and Valley, Southern Blue Ridge; uncommon summer resident in Central Hardwoods, Southeastern Coastal Plain, Mississippi Alluvial Valley; common transient and winter resident

Habitat: Weedy or shrubby fields; forest edge; yards and other urban and suburban habitats

Comments: Becoming more common in breeding season in Central Hardwoods, Southeastern Coastal Plain, and Mississippi Alluvial Valley.

High Counts – Spring
- 335 on 29 Apr 2001, Elizabethton SBC (MIG 72:31)
- 303 on 30 Apr 2005, Elizabethton SBC (MIG 76:141)
- 295 on 12 May 2001, Putnam Co. NAMC (MIG 72:21)
- 293 on 13 May 2000, Putnam Co. NAMC (MIG 71:59)

High Counts – Fall
- 163 on 5 Oct 2002, Elizabethton FBC (MIG 73:53)
- 107 on 24 Sep 2004, Elizabethton FBC (MIG 76:23)
- 105 on 26 Sep 2009, Elizabethton FBC (MIG 81:46)
- 104 on 30 Sep 2006, Elizabethton FBC (MIG 78:29)

High Counts – Winter
- 1,069 on 4 Jan 2003, Savannah CBC (MIG 74:45)
- 956 on 18 Dec 1982, Knoxville CBC (MIG 54:14)
- 940 on 1 Jan 1988, Hiwassee CBC (MIG 60:19)
- 900 on 1 Jan 1994, Hickory-Priest CBC (MIG 65:19)

Substantiation: Specimen: LSUMZ, 77482

Lincoln's Sparrow, *Melospiza lincolnii*

Status and Abundance: Uncommon transient; rare winter resident
Habitat: Weedy or brushy fields, forest edge, hedgerows
Spring Arrival: mid Apr
Spring Departure: mid May
Fall Arrival: mid Sep
Fall Departure: mid Nov

Late Spring
    28 May 1940, Nashville (BNA:41)
    28 May 1988, Shelby Co. (Robinson 1990)
    21 May 1995, Ensley (JRW, unpubl. data)
Early Fall
    1 Sep 2003, Carver's Gap (MIG 75:35)
    8 Sep 1965, Knoxville (MIG 36:96)
    10 Sep 2012, Whigg Meadow, Monroe Co. (MIG 83:158)
High Counts – Spring
    15 on 28 Apr 2009, Porter's Gap Road, Lauderdale Co. (MT, pers. comm.)
    13+ on 2 May 2000, Shelby Bottoms Park (MIG 71:90)
    8 on 5 May 1996, Ensley (JRW, unpubl. data)
    7 on 29 Apr 1989, Ensley (JRW, unpubl. data)
High Counts – Fall
    8 on 26 Sep 1972, Johnson City (MIG 43:102)
    5 on 15 Oct 1988, Ensley (JRW, unpubl. data)
    5 on 29 Oct 2013, Shady Valley (*fide* RLK)
High Counts – Winter
    4 on 21 Dec 2001, Cross Creeks CBC (MIG 72:120)
    2 on 16 Dec 2004, Cross Creeks CBC (MIG 76:68)
Substantiation: Specimen: LSUMZ, 77443

Swamp Sparrow, *Melospiza georgiana*
Status and Abundance: Common transient and winter resident; accidental summer visitor
Habitat: Marshes and in low grassy or brushy fields, often near water
Spring Departure: mid May
Fall Arrival: late Sep
Late Spring
    30 May 1977, Austin Springs (MIG 48:106)
    21 May 1995, Ensley (JRW, unpubl. data)
Early Fall
    4 Aug 1998, Orchard Bog (MIG 70:55)
    15 Sep 2008, Blount Co. FBC (MIG 79:16)
    18 Sep 2004, Hamilton Co. (MIG 76:36)
    18 Sep 2004, Roane Co. FBC (MIG 76:18)
High Counts – Spring
    162 on 15 Apr 1989, Stewart Co. (MIG 60:87)
High Counts – Fall
    121 on 8 Oct 2005, Nashville FBC (MIG 77:12)
    80 on 26 Oct 1996, Ensley (JRW, unpubl. data)

Summer Records
    1 banded on 1 Jul 1999, Radnor Lake (MIG 70:131)
High Counts – Winter
    1,036 on 4 Jan 2003, Savannah CBC (MIG 74:45)
    502 on 26 Dec 1936, Memphis CBC (MIG 8:8)
Substantiation: Specimen: LSUMZ, 77455

White-throated Sparrow, *Zonotrichia albicollis*

Status and Abundance: Common winter resident and transient; accidental summer visitor

Habitat: Forest undergrowth, forest edges, shrubby or brushy fields, yards and feeders

Spring Departure: late May

Fall Arrival: late Sep

Comments: More than 30 summer records; most are likely individuals that over-summered following the previous winter.

Late Spring
    10 Jun 2005, Nashville (MIG 76:145)
    7 Jun 1992, Davidson Co. (MIG 63:97)
Early Fall
    3 Sep 2004, Carver's Gap (MIG 76:39)
    16 Sep 1959, Nashville (MIG 30:37)
    18 Sep 2004, Greene Co. FBC (MIG 76:18)
    19 Sep 2009, Putnam Co. FBC (MIG 81:46)
    21 Sep 2002, Eagle Lake WMA (MIG 74:17)
High Counts – Spring
    188 on 27 Apr 1997, Shelby Co. SBC (MIG 68:60)
    187 on 26 Apr 1992, Knoxville SBC (MIG 63:50)
    163 on 29 Apr 2001, Knox Co. SBC (MIG 72:31)
    158 on 25 Apr 2004, Knoxville SBC (MIG 75:107)
    155 on 21 Apr 1990, Greeneville SBC (MIG 61:53)
High Counts – Fall
    50 on 9 Oct 2010, Nashville FBC (MIG 81:148)
High Counts – Winter
    2,284 on 26 Dec 1965, Memphis CBC (MIG 36:90)
    1,164 on 17 Dec 1989, Memphis CBC (MIG 61:6)
    1,107 on 20 Dec 1998, Memphis CBC (MIG 70:17)
    1,015 on 21 Dec 1996, Memphis CBC (MIG 68:23)
Substantiation: Specimen: LSUMZ, 77426

Harris's Sparrow, *Zonotrichia querula*

Status and Abundance: Rare transient and winter visitor

Habitat: Brushy thickets and hedgerows
Comments: Often found with White-crowned Sparrows.
Late Spring
    29 May 2006, Union Co. (MIG 77:105)
    8 May 2014, Millington (*fide* SGS)
    6 May 1966, Nashville (MIG 37:21)
    5 May 1999, Gallatin (MIG 70:100)
    3 May 2005 (18 Mar-3 May), Shelby Farms (MIG 76:96)
Early Fall
    30 Oct 1956, Memphis (MIG 28:6)
    6 Nov 1953, Memphis (Coffey 1956)
    6 Nov 1988, McKellar Lake, Shelby Co. (MIG 60:27)
High Counts – Winter
    11 on 26 Dec 1954, Memphis CBC (MIG 25:79)
    2 on 19 Dec 1989-6 Jan 1990, Albany (MIG 61:62)
Substantiation: Specimen: LSUMZ, 77399

White-crowned Sparrow, *Zonotrichia leucophrys*

Subspecies: *leucophrys*
Status and Abundance: Uncommon to fairly common transient and winter resident
Habitat: Brushy fields, thickets and hedgerows; particularly favors multiflora rose thickets
Spring Departure: mid May
Fall Arrival: early Oct
Comments: There are two reports of Gambel's White-crowned Sparrow (*Z. l. gambelii*): one on 9 Jan 2000, Greene Co. (MIG 71:45) and one banded 24 Oct 1989, Austin Springs (*fide* RLK). Adults are readily separable from the nominate subspecies by their pale gray lores (vs. the black lores of the nominate). Immatures are likely not distinguishable in the field.
Late Spring
    1 Jun 1964, Nashville (MIG 35:36)
    31 May 1989, Limestone, Washington Co. (MIG 60:90)
Early Fall
    19 Sep 1959, Nashville (MIG 30:37)
    22 Sep 1982, Austin Springs (MIG 54:26)
    25 Sep 2010, Elizabethton FBC (MIG 81:148)
    26 Sep 2004, Knoxville FBC (MIG 76:23)
High Counts – Spring
    51 on 29 Apr 2001, Elizabethton SBC (MIG 72:31)
    43 on 5 May 1991, Memphis SBC (MIG 62:39)

32 on 29 Apr 1989, Elizabethton SBC (MIG 60:51)
High Counts – Fall
11 on 9 Oct 2010, Nashville FBC (MIG 81:148)
High Counts – Winter
262 on 28 Dec 1985, Clarksville CBC (MIG 57:12)
250 on 13 Feb 1976, Washington Co. (MIG 47:48)
233 on 20 Dec 1998, Memphis CBC (MIG 70:17)
233 on 31 Dec 2000, Bristol CBC (MIG 72:74)
Substantiation: Specimen: LSUMZ, 7375

Golden-crowned Sparrow, *Zonotrichia atricapilla*
Status and Abundance: Accidental visitor
Records
(1) 1 on 11 Nov 2005-17 Jan 2006, Tipton Co. (Kunkel and Kunkel 2012)
Substantiation: Photograph: Todd, M.C. 2005. "Golden-crowned Sparrow". <http://www.pbase.com/mctodd/image/54031888> Accessed 25 Sep 2014.

Dark-eyed Junco, *Junco hyemalis*
Subspecies: *hyemalis* / *carolinensis*
Status and Abundance: Common transient and winter resident; locally common summer resident in Southern Blue Ridge
Habitat: Weedy or brushy fields; forest edge; yards. Nests in high elevations grassy balds and deciduous and coniferous forests
Spring Departure: late Apr
Fall Arrival: early Oct
Comments: Slate-colored Junco (*J. h. hyemalis* group) is the expected subspecies. Oregon Junco (*J. h. oreganus* group) has been reported at least 13 times beginning with a sighting of 4 birds on 10 Mar 1960 in Greene Co. (Darnell 1960); however correct identification of these subspecies is often difficult without the bird in hand (DeVore 1974). A Gray-headed Junco (*J. h. caniceps*) was reported on 24 May 1982, Maury Co. (Anderson 1984). Two White-winged Juncos (*J. h. aikeni*) were reported in Nashville in Jan and Feb 1933 (Laskey 1933). Two Pink-sided Juncos (*J. h. mearnsi*) were reported on 5 Jan 2009, Lewis Co. (MIG 80:69) and 1 on 21 Dec 2012, Carter Co. (NAB 67(2):367).
Late Spring
17 May 1969, Knoxville (MIG 40:70)
13 May 1923, Nashville (BNA:41)
10 May 1997, Walnut Log Road, Lake Co. (JRW, unpubl. data)

Early Fall
- 21 Sep 1997, Memphis (MIG 69:41)
- 23 Sep 1990, Britton Ford (JRW, unpubl. data)
- 24 Sep 1972, Cross Creeks NWR (MIG 43:100)
- 25 Sep 2006, Lewis Co. (MIG 78:36)

High Counts – Spring
- 114 on 26 Apr 1992, Elizabethton SBC (MIG 63:50)
- 93 on 1 May 1994, Elizabethton SBC (MIG 65:35)
- 74 on 24 Apr 2004, Elizabethton SBC (MIG 75:107)

High Counts – Fall
- 150 on 25 Sep 2004, Elizabethton FBC (MIG 76:23)
- 121 on 27 Sep 2003, Elizabethton FBC (MIG 75:18)
- 92 on 5 Oct 2002, Elizabethton FBC (MIG 73:53)
- 81 on 27 Sep 2008, Elizabethton FBC (MIG 80:19)
- 66 on 24 Sep 2005, Elizabethton FBC (MIG 77:12)

High Counts – Winter
- 1,700 on 4 Jan 1976, GSMNP CBC (MIG 47:37)
- 725 on 26 Dec 1992, Buffalo River CBC (MIG 64:9)

Substantiation: Specimen: LSUMZ, 77346

Cardinalidae: Cardinals, Grosbeaks, and Allies.

Eleven species have been documented in Tennessee, with most occurring annually. The recently reclassified *Piranga* tanagers now belong to this family.

Summer Tanager, *Piranga rubra*

Status and Abundance: Fairly common transient and summer resident, except rare to uncommon in Southern Blue Ridge; rare winter visitor

Habitat: Deciduous and mixed forest and forest edge

Spring Arrival: mid Apr

Fall Departure: mid Oct

Comments: At least 15 winter records.

Early Spring
 11 Mar 1966, Hamilton Co. (MIG 37:23)
 4 Apr 1988, Montgomery Co. (Robinson 1990)

Late Fall
 19 Nov-Dec 2006, Hamilton Co. (MIG 78:40)
 16 Nov 1974, Memphis (MIG 46:44)
 7 Nov 1975, Putnam Co. (MIG 47:19)
 5 Nov 1994, Shelby Bottoms Park (MIG 66:23)

High Counts – Spring
 114 on 10 May 2008, Putnam Co. NAMC (MIG 79:79)
 99 on 12 May 2001, Putnam Co. NAMC (MIG 72:21)
 95 on 8 May 2010, Putnam Co. NAMC (MIG 82:23)
 88 on 18 May 2010, DeKalb Co. SBC (MIG 82:9)
 85 on 13 May 2006, Putnam Co. NAMC (MIG 77:137)

High Counts – Fall
 59 on 17 Sep 2005, Shelby Co. FBC (MIG 77:17)
 56 on 16 Sep 2003, Shiloh NP (MIG 75:25)

Substantiation: Specimen: LSUMZ, 77084

Scarlet Tanager, *Piranga olivacea*

Status and Abundance: Fairly common transient; fairly common summer resident in Cumberland Plateau, Ridge and Valley, Southern Blue Ridge; uncommon summer resident in Central Hardwoods; locally uncommon summer resident in Southeastern Coastal Plain, Mississippi Alluvial Valley; accidental winter visitor

Habitat: Mature hardwood forest

Spring Arrival: mid Apr

Fall Departure: mid Oct

Early Spring
 1 Apr 1969, Knoxville (MIG 40:50)

2 Apr 1999, Hamilton Co. (MIG 70:103)
4 Apr 2005, Nashville (MIG 76:99)

Late Spring
8 Jun 2000, Radnor Lake (MIG 71:120)

Late Fall
27 Nov 1974, Nashville (MIG 46:71)
7 Nov 1976, Johnson City (Robinson 1990)

High Counts – Spring
114 on 10 May 2008, Putnam Co. NAMC (MIG 79:79)
110 on 7 May 2011, Cumberland Co. SBC (MIG 82:71)
100 on 7 May 1978, Knoxville SBC (MIG 49:58)
77 on 8 May 2010, Cumberland Co. NAMC (MIG 82:23)
76 on 13 May 2006, Putnam Co. NAMC (MIG 77:137)

High Counts – Fall
29 on 18 Oct 2010, White Co. FBC (MIG 81:148)
29 on 26 Sep 2010, Knoxville FBC (MIG 81:148)
27 on 20 Sep 2008, Putnam Co. FBC (MIG 80:19)
25 on 23 Sep 2006, White Co. FBC (MIG 78:29)
21 on 19 Sep 2009, Putnam Co. FBC (MIG 81:46)

High Counts – Summer
29 on 6 Jun 1993, Frozen Head SP (MIG 64:88)

Substantiation: Specimen: LSUMZ, 7970

Western Tanager, *Piranga ludoviciana*

Status and Abundance: Accidental visitor

Records
(1) 1 ad m on 23-24 Apr 1969, Dyersburg (Hudson 1960)
(2) 1 f on 9 May 1988, Ensley (JRW, unpubl. data)
(3) 1 ad m on 7 Dec 1992-28 Feb 1993, Franklin, Williamson Co. (MIG 64:49, Knight 1996)
(4) 1 on 21 Aug 1994, Dyersburg (Knight 1996)
(5) 1 f on 29 Sep 1998, Hampton, Carter Co. (MIG 70:55)

Substantiation: Photograph: 1 ad m on 7 Dec 1992-28 Feb 1993, Franklin, Williamson Co. (JRW, unpubl. photograph *fide* MAG)

Northern Cardinal, *Cardinalis cardinalis*

Status and Abundance: Common permanent resident

Habitat: Widespread generalist; shrubs, thickets, forest, forest edge, urban and suburban areas

Comments: Abundant breeding bird throughout the state. Occurs in loose flocks of over fifty individuals during winter. Nesting documented into Oct with male feeding fledglings on 7 Oct 2003 at Tremont (MIG

75:35). Rare above 4,000 ft elevation.

High Counts – Spring
    652 on 12 May 2007, Putnam Co. NAMC (MIG 78:135)
    494 on 14 May 2005, Putnam Co. NAMC (MIG 76:133)
    426 on 10 May 2008, Putnam Co. NAMC (MIG 79:80)
    421 on 7 May 2005, Nashville SBC (MIG 76:141)

High Counts – Fall
    343 on 5 Oct 2002, Putnam Co. FBC (MIG 73:53)
    340 on 8 Oct 2005, Nashville FBC (MIG 77:13)
    319 on 16 Sep 2006, Putnam Co. FBC (MIG 78:22)
    319 on 19 Sep 2009, Putnam Co. FBC (MIG 81:46)

High Counts – Winter
    1,008 on 2 Jan 2005, Knoxville CBC (MIG 76:69)
    813 on 17 Dec 1989, Memphis CBC (MIG 61:5)
    797 on 28 Dec 1985, Clarksville CBC (MIG 57:11)
    790 on 26 Dec 1983, Nashville CBC (MIG 55:10)
    704 on 26 Dec 1965, Memphis CBC (MIG 36:90)

Substantiation: Specimen: LSUMZ, 77096

Rose-breasted Grosbeak, *Pheucticus ludovicianus*

Status and Abundance: Fairly common transient; locally common summer resident in Cumberland Plateau, Southern Blue Ridge; rare winter resident

Habitat: Forest

Spring Arrival: mid Apr

Spring Departure: late May

Fall Arrival: early Sep

Fall Departure: late Oct

Early Spring
    16 Mar 1984, Columbia (MIG 55:71)
    18 Mar 2000, Cheatham Co. (MIG 71:90)
    23 Mar 1971, Dyersburg (MIG 42:43)
    1 Apr 1999, Williamson Co. (MIG 70:100)

Late Spring
    10 Jun 1986, Williamson Co. (MIG 57:110)
    7 Jun 1997, Nashville (MIG 68:136)
    31 May 1976, Cannon Co. (MIG 47:100)

Early Fall
    20 Jul 1997, Natchez Trace, Williamson Co. (MIG 68:136)
    19 Aug 1973, Lake Co. (MIG 44:99)
    29 Aug 1976, Two Jays (MIG 48:19)

Late Fall
- 28 Nov 2008, Hamilton Co. (MIG 80:71)
- 24 Nov 1988, Nashville (MIG 60:30)
- 14 Nov 2004, Collierville, Shelby Co. (MIG 76:29)
- 13 Nov 2004, Knox Co. (MIG 76:36)
- 12 Nov 2001, Bluff City (MIG 73:19)

High Counts – Spring
- 59 on 10 May 1997, Montgomery Co. NAMC (MIG 68:59)
- 54 on 30 Apr 1995, Knoxville NAMC (MIG 66:36)

High Counts – Fall
- 621 on 27 Sep 1980, Elizabethton FBC (*fide* RLK)
- 456 on 30 Sep 1990, Elizabethton FBC (MIG 62:54)
- 437 on 28 Sep 1980, Knoxville (MIG 52:26)

High Counts – Winter
- 2 on 27 Dec 1994, Dresden CBC (MIG 65:18)

Substantiation: Specimen: LSUMZ, 7974

Black-headed Grosbeak, *Pheucticus melanocephalus*

Status and Abundance: Accidental visitor

Records
- (1) 1 present mid-winter 1968-24 Apr 1969, Sevierville (Alsop 1969)
- (2) 1 on 19 Jan-1 Mar 1970, Shelby Co. (MIG 41:21)
- (3) 1 on 30 Dec 1973-9 Jan 1974, Murfreesboro (Hettish 1974)
- (4) 1 on 11-15 Jan 1974, Knoxville (MIG 45:24)
- (5) 1 on 2 Jan-21 Apr 1975, Sumner Co. (MIG 46:67)
- (6) 1 on 13-19 Jan 1975, Memphis (MIG 46:44)
- (7) 1 on 15 Mar 1975, Nashville (MIG 46:67)
- (8) 1 on winter period (no date given)-21 Apr 1975, Sumner Co. (MIG 46:67)
- (9) 1 on 25-26 Apr 1981, Chattanooga SBC (MIG 52:66)
- (10) 1 on 20-23 Mar 1986, Baylor School, Hamilton Co. (MIG 63:68)
- (11) 1 on 4 May 1986, Nashville (MIG 57:80)
- (12) 1 on 6 Sep 1987, Lake Co. (MIG 59:32)
- (13) 1 imm m on 30 Sep 1990, Ripshin Lake (MIG 62:54)
- (14) 1 on 3-8 Dec 1990, Sewanee (MIG 62:83)
- (15) 1 on 19 Sep 1992, Raccoon Mtn., Marion Co. (MIG 64:21)
- (16) 1 on 10 Oct 1996, Tipton Co. (MIG 68:27)
- (17) 1 on 27 Sep 1997, Munford (MIG 69:41)
- (18) 1 imm m on 10 Oct 2009, Lake Co. (MIG 81:50)

Substantiation: 1 present mid-winter 1968-24 Apr 1969, Sevierville (MIG 40(3):59)

Blue Grosbeak, *Passerina caerulea*

Status and Abundance: Uncommon to fairly common transient and summer resident; rare winter visitor

Habitat: Shrubby fields and adjacent yards or similar open areas

Spring Arrival: mid Apr

Fall Departure: mid Oct

Comments: Most numerous in Central Hardwoods; generally absent from the higher elevations of Cumberland Plateau and Southern Blue Ridge.

Early Spring
- 24 Mar 1993, Shelby Farms (MIG 64:65)
- 28 Mar 1972, Murfreesboro (MIG 43:51)

Late Fall
- 22 Nov 2001, Monsanto Ponds (MIG 73:14)
- 29 Oct 1995, Shelby Forest SP (MIG 67:20)
- 26 Oct 2002, Wolf River WMA (MIG 74:17)
- 25 Oct 1989, Ensley (JRW, unpubl. data)
- 24 Oct 2004, Knox Co. (MIG 76:36)

High Counts – Spring
- 67 on 1 May 2010, White Co. SBC (MIG 82:9)
- 59 on 12 May 2001, Putnam Co. NAMC (MIG 72:23)
- 53 on 30 Apr 2011, Overton Co. SBC (MIG 82:71)
- 51 on 3 May 2011, White Co. SBC (MIG 82:71)
- 44 on 13 May 2000, Putnam Co. NAMC (MIG 71:59)

High Counts – Fall
- 35 on 20 Sep 2008, Putnam Co. FBC (MIG 80:20)
- 34 on 18 Oct 2010, White Co. FBC (MIG 81:148)
- 22 on 25 Sep 2005, Knoxville FBC (MIG 77:13)

Winter Records
- 1 on 27 Dec 1970, Knoxville CBC (MIG 42:10)

Substantiation: Specimen: LSUMZ, 19668

Lazuli Bunting, *Passerina amoena*

Status and Abundance: Accidental visitor

Records
- (1) 1 f on 3-4 May 1996, Ensley Bottoms (MIG 76:93, Greene 2011)

Substantiation: Photograph: Wilson, J.R. 1996. "Lazuli Bunting". <http://www.pbase.com/ol_coot/image/105172511> Accessed 25 Sep 2014.

Indigo Bunting, *Passerina cyanea*
- Status and Abundance: Common transient and summer resident; rare winter visitor
- Habitat: Second growth, including shrubby or weedy fields, forest edge, light gaps within deciduous forest
- Spring Arrival: mid Apr
- Fall Departure: late Oct
- Comments: Over 35 winter records. Uncommon over 5,000 ft elevation.
- Early Spring
    - 8 Mar 2006, Memphis (MIG 77:99)
    - 14 Mar 2000, Radnor Lake (MIG 71:90)
    - 18 Mar 2004, Millington (MIG 75:112)
    - 19 Mar 1966, Elizabethton (MIG 37:26)
    - 21 Mar 1986, Lawrence Co. (MIG 57:80)
- Late Fall
    - 10 Dec 2003, Shelby Bottoms Park (MIG 75:76)
    - 28 Nov 1989, Washington Co. (MIG 61:19)
    - 13 Nov 1978, Columbia (MIG 50:43)
    - 13 Nov 1997, Putnam Co. (MIG 69:44)
    - 12 Nov 2003, Radnor Lake (MIG 75:28)
- High Counts – Spring
    - 891 on 13 May 2000, Putnam Co. NAMC (MIG 71:59)
    - 829 on 12 May 2001, Putnam Co. NAMC (MIG 72:23)
    - 700 on 10 May 2008, Putnam Co. NAMC (MIG 79:80)
    - 694 on 12 May 2007, Putnam Co. NAMC (MIG 78:135)
    - 656 on 9 May 1998, Putnam Co. NAMC (MIG 69:156)
- High Counts – Fall
    - 432 on 25 Sep 2005, Knoxville FBC (MIG 77:13)
- High Counts – Winter
    - 3 on 22 Dec 1992, Reelfoot Lake CBC (MIG 64:9)
- Substantiation: Specimen: LSUMZ, 77122

Painted Bunting, *Passerina ciris*
- Status and Abundance: Uncommon summer resident; accidental winter visitor
- Habitat: Shrubby thickets, forest edge
- Spring Arrival: late Apr
- Fall Departure: late Sep
- Comments: Breeds almost exclusively in Shelby and Tipton Co., but may occur in other counties along the Mississippi River. Eight records from middle and east Tennessee (Robinson 1990, *fide* RLK).

Early Spring
    11 Apr 2005, Ensley (MIG 76:96)
Late Fall
    15 Oct 1988, Ensley (DS, pers. comm.)
High Counts – Spring
    10 on 31 May 1981, President's Island (MIG 52:96)
High Counts – Winter
    1 ad m on 13 Jan 2007, Knox Co. (MIG 78:83)
Substantiation: Photograph: Somershoe, S.G. 2011. "Painted Bunting". <http://www.pbase.com/shoeman/image/134336840> Accessed 25 Sep 2014.

Dickcissel, *Spiza americana*

Status and Abundance: Uncommon to rare transient and summer resident in Cumberland Plateau, Ridge and Valley, Southern Blue Ridge; uncommon transient and summer resident in Central Hardwoods; fairly common to common transient and summer resident in Southeastern Coastal Plain, Mississippi Alluvial Valley; rare winter resident

Habitat: Shrubby fields, hedgerows adjacent to fields or agricultural areas

Spring Arrival: late Apr

Fall Departure: mid Sep

Comments: Over 50 winter records from across the state. Fall migration poorly known. Very early spring birds could have overwintered.

Early Spring
    1 Mar 2003, Wynnburg, Lake Co. (MIG 74:88)
    21 Mar 1997, Wolf River WMA (MIG 68:108)
    23 Mar 1998, Nashville (MIG 69:165)
    7 Apr 1989, Chattanooga (MIG 60:90)
    7 Apr 1990, Clarksville (MIG 61:74)
Late Fall
    19 Sep 2009, Putnam Co. FBC (MIG 81:46)
High Counts – Spring
    687 on 12 May 2001, Lake Co. NAMC (MIG 72:22)
    460 on 11 May 2002, Lake Co. NAMC (MIG 73:100)
    620 on 10 May 2003, Lake Co. NAMC (MIG 74:119)
    612 on 6 May 1970, Memphis SBC (MIG 41:38)
    556 on 13 May 2000, Lake Co. NAMC (MIG 71:58)
Substantiation: Specimen: LSUMZ, 77140

Icteridae: Blackbirds and Orioles.
This diverse group is represented by 15 species, of which five are vagrants.

Bobolink, *Dolichonyx oryzivorus*
- Status and Abundance: Fairly common spring transient; uncommon (east) to rare (west) fall transient; rare summer resident
- Habitat: Grasslands and weedy fields
- Spring Arrival: late Apr
- Spring Departure: late May
- Fall Arrival: late Aug
- Fall Departure: early Oct
- Comments: Breeds locally in Washington Co. (1998-2013) (Knight 2007a). Bred in Shady Valley in 1962 (Dubke 1963a). Likely bred at Ft. Campbell in 2003 (MIG 74:131).
- Early Spring
  - 12 Apr 1964, Bush Lake (MIG 35:36)
  - 18 Apr 1992, Ensley (JRW, unpubl. data)
- Late Spring
  - 10 Jun 1988, Cross Creeks NWR (MIG 59:126)
  - 5 Jun 1990, Gibson Co. (MIG 62:24)
  - 31 May 1988, Lake Co. (Robinson 1990)
- Early Fall
  - 6 Aug 1988, Tennessee NWR (Robinson 1990)
  - 9 Aug 1967, Amnicola Marsh (MIG 38:67)
- Late Fall
  - 12 Nov 1956, Elizabethton (MIG 28:13)
  - 7 Nov 1998, Shady Valley (MIG 70:55)
  - 6 Nov 2000, Kingston Steam Plant (MIG 72:45)
  - 29 Oct 1995, Shelby Forest SP (MIG 67:20)
  - 25 Oct 1987, Cross Creeks NWR (MIG 59:37)
- High Counts – Spring
  - 2,000 on 15 May 1950, Memphis (MIG 21:50)
  - 2,000 on 30 Apr 1994, Ensley (JRW, unpubl. data)
  - 685 on 8 May 1999, Shelby Co. NAMC (MIG 70:43)
  - 570 on 14 May 1994, Ensley (MIG 65:52)
  - 500+ on 3 May 2000, Lake Co. (MIG 73:58)
- High Counts – Fall
  - 575 on 27 Sep 2008, Shady Valley (MIG 80:33)
  - 500 on 29 Sep 2002, Greene Co. (MIG 74:24)
  - 150+ on 7 Sep 2012, Eagle Bend Fish Hatchery (MIG 83:155)

Icteridae: Blackbirds and Orioles

Winter Records
   1 on 20-28 Dec 2003, Putnam Co. CBC (Hawkins et al. 2005)
Substantiation: Specimen: LSUMZ, 76949

Red-winged Blackbird, *Agelaius phoeniceus*
Status and Abundance: Common permanent resident
Habitat: Weedy fields, marshes, and early successional forest, often near water
Comments: Less common during winter, esp. in upper east Tennessee.
High Counts – Spring
   2,006 on 13 May 2000, Lake Co. NAMC (MIG 71:58)
   895 on 8 May 2004, Lake Co. NAMC (MIG 75:101)
   886 on 21 Apr 1990, Greeneville SBC (MIG 61:53)
   678 on 30 Apr 2005, Elizabethton SBC (MIG 76:141)
   668 on 14 May 2005, Putnam Co. NAMC (MIG 76:133)
High Counts – Fall
   926 on 26 Sep 2010, Knoxville FBC (MIG 81:148)
   423 on 26 Sep 2009, Greeneville FBC (MIG 81:47)
High Counts – Winter
   5,000,000 on 30 Dec 1958, Reelfoot Lake CBC (MIG 30:16)
   1,002,032 on 20 Dec 1998, Memphis CBC (MIG 70:17)
   1,000,000 on 30 Dec 2000, Jackson CBC (MIG 72:69)
Substantiation: Specimen: LSUMZ, 76977

Eastern Meadowlark, *Sturnella magna*
Status and Abundance: Fairly common permanent resident
Habitat: Grassy fields, pastures, roadsides in agricultural areas
Comments: Irregular on high elevation grassy balds (e.g. Roan Mtn.)
High Counts – Spring
   754 on 22 Apr 1967, Nashville SBC (MIG 38:35)
   680 on 30 Apr 1972, Knoxville SBC (MIG 43:47)
   369 on 1 May 2010, White Co. SBC (MIG 82:9)
   288 on 11 May 2002, Putnam Co. NAMC (MIG 73:100)
High Counts – Fall
   402 on 4 Oct 2008, White Co. FBC (MIG 80:20)
   140 on 4 Oct 2009, White Co. FBC (MIG 81:47)
   92 on 1 Oct 2005, White Co. FBC (MIG 77:13)
High Counts – Winter
   660 on 21 Dec 1975, Memphis CBC (MIG 47:37)
   422 on 4 Jan 2003, Savannah CBC (MIG 74:45)
   401 on 2 Jan 1993, Savannah CBC (MIG 64:9)
   369 on 29 Dec 1994, Buffalo River CBC (MIG 66:16)

349 on 30 Dec 2009, Savannah CBC (MIG 81:97)

Substantiation: Specimen: LSUMZ, 6678

Western Meadowlark, *Sturnella neglecta*

Status and Abundance: Rare late fall and spring transient and winter resident in Mississippi Alluvial Valley and western portions of the Southeastern Coastal Plain; accidental summer resident in Mississippi Alluvial Valley

Habitat: Grassy fields, pastures, roadsides in agricultural areas

Spring Departure: mid Apr

Fall Arrival: late Oct

Comments: One nesting record at Shelby Farms on 20 May 1951 (Smith 1951). Two middle Tennessee records from Cross Creeks NWR in 1988 (MIG 59:99) and Putnam Co. in 2009 (MIG 80:69) and one record for east Tennessee in Knox Co. in 1959 (Robinson 1990).

Late Spring

26 May 1956, Shelby Farms (Robinson 1990)

8 May 1983, Reelfoot Lake SBC (MIG 54:54)

Early Fall

15 Oct 1955, Shelby Farms (MIG 27:16)

17 Oct 1971, Shelby Co. (MIG 42:91)

High Counts – Fall

7 on 31 Oct 1998, Ensley (JRW, unpubl. data)

6 on 28 Nov 1996, Dyer Co. (JRW, unpubl. data)

3 on 21 Nov 2004, Lake Co. (MIG 76:29)

High Counts – Winter

37 on 22 Feb 2013, near Bogota WMA (MIG, in press)

21 on 21 Dec 1996, Reelfoot Lake CBC (MIG 68:23)

21 on 6 Dec 1992, Ensley (JRW, unpubl. data)

19 on 1 Jan 2009, Black Bayou Refuge (MIG 80:67)

18 on 26 Feb 1956, Shelby Farms (MIG 27:16)

Substantiation: Specimen: LSUMZ, 8993

Yellow-headed Blackbird, *Xanthocephalus xanthocephalus*

Status and Abundance: Accidental visitor

Spring Departure: late Apr

Fall Arrival: early Dec

Comments: Over 30 records. Most records occur from December and April.

Late Spring

15 May 2000, Radnor Lake (MIG 71:90)

3 May 1975, Memphis (Coffey 1975)

3 May 2005, Shelby Farms (MIG76:96)
2 May 1995, Ensley (JRW, unpubl. data)
Early Fall
14 Aug 2002, Rankin Bottoms (MIG 74:25)
31 Aug 1991, Ensley (MIG 63:54)
18-24 Sep 1990, Limestone, Washington Co. (MIG 62:53)
23 Sep 2003, Shelby Farms (MIG 75:25)
High Counts – Spring
3 on 5 Apr 1991, Ensley (JRW, unpubl. data)
High Counts – Winter
2 on 18 Dec 2011, Memphis CBC (MIG 83:17)
Substantiation: Photograph: 1 on 29 Apr 2012, Standifer Gap Marsh (NAB 66(3):499)

Rusty Blackbird, *Euphagus carolinus*
Status and Abundance: Uncommon to fairly common transient and winter resident.
Habitat: Forests (particularly near wet areas); forested swamps; pastures and open agricultural fields
Spring Departure: mid Apr
Fall Arrival: late Oct
Comments: Populations declining rapidly in last 25 years. Rarely seen in large flocks anymore.
Late Spring
23 May 1967, Chattanooga (MIG 38:52)
23 May 1983, Nashville (MIG 54:63)
16 May 1998, Memphis (MIG 69:163)
Early Fall
19 Sep 2009, Blount Co. FBC (MIG 81:47)
26 Sep 1965, Knoxville (MIG 36:96)
9 Oct 2004, White Co. (MIG 76:31)
12 Oct 1968, Reelfoot Lake (MIG 39:89)
High Counts – Spring
500+ on 1 Mar 2009, Washington Co. (MIG 80:94)
107 on 8 Apr 1990, Shady Valley (MIG 61:79)
High Counts – Fall
500 on 28 Oct 2008, Paddle Creek, Sullivan Co. (MIG 80:30)
200 on 4 Nov 2002, Holston Valley (MIG 74:27)
22 on 9 Nov 2009, Washington Co. (MIG 81:57)
High Counts – Winter
240,000 on 30 Dec 1976, Columbia CBC (MIG 48:33)
3,000 on 18 Dec 1983, Knoxville CBC (MIG 55:10)

3,000 on 30 Dec 2000, Jackson CBC (MIG 72:69)
1,819 on 28 Dec 1985, Clarksville CBC (MIG 57:12)
Substantiation: Specimen: LSUMZ, 77010

Brewer's Blackbird, *Euphagus cyanocephalus*
Status and Abundance: Rare transient and winter resident in Central Hardwoods, Cumberland Plateau, Ridge and Valley, Southern Blue Ridge; uncommon transient and winter resident in Southeastern Coastal Plain, Mississippi Alluvial Valley
Habitat: Pastures and open agricultural fields, barnyard feedlots
Spring Departure: late Mar
Fall Arrival: mid Nov
Late Spring
19 Apr 1974, Carter Co. (MIG 45:80)
18 Apr 1959, near Nashville (BNA:42)
9 Apr 2006, Greene Co. (MIG 77:105)
Early Fall
27 Oct 1956, Memphis (MIG 28:6)
High Counts – Fall
200 on 24 Nov 2009, Black Bayou Refuge (MIG 81:50)
High Counts – Winter
3,500 on 30 Dec 2000, Jackson CBC (MIG 72:69)
1,500 on 21 Dec 2001, Jackson CBC (MIG 72:121)
350 on 3 Jan 2010, Jackson CBC (MIG 82:52)
300 on 15 Jan 1972, Carroll Co. (MIG 43:23)
256 on 18 Dec 2004, Reelfoot Lake CBC (MIG 76:69)
Substantiation: Photograph: Todd, M.C. 2014 "Brewer's Blackbird". <http://www.pbase.com/mctodd/image/154099552> Accessed 25 Sep 2014.

Common Grackle, *Quiscalus quiscula*
Status and Abundance: Common permanent resident
Habitat: Forest edge and second growth, particularly near water; sometimes in pastures and open agricultural fields
High Counts – Spring
1,600,000 on 29 Apr 1979, Knoxville SBC (MIG 50:59)
High Counts – Fall
1,412 on 29 Sep 2001, Davidson Co. FBC (MIG 73:33)
903 on 26 Sep 2004, Knoxville FBC (MIG 76:23)
High Counts – Winter
3,300,000 on 28 Dec 1974, Bristol CBC (Knight 2008)
2,500,000 on 22 Dec 1957, Memphis CBC (MIG 28:66)

2,000,000 on 27 Dec 2014, Murfreesboro CBC (SGS, pers. obs.)
2,000,000 on 29 Dec 1984, Murfreesboro CBC (MIG 56:9)
420,603 on 18 Dec 2004, Reelfoot Lake CBC (MIG 76:69)
Substantiation: Specimen: LSUMZ, 77038

Great-tailed Grackle, *Quiscalus mexicanus*
Status and Abundance: Accidental visitor
Records
(1) 2 on 3 Aug 2000, Great River Road, Dyer/Lake Co. line (JRW, unpubl. photograph)
(2) 1 ad m on 18 Aug 2002, Island 13 (MIG 74:17)
Substantiation: Photograph: 2 on 3 Aug 2000, Great River Road, Dyer/Lake Co. line (JRW, unpubl. photograph *fide* MAG)

Shiny Cowbird, *Molothrus bonariensis*
Status and Abundance: Accidental visitor
Records
(1) 1 m on 6-21 Jul 1995, President's Island (Gardler 1997, MIG 66:66)
Substantiation: Photograph: 1 m on 6-21 Jul 1995, President's Island (NAB 49(5))

Brown-headed Cowbird, *Molothrus ater*
Status and Abundance: Common permanent resident
Habitat: Open forest and forest edge; pastures and open agricultural fields; urban and suburban areas
Comments: Less common during winter, when it is sometimes absent from large regions of the state.
High Counts – Spring
272 on 14 May 2005, Putnam Co. NAMC (MIG 76:133)
245 on 10 May 2008, Putnam Co. NAMC (MIG 79:80)
243 on 7 May 2005, Nashville SBC (MIG 76:142)
232 on 11 May 2002, Shelby Co. NAMC (MIG 73:101)
High Counts – Fall
220 on 10 Oct 2009, Wilson Co. FBC (MIG 81:47)
High Counts – Winter
500,000 on 28 Dec 1962, Reelfoot Lake CBC (MIG 33:70)
150,000 on 28 Dec 1974, Bristol CBC (Knight 2008)
150,000 on 30 Dec 2000, Jackson CBC (MIG 72:69)
50,000 on 23 Dec 1923, Nashville CBC (Walker 1932)
Substantiation: Specimen: LSUMZ, 77066

Orchard Oriole, *Icterus spurius*

Status and Abundance: Fairly common spring and early fall transient and summer resident

Habitat: Semi-open areas with scattered trees (including yards); forest edge

Spring Arrival: mid Apr

Fall Departure: late Aug

Early Spring
- 25 Mar 2007, Reelfoot Lake, Lake Co. (MIG 78:100)
- 2 Apr 1945, Memphis (MIG 16:11)
- 2 Apr 1951, Lebanon (MIG 22:28)

Late Fall
- 28 Nov 1971, Davidson Co. (MIG 43:25)
- 6 Oct 2007, Rutherford Co. (MIG 79:23)
- 30 Sep 1978, Elizabethton FBC (Robinson 1990)
- 28 Sep 2008, Knoxville FBC (MIG 80:20)
- 26 Sep 1974, Memphis (MIG 46:19)

High Counts – Spring
- 253 on 8 May 2004, Lake Co. NAMC (MIG 75:101)
- 128 on 13 May 2000, Lake Co. NAMC (MIG 71:58)
- 117 on 22 Apr 1967, Nashville SBC (MIG 38:35)
- 105 on 30 Apr 2011, Overton Co. SBC (MIG 82:71)
- 101 on 12 May 2001, Putnam Co. NAMC (MIG 72:23)

High Counts – Fall
- 13 on 7 Aug 2004, Duck River Unit (MIG 76:31)

Substantiation: Specimen: LSUMZ, 76995

Hooded Oriole, *Icterus cucullatus*

Subspecies: *nelsoni*?

Status and Abundance: Accidental visitor

Habitat:

Comments: One record of an adult male on 8-14 Jul 2011 near Elora, Lincoln Co. Photographs suggest the western subspecies *nelsoni*. The TBRC rejected this record on the basis of uncertain provenance. The authors disagree. There are a number of records of vagrants of this species in eastern North America. While it is true that none (that we have found) are from mid-summer, there was no evidence of cage wear, nor any other evidence suggesting non-natural origin. Thus, in our opinion, the better decision is to treat this individual as wild, as we have done here.

Icteridae: Blackbirds and Orioles

Records
(1) 1 ad m on 8-14 Jul 2011, near Elora, Lincoln Co. (TBRC report, photos)
Substantiation: Photograph: 1 ad m on 8-14 Jul 2011, near Elora, Lincoln Co. (NAB 65(4):715)

Bullock's Oriole, *Icterus bullockii*
Status and Abundance: *Unsubstantiated*; accidental visitor
Records
(1) 1 f on 17 Dec 1983, Murfreesboro (Witt 1986)
(2) 1 ad m on 3 Dec 1994 into 1995, Nashville (Knight 1996)

Baltimore Oriole, *Icterus galbula*
Status and Abundance: Fairly common to uncommon spring and early fall transient in Central Hardwoods, Cumberland Plateau, Ridge and Valley, Southern Blue Ridge; fairly common spring and early fall transient in Southeastern Coastal Plain, Mississippi Alluvial Valley; uncommon summer resident; rare winter visitor
Habitat: Semi-open areas with tall scattered trees; riparian forest and forest edge; prefers sycamore and cottonwood trees
Spring Arrival: mid Apr
Fall Departure: late Sep
Comments: Irregular winter visitor with over 45 records. Early spring records could be birds that overwintered nearby.
Early Spring
19 Mar 1966, Elizabethton (MIG 37:26)
19 Mar 2005, Sullivan Co. (MIG 76:102)
8 Apr 1929, Nashville (BNA:42)
Late Fall
8 Nov 1968, Nashville (BNA:42)
4 Nov 1977, Dyersburg (MIG 49:41)
27 Oct 2002, Kyker Bottoms WMA (MIG 74:25)
High Counts – Spring
281 on 8 May 2004, Lake Co. NAMC (MIG 75:101)
254 on 13 May 2000, Lake Co. NAMC (MIG 71:58)
100 on 14 May 2005, Lake Co. (MIG 76:96)
High Counts – Fall
17+ on 31 Aug 2004, Shelby Bottoms Park (MIG 76:31)
16 on 5 Sep 2002, Shelby Bottoms Park (MIG 74:20)
15 on 7 Sep 2000, Radnor Lake (MIG 72:41)
Substantiation: Specimen: LSUMZ, 77000

Fringillidae: Finches and Allies. Nine species have been documented in Tennessee, of which three are very uncommon to extremely rare, while the others are permanent residents and/or found statewide in the appropriate season.

Pine Grosbeak, *Pinicola enucleator*
   Status and Abundance: *Unsubstantiated*; accidental visitor
   Comments: This record was accepted by the TBRC on the basis of written documentation. However, in the opinion of the authors, the published description does not eliminate the possibility of White-winged Crossbill. Because of that, and because of the otherwise extraordinary nature of this record, the authors question its accuracy, but include it here on account of its acceptance by the TBRC.
   Records
      (1) 4 on 28 Mar 1992, Eagle Creek, Tennessee NWR, Benton Co. (Masters et al. 1994, Knight 1993)

House Finch, *Haemorhous mexicanus*
   Status and Abundance: Common permanent resident; introduced
   Habitat: Forest edge, shrubby fields, urban and suburban areas, regularly frequents bird feeders
   Comments: Species has become established across entire state since the first state record in Greeneville in 1972 (Holt 1972). First record in Mississippi Alluvial Valley was on 4 Dec 1979, Shelby Co. (MIG 51:38).
   High Counts – Spring
      176 on 9 May 1992, Chattanooga SBC (MIG 63:50)
      143 on 1 May 1994, Elizabethton SBC (MIG 65:35)
   High Counts – Fall
      1,500 on 28 Oct 1989, Ensley (JRW, unpubl. data)
      1,200 on 13 Nov 1993, Ensley (JRW, unpubl. data)
      600 on 15 Nov 1998, President's Island (JRW, unpubl. data)
   High Counts – Winter
      714 on 2 Jan 1993, Savannah CBC (MIG 64:9)
      619 on 2 Jan 1989, Greeneville CBC (MIG 60:19)
      470 on 21 Dec 1992, Cookeville CBC (MIG 64:9)
      419 on 28 Dec 1985, Lebanon CBC (MIG 57:12)
   Substantiation: Specimen: CSM, F88-3

Purple Finch, *Haemorhous purpureus*
   Status and Abundance: Uncommon to fairly common transient and winter

resident; accidental summer visitor

Habitat: Forest and forest edge; also frequents bird feeders

Spring Departure: mid May

Fall Arrival: mid Oct

Comments: Irruptive species. Summer records only exist from Roan Mtn.: 1-15 Jul 1962 (Behrend 1962); 12 May-7 Jul 1963 (Behrend 1963); 16-19 Jun 1977 (MIG 48:107).

Late Spring
- 10 Jun 1993, Coffee Co. (MIG 64:87)
- 24 May 2005, DeKalb Co. (MIG 76:99)
- 23 May 1986, Johnson City (MIG 57:86)

Early Fall
- 20 Sep 1970, Elizabethton (MIG 41:89)
- 20 Sep 1975, White Co. (MIG 47:19)

High Counts – Spring
- 13 on 21 Apr 1990, Greeneville SBC (MIG 61:53)
- 13 on 3 Mar 2002, Brunswick, Shelby Co. (MIG 73:58)
- 9 on 9 Apr 2005, Henry Co. (MIG 76:96)

High Counts – Fall
- 17 on 5 Nov 2010, Nashville (MIG 81:157)

High Counts – Winter
- 533 on 17 Dec 1977, Lebanon CBC (MIG 49:8)
- 75 on 16 Feb 2002, Big Eagle Recreation Area, Henry Co. (JRW, unpubl. data)
- 62 on 20 Dec 2008, Cookeville CBC (MIG 80:54)

Substantiation: Specimen: LSUMZ, 77155

Red Crossbill, *Loxia curvirostra*

Status and Abundance: Rare permanent resident in Southern Blue Ridge; rare transient, summer and winter visitor; irruptive

Habitat: Spruce, hemlock, and pine forest

Spring Departure: early Apr

Fall Arrival: mid Nov

Comments: This is an interesting and somewhat enigmatic species in Tennessee for several reasons. Nesting has been suspected (if not confirmed) in GSMNP and Roan Mtn. (Knight 2010). They may be found at GSMNP and Roan Mtn. in any month, but are rarely found west of the eastern mountains. Scattered June and July records from Mississippi Alluvial Valley to Cumberland Plateau (Robinson 1990). Ten adults and two begging fledglings seen in Germantown, Shelby Co. on 23-26 May 1991 (Peeples 1991). Most Red Crossbills in Tennessee are likely Type 1, although the authors know of only one individual song that has been recorded and confirmed as Type 1 (DK, pers. comm.)

Late Spring
    24 May 2013, Van Buren Co. (MIG, in press)
    14 May 1985, Cumberland Co. (MIG 56:81)
    14 May 2006, Bristol (MIG 77:105)
    14 Apr 1974, Davidson Co. (MIG 45:76)
    14 Apr 1974, Williamson Co. (MIG 45:76)

Early Fall
    8 Aug 1981, Nashville (MIG 53:17)

High Counts – Spring
    11 on 9 Apr 1989, Ft. Campbell, Montgomery Co. (MIG 60:87)

High Counts – Fall
    20 on 27 Sep 1989, GSMNP (JRW, unpubl. data)

High Counts – Summer
    80+ on 16 Jun 2000, Roan Mtn. (Knight 2010)
    20 on 10 Jun 2004, Roan Mtn. (MIG 75:162)

High Counts – Winter
    275 on 28 Dec 1969, GSMNP CBC (MIG 41:9)
    159 on 27 Dec 1998, GSMNP CBC (MIG 70:18)
    130 on 29 Dec 2002, Cades Cove CBC (MIG 74:44)

Substantiation: Specimen: LSUMZ, 82372

White-winged Crossbill, *Loxia leucoptera*

Status and Abundance: Accidental transient and winter visitor; irruptive

Habitat: Spruce, hemlock, and fir forest

Comments: First state record on 26 Dec 1954, Memphis (MIG 25:74). Most frequently found on Roan Mtn. Few records away from the eastern mountains. More frequent before the 1980s, accidental now. One record since 1997: 1 on 20 Nov 2012, Bristol (MIG 83:156).

Late Spring
    5 Jun 1966, Roan Mtn. (MIG 37:56)
    25 May 1970, Roan Mtn. (MIG 41:72)

Early Fall
    28 Nov 1977, Martin, Weakley Co. (MIG 49:41)
    20 Nov 2012, Bristol (MIG, in press)
    5 Nov 1975, Etowah, McMinn Co. (MIG 47:48)

High Counts – Winter
    210 on 29 Dec 1965, Roan Mtn. CBC (MIG 36:92)
    20 on 29 Dec 1989, Roan Mtn. CBC (MIG 61:6)

Substantiation: Specimen: LSUMZ, 77183

Common Redpoll, *Acanthis flammea*
Subspecies: *flammea*
Status and Abundance: Accidental visitor
Habitat: Typically associated with large flocks of American Goldfinches or Pine Siskins
Comments: Most (all?) appear to be attributable to the nominate subspecies *flammea*.
High Counts – Winter
  5 on 2 Jan 1966, GSMNP CBC (MIG 36:90)
Records
  (1) 1 on winter 1933-34, Johnson City (Tyler and Lyle 1934)
  (2) 1 on 14 Dec 1965, GSMNP (DeFoe 1966)
  (3) 5 on 2 Jan 1966, GSMNP CBC (MIG 36:90)
  (4) 1 on 29 Dec 1968, Knoxville CBC (MIG 39:78)
  (5) 1 on 10 Jan 1969, Knox Co. (Alsop and Wallace 1970)
  (6) 1 on 9 Jan-11 Mar 1978, Nashville (MIG 49:43
  (7) 1 on 10 Nov 1981, Clarksville (MIG 53:17)
  (8) 1 on 21 Jan 1985, Stewart Co. (MIG 56:53)
  (9) 1 on 20 Dec 1985-14 Mar 1986, Franklin Co. (MIG 57:62)
  (10) 1 on 5 Jan 1986, Washington Co. (MIG 58:30)
  (11) 1 on 19 Jan 1994, Erwin (MIG 65:45)
  (12) 1 on 31 Dec 1995, Holston Mtn., Sullivan Co. (MIG 67:35)
  (13) 2 on early Feb through 23 Feb 1996, Greene Co. (MIG 67:33)
  (14) 1 on 23 Jan-25 Feb 2000, Shady Valley (MIG 71:46)
  (15) 1 on 9 Jan-16 Feb 2007, Munford (MIG 78:79)
  (16) 1 on 18 Feb-9 Mar 2007, Hohenwald, Lewis Co. (MIG 78:102, MIG 78:80, Edwards 2012)
  (17) 1 on 8-20 Feb 2012, Nashville (MIG 83:23)
  (18) 1 on 13-22 Feb 2012, Pleasantville, Perry Co. (MIG 83:23)
  (19) 1 on 29 Dec 2012, Antioch, Henry Co. (MIG, in press)
  (20) 1 on 17 Jan 2013, Obion Co. (MIG, in press)
Substantiation: Photograph: Todd, M.C. 2007. "Common Redpoll". <http://www.pbase.com/mctodd/image/74636822> Accessed 15 Dec 2014.

Pine Siskin, *Spinus pinus*
Status and Abundance: Uncommon transient and winter resident; rare summer resident; irruptive
Habitat: Weedy and brushy fields, forest and forest edge, suburban areas at feeders
Spring Departure: mid May

Fall Arrival: mid Oct

Comments: Nesting documented on Roan Mtn. where this species is a summer resident (Trently and Biller 2008, Knight 2010a). A pair nested (4 young) on Clingman's Dome, just yards into North Carolina, from 25 May-19 Jun 2013 (MIG, in press). Other summer records may be of undocumented breeding birds or over-summering birds.

Late Spring
    8 Jun 1984, Anderson Co. (MIG 55:95)
    6 Jun 1984, Memphis (MIG 55:88)
    31 May 1987, Wilson Co. (MIG 58:99)

Early Fall
    9 Sep 2002, Hawkins Co. (MIG 74:25)
    16 Sep 2005, Smithville (MIG 76:26)
    18 Sep 1968, Hamilton Co. (MIG 39:95)
    3 Oct 1987, Tennessee NWR (MIG 59:38)

High Counts – Spring
    750+ on 7 May 2000, Roan Mtn. (MIG 71:95)
    500 on 15 Mar 2009, Marion Co. (MIG 80:94)
    235 on 16 Apr 1988, Greeneville SBC (MIG 60:51)
    214 on 29 Apr 1990, Knoxville SBC (MIG 61:53)

High Counts – Fall
    200 on 7 Nov 1993, Hampton, Carter Co. (MIG 65:27)
    119 on 12 Nov 2012, Munford (MIG 83:148)
    60 on 13 Sep 2008, Roan Mtn. (MIG 80:33)

High Counts – Summer
    24 on 13 Jun 1992, Carter Co. (*fide* RLK)
    21 on 19 Jun 1999, Carter Co. (*fide* RLK)
    20 on 30 Jun 2008, Mt. LeConte (MIG 79:101)
    18 on 4 Jun 2011, Carter Co. (*fide* RLK)

High Counts – Winter
    4,813 on 2 Jan 1966, GSMNP CBC (MIG 36:90)
    2,800 on 29 Dec 1963, GSMNP CBC (MIG 34:85)
    1,820 on 20 Dec 1987, Roan Mtn. CBC (MIG 59:8)
    1,387 on 19 Dec 1987, Elizabethton CBC (MIG 59:8)

Substantiation: Specimen: LSUMZ, 77169

American Goldfinch, *Spinus tristis*

Status and Abundance: Common permanent resident

Habitat: Weedy and brushy fields, forest and forest edge, suburban areas at feeders

High Counts – Spring
    2,000 on 22 Apr 1978, Highland Rim SBC (MIG 49:58)

1,197 on 24 Apr 1971, Nashville SBC (MIG 42:39)
1,120 on 3 Jan 1987, Nickajack Lake CBC (MIG 58:5)

High Counts – Fall
339 on 25 Sep 2004, Elizabethton FBC (MIG 76:23)
248 on 15 Sep 2008, Putnam Co. FBC (MIG 79:16)
215 on 20 Sep 2008, Putnam Co. FBC (MIG 80:20)
201 on 9 Oct 2010, Nashville FBC (MIG 81:148)

High Counts – Winter
475 on 3 Jan 2009, Knoxville CBC (MIG 80:55)
465 on 26 Dec 2008, Kingsport CBC (MIG 80:55)
430 on 28 Dec 2008, Bristol CBC (MIG 80:54)
377 on 2 Jan 2005, Knoxville CBC (MIG 76:69)

Substantiation: Specimen: LSUMZ, 77173

Evening Grosbeak, *Coccothraustes vespertinus*

Status and Abundance: Rare winter resident and spring and late fall transient; accidental summer visitor; irruptive

Habitat: Open forest and forest edge; bird feeders

Spring Departure: late Mar

Fall Arrival: early Nov

Comments: Formerly regular winter resident, exceedingly rare in last 15 years due to severe range-wide population declines starting in the 1990s.

Late Spring
5 Jun 1962, near GSMNP (Stupka 1962)
24 May 1986, Coffee Co. (MIG 57:81)
17 May 1996, Shelby Farms (MIG 67:61)
13 May 2000, Knox Co. NAMC (MIG 71:58)
8 May 1996, Walnut Log Road, Lake Co. (JRW, unpubl. data)

Early Fall
16 Sep 1986, Chattanooga (MIG 58:29-30)
27 Sep 1971, Nashville (MIG 42:93)
17 Oct 1979, Memphis (MIG 51:16)

High Counts – Spring
200 on 1 Mar 1994, Shady Valley (MIG 65:56)
131 on 1 May 1994, Elizabethton SBC (MIG 65:35)
120 on 5 Mar 1990, Roan Mtn. (MIG 61:79)
80+ on 23 Apr 2000, Roan Mtn. (MIG 71:95)
64 on 23 Apr 1994, Greene Co. SBC (MIG 65:35)

High Counts – Fall
80+ on 23 Non 1993, Roan Mtn. (MIG 65:27)
40 on 6 Nov 1993, Holston Valley (MIG 65:27)

23 on 26 Nov 1995, Obion Co. (MIG 67:20)

High Counts – Winter

416 on 2 Jan 1994, GSMNP CBC (MIG 65:19)
250 on 23 Feb 1955, Gatlinburg (Stupka and Tanner 1955)
151 on 28 Dec 1997, GSMNP CBC (MIG 69:113)
114 on 22 Dec 1985, Memphis CBC (MIG 57:12)
110 on 25 Feb 1996, Roan Mtn. (MIG 67:35)

Substantiation: Specimen: LSUMZ, 77150

Passeridae: Old World Sparrows. This family is represented by one non-native, widespread, and abundant species. Eurasian Tree Sparrows have been reported on several occasions, but none have yet been convincingly documented.

House Sparrow, *Passer domesticus*
> Status and Abundance: Common permanent resident; introduced
> Habitat: Urban and suburban areas; farmlands, usually in close proximity to human dwellings
> High Counts – Spring
>> 218 on 9 May 1992, Chattanooga SBC (MIG 63:50)
>> 209 on 12 May 2007, Putnam Co. NAMC (MIG 78:135)
>> 156 on 12 May 2001, Putnam Co. NAMC (MIG 72:23)
>
> High Counts – Fall
>> 192 on 20 Sep 2003, Shelby Co. FBC (MIG 75:12)
>> 146 on 5 Oct 2002, Putnam Co. FBC (MIG 73:54)
>> 142 on 13 Sep 2008, Shelby Co. FBC (MIG 80:20)
>> 118 on 19 Sep 2009, Shelby Co. FBC (MIG 81:47)
>
> High Counts – Winter
>> 2,190 on 23 Dec 1962, Memphis CBC (MIG 33:69)
>> 1,370 on 21 Dec 1985, Reelfoot Lake CBC (MIG 57:12)
>
> Substantiation: Specimen: LSUMZ, 76939

References

Abernathy, B.H. 1943. The Connecticut Warbler: a spring visitant. The Migrant 14(2):27-28.

Alsop, F.J., III. 1967. Observations at a unique farm in Knox County. The Migrant 38(1):1-3.

Alsop, F.J., III. 1969. Black-headed Grosbeak in Tennessee. The Migrant 40(3):59-60.

Alsop, F.J., III. 1972. A preliminary list of Tennessee birds. The Migrant 43(3):57-64.

Alsop, F.J., III. 1978. Savannah Sparrow nesting in upper east Tennessee. The Migrant 49(1):1-4.

Alsop, F.J., III and G.O. Wallace. 1970. Addendum: the birds of Knox County, Tennessee. The Migrant 41(1):1-4.

Anderson, K.G. 1984. First sight record of a 'Gray-headed' Junco in Tennessee. The Migrant 55(3):64.

Applegate, R.D. 2006. Breeding season occurrence of sora in west Tennessee. The Migrant 77(4):111-112.

Audubon, J.J. 1929. Journal of John James Audubon made during his trip to New Orleans in 1820-1821. H. Corning, editor. The Club of Odd Volumes, Boston.

Basham, B. 1969. Brown-headed Nuthatch. The Migrant 40(1):11.

Behrend, F.W. 1954. Horned Grebe and Double-crested Cormorant on Lake Phillip Nelson. The Migrant 25(3):49.

Behrend, F.W. 1955. Evening Grosbeaks and Snow Buntings on Roan and Big Bald Mountains, Tennessee-North Carolina. The Migrant 26(1):14-16.

Behrend, F.W. 1962. Northern finches summering on Roan Mountain. The Migrant 33(3):56.

Behrend, F.W. 1963. Northern birds repeat their summer stay on Roan Mountain. The Migrant 34(2):38-39.

Behrend, F.W. 1965. Snow Bunting on Hump Mountain. The Migrant 36(2):52-53.

Bierly, M.L. 1972. Whimbrel recorded at Nashville. The Migrant 43(4):92-93.

Bierly, M.L. 1976. King Eider recorded in Tennessee. The Migrant 47(1):14.

References

Bierly, M.L. 1978. Brown Creeper nests in Nashville. The Migrant 49(4):86-87.

Bierly, M.L. 1980. Bird finding in Tennessee. Nashville: Michael L. Bierly.

Blunk, D.W. 1984. Black-legged Kittiwake in Stewart County, Tennessee. The Migrant 55(1):15.

Braun, M.J. 1988. Northern Gannet on I-65: second record for Kentucky, first record for Tennessee. The Kentucky Warbler 64:34-36.

Bridgforth, W.A., Jr. 1969. Whip-poor-will foray. The Migrant 40(3):66.

Brown, C.W. 1985. Hudsonian Godwits in Lake County, Tennessee. The Migrant 65(4):105.

Butts, W.K. 1936. A Florida (Sandhill) Crane at Chattanooga. The Migrant 7(1):24.

Calhoon, K. 1998. Late Red Phalarope at Chattanooga, Tennessee. The Migrant 69(3):131-133.

Calhoon, K. 1998a. Report of the Tennessee Bird Records Committee. The Migrant 69(3):125-126.

Calhoon, K. 1999. Report of the Tennessee Bird Records Committee. The Migrant 70(3):90-91.

Calhoon, K. 2000. Report of the Tennessee Bird Records Committee. The Migrant 71(3):82-83.

Calhoun, J.B. 1941. Notes on the summer birds of Hardeman and McNairy Counties. Journal of Tennessee Academy of Sciences 16:293-309.

Cardiff, S.W., and D. Dittmann. 1991. Comments on the first Arctic Tern record for Tennessee. The Migrant 62(3):67-68.

Clebsch, A. 1940. Mid-winter field ventures. The Migrant 11(1):5-8.

Clebsch, A. 1943. Some winter birds of the river bottoms. The Migrant 14(4):65-67.

Clebsch, A. 1950. Orange-crowned Warbler as spring migrant. The Migrant 21(2):29-30.

Clements, J.F. 2007. The Clements Checklist of Birds of the World, Sixth Edition. Comstock Publishing Associates. Including all subsequently released Updates & Corrections.

Coffey, B.B. Jr. 1935. A Piping Plover at Memphis. The Migrant 6(2):35.

Coffey, B.B. Jr. 1935a. Bell's Vireo at Memphis. The Migrant 6(3):67-68.

Coffey, B.B., Jr. 1939. Rare shorebirds at Mud Lake. The Migrant 10(1):15-16.

Coffey, B.B., Jr. 1955. The Short-eared Owl in the mid-south. The Migrant 26(2):24-25.

Coffey, B.B., Jr. 1956. Harris's Sparrow in the mid-south. The Migrant 27(2):37-39.

Coffey, J.W. 1964. An additional Snowy Owl record for 1930. The Migrant 35(3):71.

Coffey, J.W. 1964a. Northern Shrike at Bristol - a new species for Tennessee. The Migrant 35(4):90-94.

Coffey, J.W. 1970. Mute Swan in Sullivan County. The Migrant 41(3):59-60.

Coffey, B.B., Jr. 1974. Brant in Shelby County. The Migrant 45(4):93-94.

Coffey, B.B., Jr. 1975. Yellow-headed Blackbird in Memphis. The Migrant 46(1):15.

Coffey, B.B., Jr. 1981. Prairie Falcon at Memphis. The Migrant 52(1):18.

Coffey, B.B., Jr., and L. Coffey. 1980. A west Tennessee foray - June, 1979. The Migrant 51(1):12-14.

Coffey, B.B., Jr., et al. 1942. The wrens of Tennessee. The Migrant 13(1):1-13.

Crawford, P. and D. Crawford. 1975. Purple Sandpiper in Sumner County, Tennessee. The Migrant 46(4):80-81.

Crawford, D. and P. Crawford. 1977. Snowy Plover added to Tennessee state list. The Migrant 48(3):63-64.

Criswell, W.G. 1979. A heron roost in Dyersburg. The Migrant 50(2):33.

Criswell, W.G. 1986. Second Tennessee record of the Groove-billed Ani. The Migrant 57(3):70.

Criswell, W.G. 1991. Arctic Tern at Island 13, Lake County, Tennessee: the first state record. The Migrant 62(3):66.

Criswell, W.G. 1991a. The first Tennessee record of a Black-shouldered Kite. The Migrant 62(3):69.

Criswell, W.G. 1997. State's first Curlew Sandpiper sighted in west Tennessee. The Migrant 68(2):46.

Criswell, W.G. 1997a. Sabine's Gull sighted in Lake County, Tennessee. The Migrant 68(2):50.

References

Crook, C. 1935. The birds of late summer on Reelfoot Lake. J. Tenn. Acad. Sci. 10:1-18.

Crook, C. 1936. A late Golden-winged Warbler in the Cumberlands. The Migrant 7(2):48.

Cushman, J.H. and R.M. Cushman. 1997. Third Varied Thrush observed in Tennessee. The Migrant 68(1):10.

Cybert, E., Jr. 1955. Some interesting bird observations on Kentucky Lake. The Migrant 26(1):9-11.

Cypert, E., Jr. 1955a. Snowy Owl on Kentucky Lake. The Migrant 26(1):12.

Darnell, M. 1956. Kirtland's Warbler. The Migrant 27(3):53.

Darnell, C.B. 1960. Oregon Juncos near Greeneville. The Migrant 31(1):19.

Deaderick, W.H. 1940. Audubon in Tennessee. The Migrant 11(3):59-61.

DeFoe, D.H. 1966. Common Redpoll in GSMNP. The Migrant 37(1):11.

DeVore, J.E. 1966. Sandhill Crane near Chattanooga in August. The Migrant 37(1):15.

DeVore, J.E. 1969. Brant and White-fronted Geese in east Tennessee. The Migrant 40(3):61.

DeVore, J.E. 1972. The Sandhill Crane in Tennessee. The Migrant 43(2):29-34.

DeVore, J. E. 1974. Dark-headed Juncos in Rutherford and Wilson Counties. The Migrant 45(2):54.

DeVore, J. E. 1975. Middle Tennessee ornithological records of the late H. O. Todd, Jr. The Migrant 46(2):25-37.

DeVore, J.E. and K.H. Dubke. 1966. Black Brant at Hiwassee Island. The Migrant 37(1):12.

Dinsmore, M.O. 1975. Wood Stork seen in Stewart County. The Migrant 46(4):79.

Dubke, K.H. 1963. Unusually late spring waterfowl, shorebird, gull, and tern records - 1963. The Migrant 34(2):36-37.

Dubke, K.H. 1963a. First nesting record of Bobolink in Tennessee. The Migrant 34(2):17-19.

Dubke, K.H. 1968. Red Phalaropes near Chattanooga. The Migrant 39(1):13.

Dubke, K.H., and L.H. Dubke. 1975. Red-necked Grebe sighted on Chickamauga Lake. The Migrant 46(4):75-76.

Edwards, M.E. 1991. First record of a Varied Thrush in Tennessee. The Migrant 62(3):57-65.

Edwards, K.D. 2012. Report of the Tennessee Bird Records Committee. The Migrant 83(2):29-36.

Etnier, D.A. 1971. Snow Buntings, Oldsquaw, and White-winged Scoter in east Tennessee. The Migrant 42(1):5.

Fintel, W.A. 1974. Band-tailed Pigeon sighting, Nashville, Tennessee. The Migrant 45(2):49-51.

Ford, R.P. 1987. Summary of recent Brown Creeper observations in west Tennessee. The Migrant 58(2):50-51.

Foster, G., Jr. 1937. A Brown Pelican in East Tennessee. The Migrant 8(4):87.

Ganier, A.F. 1933. A Swallow-tailed Kite. The Migrant 4(4):51.

Ganier, A.F. 1933a. A distributional list of the birds of Tennessee. Tennessee Avifauna No. 1. Nashville: Tennessee Ornithological Society.

Ganier, A.F. 1933b. Water birds of Reelfoot Lake, Tennessee. Tennessee Avifauna No. 2. Nashville: Tennessee Ornithological Society.

Ganier, A.F. 1952. A Black Vulture roost. The Migrant 23(1):7.

Ganier, A.F. 1954. Spring water birds at Nashville - 1954. The Migrant 25(2):21-23.

Ganier, A.F. 1960. A new heronry in northwest Tennessee. The Migrant 31(3):48-49.

Ganier, A.F. 1962. Bird casualties at a Nashville TV tower. The Migrant 33(4):58-60.

Ganier, A.F. 1968. Swallow-tailed Kite near Nashville. The Migrant 39(4):85.

Gardler, M. 1997. First record of Shiny Cowbird in Tennessee. The Migrant 68(2):47.

Goodpasture, K.A. 1974. Fall 1972 television tower casualties in Nashville. The Migrant 45(2):29-31.

Goodpasture, K.A. 1976. Nashville television tower casualties, 1975. The Migrant 47(1):8-10.

Goodpasture, K.A. 1977. Fall banding at Basin Spring, 1975. The Migrant 48:65-69.

References

Graham, T. 2012. First accepted Inca Dove record for Tennessee. The Migrant 83(3):99.

Greene, M.A. 1997. Report of the Tennessee Bird Records Committee. The Migrant 68(3):94-95.

Greene, M.A. 2011. Lazuli Bunting in Shelby County, Tennessee. The Migrant 82(3):116.

Hassler, R.C. 1984. A Yellow Rail in Pickett County, Tennessee. The Migrant 55(1):15.

Hawkins, M.J., G.K. Ensor, and K.L. Morgan. 2005. First winter record of Bobolink in Tennessee. The Migrant 76(3):89-90.

Herndon, L.R. 1944. Notes on Prothonotary Warblers. The Migrant 15(3):58.

Herndon, L.R. 1950. Birds of Carter County, Tennessee. The Migrant 21(4):57-68.

Herndon, L.R. 1957. Green-tailed Towhee in Elizabethton, Tennessee. The Migrant 28(1):15.

Herndon, L.R. 1972. Black-throated Gray Warbler. The Migrant 43(3):67-68.

Herndon, L.R. 1973. Bird kill on Holston Mountain. The Migrant 44(1):1-4.

Hettish, A. 1974. Report on Black-headed Grosbeak, Murfreesboro. The Migrant 45(3):72-73.

Hoff, A.R. 1987. Autumn Hawk Counts - 1987. The Migrant 59(3):88-91.

Hogg, G.E. 1968. Vermilion Flycatcher at Reelfoot. The Migrant 39(1):12.

Holt, J.G. 1972. House Finches at Greeneville. The Migrant 43(4):87.

Holt, J.G. 1979. Purple Sandpiper in west Tennessee. The Migrant 50(3):63.

Howell, J.C. and M.B. Monroe. 1957. The birds of Knox County, Tennessee. Journal of Tennessee Academy of Sciences 32(4):247-322.

Howell, J.C. and M.B. Monroe. 1958. The birds of Knox County, Tennessee. The Migrant 29(2):17-27.

Howell, J.C., and J.T. Tanner. 1951. An accident to migrating birds at the Knoxville airport. The Migrant 22(4):61-62.

Howell, S.N.G., I. Lewington, and W. Russell. 2014. Rare Birds of North America. Princeton University Press.

Hoyle, S. 2011. Sage Thrasher in Knox County, Tennessee. The Migrant 82(1):1-2.

Hudson, C. 1969. Western Tanager in Dyer County. The Migrant 40(3):65-66.

Ijams, H.P. 1934. A Sooty Tern at Knoxville. The Migrant 5(3):46.

Irwin, O.F. 1958. Long-eared Owl at Memphis. The Migrant 29(3):59.

Irwin, O.F. 1961. Snow Bunting at Memphis. The Migrant 32(3):49-50.

Jacobson, D.R. 1976. The seasons: Eastern ridge and valley region. The Migrant 47(1):20-23.

Kellberg, J.M. 1956. Snowy Owl. The Migrant 27(4):74.

Kiff, L.F. 1989. Historical breeding records of the Common Merganser in the southeastern United States. The Wilson Bulletin 101(1):141-43.

Knight, R.L. 1992. Sprague's Pipit at Roan Mountain, Tennessee and North Carolina. The Migrant 63:65-67.

Knight, R.L. 1993. Report of the Tennessee Bird Records Committee. The Migrant 64(3):53-57.

Knight, R.L. 1996. Report of the Tennessee Bird Records Committee for 1995. The Migrant 67(3):37-42.

Knight, R.L. 2005. Townsend's Warbler in northeast Tennessee. The Migrant 76(1):10-11.

Knight, R.L. 2007. Pacific Loon in northeast Tennessee. The Migrant 78(2):58-59.

Knight. R.L. 2007a. Bobolinks breeding in Washington County, Tennessee. The Migrant 78(4):109-111.

Knight, R.L. 2008. The birds of northeast Tennessee, 2nd edition. Universal Printing, Bristol, VA.

Knight, R.L. 2010. Summer birds of the Roan Mountain Highlands. The Migrant 81:1-28.

Knight, R.L. 2010a. Another Pine Siskin nest at Roan Mountain, Tennessee. The Migrant 81(3): 109-110.

Knight, R.L. 2011. Summer records and first breeding of Yellow-rumped Warbler (*Setophaga coronata*) in the mountains of North Carolina and Tennessee. Chat 75:117-119.

Knight, R.L. 2011a. The 2011 TOS Shady Valley Foray. The Migrant 82(3):97-110.

Knight, R.L. 2011b. Status of Glossy and White-faced Ibises in Tennessee. The Migrant 82(4):125-128.

Knight, R.L. 2012. Cave Swallows in Northeast Tennessee. The Migrant 83(4):127-129.

Knight, R.L. and R.M. Hatcher. 1997. Recovery efforts result in returned nesting of Peregrine Falcons in Tennessee. The Migrant 68:33-39.

Knight, R.L., H.P. Langridge, B.L. Cross. 1992. Great White Heron at South Holston Lake, Tennessee and Virginia. Migrant 63(1):1-3.

Koella, J.A. 1985. Sight record of a Gyrfalcon in Jefferson County, Tennessee. The Migrant 56(1):14-15.

Kunkel, K. and P. Kunkel. 2012. Golden-crowned Sparrow: first state record. The Migrant 83(1):1.

Landis, H., Jr. 1955. Long-eared Owl in Memphis. The Migrant 26(2):33.

Langridge, H.P. and B. Cross. 1991. Hurricane Hugo brings oceanic birds to Watauga Lake, Tennessee. The Migrant 62(2):29-31.

Laskey, A.R. 1933. Juncos with white wing-bars in Tennessee. The Migrant 4(1):9.

Laskey, A.R. 1950. A Tennessee Warbler found in Nashville in January. The Migrant 21(2):29.

Laskey, A.R. 1956. Bird casualties at Smyrna and Nashville Ceilometers, 1955. The Migrant 27(1):9-10.

Laskey, A.R. 1960. Bird migration casualties and weather conditions - autumns 1958-1959-1960. The Migrant 31(4):61-65.

Laskey, A.R. 1962. Migration data from television tower casualties at Nashville. The Migrant 33(1):7-8.

Laskey, A.R. 1964. Data from the Nashville T.V. tower casualties autumn 1964. The Migrant 35(4):95-96.

Laskey, A.R. 1966. T.V. tower casualties at Nashville; spring and fall, 1966. The Migrant 37(4):61-62.

Laskey, A.R. 1969. Autumn 1969 T.V. tower casualties at Nashville. The Migrant 40(4):79-80.

Layne, J.N. 1946. Field notes from the Smyrna area. The Migrant 17(2):19-21.

Leggett, K. 1969. Groove-billed Ani. The Migrant 40(1):7-9.

Leggett, K. 1969a. Vermilion Flycatcher again recorded at Reelfoot. The Migrant 40(1):17.

Martin, K. 2012. Mid-south raptor center rehabilitation program: a ten year review 2003-2012. The Migrant 83(3):96-98.

Masters, L., K. Flowers, M. Lawrence, and J. Dodd. 1994. Pine Grosbeaks in west Tennessee. The Migrant 65(4):59.

Mayfield, G.R., Jr. 1935. A Tennessee Warbler winters in Nashville. The Migrant 6(1):14.

Mayfield, G.R., Jr. 1981. Whimbrels on Big Bald Mountain, Tennessee. The Migrant 52(4):91.

M'Camey, F. 1935. August notes from North Lake. The Migrant 6(3):51-53.

McCrary, W.L., and M. Wood. 1966. Red Phalarope near Tullahoma. The Migrant 37(1):15.

McCrary, W.L., and M. Wood. 1966a. Lark Bunting in Tennessee. The Migrant 37(2):41-42.

McKinney, G.W. and J.B. Owen. 1989. First evidence of Northern Saw-whet Owls nesting in Tennessee. The Migrant 60(1):5-6.

Monk, H.C. 1932. The water birds of Radnor Lake. Journal of Tennessee Academy of Sciences 7:217-232.

Monroe, B.L. 1945. Field notes from west Tennessee. The Migrant 15(4):76.

Monroe, M.B. 1959. Red Phalarope. The Migrant 30(4):56.

Mooney, D. and L. Mooney. 2006. Townsend's Solitaire at Seven Islands Wildlife Refuge, Knox County, Tennessee. The Migrant 77(1):1-2.

Morlan, R.E. 1961. A Limpkin at Nashville. The Migrant 32(3):48-49.

Munro, A.R. 1961. Snowy Owl. The Migrant 32(1):1-3.

Murray, C. 2012. Hooded Crane at Hiwassee Refuge. The Migrant 83(1):5.

Nevius, R. 1964. A Tennessee nesting of the Black Rail. The Migrant 35(3):59-60.

Nicholson, C.P. 1980. Birds of Decatur County. The Migrant 51(1):1-10.

Nicholson, C.P. 1983. The official list of Tennessee birds. The Migrant 54(1):2-5.

Nicholson, C.P. 1983a. Barnacle Goose in Humphreys County, Tennessee. The Migrant 54(2):39.

Nicholson, C.P. 1984. Late spring and summer birds of McNairy County, Tennessee. The Migrant 55(2):29-39.

Nicholson, C.P. 1986. Alexander Wilson's travels in Tennessee. The Migrant 57(1):1-7.

Nicholson, C.P. 1990. Recent records of Wood Storks in Knox County, Tennessee. The Migrant 61(1):10-11.

Nicholson, C.P. and A. Morton. 1972. Glaucous Gull on Fort Loudon Lake. The Migrant 43(1):21.

Nicholson, C.P. and S.J. Stedman. 1988. The official list of Tennessee birds: addendum 1. The Migrant 59(1):1-4.

Ogden, J. 1955. Lark Sparrows near Nashville. The Migrant 26(3):45-46.

Ogden, J. 1959. Northern Phalaropes at Nashville. The Migrant 30(4):55.

Olson, F.B. 1961. Cattle Egret - first Tennessee record. The Migrant 32(2):35.

Olson, F.B. 1961a. White-fronted Goose at Cove Lake. The Migrant 32(2):35-36.

Olson, F.B. 1965. Fulvous Tree Ducks below Norris Dam, Anderson County. The Migrant 36(4):104.

Owen, J.B. 1965. Vermilion Flycatcher in Knox County. The Migrant 36(1):14-15.

Pardue, P. 1997. Second record of Allen's Hummingbird in Tennessee. The Migrant 68(1):11.

Parmer, H.E. 1962. Further observations at Bush Lake. The Migrant 33(1):8-10.

Parmer, H.E. 1963. Late warblers at Nashville. The Migrant 34(2):37-38.

Parmer, H.E. and H.C. Monk. 1969. Glaucous Gull. The Migrant 40(1):12-13.

Patterson, D.E. 2006. Notes on Least Bitterns nesting at Standifer Gap Marsh, Hamilton County. The Migrant 77(3):89-94.

Patterson, D.E., and M. Patterson. 1969. Clay-colored Sparrow in Hardin County. The Migrant 40(4):84-85.

Peeples, W.R. 1991. Red Crossbill feeding young in Shelby County, Tennessee. The Migrant 62(4):107.

Pitts, T.D. 1981. European Wigeon at Reelfoot Lake, Tennessee in the early 1950s. The Migrant 52(3):68.

Pitts, T.D. 1982. First record of occurrence and possible nesting of Black-bellied Whistling Ducks in Tennessee. The Migrant 53(1):1-3.

Pitts, T.D. 1985. The breeding birds of Reelfoot Lake, Tennessee. The Migrant 56(2):29-41.

Pranty, B., J. Barry, J.L. Dunn, K.L. Garrett, D.D. Gibson, M.W. Lockwood, R. Pittway, D.A. Sibley. 2014. 25th Report of the ABA Checklist Committee 2013-2014. Birding 46(6):26-33.

Purrington, R.D. 2000. Central Southern Region (Summer 2000). North American Birds, 54:391-394.

Rauber, E.L. 1972. Cinnamon Teal sighted at Tennessee National Wildlife Refuge. The Migrant 43(3):67.

Renfrow, F. and S.J. Stedman. 2003. Red-breasted Nuthatches in the Big South Fork National River and Recreation Area: first nesting record for Tennessee's Cumberland Plateau. The Migrant 74(1):1-5.

Rhoads, S.N. 1895. Contributions to the zoology of Tennessee, No. 2. Birds. Proceedings of the Academy of Natural Sciences of Philadelphia 47:463-501.

Riggins, J.N., and H. Riggins. 1972. Second state record of Whimbrel. The Migrant 43(4):92.

Robinson, J.C. 1988. First record of Ross' Goose in Tennessee. The Migrant 59(4): 114-115.

Robinson, J.C. 1988a. Heron and egret roost discovered near Memphis. The Migrant 59(4):118-19.

Robinson, J.C. 1988b. Audubon's Yellow-rumped Warbler in Tennessee. The Migrant 59(4):117.

Robinson, J.C. 1990. An Annotated Checklist of the Birds of Tennessee. University of Tennessee Press, Knoxville.

Robinson, J.C., and D.W. Blunk. 1989. The birds of Stewart County, Tennessee. P. 70-103 in A.F. Scott, ed. Proceedings of the contributed paper session of the second annual symposium on the natural history of the lower Tennessee and Cumberland river valley.

Ryan, C. 1968. Fulvous Tree Duck near Dover. The Migrant 39(1):16.

Sargent, R.R., and M.B. Sargent. 1993. First documented occurrence of Black-chinned Hummingbird in Tennessee. The Migrant 64(1):1-3.

Sauer, J.R., J.E. Hines, J.E. Fallon, K.L. Pardieck, D.J. Ziolkowski, Jr., and W.A. Link. 2012. The North American Breeding Bird Survey, Results and Analysis 1966-2011. Version 12.13.2011 USGS Patuxent Wildlife Research Center, Laurel, MD.

References

Seahorn, C., Jr. 1953. Spotted Towhee at Germantown, Tennessee. The Migrant 24(2):42-43.

Shafer, W.L. 1972. First known record of a Ruff in Tennessee. The Migrant 43(4):86.

Shaw, J. 2004. MacGillivray's Warbler in Davidson County, Tennessee. The Migrant 75(2):37-38.

Skelton, C.E. and R. Kays. 1997. Kirtland's Warbler in Tennessee. The Migrant 68:(2):42-43.

Sloan, C. 2011. Great Shearwater found in parking lot: first Tennessee record. The Migrant 82(2):65.

Smith, R.D. Jr. 1951. Western Meadowlark nesting at Memphis. The Migrant 22(2):21-22.

Smith, R.D. Jr. 1952. Green-tailed Towhee in Memphis, Tennessee. The Migrant 23(4):76.

Smith, A.I. 1965. Vermilion Flycatchers at Reelfoot Lake. The Migrant 36(1):14.

Snyder, D.H. 1974. Second record of Cinnamon Teal in Tennessee. The Migrant 45(4):94.

Spofford, W.R. 1945. Bald Eagle notes from Reelfoot Lake. The Migrant 16(4):65.

Spofford, W.R. 1948. Some additional notes on the birds of Pickett Forest, Tennessee. The Migrant 19(1):12-13.

Stedman, S.J. 1980. Recent records and status of the Whimbrel in Tennessee. The Migrant 51(4):88-89.

Stedman, S.J. 1985. First record of Long-tailed Jaeger in Tennessee. The Migrant 56(3):64-66.

Stedman, S. J. 1995a. Central Southern Region [Winter 1994–1995]. National Audubon Society Field Notes 49: 155–159.

Stedman, S.J. and M.J. Hawkins. 2003. Winter records of Yellow-breasted Chat in Tennessee. The Migrant 74(4):104-108.

Stedman, S.J. and J.C. Robinson. 1986. First record of Parasitic Jaeger in Tennessee. The Migrant 57(2):44-46.

Stedman, S.J. and J.C. Robinson. 1987. First record of Parasitic Jaeger in Tennessee: addenda. The Migrant 58(3):89-90.

Stedman, B.H. and S.J. Stedman. 1981. Notes on the raptor migration at Chilhowee Mountain. The Migrant 52(2):38-40.

Stedman, S.J. and B.H. Stedman. 2002. Notes on the Birds of the Big South Fork National River and Recreation Area and Obed National Wild and Scenic River. Tennessee Technological University, Cookeville, Tennessee.

Steenis, J.H. 1946. An Old Squaw duck on Reelfoot Lake. The Migrant 17(2):26.

Stupka, A. 1962. Late Evening Grosbeaks in Gatlinburg. The Migrant 33(2):35.

Stupka, A. 1963. Notes on the Birds of the Great Smoky Mountains National Park. Knoxville: University of Tennessee Press.

Stupka, A. and J. T. Tanner. 1955. Evening Grosbeaks in the Gatlinburg-Knoxville area. The Migrant 26(1):13-14.

Switzer, A.H. 1957. Observations at a fish hatchery. The Migrant 28(4):60-61.

Thompson, B. 1937. Two Snowy Owl records. The Migrant 8(2):35.

Todd, H.O. 1937. Upland Plovers at Murfreesboro. The Migrant 8(3):64.

Todd, M. 2004. Report of the Tennessee Bird Records Committee. The Migrant 75(1):6-7.

Trently, A.J. 2003. Breeding season record for the Mourning Warbler on Roan Mountain. The Migrant 74:83-84.

Trently, A.J. and R. Biller. 2008. Confirmed nesting of the Pine Siskin in Tennessee. The Migrant 79(1):2-3.

Tucker, R.E. 1950. Notes of some specimens of birds from Shelby County, Tennessee. The Migrant 21(3):41-45.

Tyler, B.P. 1933. Clay-colored Sparrow at Johnson City. The Migrant 42(2):23.

Tyler, B.P. and R.B. Lyle. 1934. Additions to the list of winter birds of northeast Tennessee. The Migrant 5(1):14.

Tyler, B.P. and R.B. Lyle. 1936. Additions to the winter birds of northeast Tennessee. The Migrant 7(1):25-26.

U.S. Fish and Wildlife Service. 2010. Recovery Plan for the Ivory-billed Woodpecker (*Campephilus principalis*). U.S. Fish and Wildlife Service, Atlanta, Georgia. 156 pp.

Waldron, M.G. 1980. Anhinga nesting at Big Hill Pond, McNairy Co. The Migrant 51(4):86.

References

Waldron, M.G. 1987. Seasonal occurrences of Shelby County, Tennessee birds. Memphis Chapter Tennessee Ornithological Society.

Waldron, M. 1989. Second record of Ruff in Tennessee. The Migrant 60:51.

Waldron, M. 1989a. Wilson's Plover sighting in Shelby County, Tennessee. The Migrant 60:56.

Waldron, M. 1990. First Tennessee record of White-faced Ibis. The Migrant 61(3): 65-66.

Walker, W.M., Jr. 1932. Nashville Christmas census for 17 years. The Migrant 3(4):42-43.

Walker, W.M., Jr. 1935. A collection of birds from Cocke County, Tennessee. The Migrant 6(3):48-50.

Weise, C.M. 1958. Spring shorebird migration at Nashville, 1954-56. The Migrant 29(3):42-50.

West, E.M. 1959. Whistling Swan. The Migrant 30(4):56.

West, E.M. 1959a. Brant in Chattanooga. The Migrant 30(4):54.

Wetmore, A. 1939. Notes on the birds of Tennessee. Proceedings of the United States National Museum 86:175-243.

White, R.L. 1944. European Widgeons in west Tennessee. The Migrant 15(1):14.

Williams, M.D. 1976. Nest of Olive-sided Flycatcher in the southern Appalachian Mountains. The Migrant 47(3):69-71.

Williams, M.D. 1978. A late May sighting of Fox Sparrow in Tennessee. The Migrant 49(4):87-88.

Witt, T.J. 1986. A sight record of a "Bullock's" Oriole in Tennessee. The Migrant 57(2):47.

Witt, T. 2006. Gull-billed Tern in Tennessee. The Migrant 77(4):109-110.

Yeatman, H.C. 1965. Swallow-tailed Kite in Franklin County, Tennessee. The Migrant 36(3):58-59.

Index of English Names

Anhinga, 64
Ani, Groove-billed, 167
Avocet, American, 106

Bittern
   American, 67
   Least, 68
Black-bellied Whistling-Duck, 15
Blackbird
   Brewer's, 314
   Red-winged, 311
   Rusty, 313
   Yellow-headed, 312
Bluebird, Eastern, 233
Bobolink, 310
Bobwhite, Northern, 46
Brant, 18
Bufflehead, 40
Bunting
   Indigo, 308
   Lark, 291
   Lazuli, 307
   Painted, 308, 309
   Snow, 248

Canvasback, 33
Cardinal, Northern, 304
Catbird, Gray, 240
Chat, Yellow-breasted, 284
Chickadee
   Black-capped, 219
   Carolina, 219
Chuck-wills-widow, 174
Collared-Dove, Eurasian, 163
Coot, American, 99
Cormorant
   Double-crested, 62
   Neotropic, 62
Cowbird
   Brown-headed, 315
   Shiny, 315
Crane
   Hooded, 102
   Sandhill, 102
   Whooping, 103
Creeper, Brown, 224
Crossbill
   Red, 319
   White-winged, 320
Crow
   American, 209
   Fish, 210
Cuckoo
   Black-billed, 166
   Yellow-billed, 166
Curlew, Long-billed, 121

Dickcissel, 309
Dove
   Inca, 164
   Mourning, 165
   White-winged, 164
Dowitcher
   Long-billed, 137
   Short-billed, 136
Duck
   American Black, 26
   Harlequin, 37
   Long-tailed, 40
   Mottled, 27
   Ring-necked, 34
   Ruddy, 44
   Wood, 22
Dunlin, 127

Eagle
   Bald, 85
   Golden, 92
Eastern Whip-poor-will, 174
Egret
   Cattle, 73
   Great, 69
   Reddish, 73
   Snowy, 70

Index of English Names

Eider, King, 37

Falcon
  Peregrine, 188
  Prairie, 189
Finch
  House, 318
  Purple, 318
Flicker, Northern, 185
Flycatcher
  Acadian, 193
  Alder, 194
  Ash-throated, 198
  Great Crested, 198
  Least, 195
  Olive-sided, 191
  Scissor-tailed, 200
  Variegated, 199
  Vermilion, 197
  Willow, 195
  Yellow-bellied, 192
Frigatebird, Magnificent, 60
Fulvous Whistling-Duck, 15

Gadwall, 23
Gallinule
  Common, 98
  Purple, 98
Gannet, Northern, 61
Garganey, 31
Gnatcatcher, Blue-gray, 230
Godwit
  Hudsonian, 121
  Marbled, 122
Goldeneye
  Common, 41
Golden-Plover, American, 109
Goldfinch, American, 322
Goose
  Barnacle, 19
  Cackling, 19
  Canada, 20
  Greater White-fronted, 16
  Ross's, 18
  Snow, 17, 18
Goshawk, Northern, 87
Grackle
  Common, 314
  Great-tailed, 315
Greater White-fronted Goose, 16
Grebe
  Eared, 54
  Horned, 52
  Pied-billed, 52
  Red-necked, 53
  Western, 55
Grosbeak
  Black-headed, 306
  Blue, 307
  Evening, 323
  Pine, 318
  Rose-breasted, 305
Ground-Dove, Common, 164
Grouse, Ruffed, 47
Gull
  Black-headed Gull, 147
  Bonaparte's, 146
  California, 150
  Franklin's, 149
  Glaucous, 153
  Great Black-backed, 154
  Herring, 151
  Iceland, 152
  Ivory, 145
  Laughing, 148
  Lesser Black-backed, 152
  Little, 147
  Ring-billed, 150
  Sabine's, 146
  Thayer's, 151
Gyrfalcon, 188

Harrier, Northern, 85
Hawk
  Broad-winged, 89
  Ferruginous, 91
  Red-shouldered, 88
  Red-tailed, 90

Rough-legged, 91
Sharp-shinned, 86
Heron
   Great Blue, 68
   Green, 74
   Little Blue, 71
   Tricolored, 72
Hummingbird
   Allen's, 180
   Anna's, 179
   Black-chinned, 179
   Broad-tailed, 181
   Calliope, 179
   Ruby-throated, 178
   Rufous, 180

Ibis
   Glossy, 77, 78
   White, 77
   White-faced, 78

Jaeger
   Long-tailed, 143
   Parasitic, 142
   Pomarine, 142
Jay, Blue, 209
Junco, Dark-eyed, 301

Kestrel, American, 187
Killdeer, 112
Kingbird
   Eastern, 200
   Western, 199
Kingfisher, Belted, 182
Kinglet
   Golden-crowned, 231
   Ruby-crowned, 231
Kite
   Mississippi, 84
   Swallow-tailed, 83
   White-tailed, 83
Kittiwake, Black-legged, 145
Knot, Red, 123

Lark, Horned, 212
Limpkin, 101
Longspur
   Chestnut-collared, 247
   Lapland, 247
   McCown's, 248
   Smith's, 248
Loon
   Common, 50
   Pacific, 49
   Red-throated, 49
   Yellow-billed, 51

Mallard, 27
Martin, Purple, 213
Meadowlark
   Eastern, 311
   Western, 312
Merganser
   Common, 43
   Hooded, 42
   Red-breasted, 43
Merlin, 187
Mockingbird, Northern, 241
Murrelet, Long-billed, 144

Nighthawk, Common, 173
Night-Heron
   Black-crowned, 74
   Yellow-crowned, 75
Nuthatch
   Brown-headed, 222
   Red-breasted, 221
   White-breasted, 222

Oriole
   Baltimore, 317
   Bullock's, 317
   Hooded, 316
   Orchard, 316
Osprey, 82
Ovenbird, 250
Owl
   Barn, 168

Index of English Names

Barred, 170
Great Horned, 169
Long-eared, 171
Northern Saw-whet, 172
Short-eared, 171
Snowy, 170

Parakeet, Carolina, 190
Parula, Northern, 269
Pelican, American White, 65
Pelican, Brown, 66
Phalarope
  Red, 141
  Red-necked, 140
  Wilson's, 139
Phoebe
  Eastern, 196
  Say's, 197
Pigeon
  Band-tailed, 163
  Passenger, 164
  Rock, 163
Pintail, Northern, 30
Pipit
  American, 244
  Sprague's, 245
Plover
  Black-bellied, 108
  Piping, 112
  Semipalmated, 111
  Snowy, 110

Rail
  Black, 94
  Clapper, 95
  King, 95
  Virginia, 96
  Yellow, 94
Raven, Common, 210
Redhead, 33
Redpoll, Common, 321
Redstart, American, 265
Robin, American, 238
Ruff, 124

Sanderling, 126
Sandpiper
  Baird's, 128
  Buff-breasted, 132
  Curlew, 126
  Least, 129
  Pectoral, 132
  Purple, 128
  Semipalmated, 134
  Sharp-tailed, 124
  Solitary, 115
  Spotted, 114
  Stilt, 125
  Upland, 119
  Western, 135
  White-rumped, 131
Sapsucker, Yellow-bellied, 183
Scaup
  Greater, 35
  Lesser, 36
Scoter
  Black, 39
  Surf, 37
  White-winged, 38
Screech-Owl, Eastern, 169
Shearwater, Great, 57
Shoveler, Northern, 29
Shrike
  Loggerhead, 202
  Northern, 202
Siskin, Pine, 321
Skimmer, Black, 162
Skua, South Polar, 142
Snipe, Wilson's, 138
Solitaire, Townsend's, 233
Sora, 97
Sparrow
  American Tree, 288
  Bachman's, 287
  Black-throated, 291
  Chipping, 288
  Clay-colored, 289
  Field, 289

Fox, 296
　　Golden-crowned, 301
　　Grasshopper, 293
　　Harris's, 299
　　Henslow's, 293
　　House, 325
　　Lark, 291
　　Le Conte's, 294
　　Lincoln's, 297
　　Nelsons's, 295
　　Savannah, 292
　　Song, 297
　　Swamp, 298
　　Vesper, 290
　　White-crowned, 300
　　White-throated, 299
Spoonbill, Roseate, 79
Starling, European, 243
Stilt, Black-necked, 105
Stint, Red-necked, 126
Stork, Wood, 59
Storm-Petrel, Band-rumped, 58
Swallow
　　Bank, 215
　　Barn, 217
　　Cave, 217
　　Cliff, 216
　　Northern Rough-winged, 215
　　Tree, 214
　　Violet-green, 215
Swan
　　Mute, 21
　　Trumpeter, 21
　　Tundra, 22
Swift, Chimney, 176

Tanager
　　Scarlet, 303
　　Summer, 303
　　Western, 304
Teal
　　Blue-winged, 28
　　Cinnamon, 28
　　Green-winged, 31

Tern
　　Arctic, 160
　　Black, 158
　　Bridled, 155
　　Caspian, 156
　　Common, 159
　　Forster's, 160
　　Gull-billed, 156
　　Least, 155
　　Royal, 161
　　Sooty, 154
Thrasher
　　Brown, 240
　　Sage, 241
Thrush
　　Gray-cheeked, 234
　　Hermit, 236
　　Swainson's, 235
　　Varied, 238
　　Wood, 237
Titmouse, Tufted, 219
Towhee
　　Eastern, 287
　　Green-tailed, 286
　　Spotted, 286
Turkey, Wild, 47
Turnstone, Ruddy, 122

Veery, 233
Violetear, Green, 178
Vireo
　　Bell's, 203
　　Blue-headed, 205
　　Philadelphia, 207
　　Red-eyed, 207
　　Warbling, 206
　　White-eyed, 203
　　Yellow-throated, 204
Vulture
　　Black, 80
　　Turkey, 80

Warbler
　　Bay-breasted, 271

Index of English Names

Black-and-white, 255
Blackburnian, 272
Blackpoll, 275
Black-throated Blue, 275
Black-throated Gray, 281
Black-throated Green, 281
Blue-winged, 253, 254
Canada, 282
Cape May, 267
Cerulean, 268
Chestnut-sided, 274
Connecticut, 261
Golden-winged, 253
Hooded, 265
Kentucky, 263
Kirtland's, 267
MacGillivray's, 262
Magnolia, 270
Mourning, 262
Nashville, 260
Orange-crowned, 259
Palm, 276
Pine, 277
Prairie, 280
Prothonotary, 256
Swainson's, 257
Tennessee, 258
Townsend's, 281
Wilson's, 283
Worm-eating, 251
Yellow, 273
Yellow-rumped, 278
Yellow-throated, 279
Waterthrush
    Louisiana, 251
    Northern, 252
Waxwing, Cedar, 246
Whimbrel, 120
Whistling-Duck
    Black-bellied, 15
    Fulvous, 15
Wigeon
    American, 24
    Eurasian, 24
Willet, 117
Woodcock, American, 139
Woodpecker
    Downy, 184
    Hairy, 184
    Ivory-billed, 186
    Pileated, 185
    Red-bellied, 183
    Red-cockaded, 185
    Red-headed, 183
Wood-Pewee, Eastern, 192
Wren
    Bewick's, 229
    Carolina, 228
    House, 225
    Marsh, 227
    Rock, 225
    Sedge, 226
    Winter, 226

Yellowlegs
    Greater, 116
    Lesser, 118
Yellowthroat, Common, 264

Made in the USA
Columbia, SC
05 April 2025